I0825475

WATERFRONT LIVING

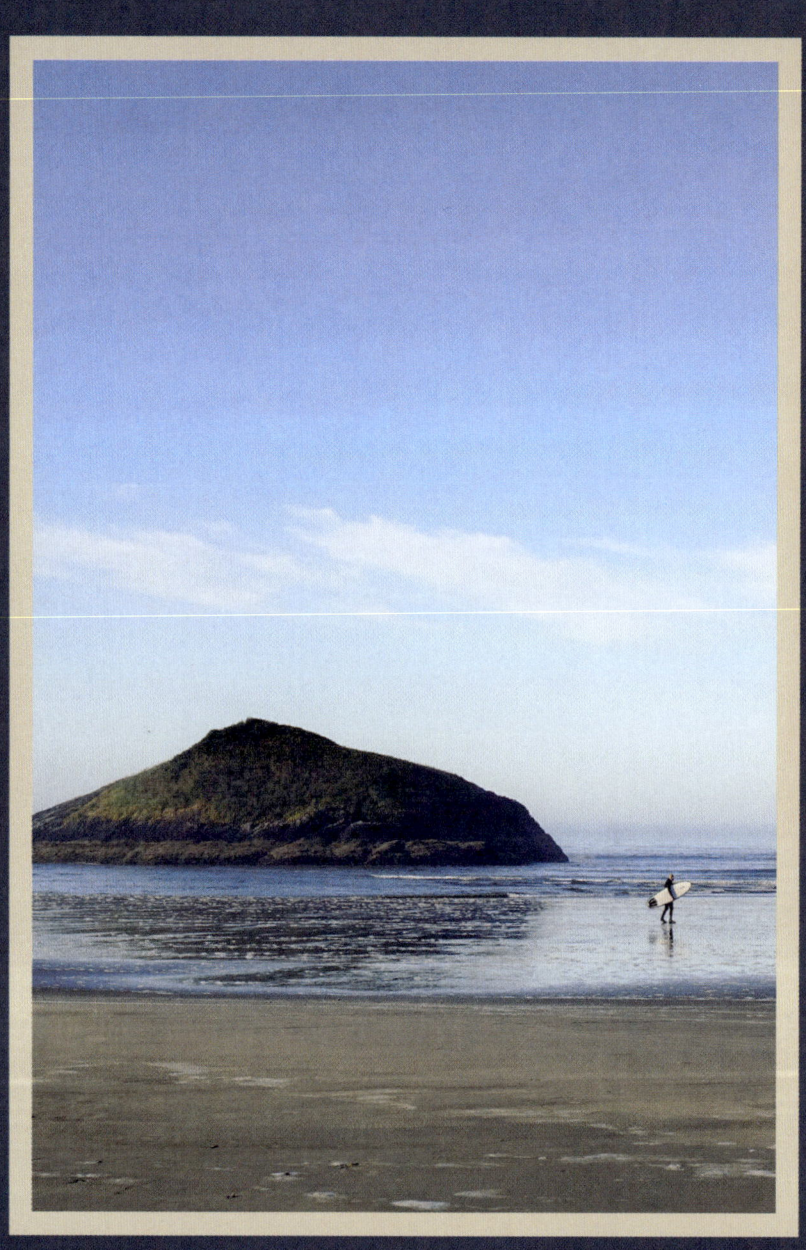

WATERFRONT LIVING

Inspired Coastal Homes & Small Town Lifestyles

ERIN AUSTEN ABBOTT

RUNNING PRESS
PHILADELPHIA

Running Press
Hachette Book Group
1290 Avenue of the Americas, New York, NY 10104
www.runningpress.com
@Running_Press

First Edition: May 2026

Published by Running Press, an imprint of Hachette Book Group, Inc. The Running Press name and logo are trademarks of Hachette Book Group, Inc.

Print book cover and interior design by Jenna McBride

Library of Congress Cataloging-in-Publication Data has been applied for.

ISBNs: 979-8-89414-137-4 (hardcover), 979-8-89414-138-1 (ebook)

Printed in China

1010

10 9 8 7 6 5 4 3 2 1

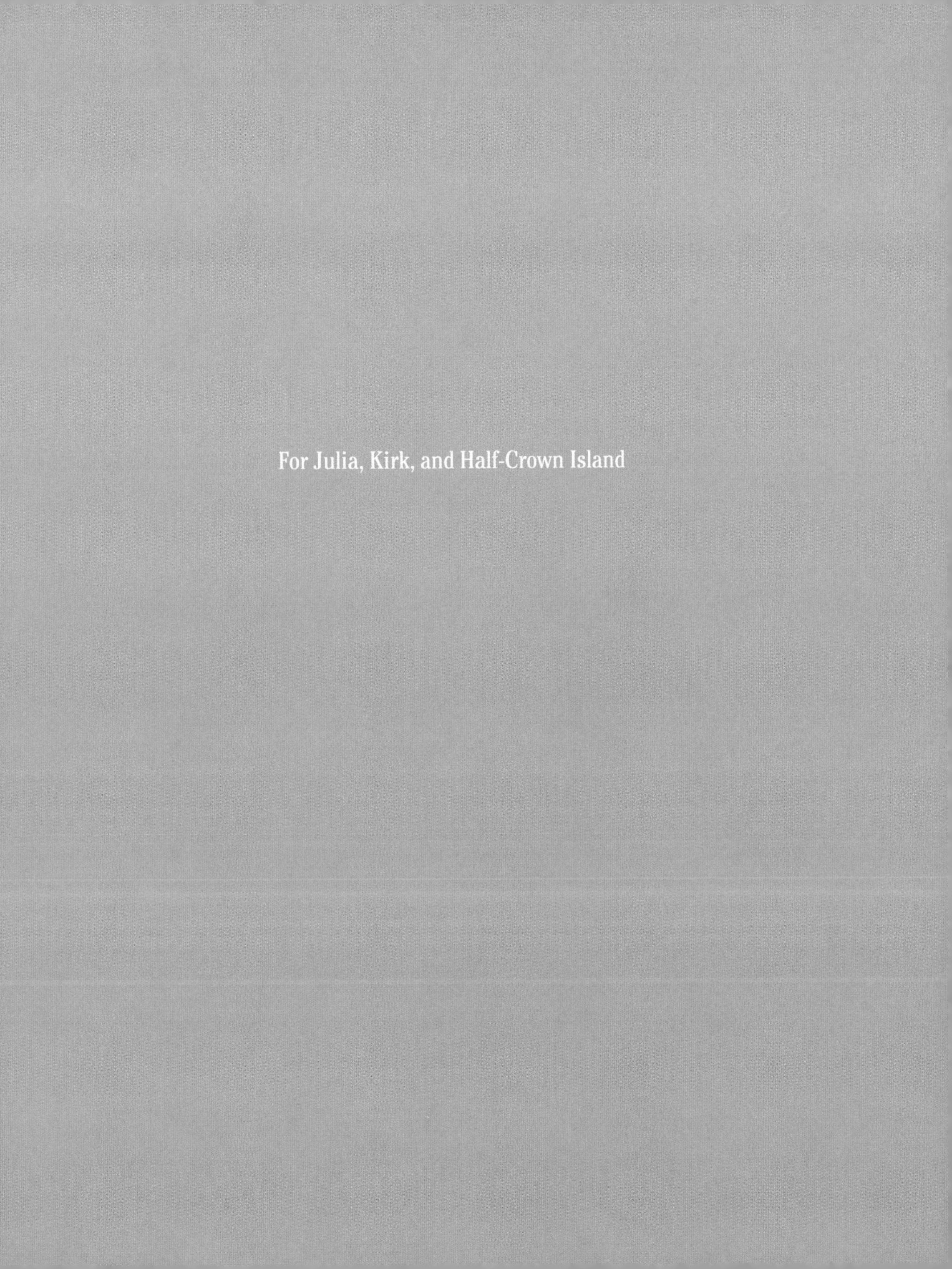

For Julia, Kirk, and Half-Crown Island

CONTENTS

OCEANS, INLETS, SOUNDS, AND BAYS 123

ISLANDS 167

Bonus Section:

BICOASTAL LIVING 227

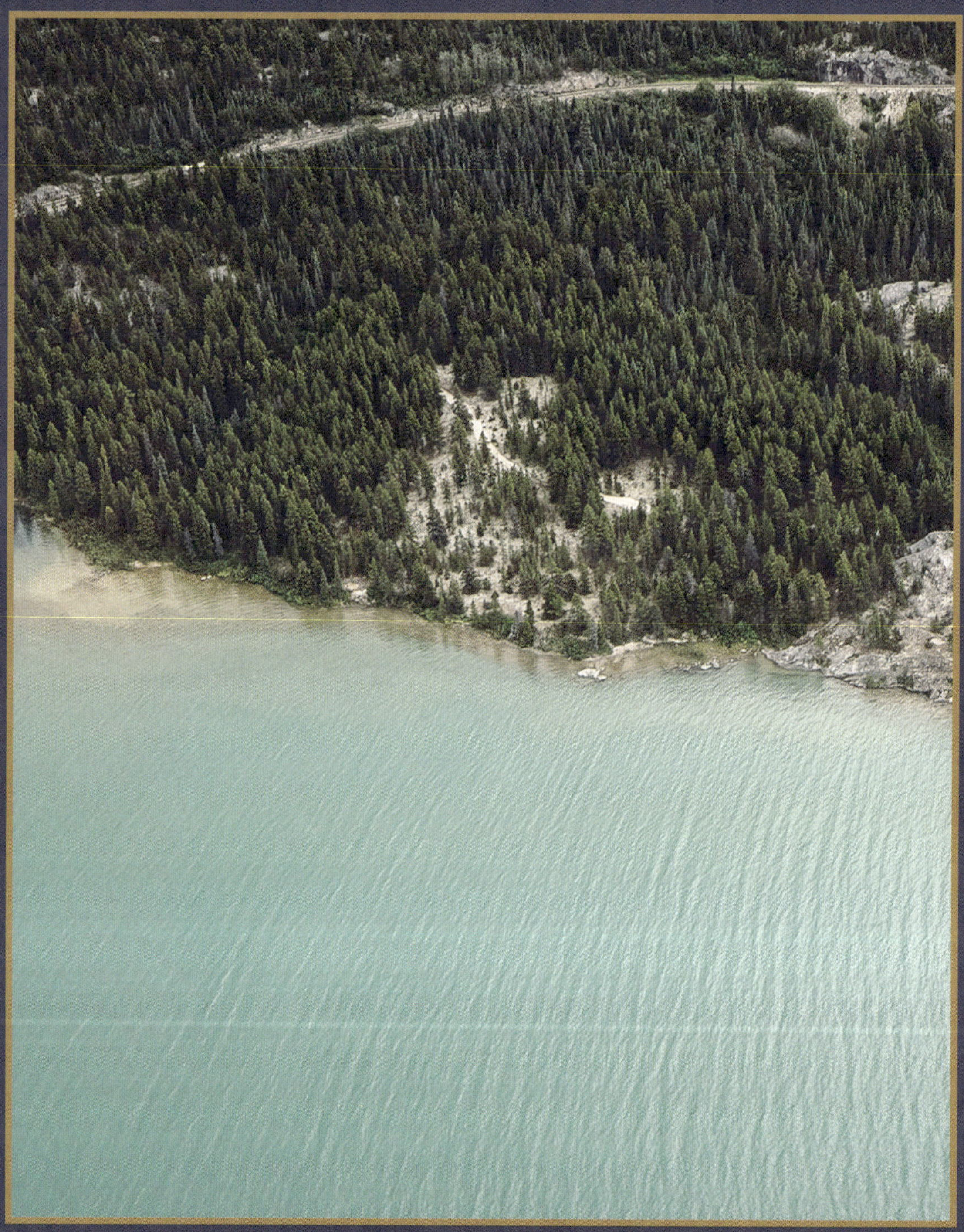

MY RELATIONSHIP WITH WATER

Born in Mississippi, I always thought of myself as landlocked. I would listen to the adults around me say, "I miss the water," and "We are so far from water," forgetting the state's name means "great river." What I was really hearing was that they missed the *ocean*; they were longing for the *beach*. I can understand this sentiment as I get older because I feel that way about rivers and lakes. When you change the conversation to include water of all types, we begin to understand we are less landlocked than we might have thought. I've been surrounded by water my whole life, bouncing from Oxford, Mississippi, near Sardis Lake and the Yocona River; to spending summers on Longboat Key, Florida, overlooking the ocean, burning my skin under the sun day after day; to summer camp in Brevard, North Carolina, with rushing creeks just outside the cabins, where I went from camper to counselor over seventeen summers at Gwynn Valley Summer Camp. We'd swim in the camp lake each day, and on special trips, we'd go tubing down the French Broad River or whitewater rafting down the Nantahala River.

We moved to Land O' Lakes, Florida, in 1985, where a lake was right outside the back door. I would watch alligators sunning themselves on our deck with fear and excitement at such a wild creature being on the other side of a hot-to-the-touch chain-link fence. At just ten years old, one of my favorite hobbies was waterskiing with the neighborhood kids. My friend's dad would take us often, and I'd always have one eye on the boat and one eye on the smooth water, just past the wake, watching for alligator eyes popping out ever so slightly. I knew I would have to stay up when I saw those eyes.

We then moved to the peninsula city of St. Petersburg, Florida, in Tampa Bay. The bay was just across the street; I couldn't get away from it if I tried. I later moved to Tampa itself, surrounded by the Hillsborough River and again the bay. The water was quite literally all around us. In college, friends and I would head north to swim in the clear blue water of the springs on days off from my waitress job and between classes.

After college, I moved to Boston, Massachusetts, where I would walk daily along the Back Bay Fens on my way to my grad school classes at the Museum School of Fine Arts or take early morning strolls along the Charles River to watch the rowers. I also made special trips to the harbor with the small boy I nannied for where we'd watch the boats while sharing a picnic.

I later moved to Seattle, where I could see the water at any given time, whether driving through town, walking down to Lake Union from my apartment, or swimming in Lake Washington late at night with friends. The fear of running into alligators was long behind me. Sometimes, I'd take the ferry across Puget Sound to Bainbridge Island or go camping in the Olympic National Forest. There was a spot near Ozette Lake that was almost on the beach I loved to visit. The campsite was a good three miles from the car; hiking down, it felt like no one else was around. You'd wake up to the sounds of seals calling out and water hitting the rocks nearby. I'd spot deer walking through the sand when I got up early enough.

After I left Seattle, I moved to San Francisco. Living in the Mission, I couldn't see the water like in previous places I'd lived, but I knew I could get to it quickly on any given drive. I would often drive out to the cliffs overlooking the ocean in the Outer Richmond, coming home along Ocean Beach. It was near the record store I liked to visit, and I had the loop from home and back down to a science: through the Castro and Ashbury Heights, over to Haight Street, buy records, drive through Golden Gate Park, and arrive at the ocean. I'd go home through the Outer Sunset and Noe Valley, only a twelve-mile round trip.

I moved to Memphis, Tennessee, in 2003, but I had spent so much time there visiting my grandparents and uncle it felt like I'd lived there before. There was no learning curve. I knew how to get around; I could converse with people talking about the old days and chime in on places that had since closed. I knew the lingo; it felt more like home than any other place I'd lived. I used to drive downtown along the Mississippi River, watching the tugboats and hearing my grandmother's voice in my head, "We never get hit with bad storms because the bluffs along the river protect us." I would cross the bridge to Harbor Town, just off downtown, to walk through Greenbelt Park along the river.

When I decided I was ready to buy a house, I found my home in a tiny town called Water Valley, Mississippi, just an hour and a half south of Memphis. "Water Valley," I thought, sounded like a sweet town, and it was only twenty miles from where I'd grown up in Oxford. Water Valley is situated near three large lakes: Enid Lake, Sardis Lake, and Grenada Lake. And there are hundreds of smaller lakes, ponds, creeks, and rivers everywhere in between.

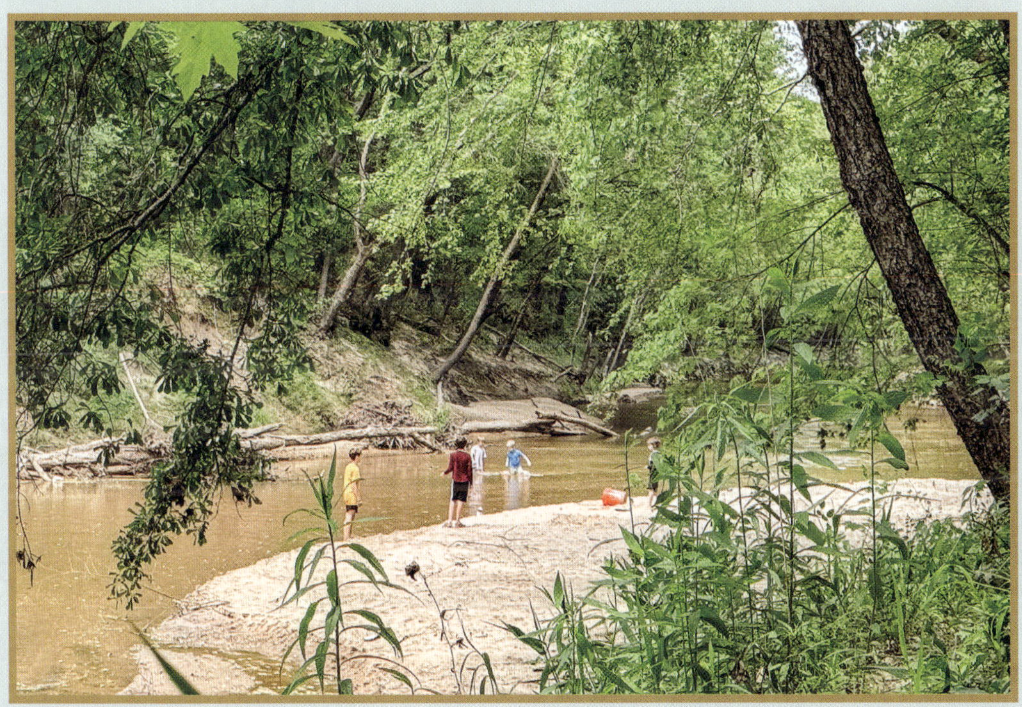

We have raised our son Tom Otis on the water, from the lakes around us in Mississippi to those of Canada where my husband's family convened each year on 31 Mile Lake in Quebec. Starting when Tom was very young, we made a point to get out into nature as much as possible, often with long walks along the Yocona River not far from our home. Something about those walks left me grounded to the Earth and this place. The peacefulness of the river allows my mind to settle and be present. And it will always remind me of those long walks with my family.

It's all about perspective. What land is pulling you in? How do we treat the water around us? How do we gravitate toward it? And how do we embrace it? It drives us, sparks creativity, and invigorates us in ways we can only imagine otherwise. Some people are called to the desert, others the mountains, and some are called to the water. The stories in this book are those of the last—those who reach for the water when they need a little reprieve.

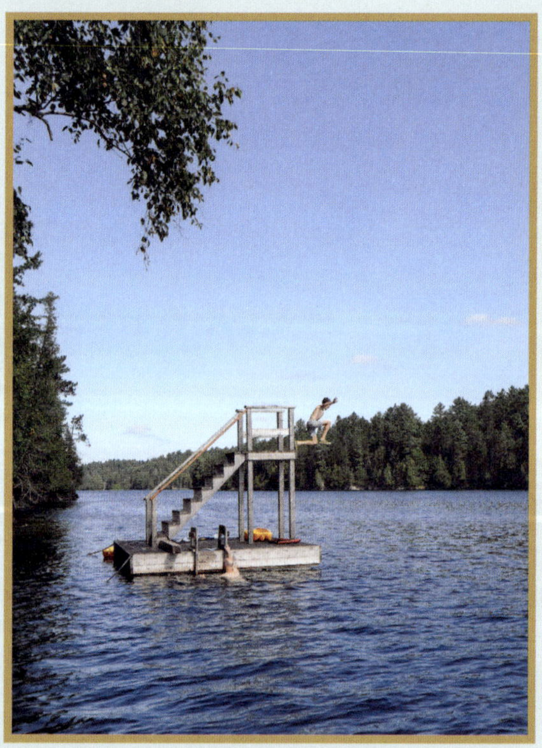

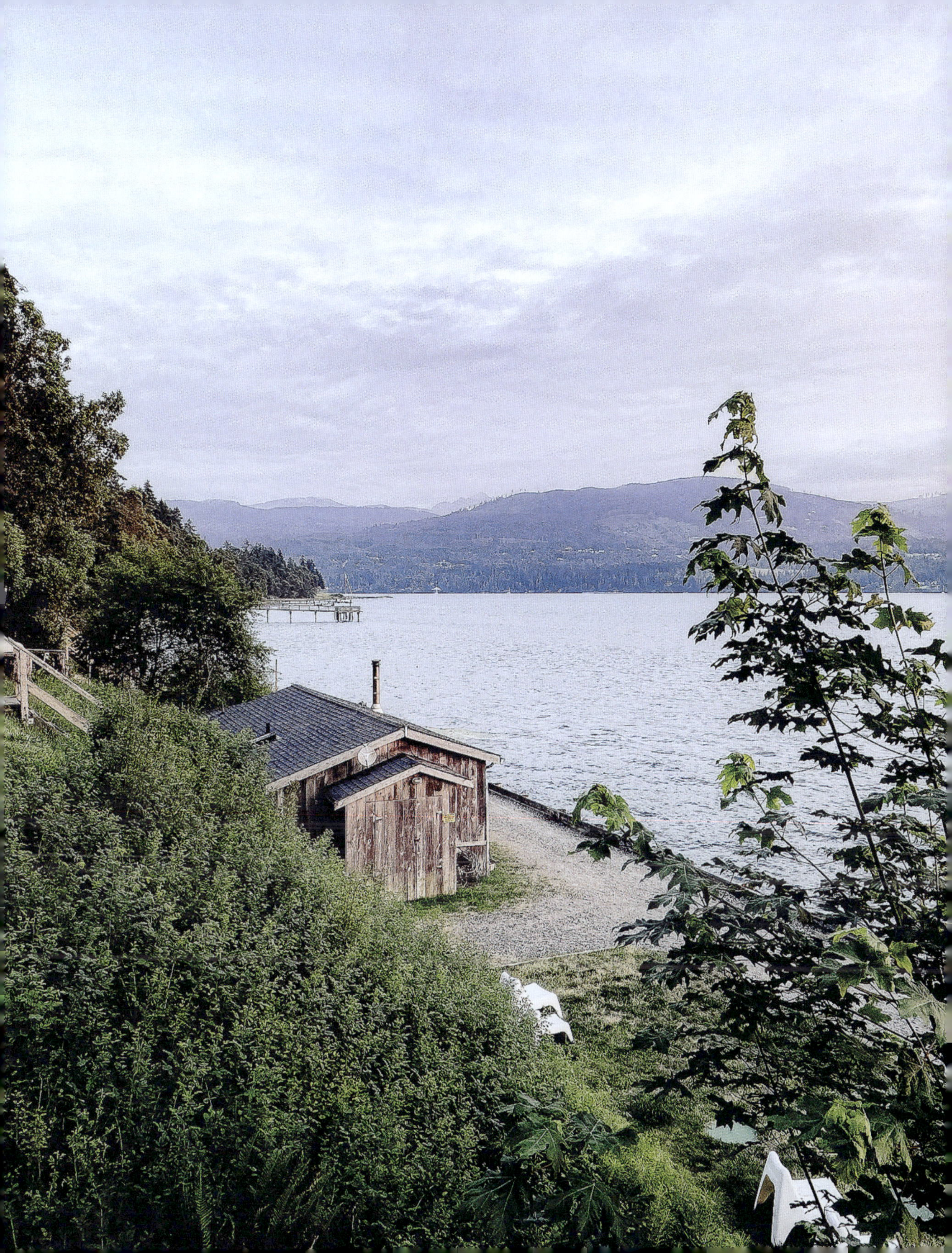

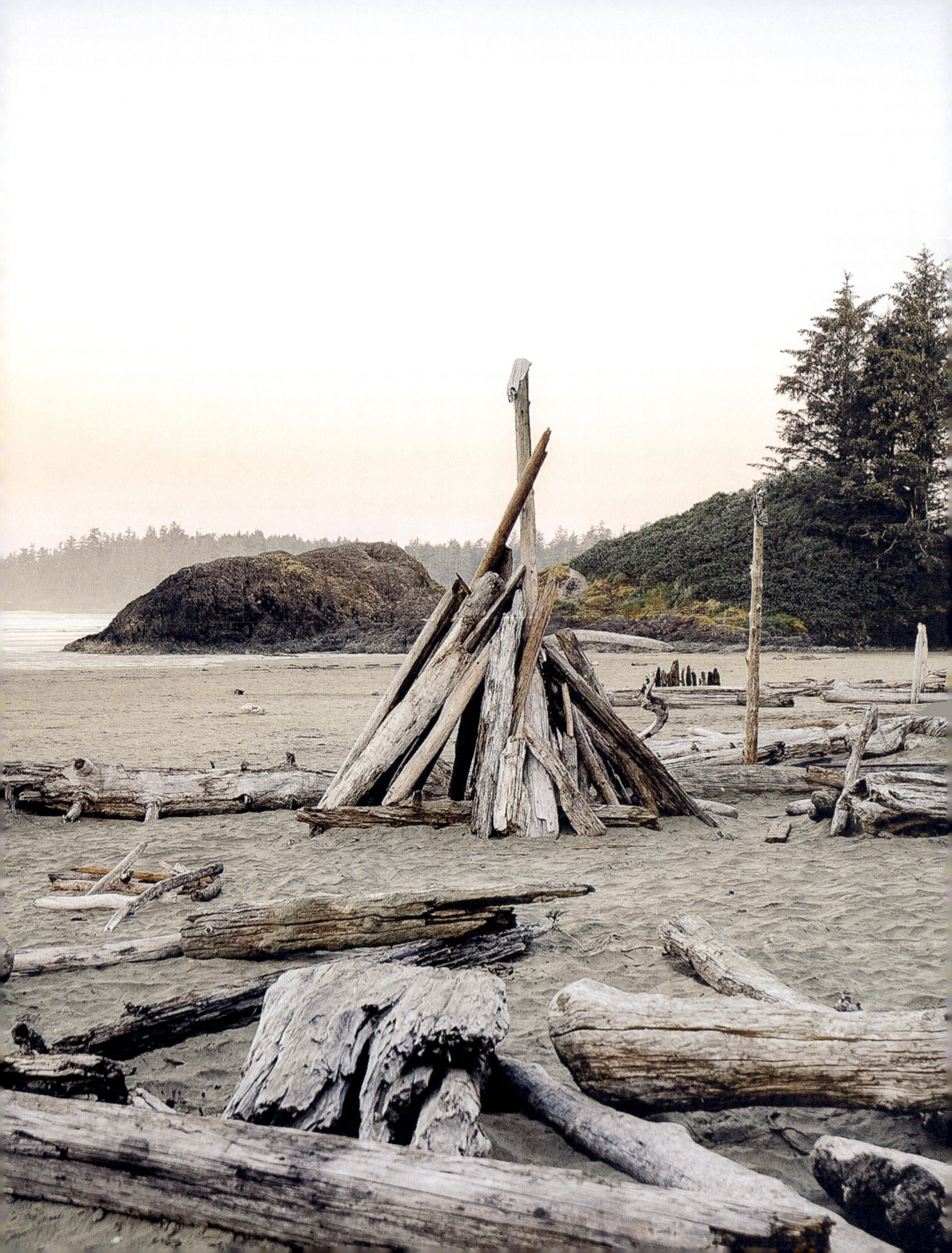

EFFECTS OF WATER ON CREATIVITY

When I look at the water, I hear music in my mind. It's transportive, like a back-road drive. Different bodies of water bring to my mind different songs and different genres of music. Rivers lead me to folk music or indie electronic, and I think about songs by Iron & Wine, Cat Stevens, Sam Amidon, Tycho, or MJ Lenderman. Standing before an ocean, I hear old jazz, such as Billie Holiday or Sun Ra, or conscious hip-hop, like A Tribe Called Quest, Digable Planets, or Kendrick Lamar. When I'm around a lake, I lean into my indie rock side and think about Frankie Cosmos, Yo La Tengo, 22° Halo, Colour Revolt, Built to Spill, and old Modest Mouse, or classical music comes to mind—Bach, specifically Cello Suite No. 1 in G Minor, or The Rachel's.

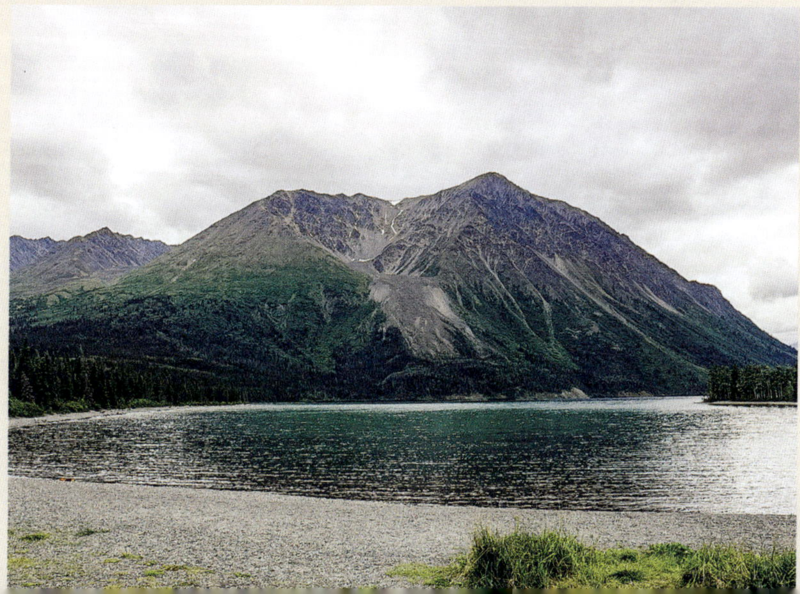

I can't turn it off; it's as if the music is embedded in my mind. I drive along a quiet road, winding with the natural shape of the water moving me along like a wave without uniformity, as if I'm moving to the beat, each turn unpredictable, each song unplanned. Water has that effect on me . . . and on you.

You might not realize it, though. It's called the Blue Mind, meaning water is affecting you and your mood, health, and creativity without your knowledge. Water calms you, pushes down your anxiety, and helps with focus and overall connectedness. Marine biologist Dr. Wallace J. Nichols developed the idea of the Blue Mind, which states that being in or near water allows our minds to enter a semimeditative state, which can affect us in healthy and positive ways. If you feel writer's block or some other form of creative standstill, find a nearby body of water or take a bath. Sitting at the edge of the water or immersing yourself in the water, even for just twenty minutes, is said to unblock our minds and open us up to new creative paths.

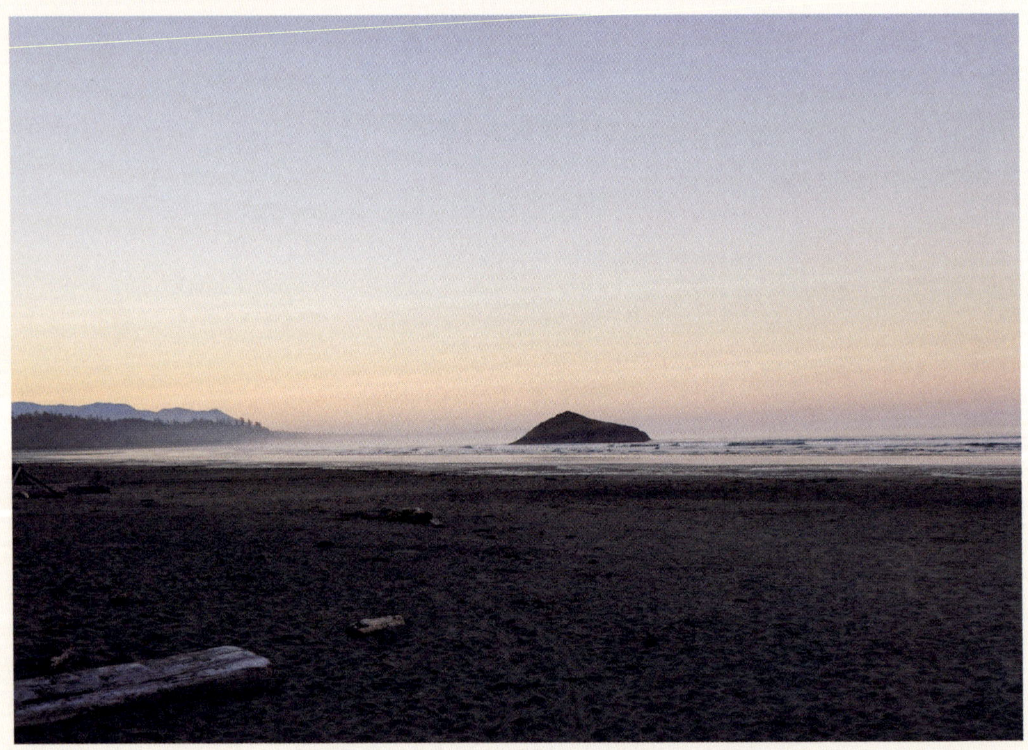

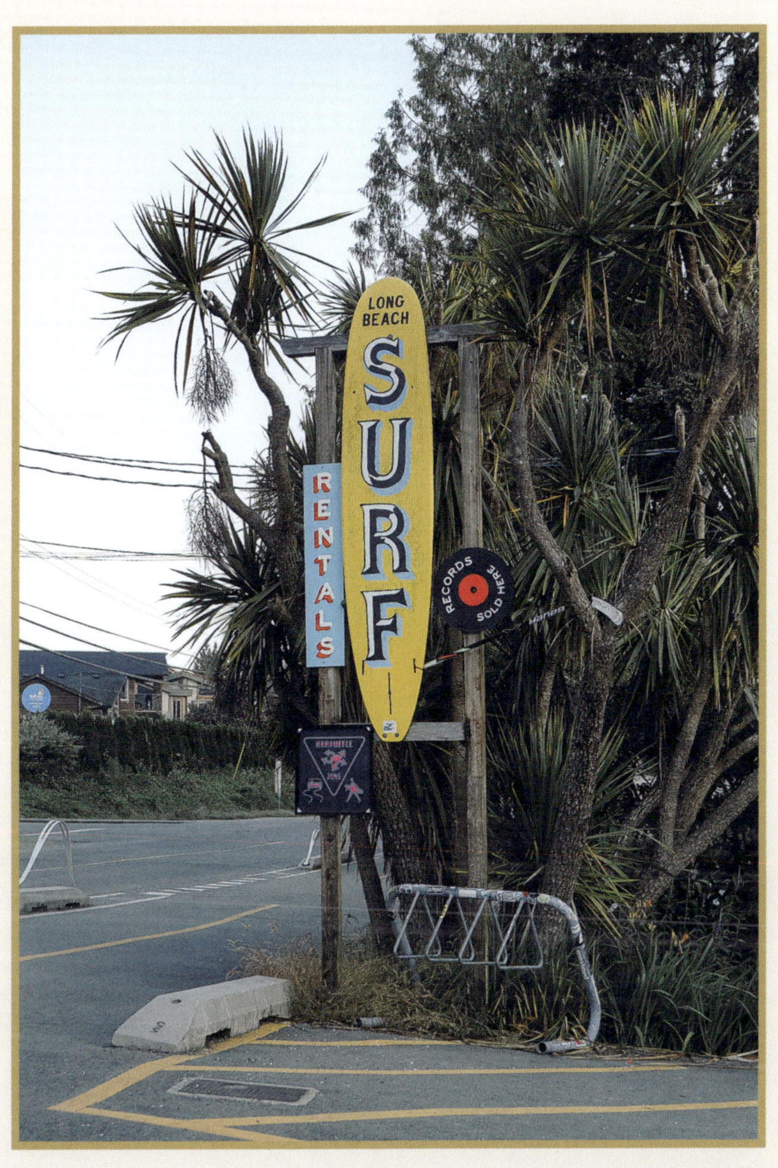
LONG BEACH
SURF
RENTALS
RECORDS SOLD HERE

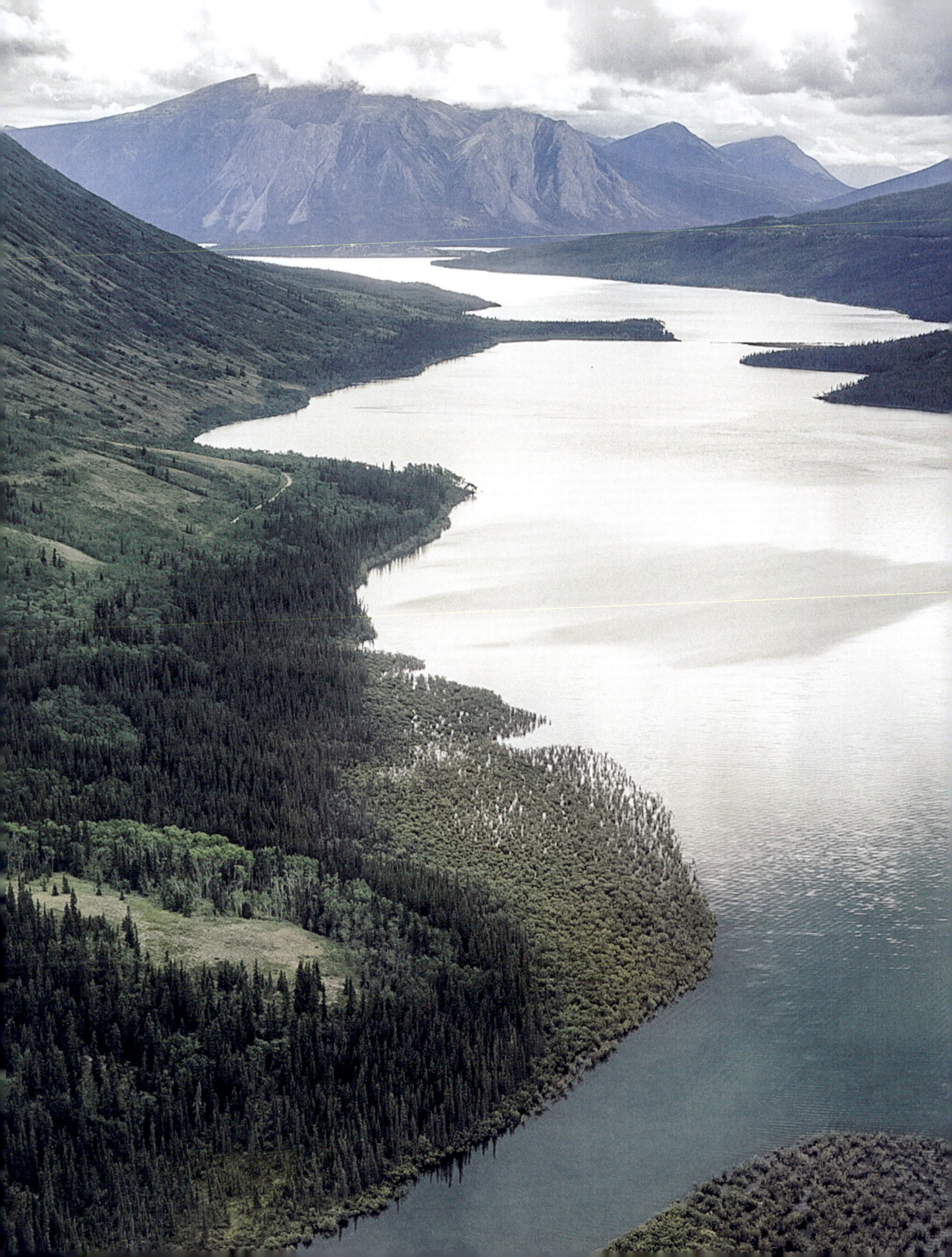

THE THROUGH LINE

Between *Small Town Living* and now *Waterfront Living*, I have talked to hundreds of people about their small towns, from those interviewed in the books to shopkeepers, restaurant workers, oyster divers, gas station attendants, etc. striking up conversations any chance I found. I've discovered people have the same concerns and similar things they want for their towns: good schools and a safe place for the children to ride bikes and play outside freely, job security within their locale, jobs for youth, more food and affordable home options.

People moving from cities to small towns are driving up costs, but this is happening everywhere, not just in small towns. However, locals are faced with the inability to return to their small town and buy property, and then they can't afford to live where they've been calling home for many generations. It happened to me, too: I couldn't afford to move back to Oxford, Mississippi, so I went one county over and found a great home and community in Water Valley. This is not a new concern, but my hope is that this book gives you the tools and knowledge to be part of the solution when moving, rather than adding to the growing issues.

When I asked people what they miss most about living in a city versus being in a small town, the number one answer from almost everyone is always the food. They miss the culture of good food, the variety, the smells pouring out onto the street, running into friends randomly out at a restaurant, and the simple, often overlooked task of getting takeout delivered to their homes. These are things taken for granted living in a city, but something people in small towns may not have.

If you are reading this book and want to move to a smaller place and open a business, think about the food culture of a place. What do they already have, and what could you add to the community that doesn't yet exist? Think outside the box about what you could bring about. Think about what will unify the town and be inclusive to everyone.

Shifting gears, the teenagers in small towns are often overlooked. Is there anything for them to do besides play sports? Maybe you could open a small movie theater, minigolf course, or ice cream shop, which would offer jobs and life skills to the town's teens and give them something to do in their downtime.

Lastly, the through line for every person interviewed in this book and in *Small Town Living*—and something that certainly sets small towns apart—is the intergenerational friendships that form out of small towns. People of all ages come together with a shared interest or common belief. These friendships are so special for many reasons: They guide the younger generation to learn and improve while giving the older generation hope for what they will be leaving behind. They impress their stewardship of the land and culture onto the new generation to carry on the traditions of a place. They support the younger people who have decided to move to a smaller place while sharing their perspectives.

QUESTIONS TO CONSIDER WHEN MAKING A MOVE

How can small town living be afforded, especially when cities push the creatives out and costs rise?

How can the locals of small towns be satisfied with the growth while people escaping the cities are just looking for something more affordable?

If this is a second home, can I find a piece of property that doesn't appeal to the locals, like a two- or three-season home?

Am I displacing someone by moving here?

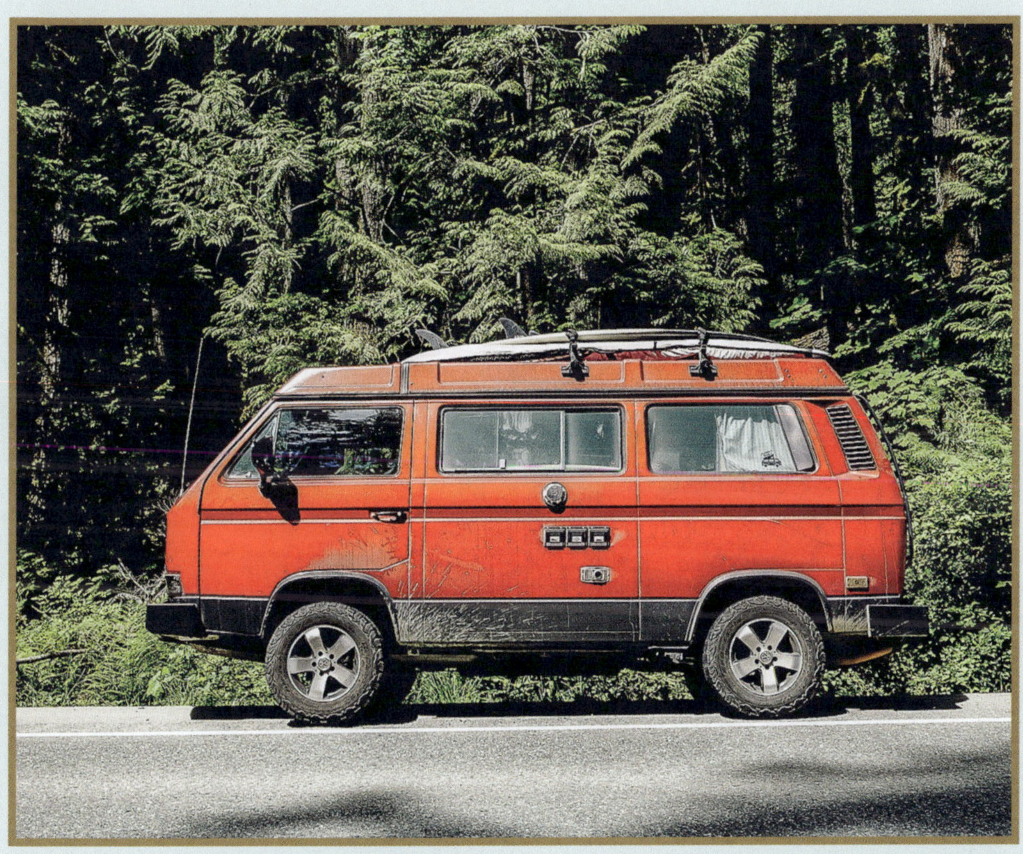

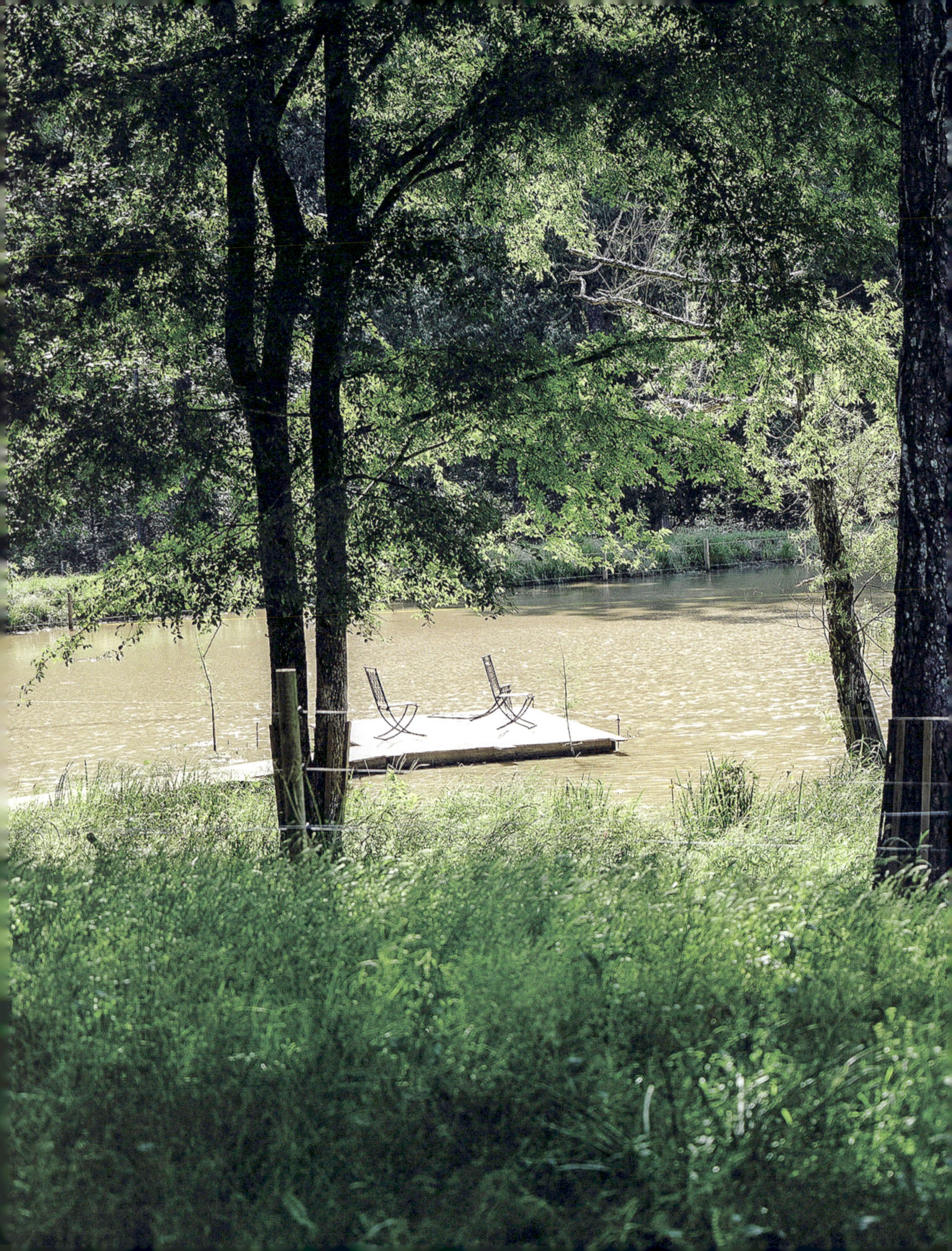

RIVERS
AND
BAYOUS

"I started coming to Mountain View a few times a year, and it was just gorgeous. I loved the feel of the town, the landscape, and the water. I think in my soul, I'm a mountain person, and I didn't know it. Looking back, a lot of my ancestors came from Appalachia, so it's similar."

—BRIT MCDANIEL

BRIT MCDANIEL

Ceramic Artist

MOUNTAIN VIEW, ARKANSAS

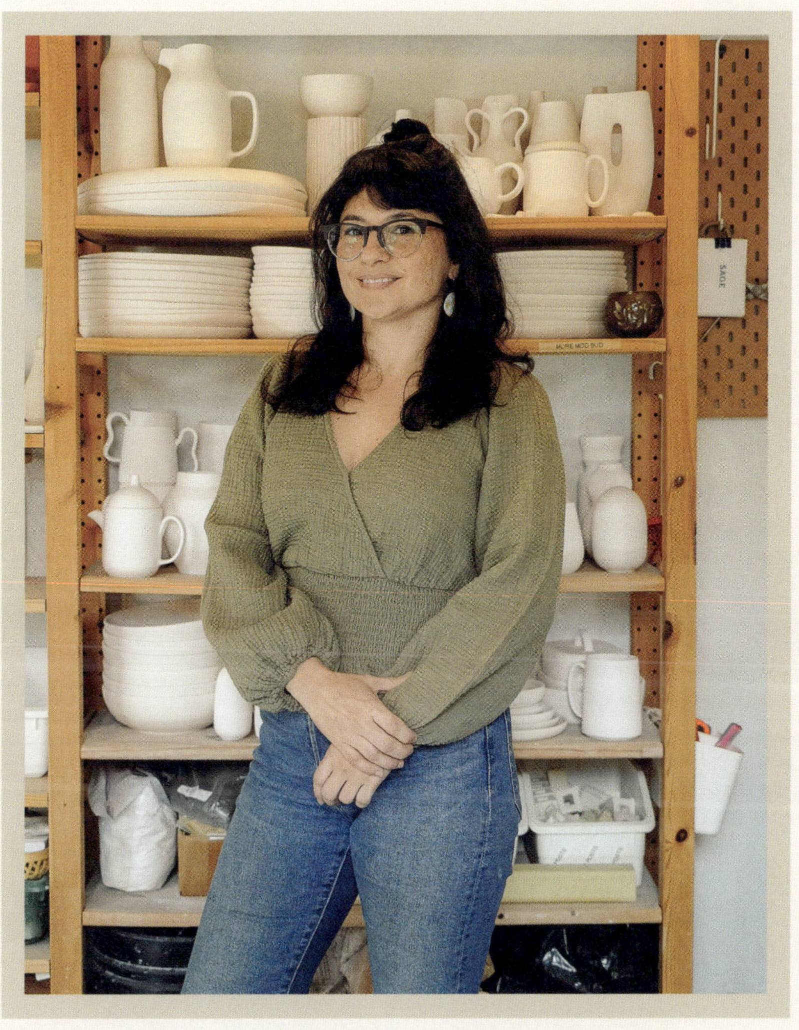

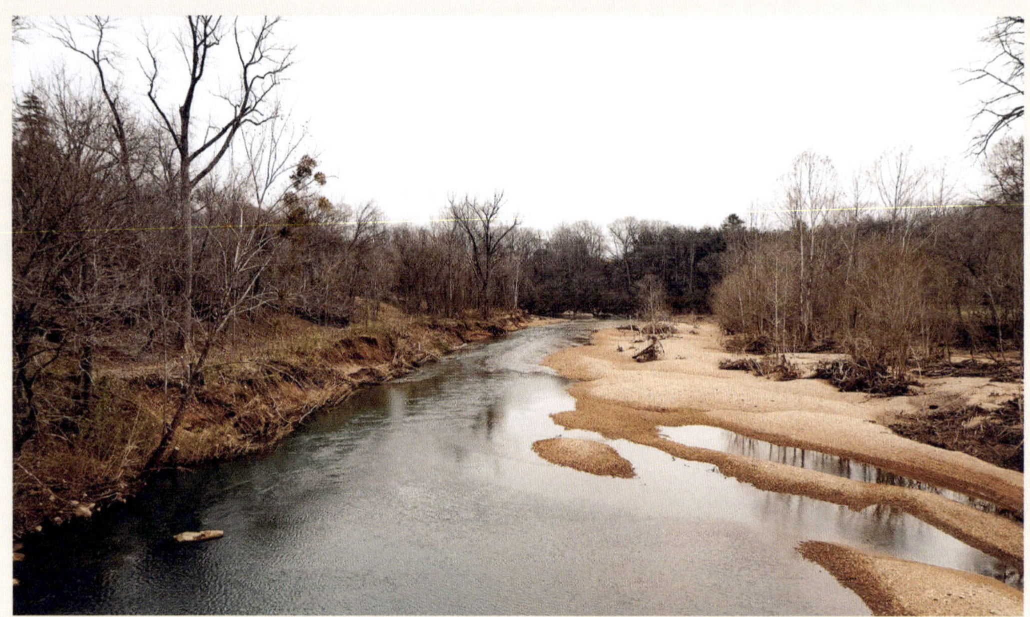

Mountain View, Arkansas, situated in the Ozark Highlands, has been pulling in ceramics artist Brit McDaniel, a Memphis, Tennessee, resident, for a long time. She had been visiting Mountain View a few times a year for many years, with what started as a weekend away, looking for a different landscape entirely from the city she'd lived in for so many years. She'd heard a lot about people from Memphis visiting Heber Springs, which was not far, but it still wasn't what she was looking for. Brit wanted less popular and less populated: a place to quiet the city's noise and allow her to reconnect with nature and her creativity. Her weekend visits to Mountain View became a few weeks long, leading to her looking for land to build a small second home. Today, Brit has left her city life behind and calls Mountain View home full time. She marvels how she's in her thirty-fourth residence across seven different states. All that moving throughout her life has left her wanting to feel more grounded in Mountain View.

With many creeks meandering through the town and the White River close by, this tiny mountain enclave in Northeast Arkansas is a nature lover's dream. Music and a creative culture thrive in tandem with the forest and water that surround the community.

CHALLENGES OF WINTER AND SOCIAL ADJUSTMENT

Facing severe burnout within her business, Brit thought she might move to Mountain View for a small amount of time, possibly six months tops, and then find her way back to

Memphis. But after relocating there in August of 2023 and settling in, she found it's a great place to slow down, think about intentionality, and prioritize life. She's noticed herself asking, *Why do I do this thing I've been doing? Why are these things important?* She's allowed herself to reconnect to the basics of being a human separate from the consumerism and social pressures that sometimes come with living in a livelier, busier place.

"When I moved here, I only had a couple of months before winter came, and the whole area hibernates. My first winter was, socially, very hard because I went from living in the middle of a city to being alone in the woods. And as much as that sounded like a dream to me, I didn't realize how much it was going to impact my mental health. I think the idea of not having social engagements and being able to do whatever I want sounded dreamy. But then I realized I got so much good social stimulation in Memphis just from existing around other people," shared Brit. When people started coming out of the woodwork, she could find community again, and she could envision the balance she was seeking. Now, she can plan for down seasons, give herself time to rest, and change her perspective.

CHOOSING MOUNTAIN VIEW

Brit has moved around a lot over the years, spending most of her time in Memphis. She

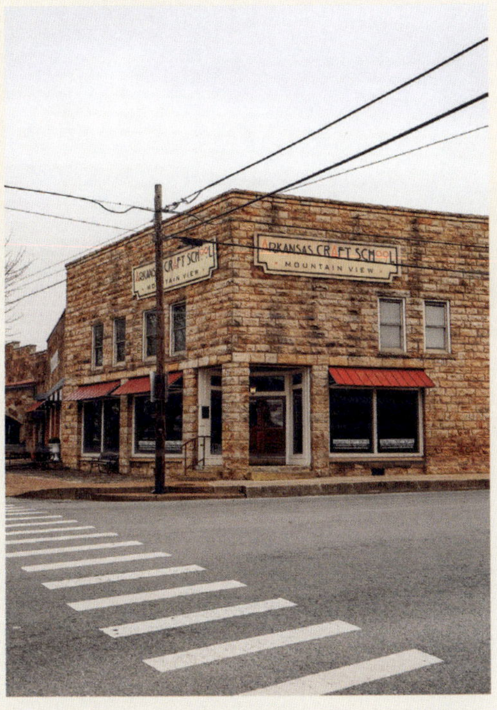

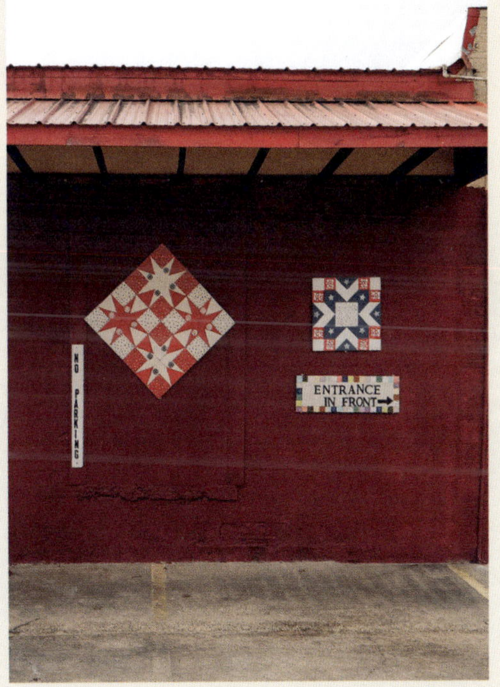

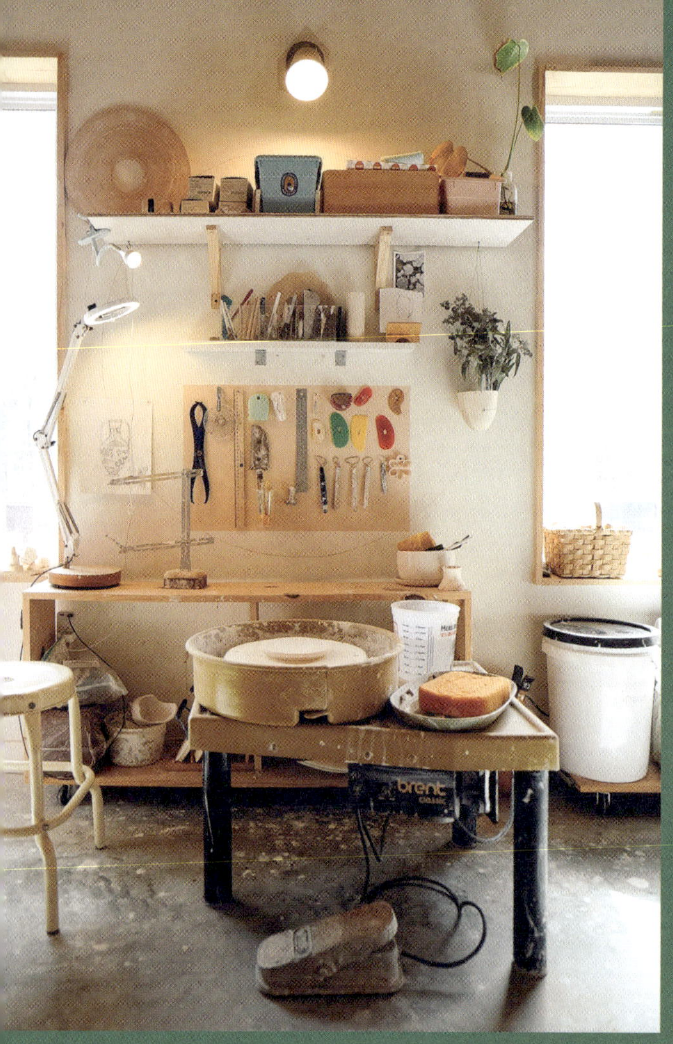
brent

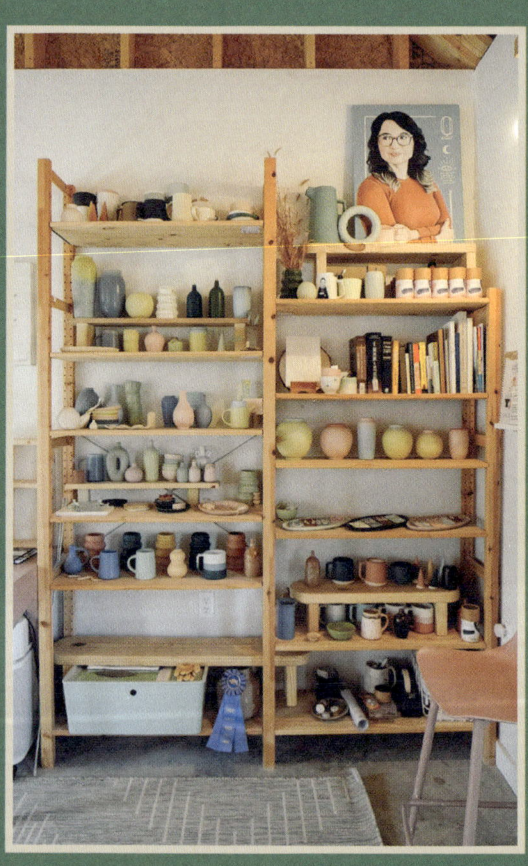

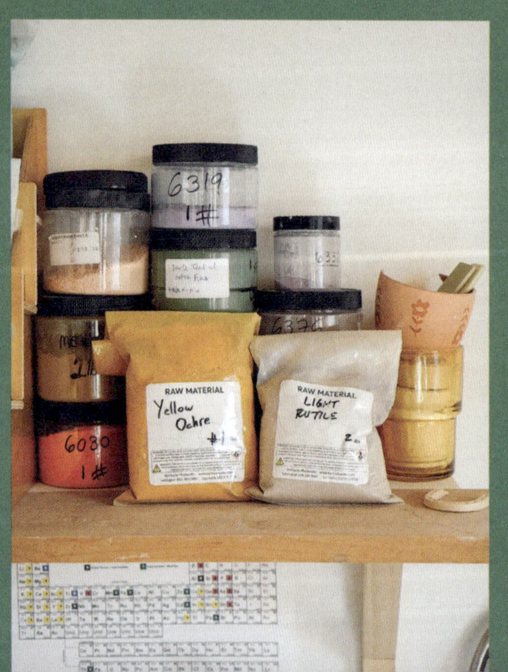
6319
1#
RAW MATERIAL
Yellow Ochre
#1
RAW MATERIAL
LIGHT
RUTILE
6030
1#

considered relocating to the Hudson Valley of New York, but that would also have meant leaving behind the community she loved so much in Memphis. With Mountain View filling a need similar to the Hudson Valley yet only three hours from the city for a fraction of the price, she still feels bound to what was important in her former life. "I'm still able to see friends and go to events in Memphis," Brit shared.

It's hard to not feel envious of a place when you see all that a community is creating. You may think you want to live there without ever even visiting. But finding your own location and creating what you want in a place is also magical. Maybe you are the subject of envy someone else feels. When you think about a place where a lot of transforming is happening quickly, you risk not only putting yourself back into a bubble but also making it unrecognizable to the people who have been there their whole lives. Considering what locals did and didn't ask for within their communities makes new people better stewards in growing the community.

CREATIVE PROCESS AND CONNECTION TO NATURE

The clear and cold White River runs right along Mountain View and through the entire area. But for Brit, it's the creeks she loves most. "Since I was a kid, I've been drawn to creeks. I love just being near the water. Seeing the ocean is cool, but being next to a creek—I feel it in my

WAYS TOWN OFFICIALS COULD ENCOURAGE PEOPLE MOVING TO TOWN

Make grants available for artists to relocate.

Ask landlords to delay rental payments for the first few months to new businesses.

Offer incentives for affordable housing.

Encourage restaurants to use local produce and proteins. Turn it into a local campaign in your town. People will be more drawn to opening new restaurants or starting a small farm.

Offer grants to programs that are teaching a craft or a trade in your town.

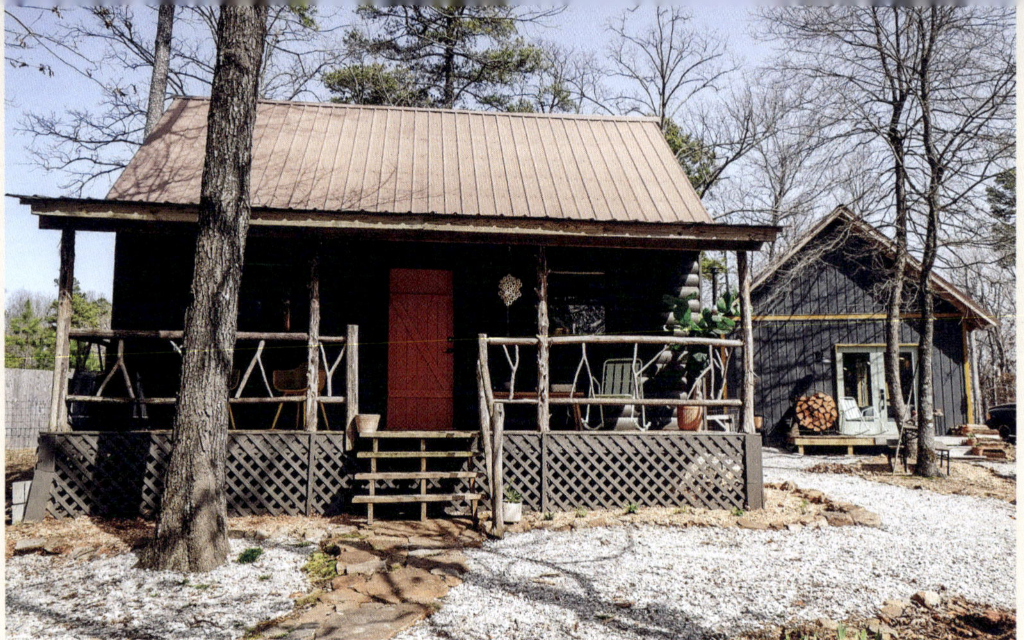

LOCATION DUPE IDEAS

When you are thinking about a new-to-you location, you may love a popular town out of your price range. Make a list of all the things that appeal to you about that town, and then begin to look for other towns that offer similar attractors. Or it could be something *you* could bring to a community. If you want to be in that same area, consider a town farther out that is more economical.

If you want to live on a beautiful yet popular lake but don't love the crowds or cost, look for a smaller lake nearby. Or check out a river that connects to the lake and see if you can find property.

Do you love live music, but the town you have your eye on isn't the right scene for traveling bands? Think about a small college town and start a venue to promote bands. Host a live radio show during off-hours or set up a place where podcasts are recorded. Turn your idea into a multipurpose location.

Is the town you are considering one with a bustling Main Street? Do you dream of opening a shop, but what you want to do is already being done or you aren't sure it's the right spot for it? There's another town that could use your ideas and direction. Don't do what's already being done. Small towns need community over competition. You will thrive setting up shop in a different location.

soul." A big creek in Mountain View that has a big impact on her is Sylamore Creek. It's massive and runs for miles, with trails meandering along the edge.

"I love hunting for cool rocks. I become a super-nerd when it comes to that stuff, and if you want to really get into it, rocks and geology are basically the basis of ceramics. But also, the red clay here! I even have a deposit on my

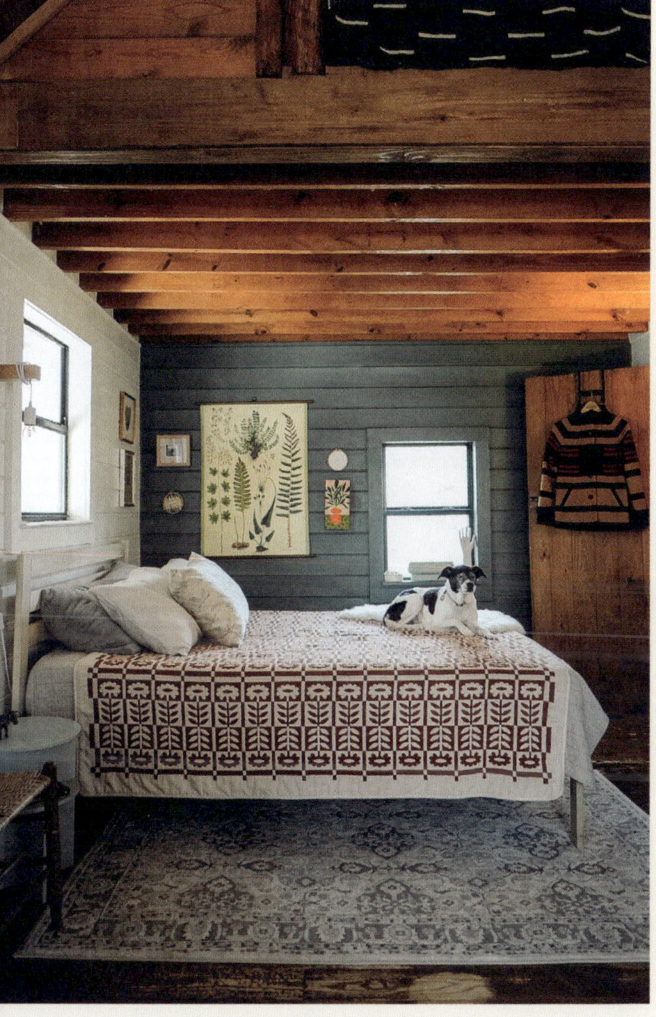

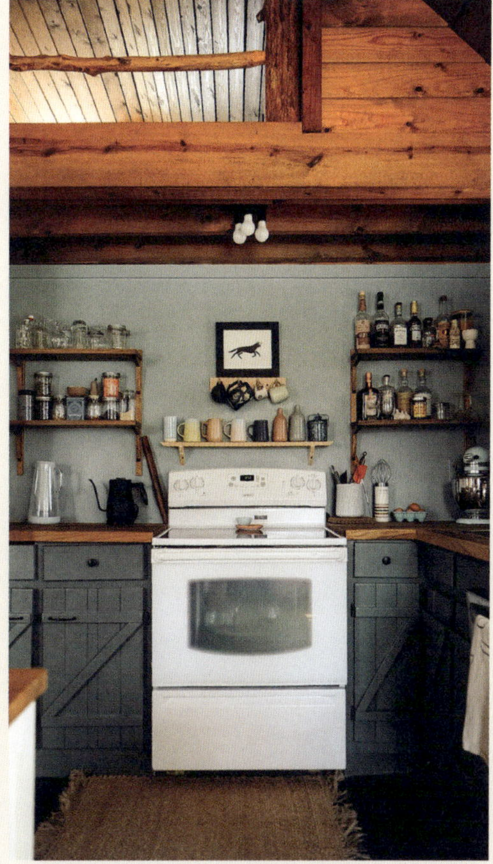

property. I can dig usable clay out of my own ground and process it. And that's remarkable," Brit described. "Thinking about your connection to the Earth and the whole process of turning this into something usable, and then turning it into something creative, and then turning it into something that supports you, it's incredible."

Watching water is like watching nature in action. Many other things happen so slowly, but with water, it happens quickly. You can see the flow and how a rock is being carved out by the water over time.

ADAPTING TO RURAL LIVING AND REDUCING COSTS

Small towns tend to lack job opportunities for younger people, leaving them with only options to move away and look for work elsewhere. How we, as a community, approach this across-the-board problem is twofold. Brit's outlook on this issue, which Mountain View could certainly benefit from, is this: first and foremost, boots on the ground, encouraging people to get out and share and talk about the town. In an almost recruitment-like stance, people who would be good stewards of the land would be invited to visit and move to the town. "I think a balance that you must strike coming from a city to a small town is seeing places for improvement but also respecting the traditions in the town. It's the classic problem of gentrification and growth. How do you improve an area without taking away all the things that make it unique for the people before you?" said Brit.

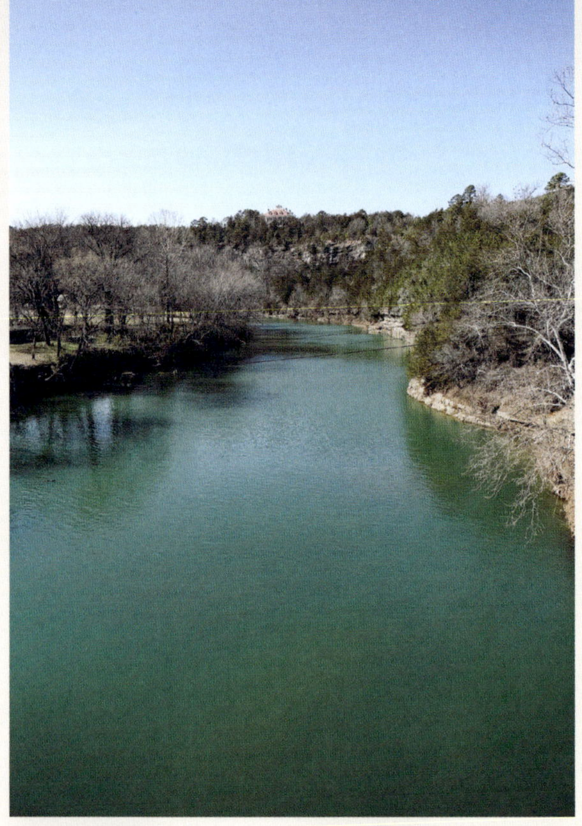

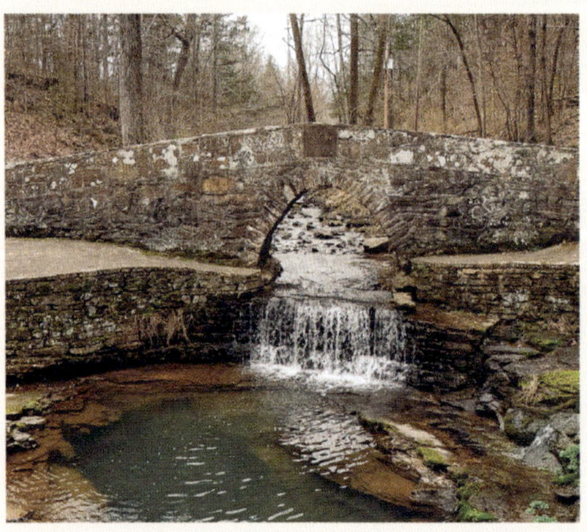

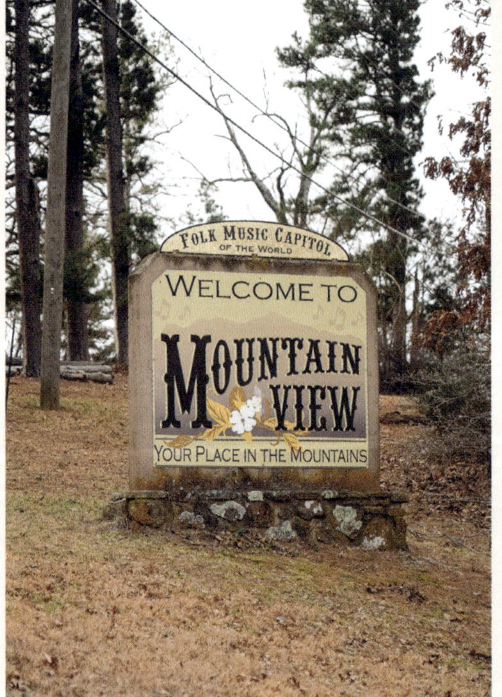

MOUNTAIN VIEW, ARKANSAS

POPULATION: 2,931 full-time residents in 2024

TOWN SIZE: 6.8 square miles

CLOSEST INTERNATIONAL AIRPORT: Memphis International Airport, Tennessee (161 miles)

CLOSEST REGIONAL AIRPORT: Clinton National Airport, Little Rock (104 miles)

CLOSEST LARGE CITY: Memphis, Tennessee (152 miles)

BONUS TOWNS NEARBY: Mountain Home, Leslie, Batesville

ANIMALS TO SPOT: black bears, bald eagles

TOWN FACTS: Mountain View is the folk music capital of the world, with many folk music festivals and weekly gatherings on the courthouse lawn. The town once held the world record for the largest gathering of folk musicians together at once. Along with music, it's also home to the Arkansas Craft School. Mountain View is so invested in the craft that school children are taught traditional mountain string instruments. There is a dulcimer shop in town where they handmake the instruments. Mountain View is a dry county, meaning you can't buy or sell alcohol. There was a folk revival in the 1970s, complete with a *LIFE* magazine article about the town and the crafts created there.

SEASONS: Mountain View is a four-season town.

WATER ACTIVITIES: kayaking, rafting, shore fishing, fly-fishing, canoeing, tubing, paddleboarding

WATER SPOTS TO VISIT: White River and Sylamore Creek

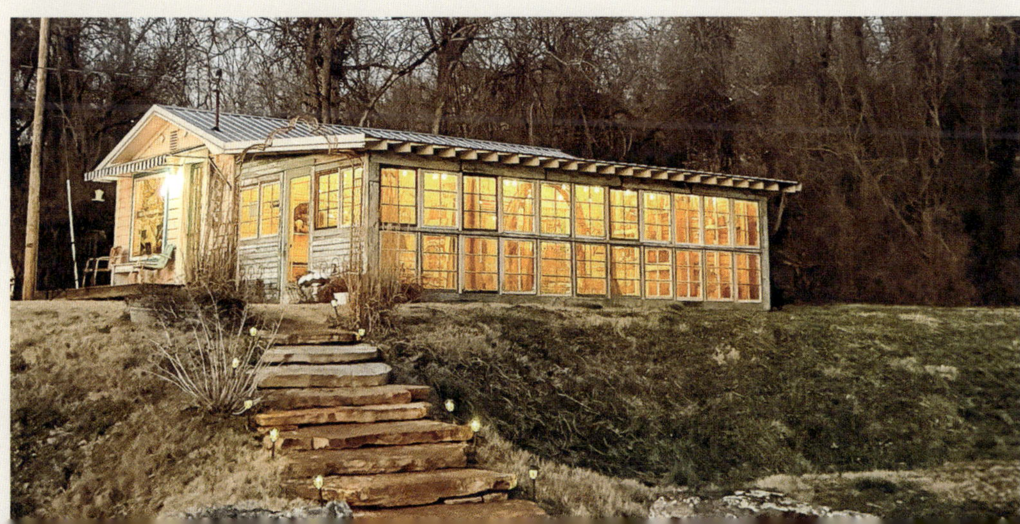

"If you had told me twenty years ago that I was going to move to a tiny town, I would have been like, 'What happened? Am I okay?'"

—AUDREY LEARY

AUDREY LEARY

Chef, Co-Owner of Blackberry River Bistro, and Artist

NORTH CANAAN, CONNECTICUT

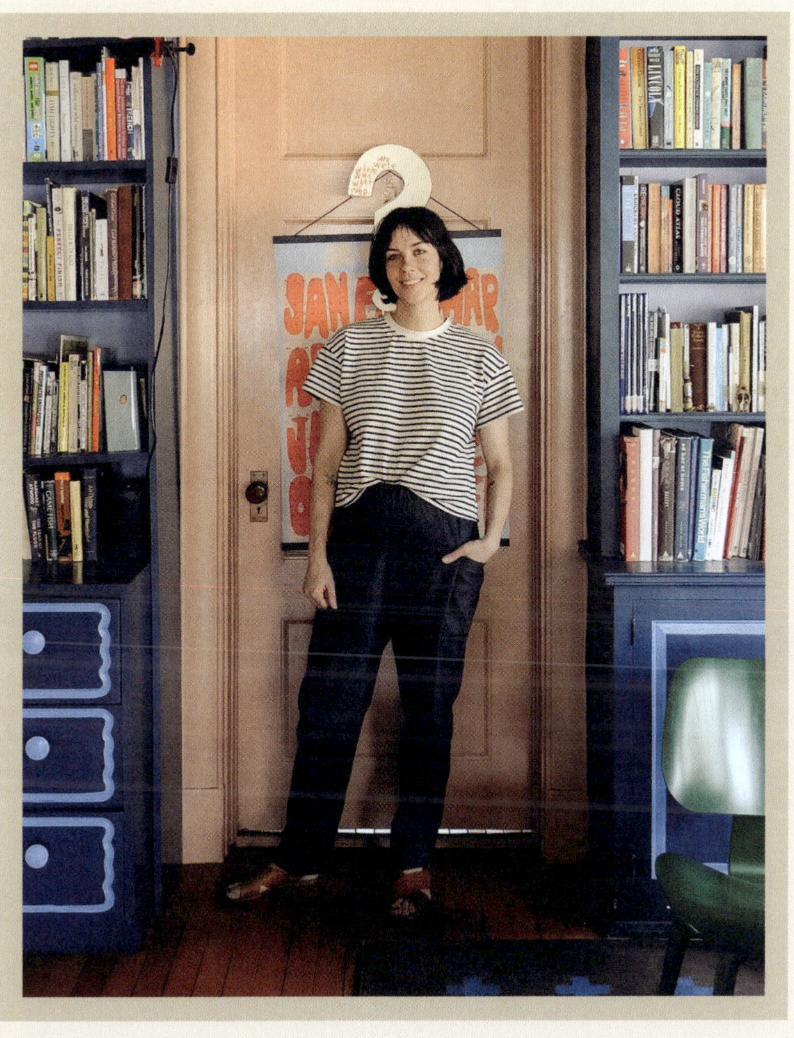

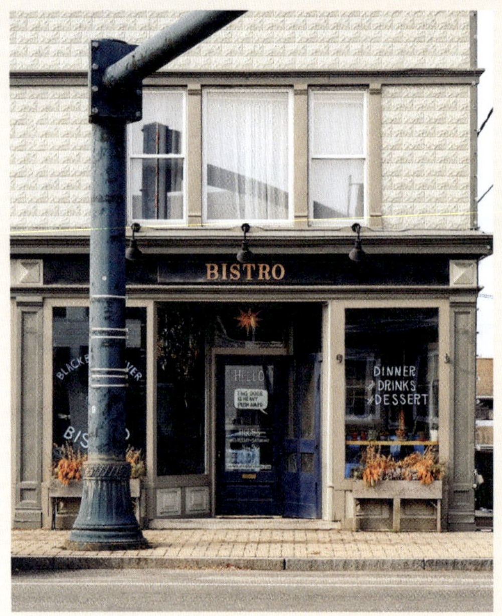

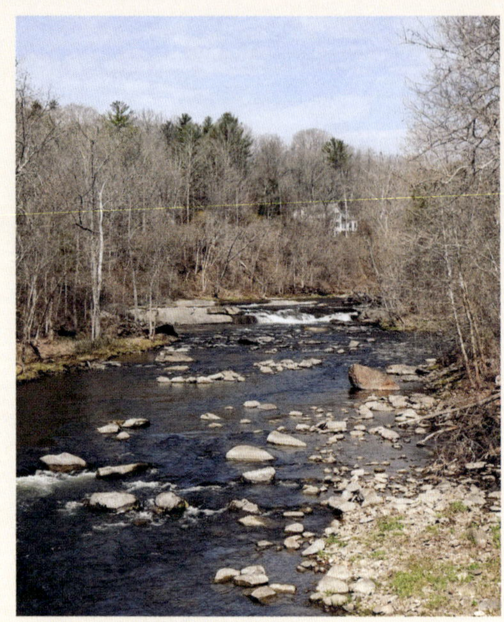

Audrey Leary, the daughter of an English professor, moved around a lot as a child. The family bounced from Los Angeles, California, to Clemson, South Carolina, to the small town of Carbondale in southern Illinois. After high school, Audrey went to Chicago, where she lived for a few years before moving to New York City for culinary school, where she met her husband Sam. In 2012, the couple moved to North Canaan, Connecticut, which sits right on the Housatonic River, a meandering waterway that flows through Massachusetts and Connecticut and is a big draw to people visiting the town. Fishing and canoeing are popular in North Canaan, but hiking year-round and watching the leaves turn golden, yellow, and red in the fall are also popular. It's where you get on single-lane roads and drive for miles without seeing anyone, meandering down back roads past old barns and churches from the 1700s, surrounded by so much natural beauty.

BUILDING A COMMUNITY AND ADJUSTING TO SMALL TOWN LIFE

"I thought I was going to be in cities forever. I love living in cities, but I hope we never move. I absolutely love it here," said Audrey. The path to the slowed-down, small town life was a whirlwind. Audrey and Sam met while they were both living in Brooklyn and quickly fell in love and got engaged. Sam was working at a hospital then and was laid off after refusing to cross a picket line. This set the couple on a path to figure out their next steps. Audrey is a professional chef and Sam loved to cook, so they started thinking about opening a bakery. The overhead on place after place the couple visited looking for a space pushed them farther and farther out of the city into smaller communities.

Audrey's in-laws spotted an existing bakery for sale for under six figures in North Canaan, and she and Sam decided to give it a look. Once they arrived, they asked themselves, *Can we imagine living here?* Coming from the grind of New York City, living hand to mouth, Audrey had to remind herself, "It's great living in New York City, except we don't get to do any of the stuff that is good about living there, so we decided to just go for it." They are close enough to get back to a city when they want—three hours from New York City and Boston in either direction.

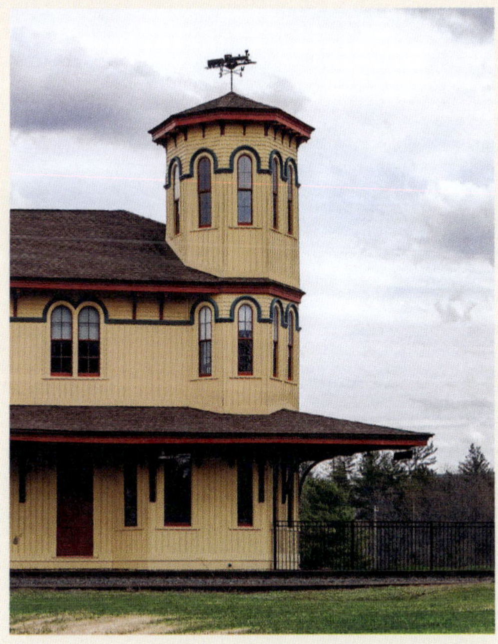

They got to work, running the bakery, making all the baked goods, serving breakfast and lunch, leaving little to no time to make friends in their new town. Slowly, as people started to find them, they began to meet more and more people, many of whom, come to find out, were also New York City expats. "We ended up finding wonderful, like-minded friends here," shared Audrey.

Once they reached a point where they could scale back a bit, they were able to evaluate their quality of life compared to the hustle and bustle they had become so accustomed to. It was evident to the couple they'd made the right choice.

Now, years later, the bakery has evolved solely into the Blackberry River Bistro, a seventeen-seat scratch-made restaurant run by just the two of them: Audrey in the back of the house, while Sam oversees the front of the house. They have a work-life balance in a place that allows them more time with their two boys. Sam can fish alone and as a guide to tourists and skateboard. Audrey enjoys working on home projects, picking up hobbies she thought were a part of her past, and hand-painting murals in private homes.

MAKING A COLORFUL HOME

They bought a house after bouncing from rental to rental for the first year in town. "It's a seasonal area, which makes it hard to find anything affordable to rent. But buying a

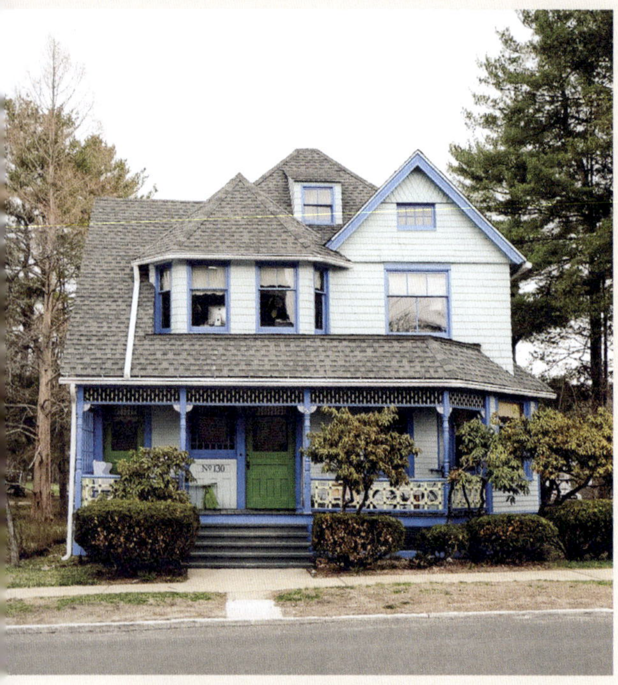

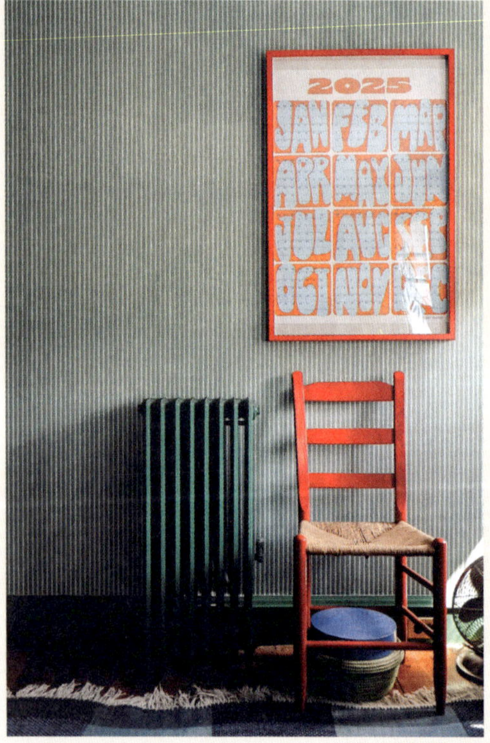

house in North Canaan was super-affordable," expressed Audrey. Their 1894 Victorian has become an extension and an expression of her personality, just 450 feet from the bistro. The proximity makes it great for their boys, knowing their parents are nearby. With a coffee shop close by, the bistro on the corner, school and the grocery store just a bike ride away, and the library across the street, the couple feels like they are back in their old Brooklyn neighborhood on a much smaller scale.

Moving into a white house did not fit Audrey's personality. Drawn to a lot of color, she got to work painting and creating an environment full of many hues and patterns that turned their home into a bold example of using color well. From the outside, you are instantly curious about who might live in the house with a bright two-tone blue and a pop of green on the front door. With the pink rhododendron lining the front of the home, you could plop it down in San Francisco or New Orleans and it would fit right in. It's color-forward, and that's by design. Each detail is thought about, such as the pink trim to match the trees on the porch railing.

Once inside, you are treated to shades of blue, peach, green, and red, to name a few, but also stripes on the walls, painted ceilings, shelves, and drawers with painted trim. Audrey also tiled her own kitchen floor with maroon, periwinkle, and blue tiles in a pattern usually only seen in large city hotels or restaurants, and

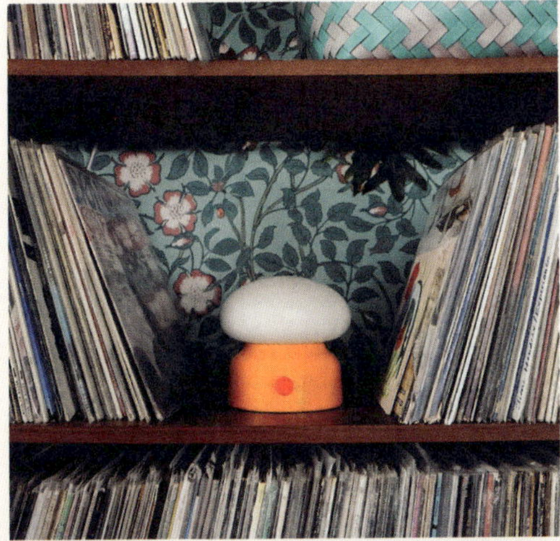

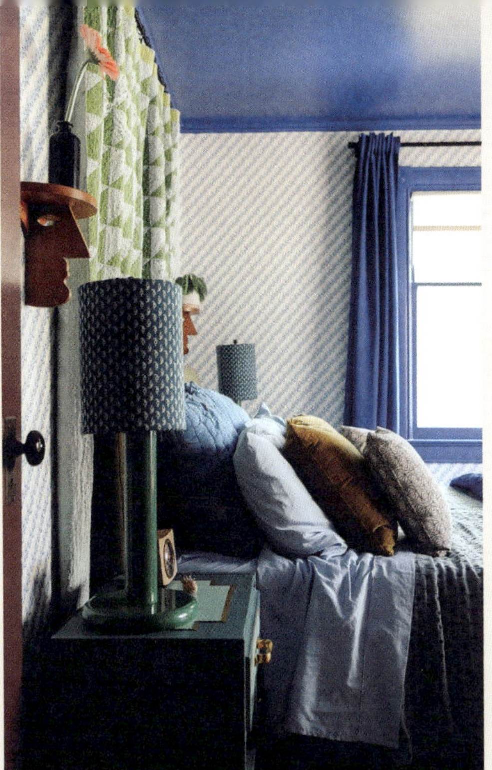

it is utterly stunning, to say the least. Pink and yellow stained-glass windows line the landing at the top of the stairs, and while these came with the house, you'd think it was Audrey's doing since they are so perfectly placed. She has created a home for her family and herself that she doesn't see leaving and one a big city could never give them.

AUDREY'S TOP FIVE FAVORITE PAINT COLORS

- Benjamin Moore — Amazon Moss
- Farrow & Ball — Babouche
- Farrow & Ball — Blue Maize
- Farrow & Ball — Dinnerware
- Farrow & Ball — Pea Flower Tea

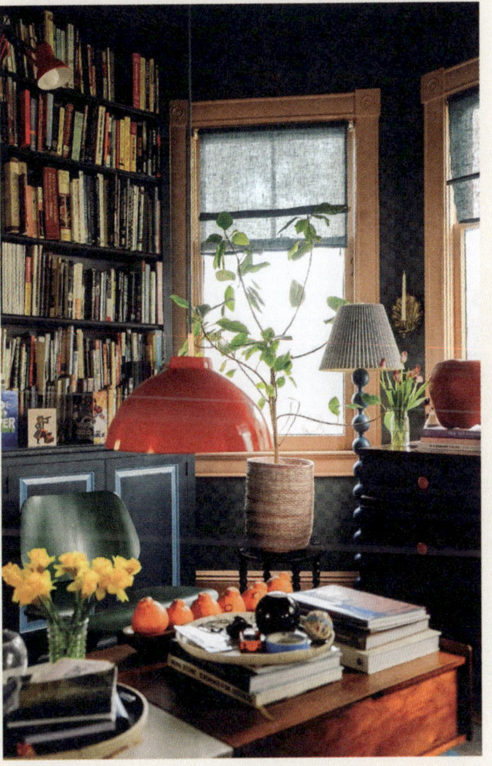

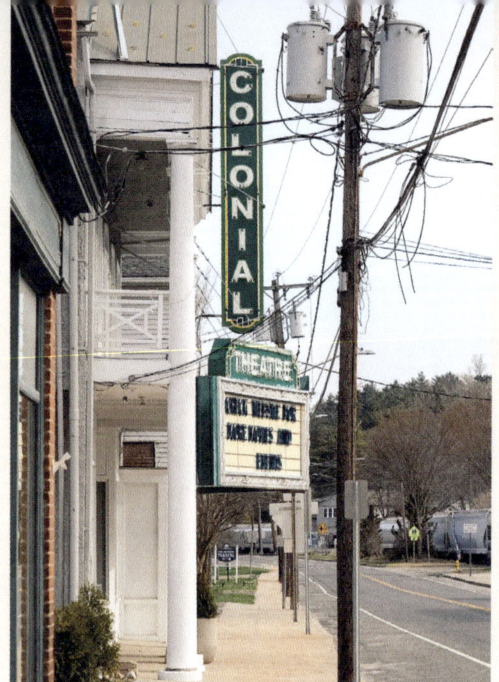

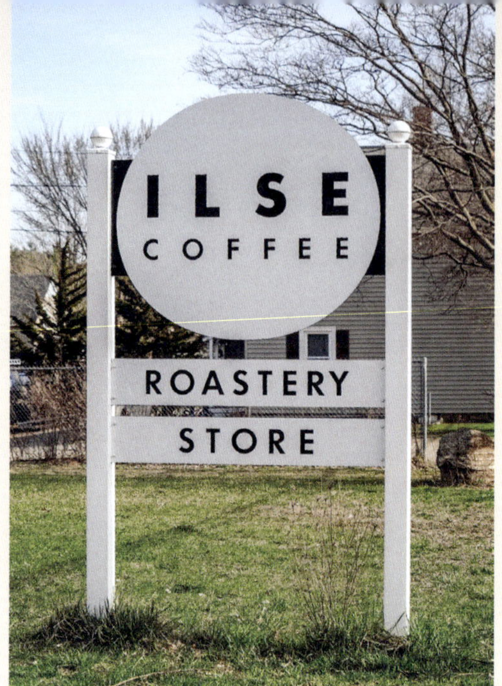

NORTH CANAAN, CONNECTICUT

POPULATION: 1,353 full-time residents in 2024

TOWN SIZE: 33.2 square miles

CLOSEST INTERNATIONAL AIRPORT: Bradley International Airport, Hartford (51.7 miles)

CLOSEST REGIONAL AIRPORT: Danbury Municipal Airport (53.5 miles)

CLOSEST LARGE CITIES: Hartford (42.7 miles); Springfield, Massachusetts (52.9 miles)

BONUS TOWNS NEARBY: Great Barrington and Sheffield, Massachusetts; Millerton, New York; Salisbury, Connecticut

TOWN FACTS: North Canaan was first settled in 1738. You can join a whitewater rafting tour just thirteen miles from town. Northwest Connecticut is one of the most popular spots for fly-fishing, where people fish for trout, bass, and perch.

SEASONS: North Canaan is a four-season town.

WATER ACTIVITIES: fly-fishing, whitewater rafting, canoeing, kayaking, swimming

WATER SPOTS TO VISIT: Blackberry River, Housatonic River, Washinee Lake, and Twin Lakes

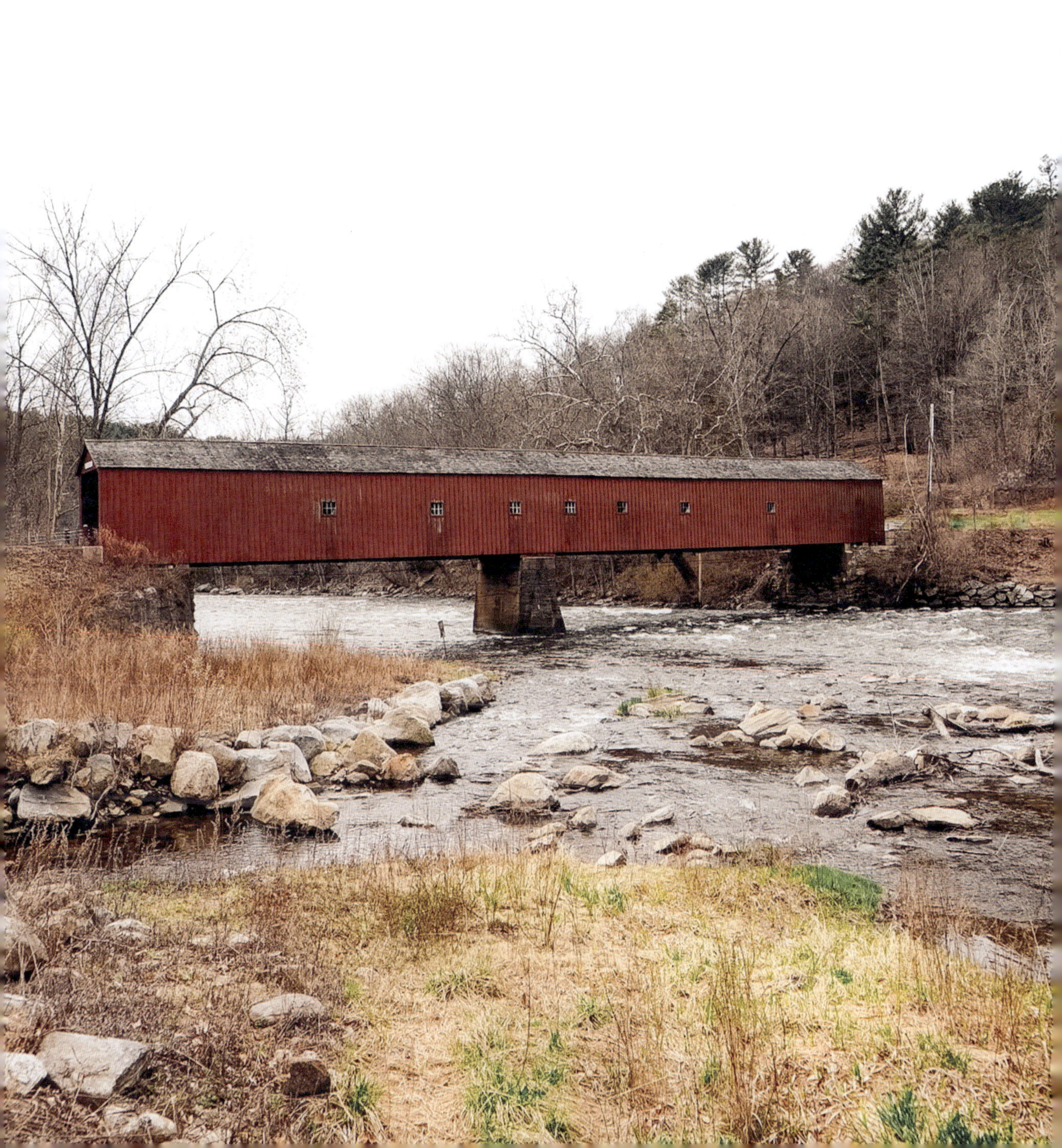

"Saint Francisville is such a desirable place to live, and prices are getting so high that I could see it being gentrified and many people being pushed out. And it just changes the culture and community entirely."

—SARAH ROLAND

SARAH ROLAND

Water Buffalo, Honey, and Blueberry Farmer at Bayou Sarah Farms

SAINT FRANCISVILLE, LOUISIANA

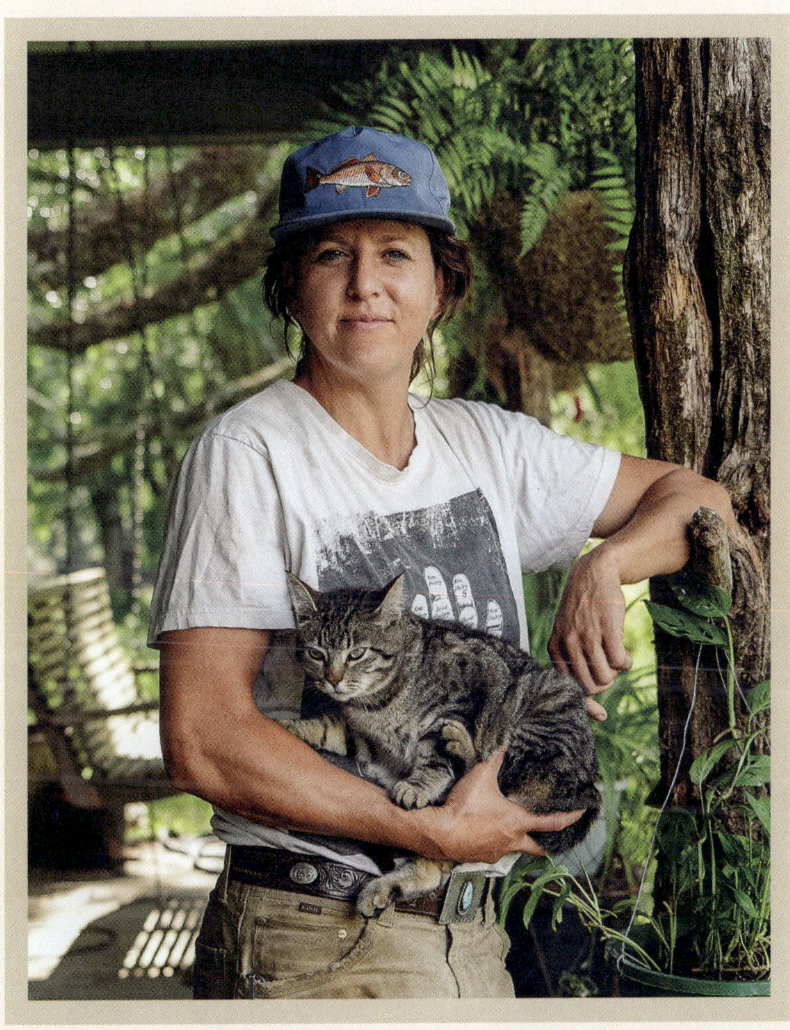

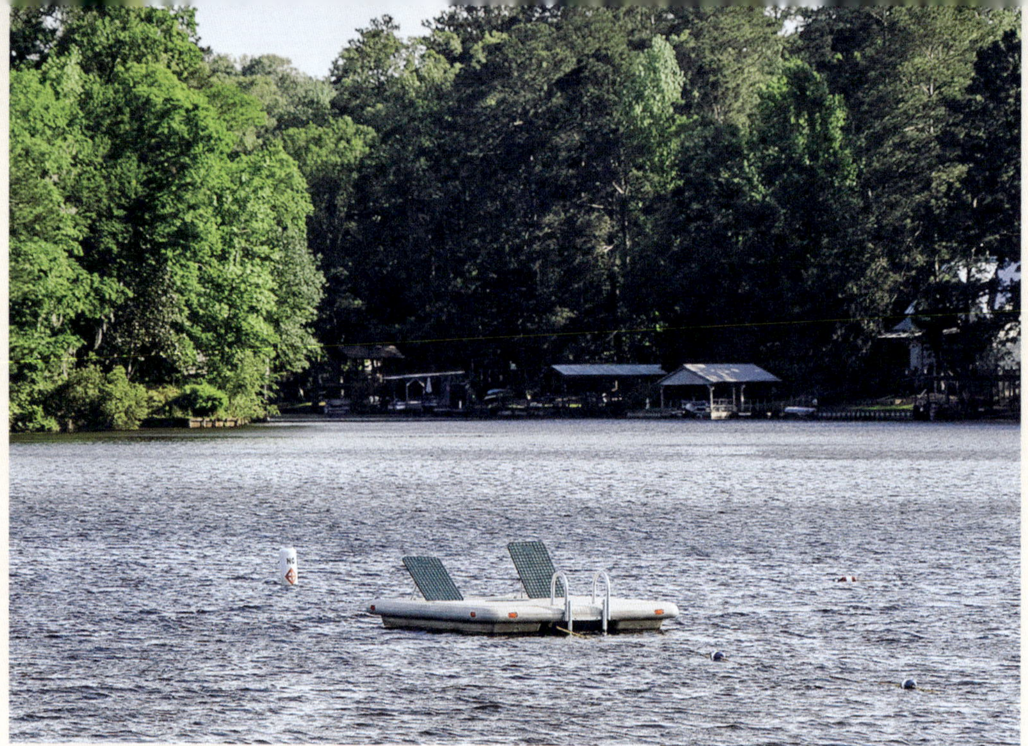

Sarah Roland spent her whole life visiting the property her grandmother bought in Saint Francisville in the 1970s. Her grandmother, from North Louisiana, went to school in Baton Rouge, driving through Saint Francisville on her way to and from school along Highway 61. Drawn to the area's natural beauty, she first bought thirty-five acres, then twenty-five more, adding another fifteen acres, and finishing it out with another seventeen acres. Then, in 1973, she built a home and began cultivating the land to plant gardens and longleaf pines, and because the land was eroded by cow pastures, she started a soil conservation project. It grew to include multiple homes, a thriving garden, and, all these years later, more plants native to Louisiana than any other garden in the state. Setting Sarah up for success, her grandmother left her with land that was well cared for.

REGENERATIVE AGRICULTURE JOURNEY

When Sarah was in the fourth grade, she and her family moved to her grandmother's land. It became a significant place for her, but for the next decade after college, she moved away, traveling in search of where to settle much like her grandmother had done. Sarah went to college in North Carolina and after that moved to Montana, Colorado, Texas, and then back to Louisiana.

In 2018, she began buying land outside of Asheville, North Carolina, but ultimately returned to the area that had left such an impression on her as a child. "While I had a contract for that land, I was planting a big organic fruit orchard with 360 blueberries on my family's land in Louisiana. While doing that, I realized how difficult it would be to start a farm and build a community simultaneously because you need to invest in the farm all the time. You're not out meeting people, and if you don't know anybody and you move somewhere, I think that's the most daunting concept of just starting out," said Sarah. With 360 flags in the ground and blueberries ready to be planted, she called out to friends and family. Even with her offer of wine and dinner in exchange for help, Sarah wasn't sure how many would show up. Thirty people gathered, ready to plant, and Sarah felt surrounded and supported by her community. "I had taken for granted the community I had in Saint Francisville," said Sarah.

Sarah had always known she wanted to have a farm, but she always told herself it would be when she was older. After living in Baton Rouge, stuck in traffic and working a job she didn't love, she began to move up the marker on her self-imposed timeline. *I need to do it now while I have my body,* Sarah told herself. She gave herself two years to learn from those ahead of her, already farming and working on cattle ranches as she moved around the country and down to Costa Rica.

The property she's currently on neighbors the entire north side of her family's land, complete with a home, ponds, and pastures. That's where Bayou Sarah Farms was born. Initially, she thought she'd have a goat farm due to the size of her family's land, but on her drive back

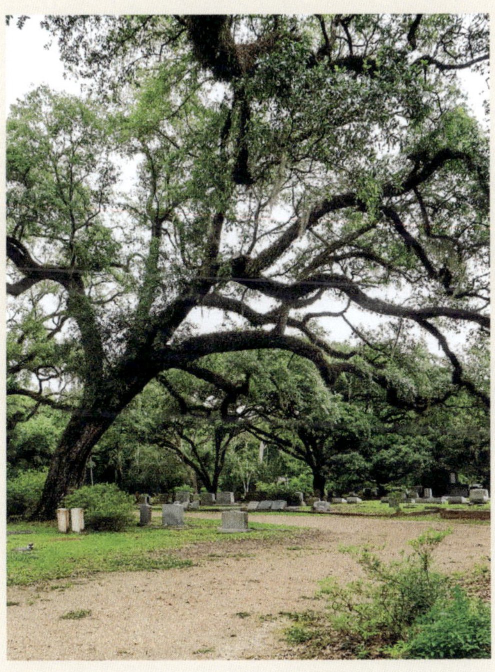

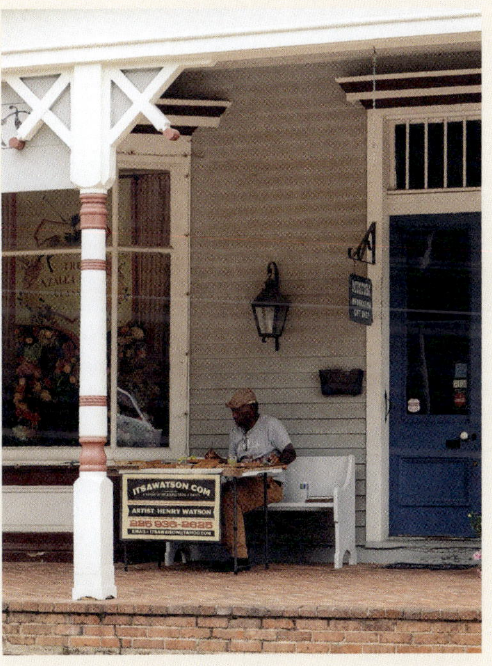

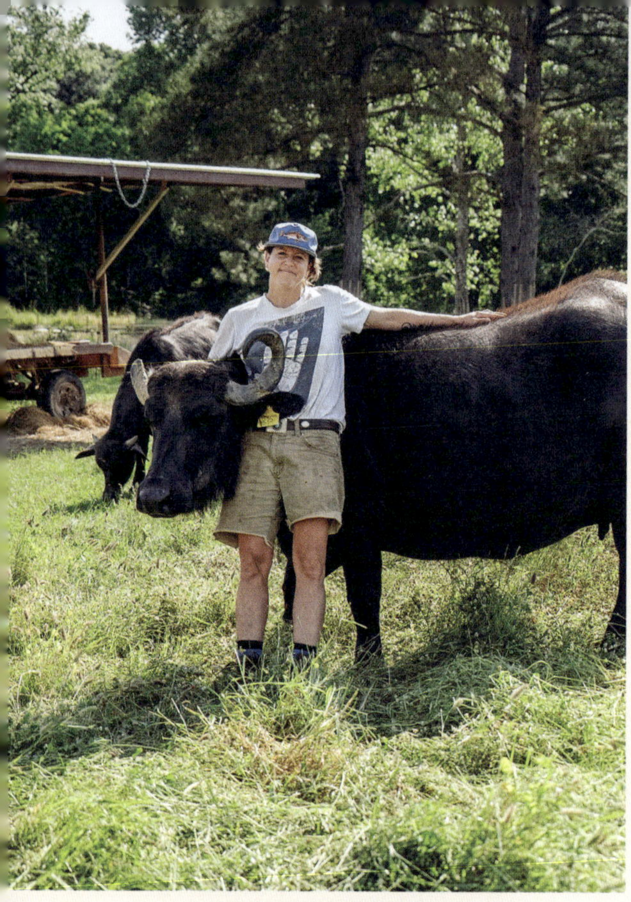

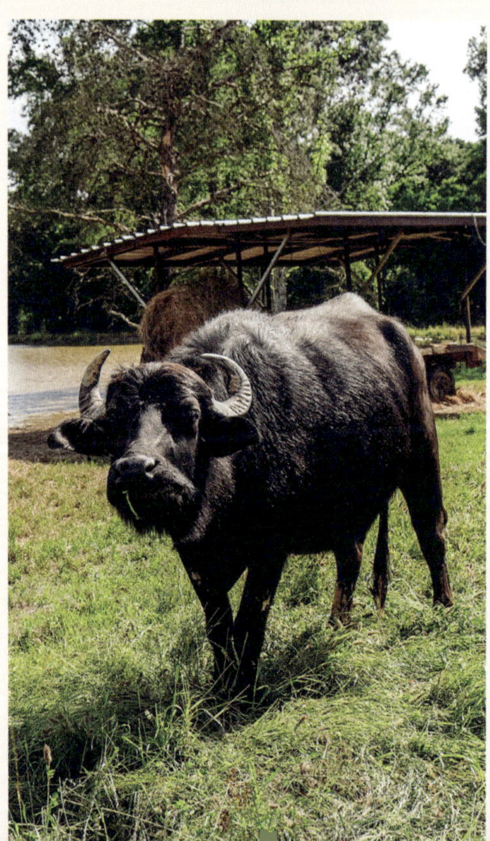

down to Louisiana from working in California, she met water buffalo. "I started a water buffalo dairy impulsively because I had just met the water buffalo. I kind of fell in love with their spirit and energy. As far as having farm animals, if you're not connected to the animals in any kind of way, they become a cog in a machine. You can lose interest very quickly. I really liked the water buffalo but didn't have space for them. When this [current] property came up, the first time I drove down this driveway I could see water buffalo in the pond and was on a dead-set track to do it. I'd figure out the business plan later," shared Sarah.

Water buffalo have proved to be very self-sufficient creatures to raise. Sarah doesn't have to trim hoofs, float their teeth, or aid in the birth of calves. Her herd has survived droughts and is fully grass-fed. "I'm doing regenerative grazing, moving them around and rotating them through the land. I also have chickens on the land. I'm working on improving my pastures. But it's been a testament to the systems that I'm practicing and the animal species how well they do." While water buffalo don't produce as much milk as dairy cows, simply because humans have restructured cows, they are perfect for homesteading and small, local farms like Bayou Sarah Farms.

The land where her farm now sits was once part of a plantation filled with crops. Then it was privately owned and used just for cutting hay, with all the nutrients taken out.

Sarah has worked hard to reestablish the land, giving it back to the native trees and species that want to live there. "I used to see maybe four or five cardinals, and a few days ago, I saw a little flock of twenty. Seeing the bugs, the birds, and the different species that want to thrive here and are being fostered to live here is special," said Sarah.

Living near large urban areas has combated the isolation of a small, rural setting. Sarah points out that she also loves getting back to the quiet when she returns from the city: "I like being able to see more trees than people."

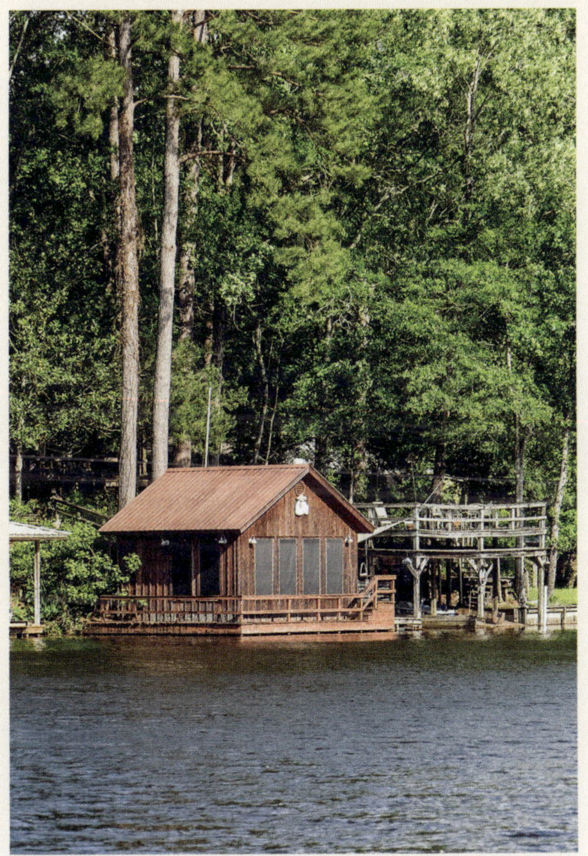

SMALL TOWN ECONOMIC OPPORTUNITIES AND CHALLENGES

In the summer, using eggs from her chickens and milk from her water buffalo, Sarah makes gelato, alongside water buffalo meat and cheese, through private membership sales. Sarah hopes the laws will change so young farmers leasing land in small town America can make a living from the goods they can produce. As it stands, too much infrastructure is required for it to be worth it for the young person just getting their start to sell milk and cheese. Sarah legally sells blueberries, honey, and water buffalo meat to grocery stores and restaurants around Saint Francisville and makes deliveries to Baton Rouge and New Orleans every one to two weeks.

If Sarah had it her way, the regulations on growing, baking, cooking, or prepping food as a cottage industry would shift drastically, and she'd have a little store and sell to the public. Sarah could then increase her herd size and hire someone to work with her. "That would be my trickle down," she said, "But then outside of that, you have the kid that graduated from high school and doesn't want to go to college, or their mom gets sick and they don't want to leave town, but they don't have a job, and they don't want to go work at a factory. But they're good at baking cupcakes. If that could be legal and available and they could do that in their own kitchen, then that would allow that person to have income and keep money in the community instead of everyone having to drive to Baton Rouge to buy cupcakes. I think that if consumers could have more authority over what they're choosing to consume and where they're choosing to get it from, instead of the federal government telling us what is available or not, it would open a lot more doors and bring a lot of economy to the community."

THINK OUTSIDE THE BOX FOR YOUR COTTAGE KITCHEN

If you are without a kitchen and have a cottage industry kitchen product, approach a local church. Many of them have kitchens sitting empty several days a week. Maybe they would be open to you making a church donation in exchange for the space. This could free you from significant overhead for several months while you get your bearings and establish your customer base.

A TOWN TIED TO WATER

Bayou Sara, for which Bayou Sarah Farms is named, connects to the Mississippi River in the heart of town, leaving Saint Francisville nestled into the corner where the two free-flowing rivers meet. Before the town was called Saint Francisville, it was called Town of Bayou Sara. It was a port town for many years before goods were transported by truck. "Like someone who lives in the mountains and goes on a hike, I always get out and explore the swamps. I'll take my canoe, go to the nearby waterway, and explore the swamp or the Mississippi River's edges. We'll go to Bayou Sara, take our four-wheelers up and down the creek, and splash through the water and sandbars. It's a fun little way to spend an afternoon," shared Sarah.

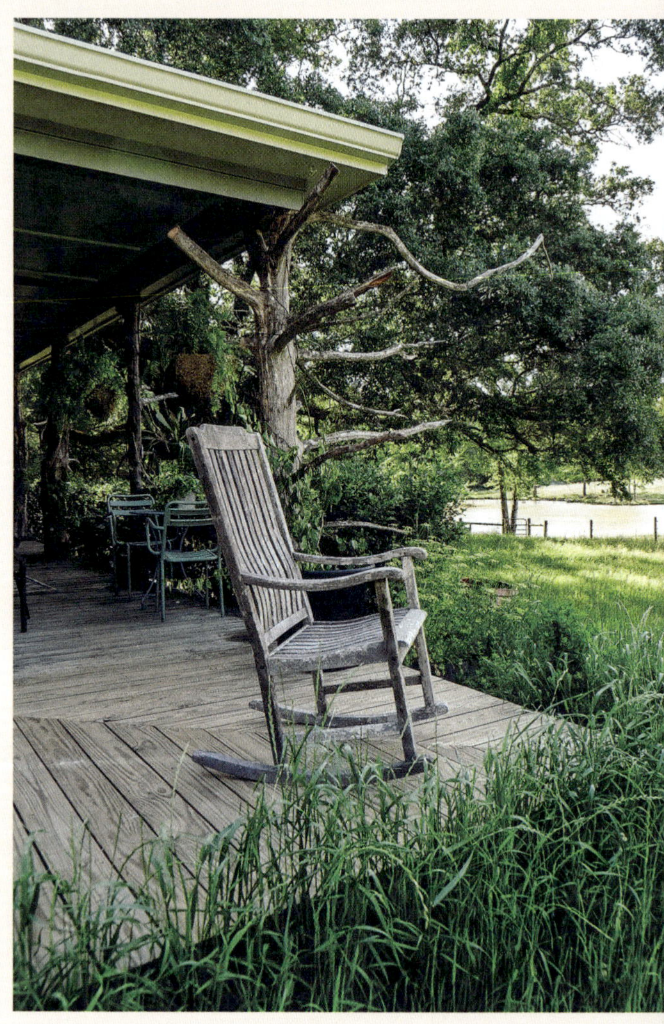

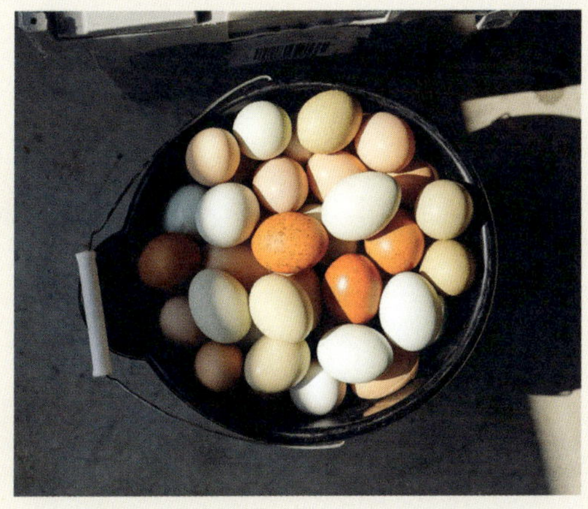

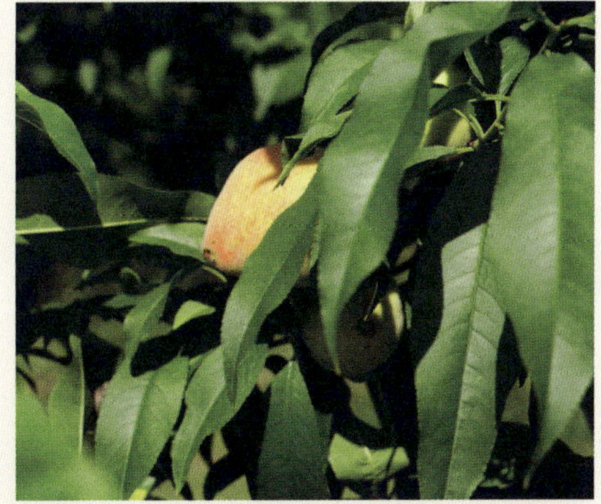

SAINT FRANCISVILLE, LOUISIANA

POPULATION: 1,517 full-time residents in 2024

TOWN SIZE: 1.8 square miles

CLOSEST INTERNATIONAL AIRPORT: Louis Armstrong New Orleans International Airport (99 miles)

CLOSEST REGIONAL AIRPORT: Baton Rouge Metropolitan Airport (25.1 miles)

CLOSEST LARGE CITY: Baton Rouge (31.3 miles)

BONUS TOWNS NEARBY: New Roads, Jackson, Zachary

ANIMALS TO SPOT: alligators, black bears, river otters

TOWN FACTS: In 2024, the town green-lighted Meta to build a 900,000-square-foot AI data center in Saint Francisville. Louisiana is set up in parishes rather than counties like the rest of the United States, and Saint Francisville is the only town incorporated into West Feliciana Parish. A dust storm during the Glacier Period created the ridge where the town was built. The Cat Island National Wildlife Refuge is less than ten miles from Saint Francisville. The Mississippi River is only about two miles from the town center.

SEASONS: Saint Francisville is a four-season town.

WATER ACTIVITIES: kayaking, paddleboarding, flat-bottom boating, canoeing

WATER SPOTS TO VISIT: Mississippi River and Bayou Sara

"I think there's an idea of folks who aren't familiar with the desert that it's only sand dunes and drifts and no life whatsoever. There's still an ecosystem. There are still animals and plants that can find enough water to survive. Visitors are often surprised by how green it is here."

—KYLE DURRIE

KYLE DURRIE

Letterpress and Shop Owner of Power & Light Press

SILVER CITY, NEW MEXICO

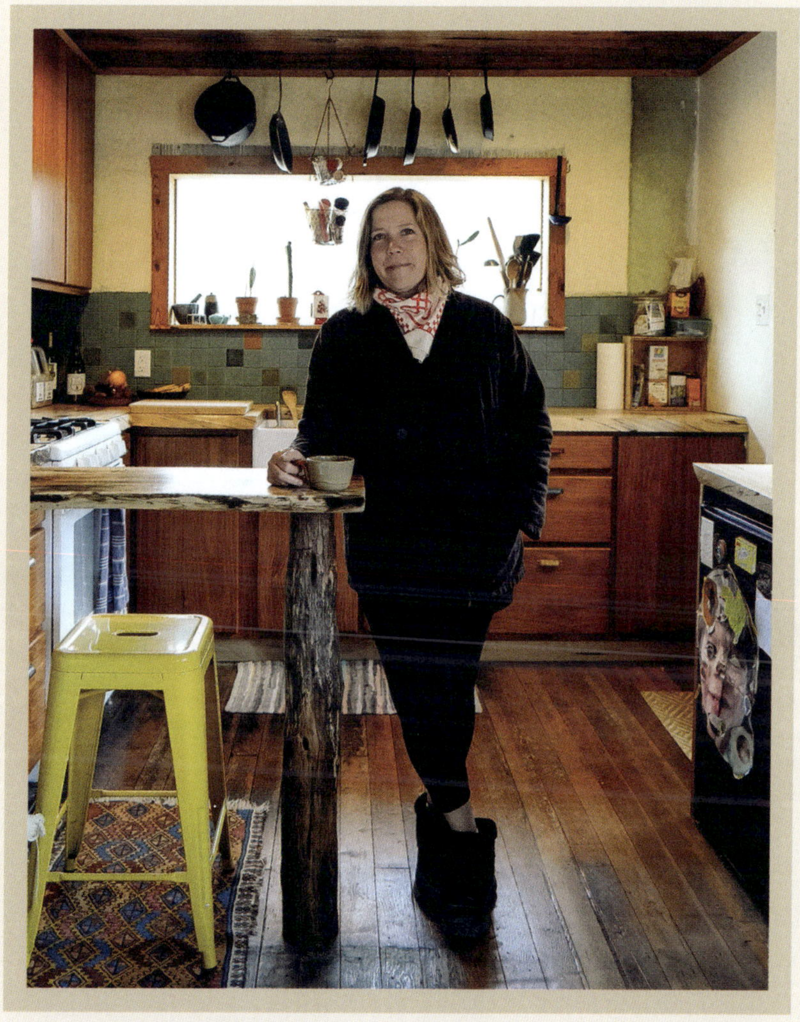

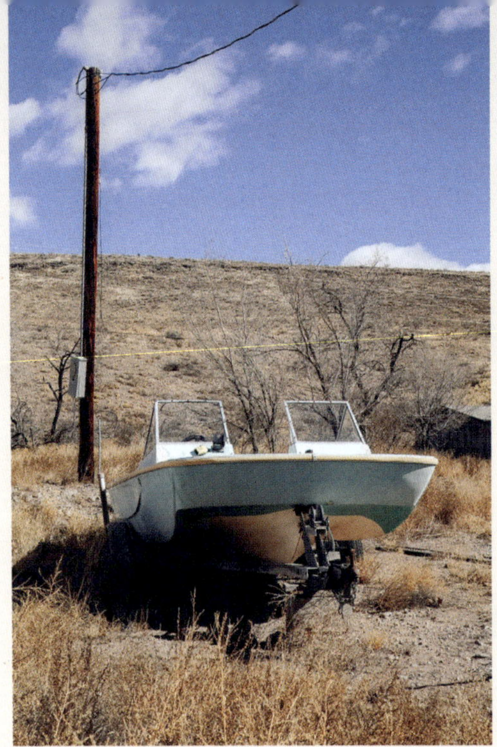

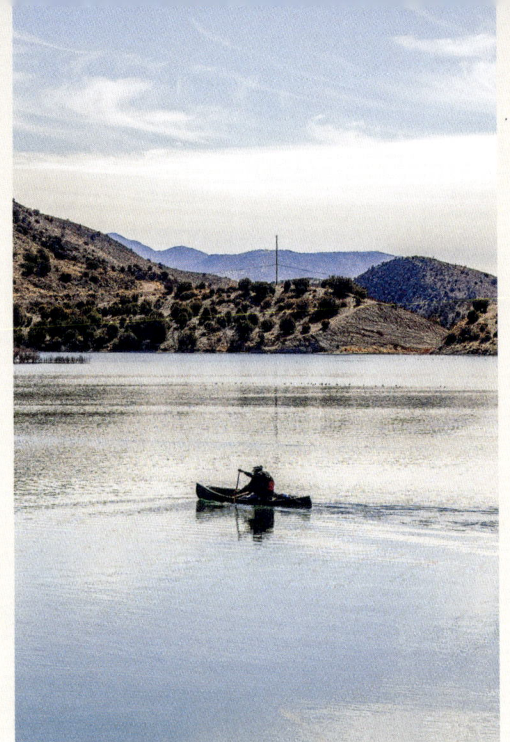

Kyle Durrie, originally from New York City before relocating to Washington, D.C., and then to Maine to attend college, eventually made her way to Portland, Oregon, with a yearlong interlude in Asheville, North Carolina, where Kyle worked for a stationery wholesale business. It was in North Carolina that she discovered she really loved the world of paper goods. Following her time in Asheville, she started her greeting card business Power & Light Press in 2009 in Portland.

Leaning on her DIY counterculture, Kyle joined a cooperative printshop in Portland. "There were several presses that were all contributed to by members, with the understanding that they would be used by other members if we had proper training. So before I ever bought my own press, I had this great printshop to work out of, which was such a formative time for me because it took all that weight of overhead off. I could just start working and not be faced with, 'I only have to save up $3,000 to buy my first press,'" explained Kyle. It also gave her the ethos for how she wanted to run her business.

Kyle and her partner Dustin Hamman, a musician, moved Power & Light Press to Silver City in 2013. They were drawn to Silver City by its affordability and natural beauty. She and Dustin chose Silver City for the local hot springs, like Faywood Hot Springs to the south of town and the Gila River Hot Springs up in the mountains not far from town. "It's way up in the wilderness and my favorite. You're up in the trees and the canyons, and it's right on the river. It's just spectacular," shared Kyle. It wasn't a completely foreign jump for Kyle, who spent her childhood visiting family in New Mexico. The state was always a big part of her life. But Silver City and the whole southern part of the state were new to her until she and Dustin started going there to get out of Portland each winter. "It gets wintery in Silver City, but there are hot springs. It's sunny, and it's just a beautiful place," remarked Kyle.

Wanting to grow the business was also a factor, and Portland just didn't meet those needs anymore as prices continued to climb. The couple also felt the relaxed environment of Silver City was exactly what they were searching for. More than that, Silver City is often described as a creative enclave, full of diversity with a mix of transplants and longtime residents alike, something Kyle and Dustin felt welcomed by right away.

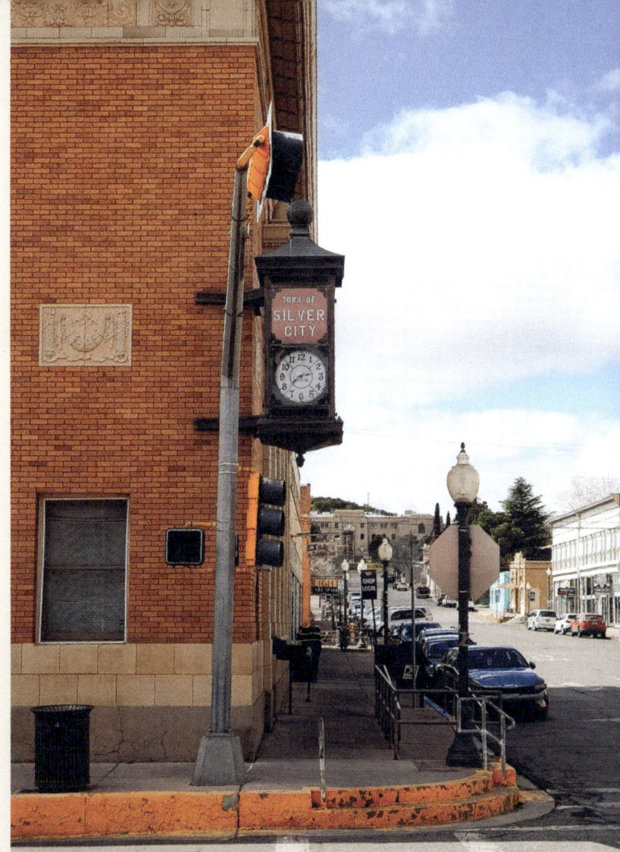

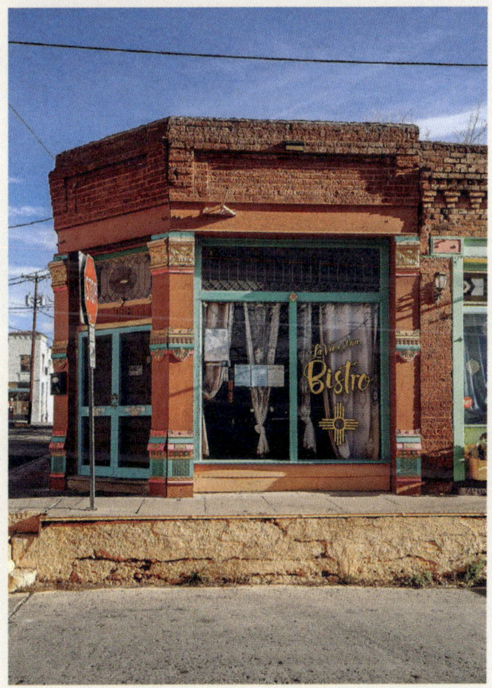

BRINGING THE CITY AND BUSINESS TO A SMALL TOWN

There's an ecosystem born out of the underground music and independent arts scene in a city that puts the outliers into a category of their own. Bringing that mindset with you when you move from a city to a small town can feel daunting, but leaning on that mentality, along with the "if you build it, they will come" philosophy, it's not as difficult as one might think.

The couple began looking for a space outside the city, needing a bit more room, a dedicated press, and a bit less overhead for the change Kyle sought. "All I needed was to be able to ship my products out, and I could do that from anywhere. So it felt okay to move to this tiny town in the middle of nowhere," said Kyle. Having made the trip from Portland to Silver City for years, they felt ready for the full-on move. It wasn't until 2018 that the retail shop was added to the Power & Light Press equation.

What Kyle is doing is very different in comparison to others in town, but with a baseline of curiosity mixed with people who are generationally at different stages in their lives, they are now playing music or painting and opening their lives up to something different. "So I think there is a very curious community, and people seem excited to try new things and grateful when things are happening in Silver City. I found hosting events and having bands play in my shop—people come out and show up for that. It's kind of like they didn't know that's what they wanted, but then you give it to them and they're intrigued," said Kyle. "I think living in a small town has allowed me to pursue what I like to think of as a more original path creatively, rather than just kind of regurgitating what else I'm seeing around me. I think the joke is that I feel more socially obligated than I ever did in Portland, which I didn't think would happen. I was thinking, *I'm just going to move to this little town. I'm going to have two friends, and I'm going to just make my art all the time.* Then you get to know more people

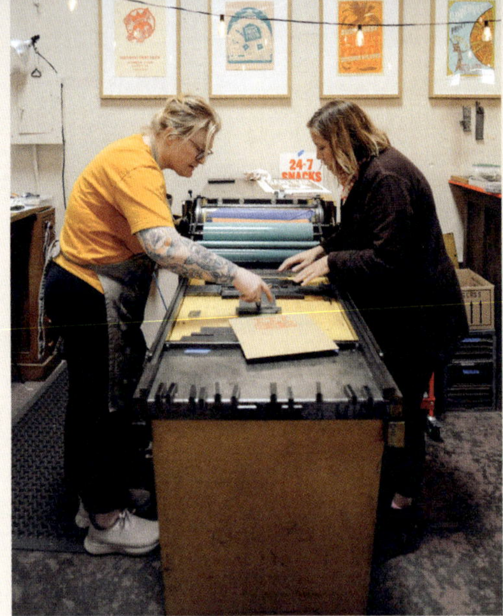

and want to support what they're doing. It all feels like, because the community is small, that support is more important. For example, if I missed a friend's show in Portland, it didn't matter. They had a good turnout. Here I'm like, *No, we have to show up for each other.* We want to survive."

Another business evoking the same sense of community wrapped in big-city ideas is the Whiskey Creek Zócalo, a bar, restaurant, and music venue on the outskirts of town. Longtime residents of Silver City tapped their adult son to move to town and bring his bartender friends with him. Collectively, the family has started to put Silver City on the map for touring musicians. "I know they've worked hard to make the bar happen, but it's that same feeling of like, hey, if you do a thing you're really excited about doing and try to make it available to other people, you're probably going to be well received. It might not always be true, but that's been my experience," expressed Kyle.

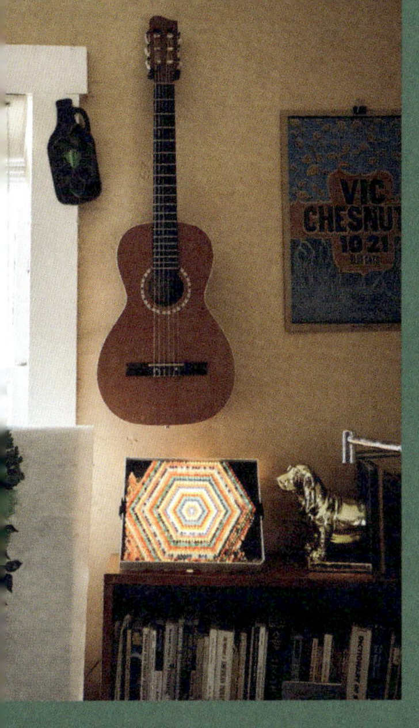
VIC
CHESNUT
10.21

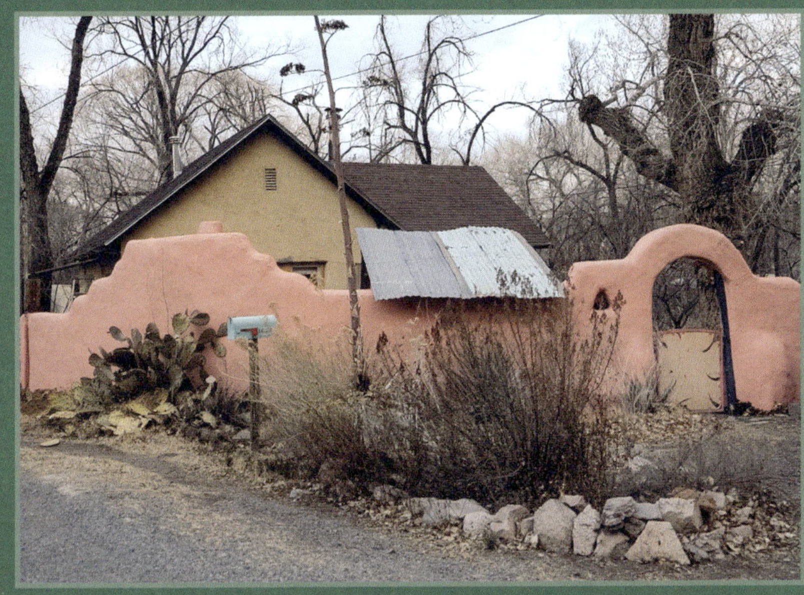

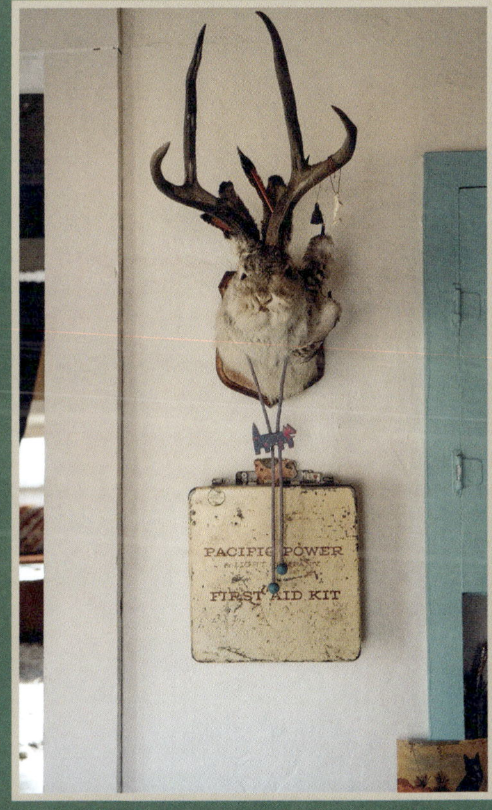
PACIFIC POWER
FIRST AID KIT

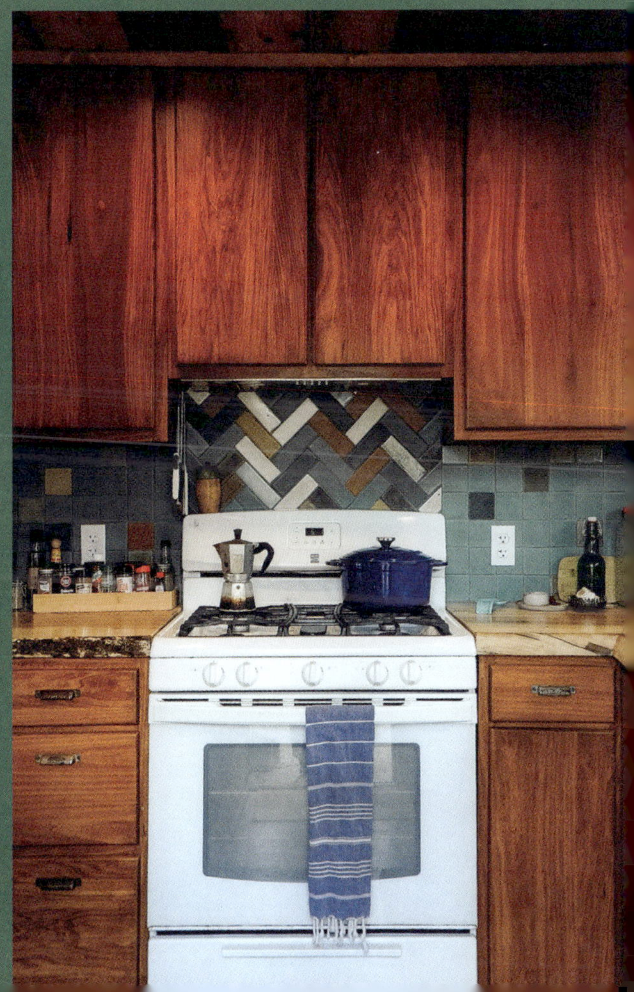

BIG-CITY BUSINESS IDEAS THAT THRIVE IN A SMALL TOWN

BAR: A gathering place for locals that offers game night, trivia night, karaoke, a good jukebox, fun bar food, etc.

GROCERY STORE: Offer items you can't find anywhere else, including local fruits and vegetables, seasonal items, gifts, and dinner party goods. Host cooking classes for children and adults and a supper club. Sell breakfast or lunch and bakery goods, depending on the town's needs. Keep your customers in mind when it comes to cost and what you offer. Stock cloth napkins, greeting cards, and candles—anything a host might need, but also items for hostess gifts.

COFFEE SHOP: Think well-designed, local-as-possible coffee beans and a calm environment. Think about the coffee shop you seek out when you travel and how you could bring that same environment to your town.

CLEANING SERVICE: Focus on green cleaning. It's the future wave, and people are looking for eco-friendliness.

THE ARCHITECTURE OF SILVER CITY

Silver City was founded as a mining town in the late 1800s. That brought an ode to the East Coast where much of the historic brick Victorian architecture still stands. Some of the structures have been lost to floods and fires over the years, but many original buildings remain. Mixed with the Victorians are homemade adobe houses. Chihuahua Hill is historically a Mexican American neighborhood, lined with family compounds that grew over the years as the families did. Near Western New Mexico University, midcentury modern architecture popped up in the 1960s. "There's just an interesting mix of eras. And you can kind of mark the eras of growth in town by the architecture around," added Kyle.

GIVING VISITING ARTISTS A PLACE TO CREATE

Kyle didn't always have running a creative residency as part of her business plan, but through a random conversation with an acquaintance who moved away, Kyle took over a beautiful Victorian apartment to house visiting artists. The landlord, an artist herself, loved Kyle's idea and what that would mean for their creative community. Three people from the residency have gone on to be full-time residents of Silver City. Charging just enough to pay the bills, Kyle never planned to make money from the additional endeavor. "I want to create a space for my people. I know how much I get out of going to a new place to have some creative, personal time, and I just would love nothing more than to share that with someone else," said Kyle.

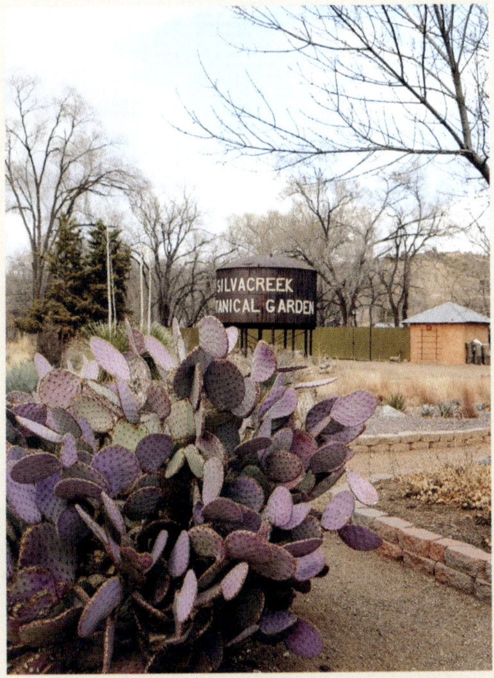

THE NATURE THAT SURROUNDS

When we think of the desert, we don't often think of wilderness, but Silver City sits just over six miles from the footbed of the Gila National Forest, which is the largest wilderness region in the Southwest at 3.3 million acres and home to the Gila River, the first protected waterway in the United States. The nearby Gila River Preserve currently protects more than 1,200 acres of habitat along the river, the last major free-flowing waterway in the Southwest. The Nature Conservancy stated its *"long-term vision for the preserve is simple: let the river rediscover its natural floodplain and enable new cottonwoods and willows to spring up, providing habitat for neotropical migratory songbirds, especially the southwestern willow flycatcher—a species whose population is in trouble. A host of other rare animal species also use the preserve's habitats."*

POSITIVE EFFECTS OF PLANTING NATIVE PLANTS IN YOUR COMMUNITY

Native plants are natural water conservationists.

Erosion is combated with native plants.

Growing native plants supports biodiversity.

Native plants promote healthy soil.

Native plantings adapt easily to local climate and seasonal changes.

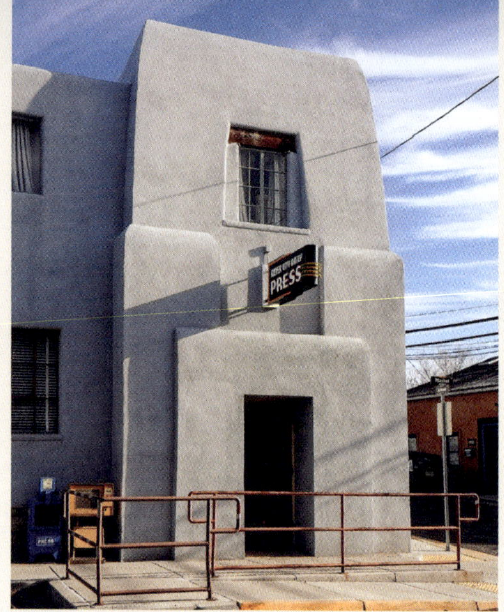

The large Silva Creek also meanders through town, and even though it's sometimes dry at certain parts of the year, it still raises the water table. Trees grow there, and life still breathes there. Even if the water isn't visibly flowing, it creates a unique ecosystem important to the desert. Together with a group of loyal volunteers, the Silva Creek Botanical Garden, managed by the Gila Native Plant Society, is thriving as a secret gem, working to educate the community about native plant uses in home gardens and landscapes. Water or no water, the town of Silver City has made a commitment to encouraging its locals to get outside and embrace the creek along San Vicente Creek Trail, which runs the length of town all through the downtown.

SILVER CITY, NEW MEXICO

POPULATION: 9,377 full-time residents in 2024

TOWN SIZE: 10.1 square miles

CLOSEST INTERNATIONAL AIRPORTS: Las Cruces International Airport (103 miles); El Paso International Airport, Texas (161 miles)

CLOSEST LARGE CITY: Las Cruces (113 miles)

BONUS TOWNS NEARBY: Arenas Valley, Santa Clara, Bayard

TOWN FACTS: Billy the Kid was arrested twice in Silver City. The town is also home to Western New Mexico University. The elevation is almost 6,000 feet, so the summers are mild. It's rare to break 100 degrees.

SEASONS: Silver City has four seasons.

WATER ACTIVITIES: dipping in the hot springs, swimming, fishing, birding

WATER SPOTS TO VISIT: Silva Creek, Whiskey Creek, Gila National Forest, Bill Evans Lake, Lake Roberts, and Gila River Hot Springs

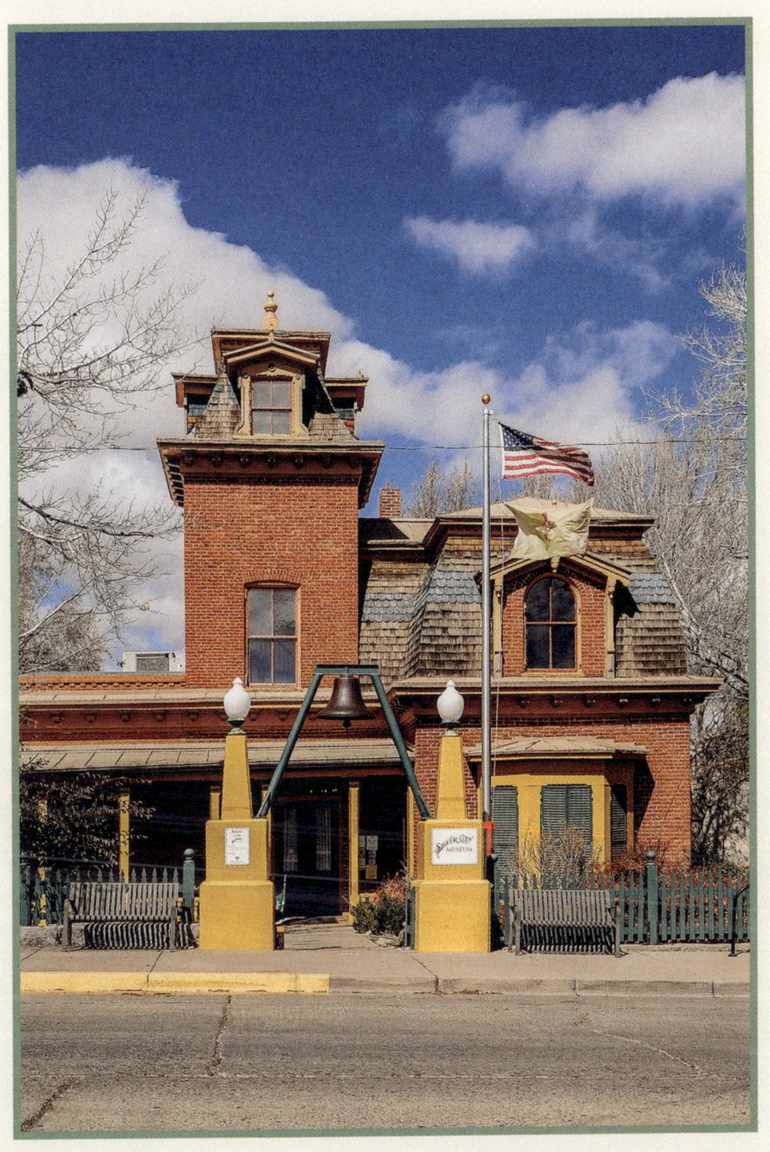
Silver City
MUSEUM

"I think there's really something special in knowing your neighbors and having a more candid conversation about things than I would be able to in a city: being able to be a change within a community, to see the effects of helping other people or different organizations, and having the ability to immediately spot a difference or an impact is something that I don't think could happen anywhere else."

—ALEESHA SERRITA NEDD

ALEESHA SERRITA NEDD

Baker and Owner at Naked Lemon Bakery

ASTORIA, OREGON

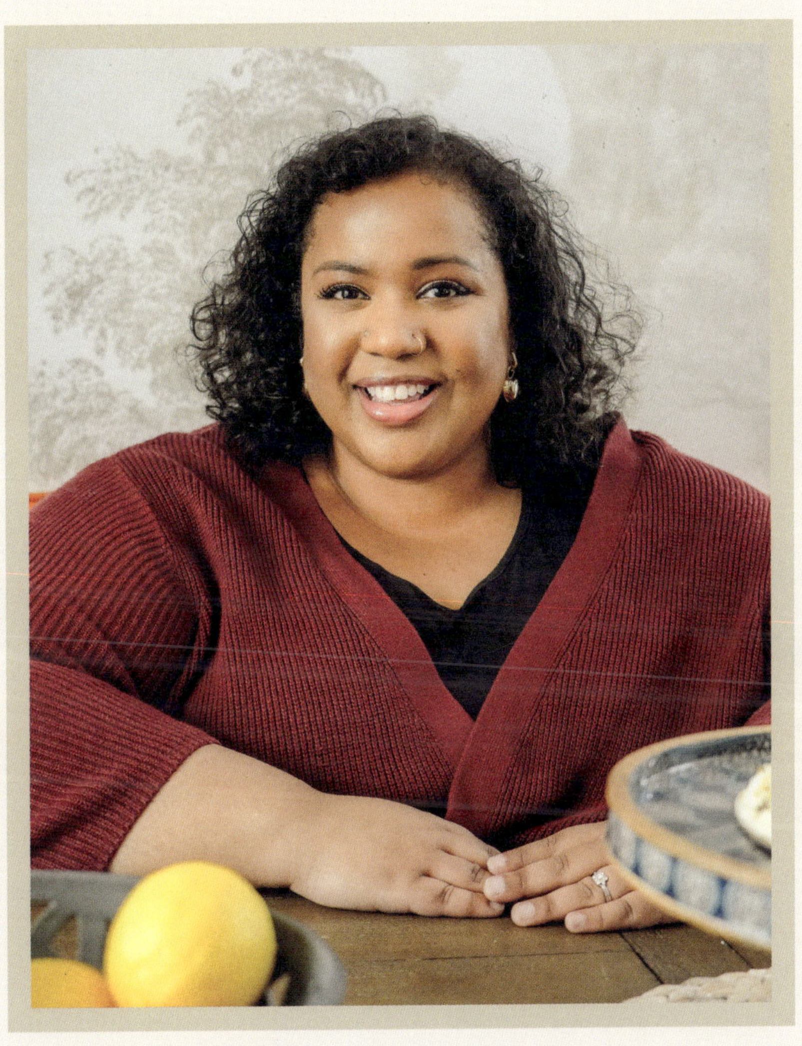

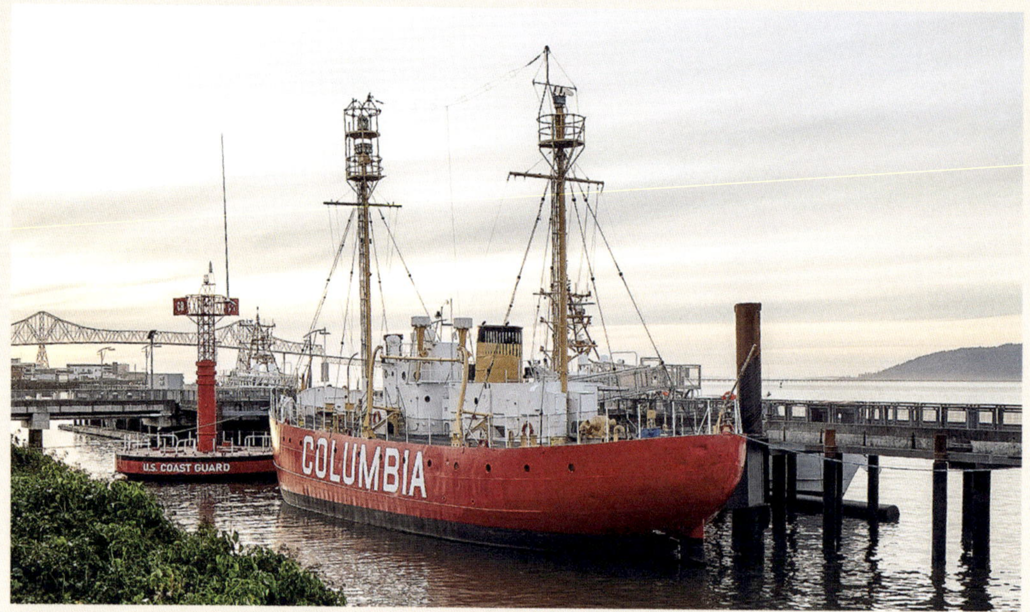

River town Astoria, Oregon, is familiar to many as the setting of the 1980s cult film *The Goonies*. While most of the film takes place belowground hunting for treasure, aboveground the town is full of a bustling community with almost 10,000 full-time residents. One of them, Aleesha Serrita Nedd, has lived in Astoria for most of her life. Growing up in Astoria, Aleesha often had the mindset of getting out of town after high school, like many young people from small towns. "My goal was to go to college, move away, and only return to visit on Thanksgiving and Christmas. And the whole thing turned into I went to college in Portland, graduated from Portland State University, and couldn't find a job. Around 2012, I ended up moving back home and working a lot of food service jobs. And during those years, I saw the niche for a bakery and decided to go for it," explained Aleesha. Naked Lemon Bakery was born out of a need within the community and her desire to create something in her hometown with French-inspired baked goods.

Aleesha's family ended up in Astoria by happenstance. Her maternal grandfather, a military meteorologist, was stationed in the area in the late 1980s. Because they loved the place so much, he and his wife decided to stay when he retired. And the family all moved, too, to be near their parents. "We all just kind of planted ourselves here," said Aleesha. Drawn to baking by the women in her family—"a product of their time," remarked Aleesha, of leaning on the homesteading and self-reliance of the generations of familial women—"I always thought it was so cool to know how to take care of your family and not rely on other people or resources." Although learning a trade would have suited Aleesha just as well, family expectations made attending college a no-brainer. But with her degree in communications and marketing, she's been able to grow her bakery in a way she might not have done otherwise.

SMALL TOWN TOURIST SEASON VS. THE COMMUNITY INFRASTRUCTURE

"Off-season feels very much classic Astoria—a small town vibe and feel—but summertime gets a little wild with traffic and the infrastructure is not keeping up with the people who want to visit. It feels a little unrecognizable, where you can walk down the street in any part of town and start seeing folks you don't recognize. You just kind of know, after a while, who lives there and who doesn't. And that feeling disappears in the town in the summertime, especially high summertime," lamented Aleesha.

How do towns combat this problem? Tourists are great for a town, but how do they also make it comfortable for those who have a home there? A town can start by prioritizing local businesses and culture, ensuring the tourists put their money into the community. Education is vital to a simpatico relationship if the town is big on local customs. Have signage

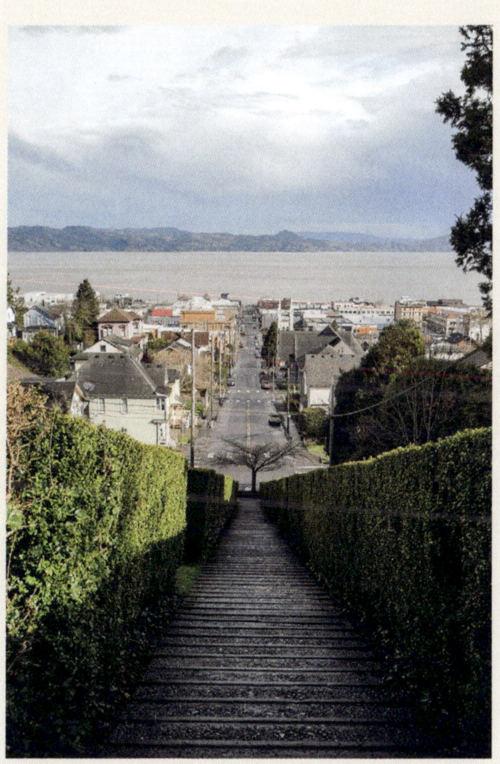

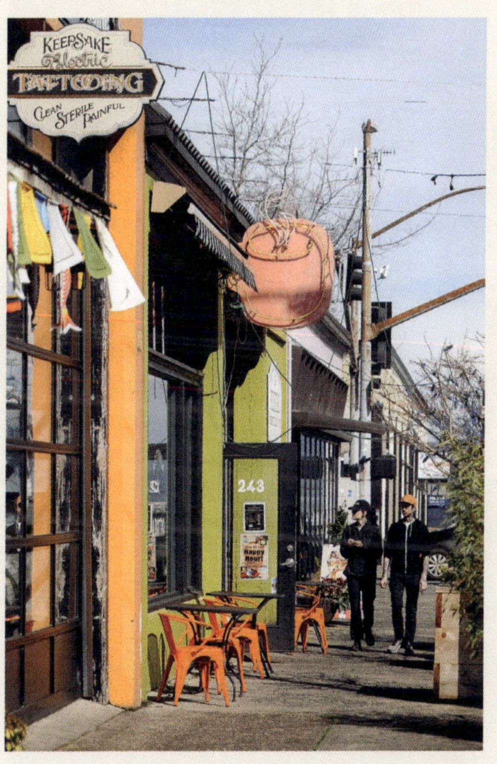

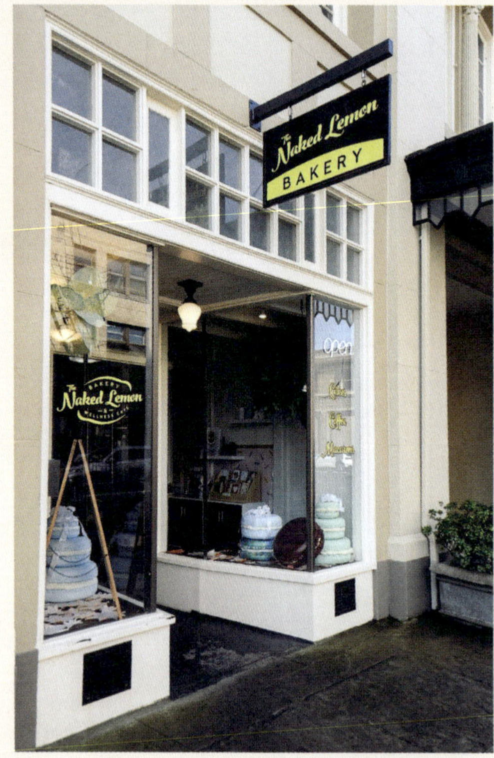

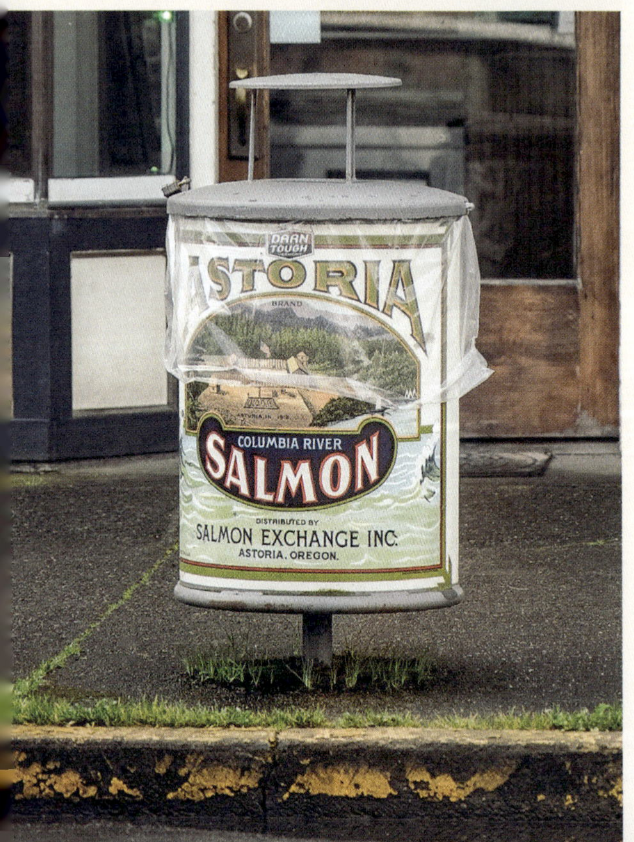

and brochures to ensure your message is clear and concise. Another aspect is holding town meetings to discuss community planning. Give the locals a place and the time to voice their needs and be heard. Offer parking for locals, if space in town allows. Workers should never have to fight to get to work to serve the tourists who have made it hard to find parking in the first place. Taking this into consideration is important to a happy community. Offer more pedestrian-friendly areas and bike lanes, with bike rentals readily available. For homes in popular areas, offer free street parking for residents only. Hire local guides and local-led tours while also developing community-led tourist experiences. In the off-season, hold events that feel more centered on locals.

One of the reasons people visit a small town is the small businesses. The same small businesses are also the ones keeping the town feeling alive. They are crucial, and when we stop supporting them, we start to see the crumble begin.

Aleesha is working to incorporate the local population of Scandinavian folks at Naked Lemon Bakery. Drawn to the town by the fishing boom, Scandinavian locals tend to have a lot of influence with different foods and flavors in Astoria. "We've incorporated those flavors into the bakery, especially around the holidays," shared Aleesha. Working with the local Finnish society, Aleesha has always wanted to ensure she is representing the heritage adequately, so she invited a local woman to teach her how to make plum tarts. "I don't think this would have happened anywhere else where we just have a regular customer who said, 'We would love to come in and show you how to do it, and then you can sell it here during like holiday times, winter, or during the Scandinavian festival time,'" remarked Aleesha, adding with laughter that the woman didn't want to make them herself, but instead have a place to purchase the efforts.

COMMUNITY IMPACT AND LOCAL INVOLVEMENT

Small towns aren't immune to issues surrounding social justice, and unhoused people also live in them. Aleesha has been passionate about contributing to a local group called Filling Empty Bellies, who provide warm meals and warming shelters for those who have been displaced and suffer from mental health and addiction issues. The Naked Lemon Bakery is committed to doing its part by sending all remaining pastries to the organization at the end of the day. She and some of her employees volunteer their time to help the organization sort supplies and donations.

The town is also home to KMUN, Astoria's active, community-led, NPR-affiliated station. Aside from donating products for auctions, Aleesha and her team are not shy about keeping the volunteers and DJs fed during their fundraisers. Public radio is rare in a small town

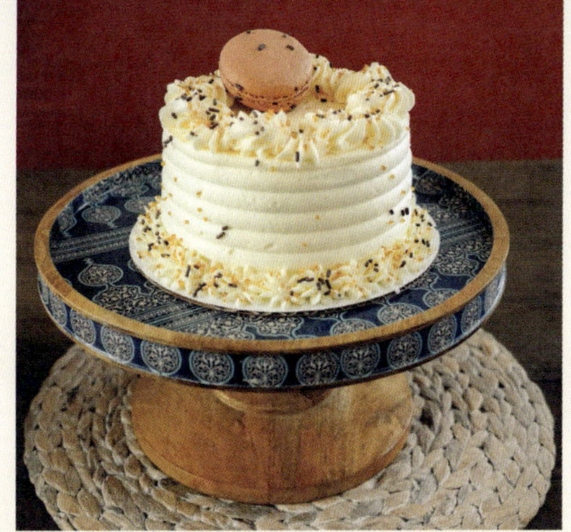

but also needed, as not everyone has access to free and public news and music otherwise. "We're talking in different community groups about how important it is now to look into what we can control, which is our local communities, and make sure local radio and these resources don't die and don't waver in a time when local elections are going to be just as important as anything else," expressed Aleesha.

LOOKING BEYOND SOCIAL MEDIA

As a town, think about how you get calendar events and information to the residents. It could be a community bulletin board or a listing in the local paper. It could be a postcard that can be picked up at local businesses around town. Give a rundown on the radio station if you are fortunate enough to have one. Consider offering options beyond social media, as not everyone has access to those channels.

CHALLENGES OF SMALL TOWN BUSINESS

Day-to-day for Aleesha means wearing all the hats in a life revolving around Naked Lemon Bakery. From her downtown storefront, where the glass cases are filled with cookies, cakes, French macarons, and scones, to her wholesale business, where she sells to local coffee shops and the community college, Aleesha has built a successful business. While her space is small at around 650 square feet, it's been exactly what she needed for the walking traffic in the area. As for scaling up and expanding outward to other communities, Aleesha moved into a production kitchen. This will allow her to take her goods down the Oregon Coast, with wholesale first in line for the revamping and then an expansion on the retail side of things to follow. "The Oregon Coast and along the 101, all the towns have their own identity, and they're spaced apart well to accommodate wholesale. You don't want to saturate a space with a product. That wouldn't be fair to the retailer or sustainable for wholesale," said Aleesha.

Every business has little fires to put out, from employee issues to coverage to cost of goods. But Aleesha shared, "When I pull back and look at things, the fact that I can do this for a living is amazing. To be able to creatively do something that I really like and enjoy, I'm grateful and thankful in a lot of ways."

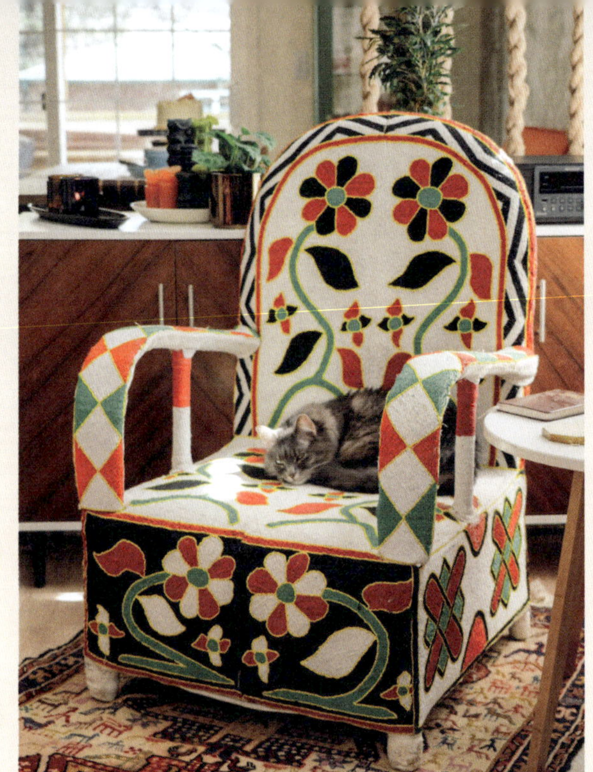

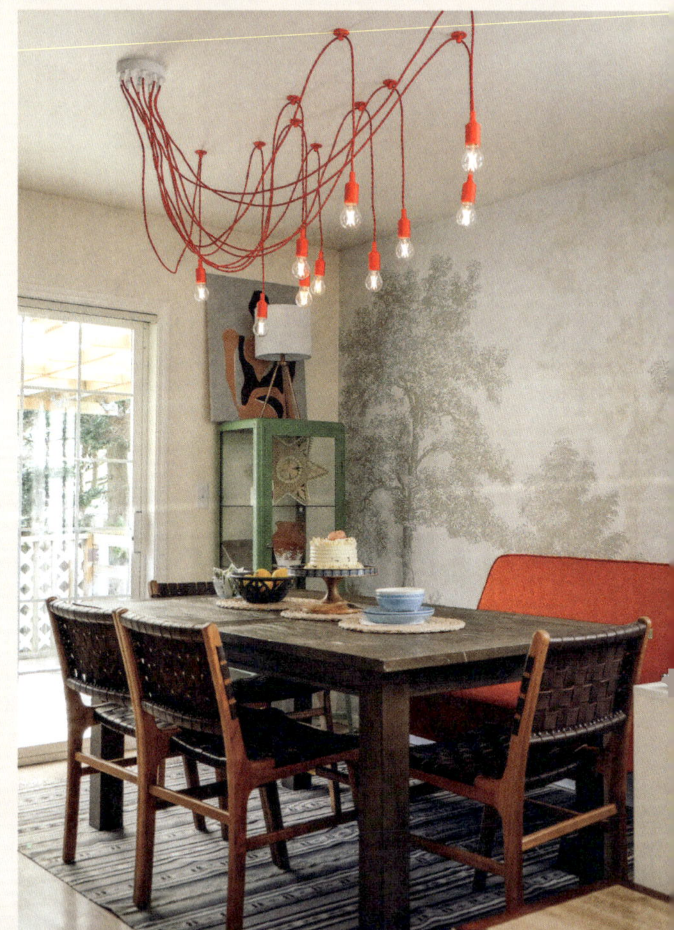

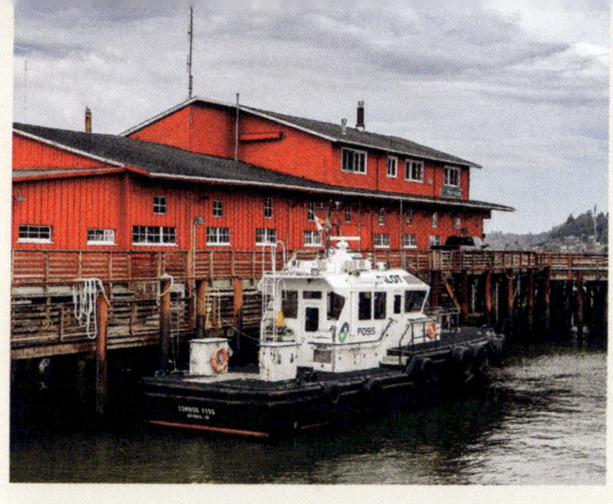

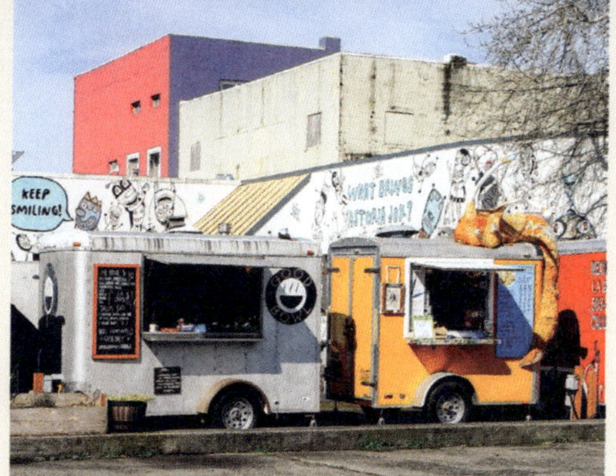

ASTORIA, OREGON

POPULATION: 9,986 full-time residents in 2024

TOWN SIZE: 10.6 square miles

CLOSEST INTERNATIONAL AIRPORT: Portland International Airport (96.9 miles)

CLOSEST REGIONAL AIRPORT: Astoria Regional Airport (6.6 miles)

CLOSEST LARGE CITIES: Vancouver, Washington (89.1 miles); Portland (97.6 miles)

BONUS TOWNS NEARBY: Warrenton, Gearhart, Seaside

BEST TIME TO WHALE-WATCH: Watch for gray whales during their migration, mid-December to mid-January and late March until June.

TOWN FACTS: Astoria was the last destination of the Lewis and Clark Expedition in 1805. The town is the oldest American settlement west of the Rocky Mountains. The 1980s cult classic *The Goonies* was filmed in Astoria, along with *Kindergarten Cop*, *Short Circuit*, and *Free Willy*, to name a few. One foot of the longest continuous truss bridge in North America—the Astoria-Megler Bridge at four miles long—is in Astoria. Astoria has a riverfront trolley line built with repurposed railroad tracks from the Columbia River train line. Astoria has a very active NPR affiliate community-led public radio station, KMUN. There is a vast population of Scandinavian residents who immigrated to the area many years ago following the fishing boom of the town.

SEASONS: Astoria is a two-season town.

WATER ACTIVITIES: scuba diving, boating to explore islands and the wildlife refuge nearby, kayaking, swimming, visiting the beach not too far away

WATER SPOTS TO VISIT: Youngs River, Youngs Bay, and Columbia River

"I took for granted how gorgeous aesthetically Vermont is, and it works its way into your artwork. When you have this type of surroundings, it's very easy to get people in a creative zone."

—WILL KASSO CONDRY

WILL KASSO CONDRY, JENNIFER HERRERA CONDRY, AND ALEXA HERRERA CONDRY

Juniper Creative: Visual Artist, Mural Artist, Herbalist, Massage Therapist, Creative Director

BRANDON, VERMONT

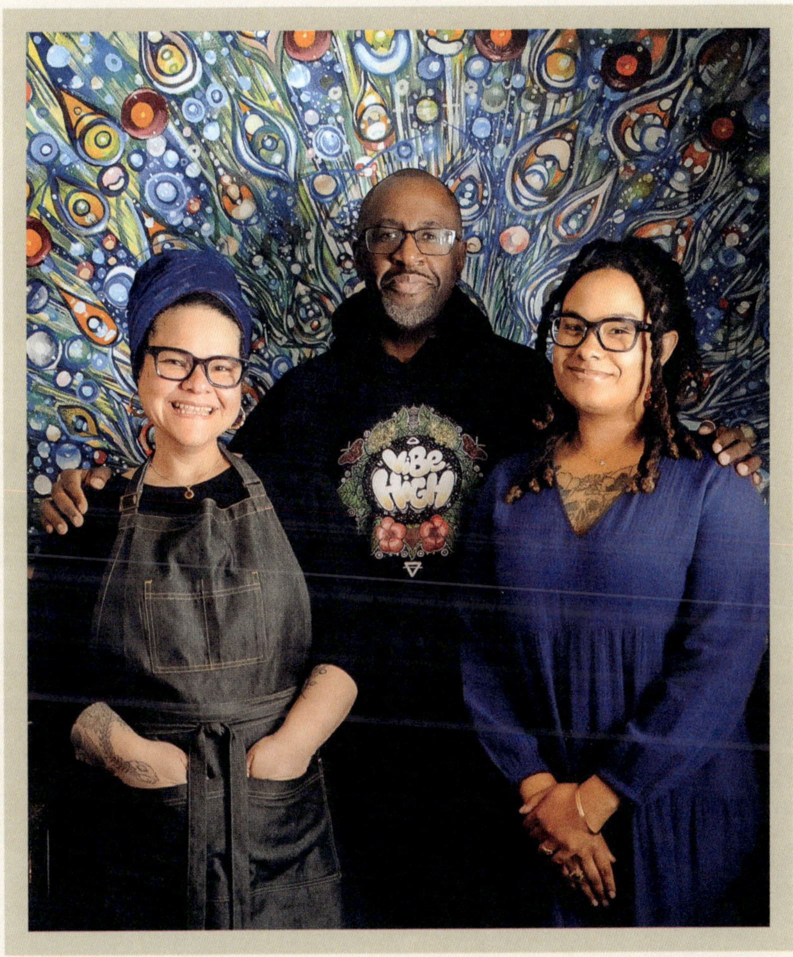

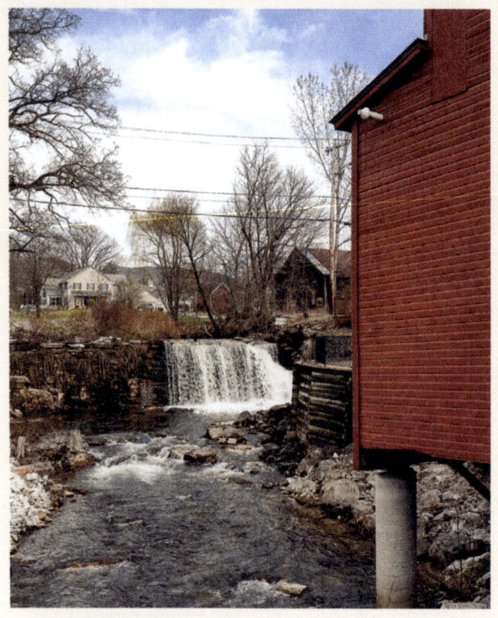

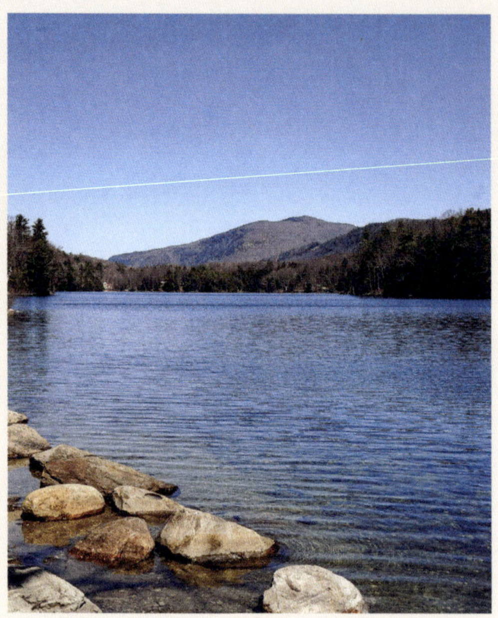

Jennifer Herrera, a college professor who grew up in Harlem in New York City, moved to Tempe, Arizona, and to Washington, D.C., where her daughter Alexa was born. Shortly after Alexa's birth, Jennifer took a teaching job at Penn State in State College, Pennsylvania, before transferring to teach at Middlebury College in Middlebury, Vermont, where she was a founding member of Middlebury College's first multicultural center.

Jennifer met Will Kasso Condry, a street artist from Trenton, New Jersey, in 2012 in an off-chance encounter. He was the guest speaker at Middlebury College, and coincidently, his niece was one of Jennifer's students and encouraged the two to get together. They became fast friends, talking about art, their lives, and how art intersects with everything in their lives. Jennifer and Will stayed close over the next four years, but it wasn't until Will described hitting a creative ceiling in Trenton that Jennifer invited him to come to Vermont for a little respite. Jennifer's advocacy also brought him back to Vermont to do a TEDx Talk. Still hitting that wall in New Jersey, Will took an extended trip to California to ensure Vermont was really the place he was supposed to move to. "I thought maybe Los Angeles or Oakland was where I needed to be, the pace that I was looking for. But I found it here in Vermont," shared Will. He moved to Vermont in January 2017, and the two started collaborating almost instantly.

THE EVOLUTION FROM FREESTYLE MURALS TO STRUCTURED, COHESIVE DESIGNS

"Before moving to Vermont, a lot of my art was done in Trenton, mostly around community rejuvenation, getting people into the power of what art can do for them," said Will. In 2012, he started a nonprofit called SAGE Coalition, where styles advanced graffiti evolution. During that time, he was heavily involved in the graffiti and street art scenes. "I organized other graffiti and street artists, traditional artists, poets, and teachers to come together and do inner city beautification projects. I would go into an area of the city that was hard hit economically and socially, and we would do public art campaigns. Those public art campaigns would be held over a three-day weekend as a block party, and we would paint all the abandoned buildings with public art. We were basically turning blocks into outside art galleries."

With the attention Will's work was receiving, it looked as if he'd just popped up out of nowhere to an outsider, especially politicians and local officials. But to those who knew him as a street artist before starting SAGE Coalition, Will had already garnered his community's support for the work to come by building those community relations for many years.

Then in the fall of 2012, Will took his street art initiative, called Windows of Soul, on the road. He traveled to Vermont, where his niece was in school, to talk about using street art as a form of activism.

A DREAM THAT LED TO BRANDON

"In August 2018, a year after we were married, I had a dream that led us to Brandon and this house. We began looking for a new house with more water around us because that was the dream. We went to the ocean to talk about this dream, but it wasn't there. Within months,

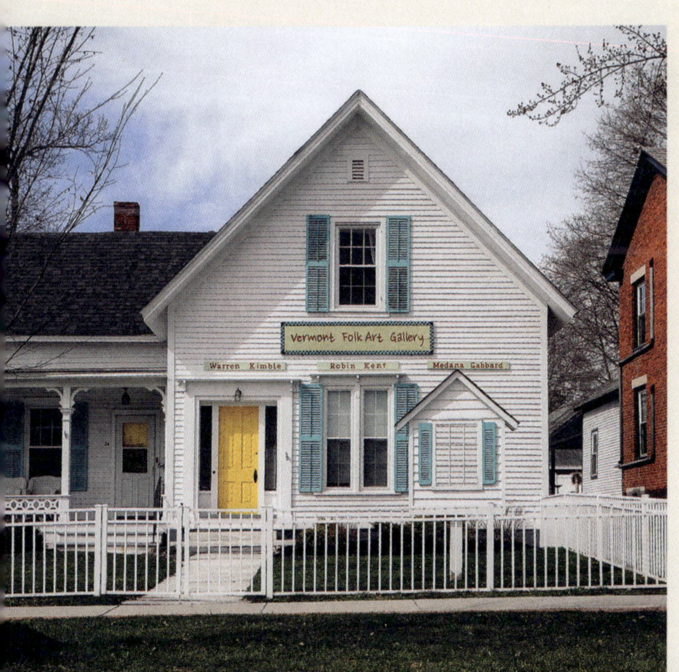

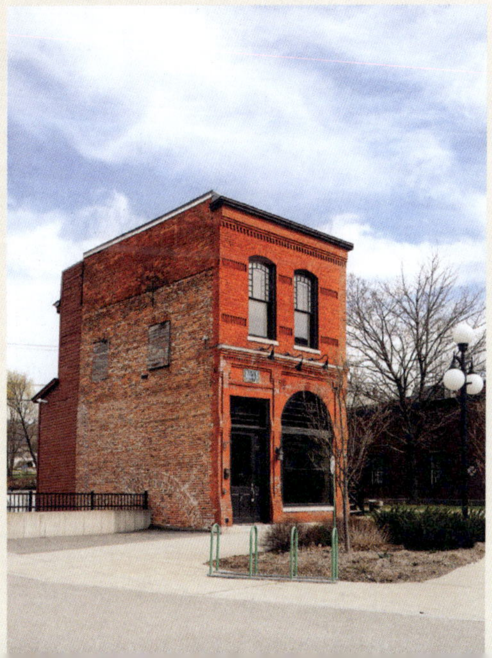

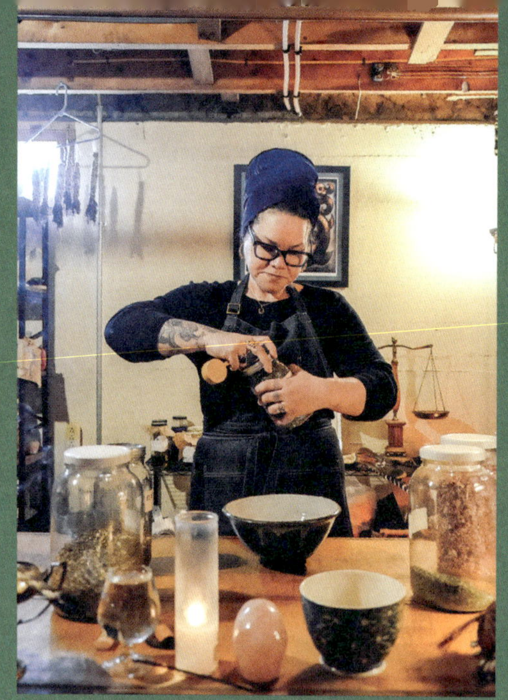

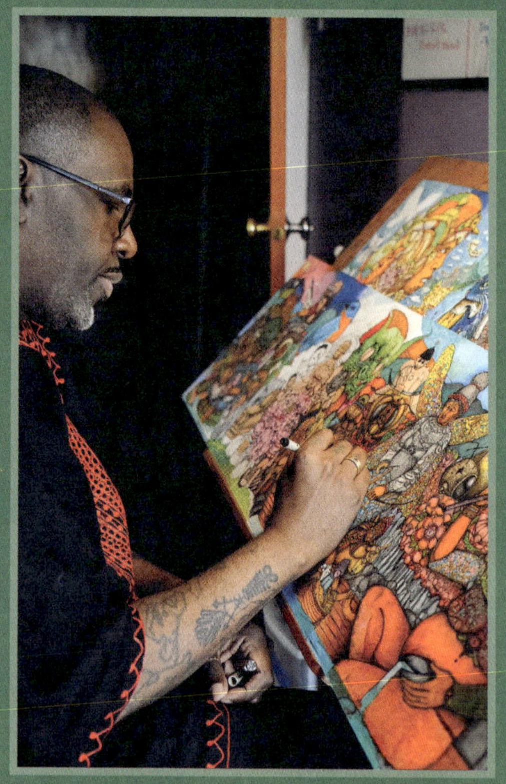

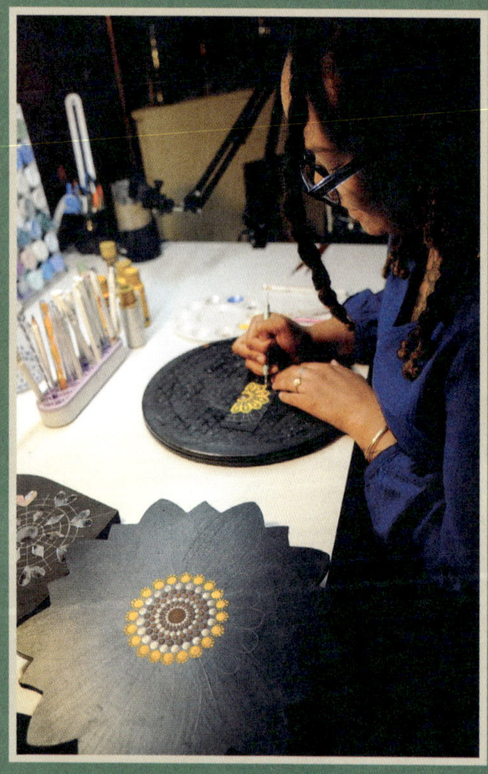

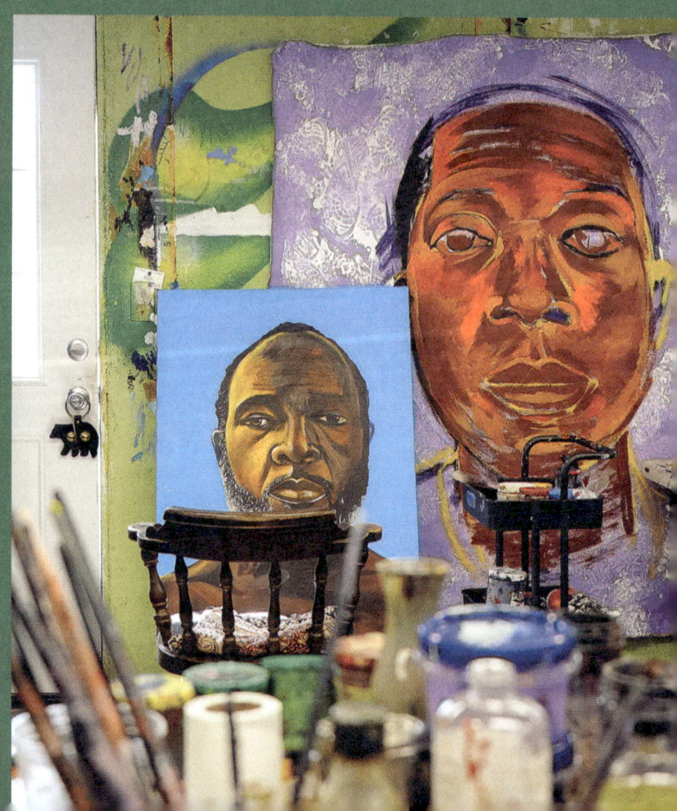

the house showed up, and we made that decision. By October of 2018, we had our home," said Jennifer.

Brandon, Vermont, is often called the *Art and Soul* of Vermont because of the volume of artists residing there. Surrounded by Otter Creek on the border and with the Neshobe River running through the town, water is all around, just as Jennifer's dream led her to find. It's not just creeks and rivers, though. Lake Bomoseen to the southwest and Lake Dunmore, accessed through Bradbury State Park to the northeast, add another layer to the water enjoyed in the town. The Brandon Swamp Wildlife Management Area is 278 acres of trails engulfed in nature to the northwest of Brandon along Otter Creek. Not far from Brandon, Lake Champlain is one of the largest lakes in the country, bordered by Vermont, New York, and Quebec, Canada. In any direction Will, Jennifer, or Alexa go, they are led to water—the dream come to life.

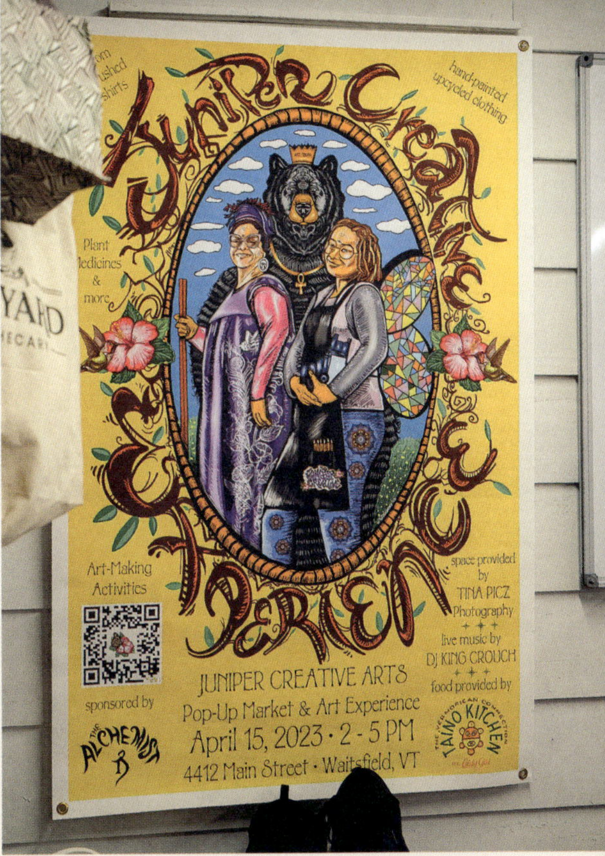

DEVELOPMENT AND GROWTH OF JUNIPER CREATIVE

Early on in Will's move to Vermont, he and Jennifer started working closely together on murals at both Middlebury College and Princeton. Time and time again, people remarked on how well they worked together and how they could make it a business. Those remarks compounded into what we know today as Juniper Creative, founded in 2020, focusing on community-based mural projects throughout the state. They emphasized the importance of community engagement, especially in schools, and the impact of their projects on reconnecting people during the 2020 COVID pandemic.

Leading up to forming Juniper Creative, Will was teaching a hip-hop class at Middlebury; Jennifer was full-steam running the multicultural center while the two were also working on the art residencies; and Alexa was a full-time college student at the University of Vermont. They were all approaching full burnout, and they knew something needed to change.

Their first project was a mural at Middlebury Union High School, which collaborated

"There's so much creativity in the quiet, the silence. You need that silence. That's how real communication happens: in the silence."
—JENNIFER

between the high school, the art students, the seniors, and the students who wanted to do volunteer work, starting a month before the 2020 COVID pandemic. Quickly shifting gears, the three all used that time to develop their website and online store, photograph their artwork, sell tea blends, and when they could, create public art again. In the fall of 2020 alone, they produced ten murals, leading them into 2021, where everything competently broke wide open and all their projects were massive, including a 1,100-square-foot vaulted ceiling mural, which took eleven months to produce.

"In 2020, major funding was coming into school districts to support belonging, retention, and community-building. In the middle of a pandemic where there was a lack of connection and learning loss, since our wheelhouse is murals everything was a community-based mural project," shared Jennifer about carrying art education throughout every project that goes back into the community. "We collaborate with the art programs in the schools, working with the districts, the principal, and the art teacher to take over the art classes." Involving the students in the projects has been so affirming for Juniper Creative. They have created over forty murals in Vermont, with a significant emphasis on our relationship to nature. "We are always looking at how to remind folks that we cannot live disconnected from nature," said Jennifer.

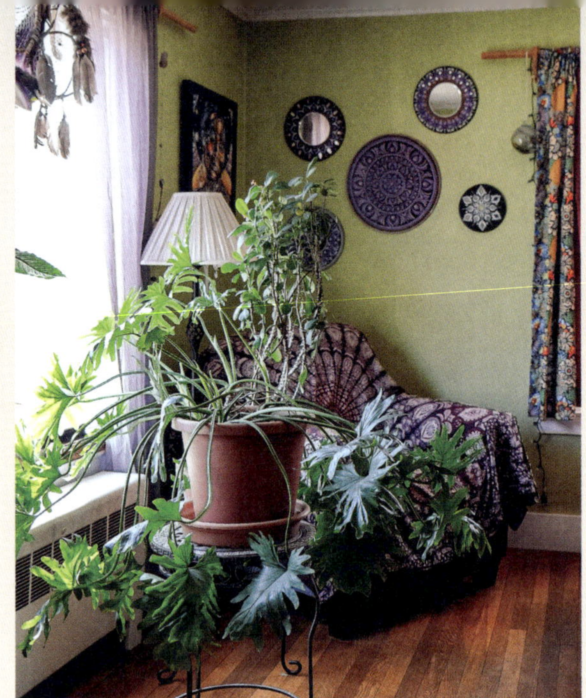

IMPACT OF RURAL LIFE ON ARTISTIC DEVELOPMENT

Like many small towns, Brandon faces some of the same push and pull from its constituents. Creatives are looking for and finding solace in the quiet parts of the rural setting, while generational poverty still exists even if it looks different in many ways from generational poverty in a city. An agrarian society's problems come with its own experiences and mindsets. "There's palpable tension around that in Brandon," shared Jennifer.

"I believe being here in a rural climate gives us that space to say, 'You know what? I'm going to go and try this in the studio today.' And if that sparks something, maybe it's something we could bring into a public art project," expressed Will. Aside from their murals, Jennifer also makes medicinal teas. Had she been in a city where the days were rushed or money was more of an issue, she might not have taken the time for herself to craft this component of their business. "New ideas come so much faster in a quiet, rural environment. There aren't any distractions," added Will.

BECOMING PART OF THE SOLUTION

Questions to ask yourself in your own community: How do you unify creatives within the town? How do you make a more inclusive environment for the town, those working the trades, and those working as creatives?

CREATING THE MURAL ARTS ACADEMY

Figuring out the most efficient ways to execute the planning, time, cost, and bid that go into a mural has been years in the making for Juniper Creative. Along with the items on their website, from sourcing the materials and sourcing printing out of house or buying a printer, a thousand other questions go into running your own art business. The collective created the Mural Arts Academy for high school, career, and technology students. They aim to teach artistic skills and the business and teamwork aspects of a career in the arts.

The monthlong program takes on ten students for the tech center's art career track. Along the way, the program answers questions and covers topics such as how to become a working artist and prepare for that path, the business of art, how to start an art business, how to file taxes, how to pay yourself, and how to work with a team.

"There is a lot of disconnection between what it really takes to have a sustainable career in the arts, as opposed to thinking, *I want to work on this project. I want to do this one thing.* It's like you must look at the long game because the art world is a $500 billion entity, but within that art world, it's different communities. You must figure out what community you want to be a part of, and then you must work your way into that community," said Will. Helping the students understand the importance of working together is the main goal of the class.

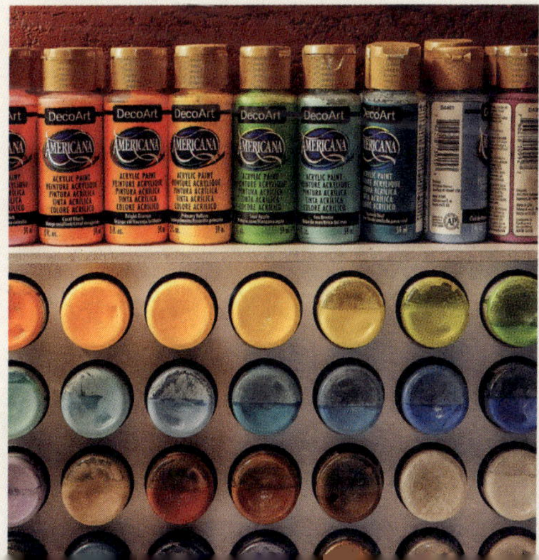

Creative Freelance Lesson

"There's no point in doing the work if your heart isn't in it or if you're too exhausted to even do it well. We intentionally started to take a step back and be a little bit more intentional. We took the first mural projects as they came in. But after a while, we realized we need to curate how we go out and do these projects a little more so that we can have sustainability for the long term. This work is important for us. This work is what brought us together, so it's bigger than just a project. It's a lifestyle."
—WILL

The skills are transferable, no matter what career aspirations you have. "They are challenged with how to collaboratively come up with a design idea, work in groups, illustrate that idea together with a pencil on paper, measure a wall to determine the square footage, and then mock it up on a piece of paper that was the equivalent of a square inch to the square footage, gridding, and translate that grid from paper manually to the wall. We didn't even bring out the projector," shared Jennifer.

HELPING PAVE THE WAY FOR DIVERSE ART IN VERMONT

From the time Alexa was a little girl in the Vermont school system to where she is today creating alongside her parents, the differences are palpable. "There is a higher population of Black and brown students in Winooski. I was one of five Black students that graduated from my high school. I have always been the only Black kid in every room I have walked into since I was in kindergarten. Working in Winooski, I thought, *You have no idea what being in this space right now, what a gift you have,*" shared Alexa.

She wasn't exposed to art in school growing up, other than art class, so going into these schools and making art that explicitly represents Black and brown children in these pieces is incredible for her. "If there was art, it was always white-centered. You would be like speckles in the background if they even thought to include Black people. If you tried to speak out about stuff like that, then you were labeled the problem. I'm happy now that I am a part of a collective with my parents, and we're able to make active changes in lives that they will remember twenty years later," said Alexa.

"The work I was doing at Middlebury College was a lot of belonging work, and I was working with traditionally unrepresented students at Middlebury College, finding their sense of place and belonging within a hundred-year-old, historically white institution. We had a growing diversity in the student body between Black and brown students coming out of urban centers to a very rural school in the mountains of Vermont," shared Jennifer. She developed belonging-related programs, student empowerment, and development programs, resources, and support to help the students thrive and persist to graduation.

Since Jennifer and Will started to collaborate through community-based art initiatives, everything she'd been a part of facilitating at the college she's been able to apply to the pockets of communities where they are doing work, helping to tell the stories. Will, a master illustrator, is able to translate the story into visuals, which make up much of the work the couple is doing.

BRANDON, VERMONT

POPULATION: 4,106 full-time residents in 2024

TOWN SIZE: 40.2 square miles

CLOSEST INTERNATIONAL AIRPORT: Patrick Leahy Burlington International Airport (50.1 miles)

CLOSEST REGIONAL AIRPORT: Middlebury State Airport (14.3 miles)

CLOSEST LARGE CITY: Albany, New York (95.6 miles)

BONUS TOWNS NEARBY: Middlebury, Rutland, Rochester

ANIMALS TO SPOT: beavers, otters, weasels, red foxes, hooded mergansers

TOWN FACTS: Thomas Davenport invented the electric motor in Brandon in 1834. There are 246 buildings on the National Register of Historic Places in Brandon. The town is the gateway to the Moosalamoo National Recreation Area. Brandon is about seventeen miles from Middlebury College. Neshobe River Winery and Otter Valley Winery in Brandon are two of the few wineries in the state. Vermont ranks second in the country for employment and retention of artists per capita. Folk artist Warren Kimble lives and works in Brandon. In Vermont, the creative sector is the number one factor in the economy.

SEASONS: Brandon has four seasons.

WATER ACTIVITIES: fishing, canoeing, paddleboarding, kayaking, boating

WATER SPOTS TO VISIT: Neshobe River, Otter Creek, Lake Dunmore, and Fern Lake

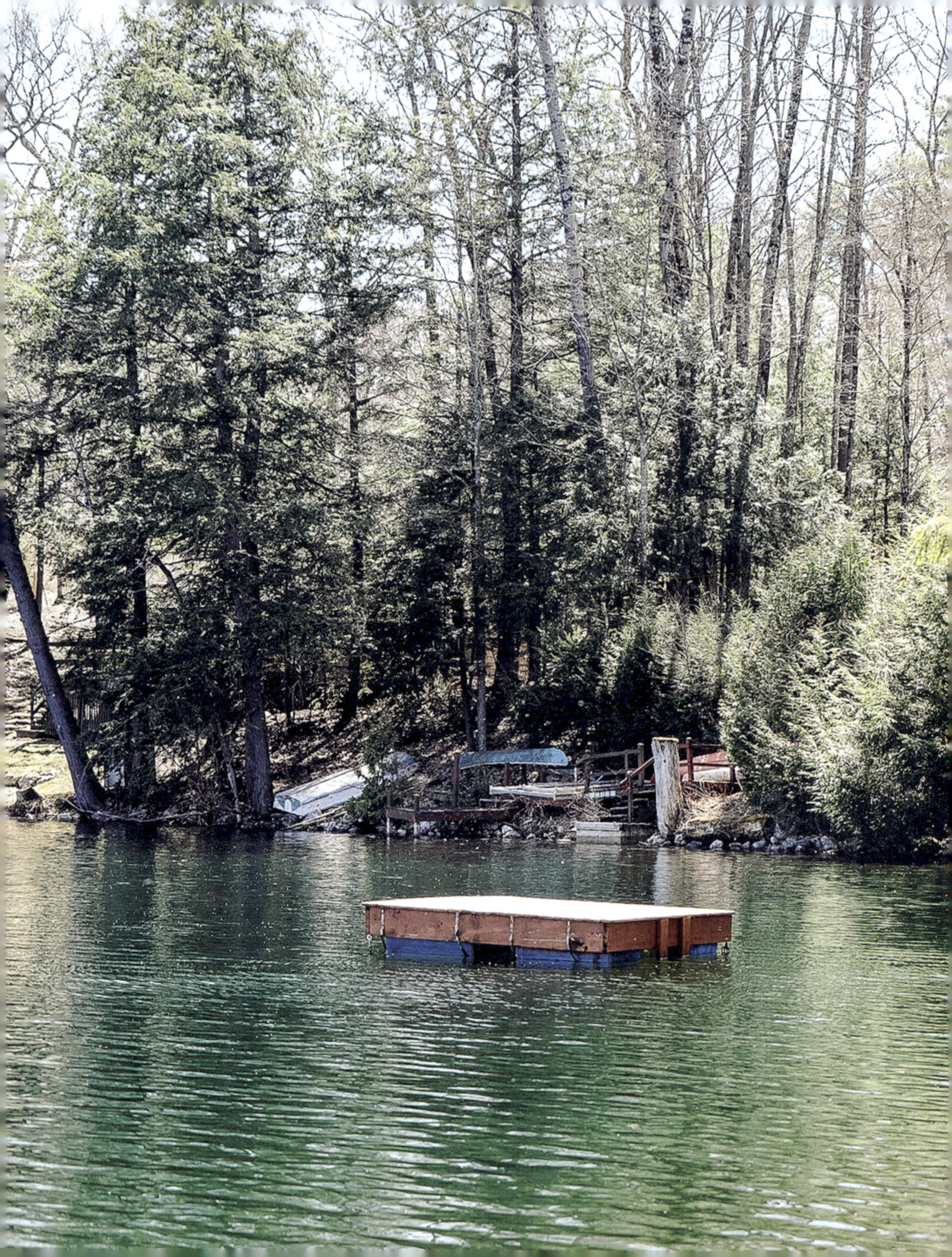

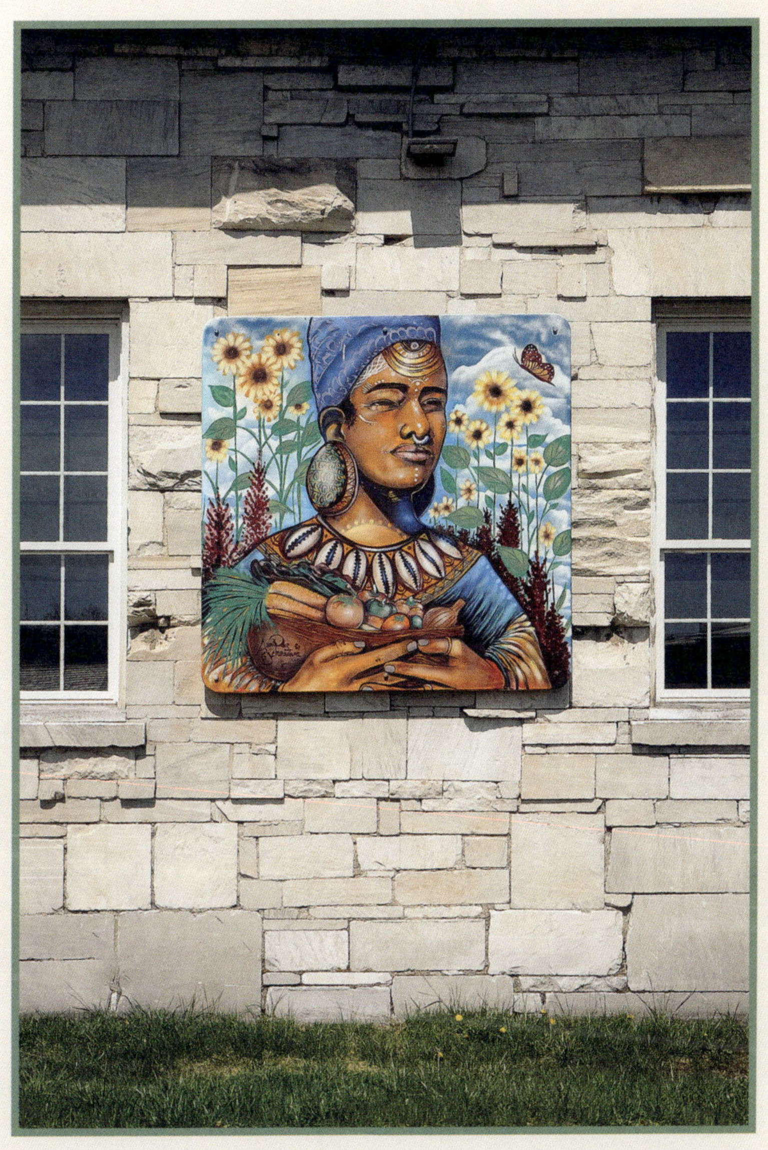

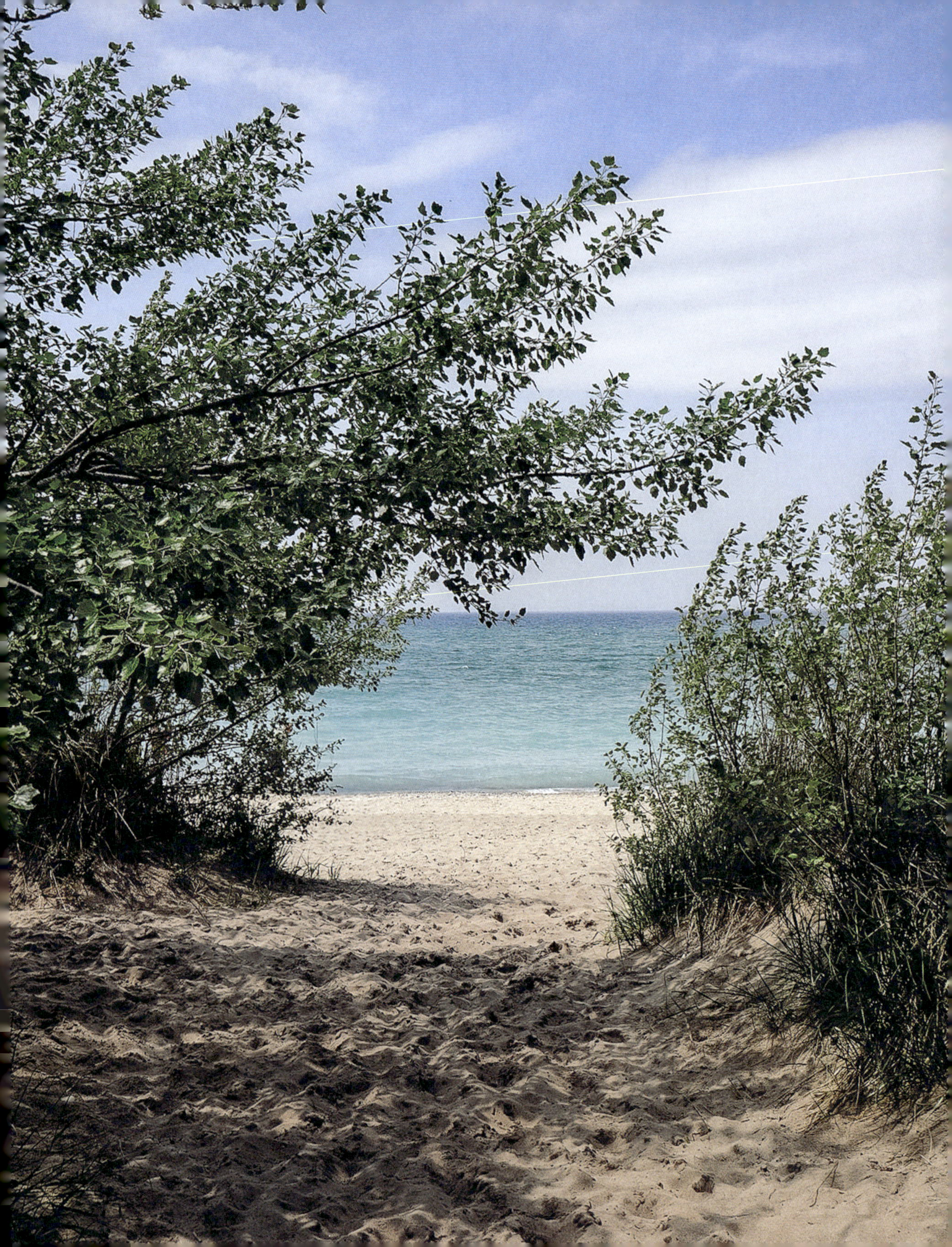

LAKES

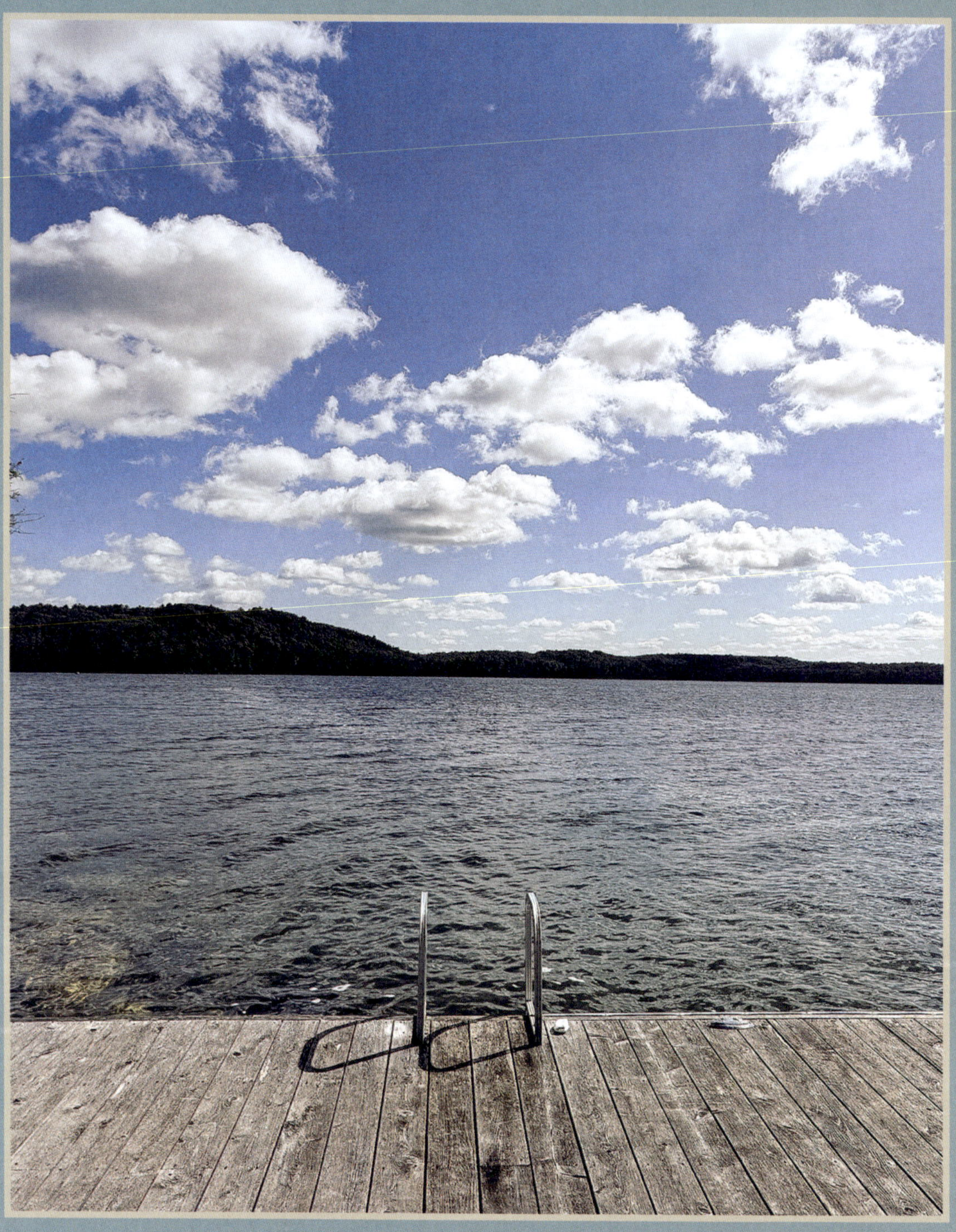

A TRIBUTE TO HALF-CROWN ISLAND AT 31 MILE LAKE

POINT COMFORT, QUEBEC, CANADA

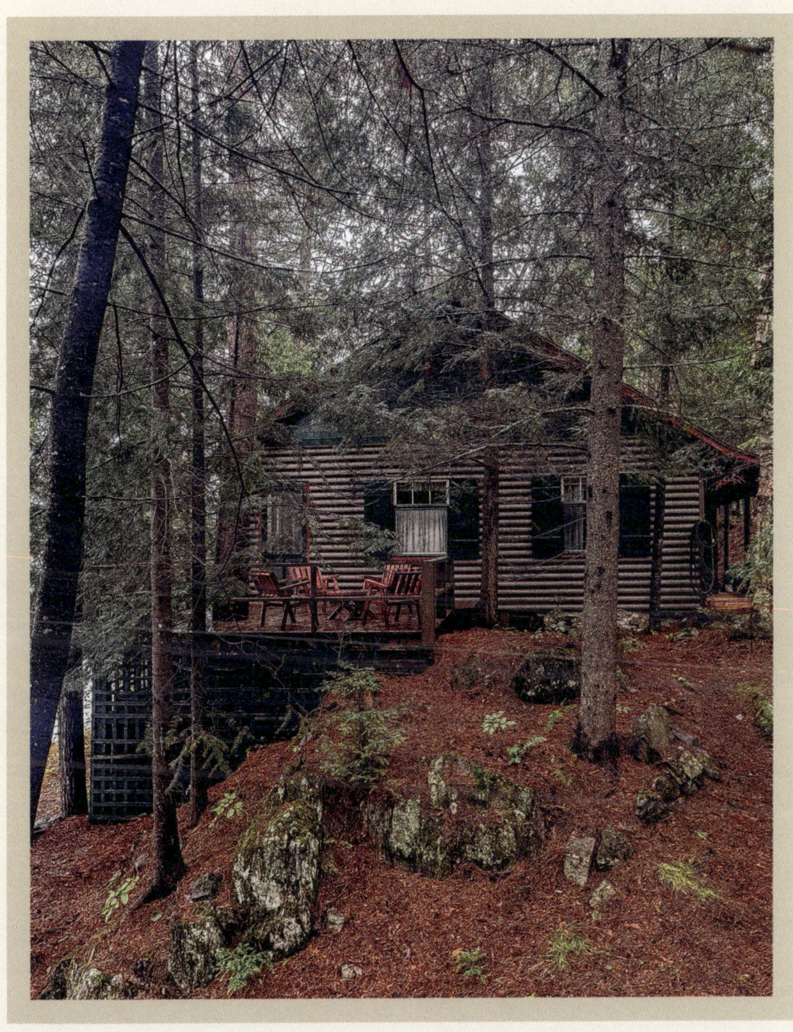

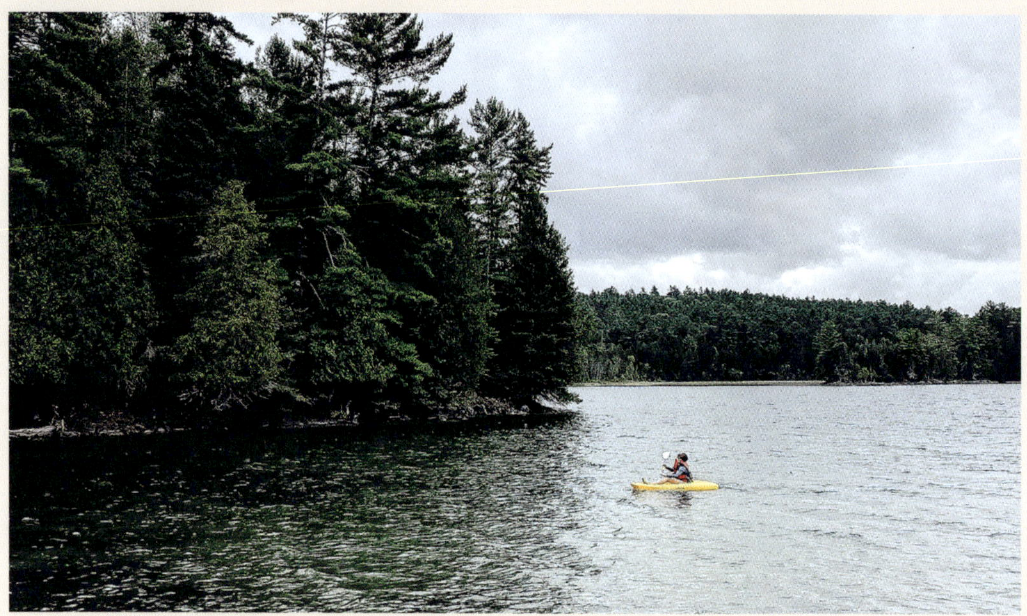

On a hot day in Houston, Texas, in 1979, O.L. Kirkpatrick, or "Kirk" as his friends call him, was sitting in the barbershop flipping through the latest issue of *Ducks Unlimited*. In the back was a lengthy ad describing a lake island ninety miles north of Ottawa, in the middle of nowhere in Quebec, Canada, for rent. It promised a beautiful, serene lake where you could hike, boat, fish, swim, and more.

With a chuckle to his question, Kirk asked his wife Julia and his son Stephen what they thought about it and called the number. First renting, then eventually purchasing the island, the Kirkpatricks and their family and friends enjoyed visiting the island in the middle of an aptly named 31 Mile Lake for forty-five years.

It's interesting when a home becomes the protagonist in a story—a place all the characters' lives revolve around and intersect with in different ways and at different times. That's what the main house is for me at Half-Crown Island: it's the lead character in our time there.

I grew up in a rather broken home, never living with my dad or knowing him very well. I was raised by a single mom, moved from home to home, town to town every few years. I never felt settled, nor did I have consistency in my life.

When I met my husband, Sean Kirkpatrick, in 2008, we talked about our families and childhoods. His face lit up describing the island in a lake in Canada where he'd spent all his summers since he was born. I was intrigued. He told me stories of his Canadian friends, the lake camp he and his brothers went to, the Loon Count his dad helped to start, the boating, the shore lunches, the fishing, and an endless list of other times spent in what could only be described as an idyllic place.

The summer after we were married in March of 2010, I went to the island for the first time, and the moment I saw the reflection of the towering trees on the still water, I was instantly hooked. It wasn't like anything I had experienced before. It wasn't fancy, but it was pure. We rode on the water for thirty minutes to reach the island, my father-in-law Stephen pulling the wooden boat into a slip inside a classic boathouse straight out of *On Golden Pond*. My husband's grandparents, Kirk and Julia, and his stepmom Marlo greeted us. We dropped our bags into a modest cabin on the island and walked down the path to the midcentury modern main house, the pillar of the island. Dinner was underway, collectively being cooked by whoever was on the island in an almost unspoken rule I'd come to learn. To use the word *rule* seems harsh because it was so much more than that. It was preparing memories around the large dining room table and storytelling through hors d'oeuvres. After dinner, we gathered in the living room to talk for hours. I was an observer at first, learning the ways of my new family and quickly falling right into place with them.

When my husband and I welcomed our son Tom, he, too, loved the island. I could see him looking for anything to connect himself to the memories Sean shared, hoping to make them his own.

"Dad, is this where you would catch crawdads?"

"Yes, Uncle Ryan and I would catch crawdads down by the boathouse."

"I'm going to go catch them there too."

"Dad, want to go swimming on the swim dock like you and Uncle Ian used to," or *"Dad, did you take this same boat to get to camp each day?"*

The questions came in the rapid-fire way a young child has.

There's something magical about watching your husband and child have a shared connection to their childhoods. It's where my son learned to walk, swim, fish, and drive a boat. It's where he got to connect with his great-grandparents, grandparents, great-aunt Susan, and uncle, all at the same time in the same place. His love of nature was discovered there, as was my husband's.

I thank Kirk and Julia for giving us that time on the lake and for making the main house a part of our family and our story. We said goodbye to the island in 2024 as getting to a remote island in another country became harder and harder, and living on an island in the dense wilderness of Canada also proved to be tricky. It was time to move on, but I know the memories of the place and the fourteen years I spent with her will live on with our family and me forever.

PLAN YOUR OWN SHORE LUNCH

If you are wondering what a shore lunch is, well, in the most basic terms, it's a fresh fish fry next to water. Lakeside, riverside, or ocean—it doesn't matter. It's a Canadian tradition.

- Freshly caught fish, prepared and cooked in a cast-iron frying pan over the campfire
- Enough fish for each person to have two to three fillets
- Baked beans
- Fried potatoes and onions, sliced thin
- Hot coffee, brewed over the fire

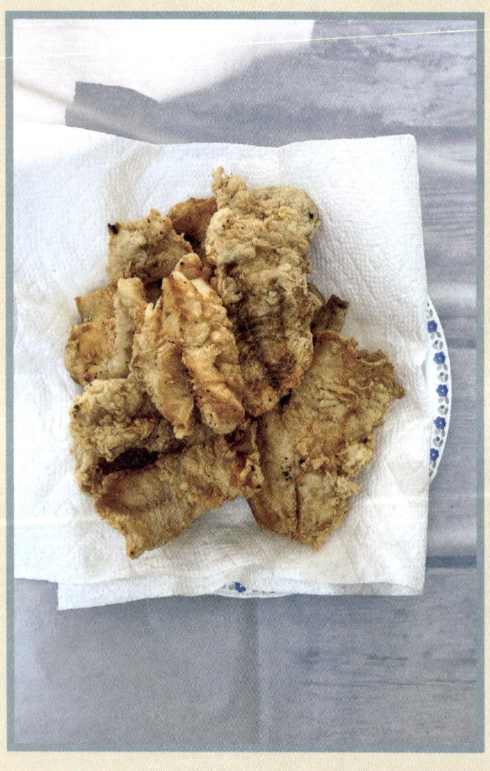

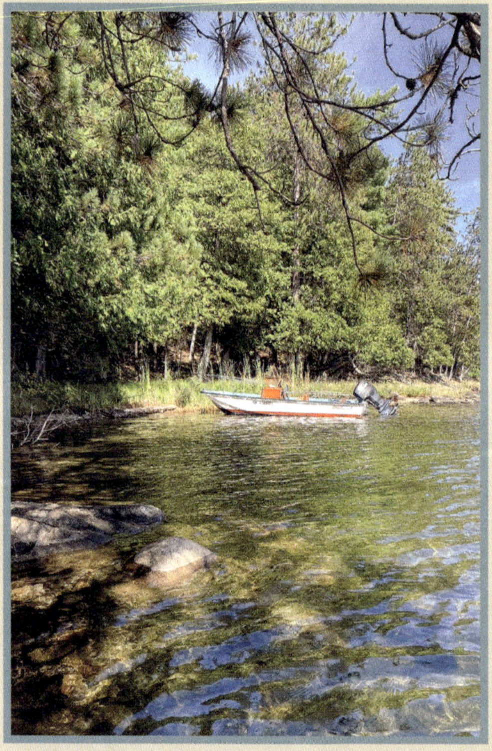

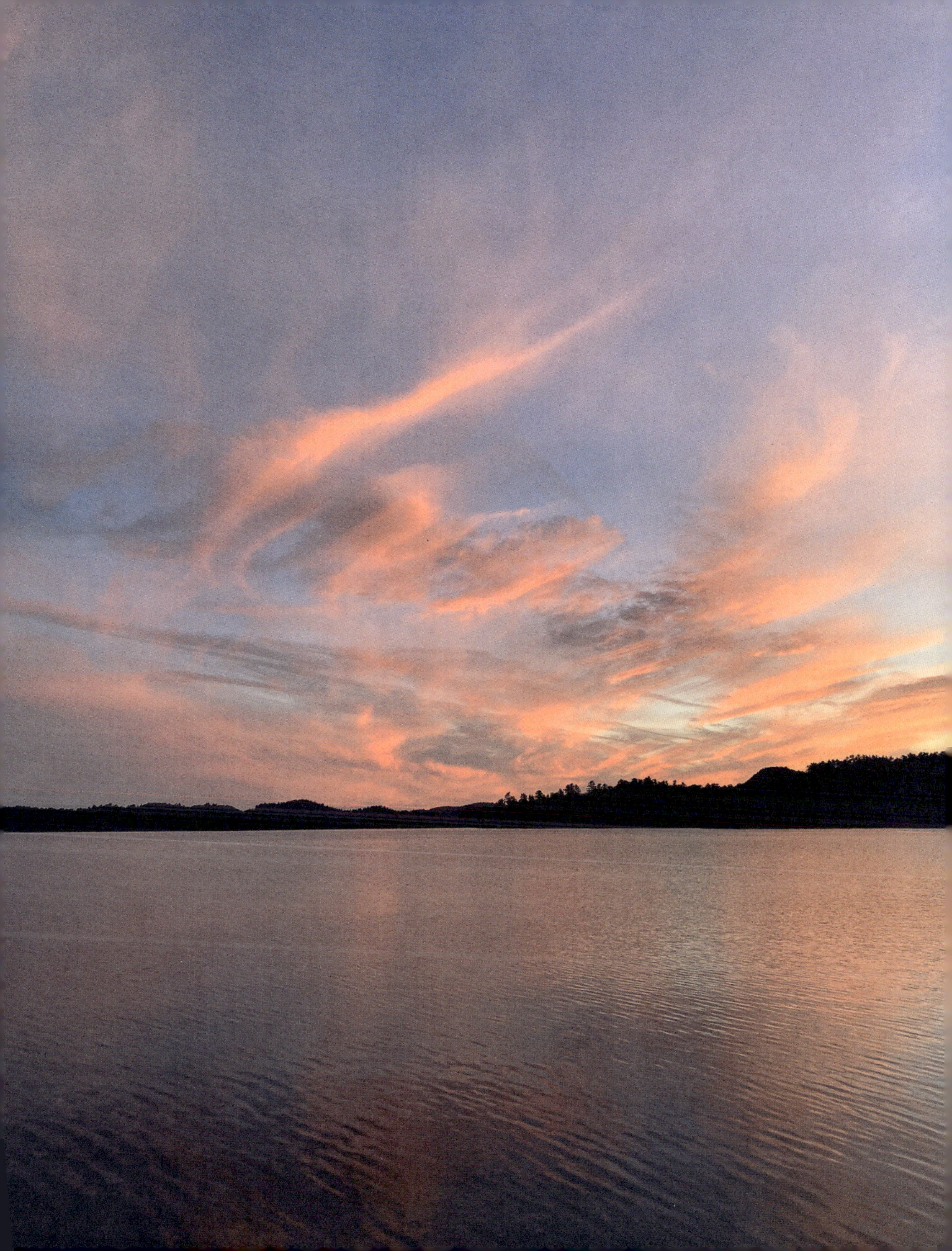

"Learn about the ethos of the community, authenticity and individuality and expression, and honor that. People move here because they feel that. It's a draw, very honoring and respectful of the land that we're on, and that really unites us. The more I talk about it, the more enchanted I become with the reality. More intensely, I want to work with those protecting the land."

—ADRIENNE HALPERT

ADRIENNE HALPERT

Shop Owner at Global Art Gallery and Artist

PATAGONIA, ARIZONA

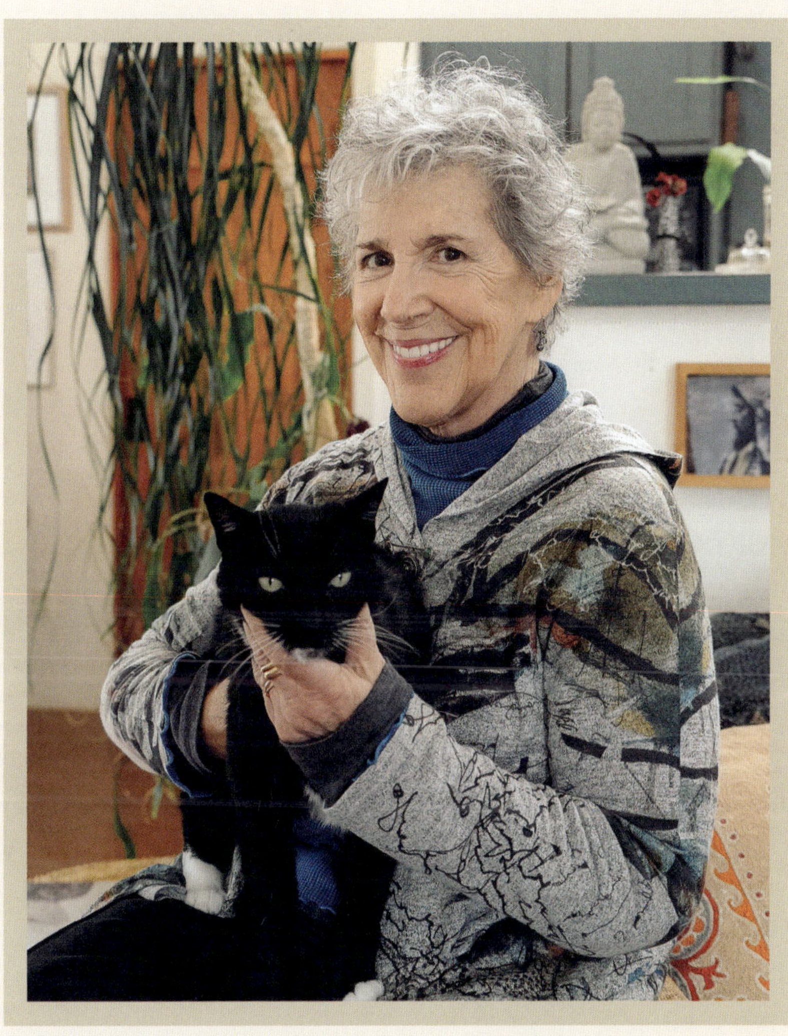

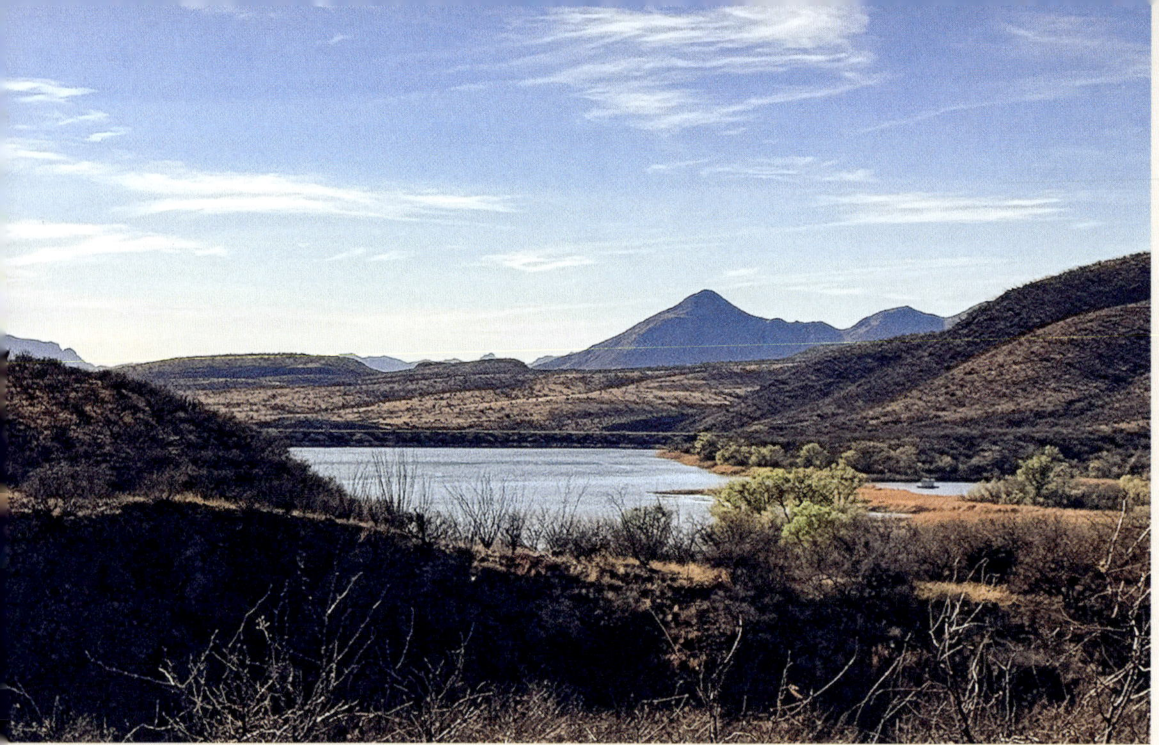

Adrienne Halpert never expected to settle in the desert unicorn town of Patagonia, Arizona, sitting in the Sonoran Desert, and certainly not for the past thirty years. She was born in New York City, leaving to bounce from Tucson, Arizona, to Houston, Texas. From there she moved on to San Francisco and then back to New York City. She went on to explore Europe, getting a view of the world at a very young age. She returned to San Francisco before relocating back to Tucson, and for the last thirty years, she's been living in the small town of Patagonia, where the desert caught her heart. "I have a beautiful view of the mountains from all directions as I look around. I'm delighted to be here where the wild ones roam—javelina, deer, coatimundi, ravens, and all manner of unnameable birds. The natural world sustains me as well as art, beauty, conversation, and connection to it all," shared Adrienne.

Patagonia is a birder's dream location and a world-renowned destination for the community, as it attracts more than 300 migrating bird species each year. Birds are attracted to the creek which runs at the edge of this desert town. Sonoita Creek State Natural Area is situated on almost 10,000 acres of protected land near the artificial lake at Patagonia Lake State Park, just twelve miles from the town center. It's also home to the Audubon Society's Paton Center for Hummingbirds.

WATER IS LIFE

"Water is life. I have deep concerns about how water is being drained from our precious aquifer by mining activities ramping up in our region. . . . They're draining the aquifer so they can drill for the mine, and they are treating the water and then dumping it into the creek. So it's changing the whole balance," said Adrienne. The town's connection with nature sits precariously alongside those with more money, resources, and a bottom line. This is something the locals are passionate about protecting and saving.

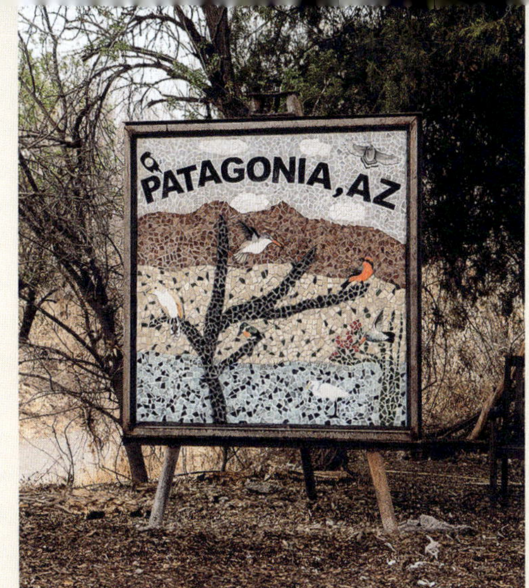

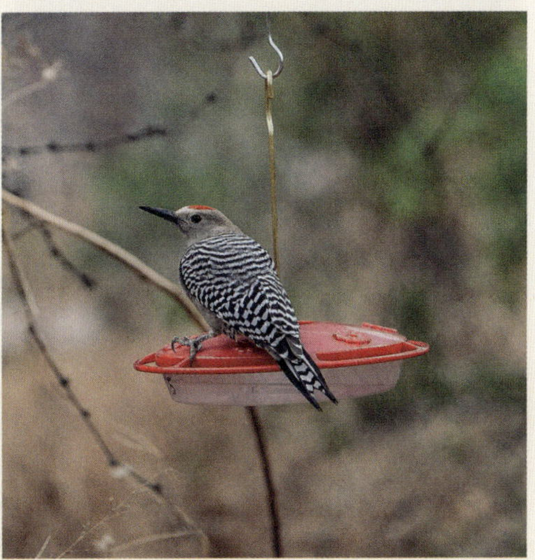

We are stewards of the land, and how we work with the people who are effecting change and can make the right decisions is important for us, as citizens, to know. We need to understand how to tackle these topics and how to approach them with corporations. We must work to educate them as much as ourselves. "The water around me is the artery that supports me. It brings a connection. I can sit by the side of the Blue Heaven Road, just beyond the Audubon Society, along the 100-year-old cottonwood trees, and everything has gone

BEST PLACES TO BIRD-WATCH IN PATAGONIA

Borderlands Wildlife Preserve

Patagonia Lake State Park

Patagonia-Sonoita Creek Preserve Visitor Center

Paton Center for Hummingbirds

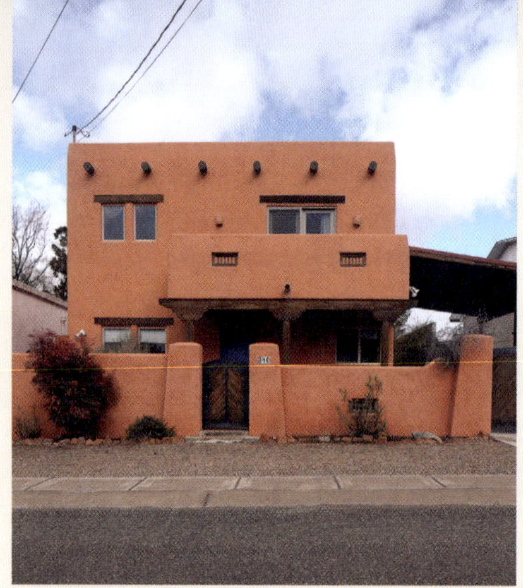

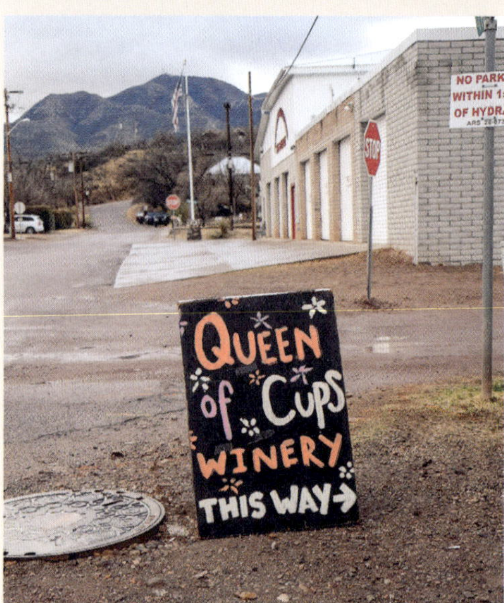

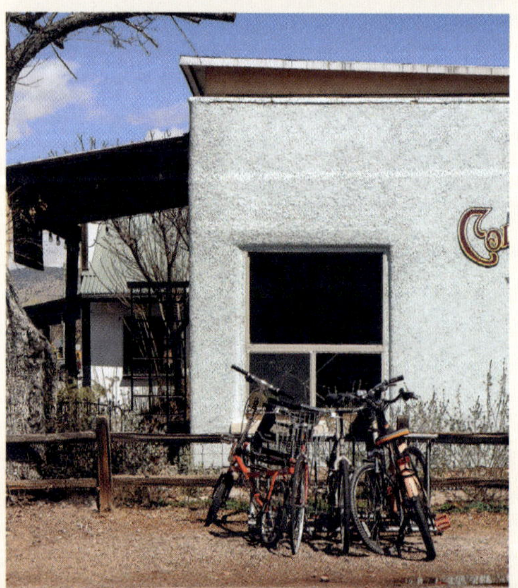

by as I'm sitting there: the creek, the water, animals. It's stillness and it's movement at the same time. If I'm stuck, it unsticks me," expressed Adrienne.

SMALL BUT MIGHTY

Patagonia is an anomaly. With under 1,000 residents, the community is thriving. It boasts a radio station, KPUP 100.5 FM; a newspaper called *Patagonia Regional Times*; a youth center; a senior center; a community garden; and an opera house that's part of the Santa Cruz Foundation for the Performing Arts. That sense of community gives Adrienne the drive to stay put and continue working to be a connector within her town. When describing Patagonia, Adrienne remarked on the continued support that everyone has for one another within the town, championing each other's creative endeavors and the environment alike.

AN ART CAREER BUILT ON COMMUNITY

Before Patagonia, Adrienne worked diligently in Tucson to preserve historic buildings. She was on committee after committee—"save this, do that" she remarked—but feeling burnt out, Adrienne began looking for a space nearby to create her artwork. Landing in Patagonia, she started her creative career making jewelry. Together with other creatives, she rented a building in hopes of each having space to make and sell work. Her area was 10 by 15 of the significant 2,000-square-foot location.

Commuting back and forth between Tucson and Patagonia for the first three years of her thirty in Patagonia, she quickly learned she couldn't make enough inventory to support her art career, so she slowly began taking over more and more space within the 2,000 square feet and filling it with her friends' artwork and crafts. A weaver, a furniture maker, a coffee shop, an herbalist . . . over time, they consumed the entire location. The community she built little by little still sits there today inside the Global Arts Gallery. The shop has a certain artfulness, from apparel, home goods, accessories, jewelry, folk art, and art. "Items in the shop may have some humor, but it's the mark of the hand, of the echo of time. It could have been made 100 years ago, could have been made yesterday, but it has the mark of the hand," shared Adrienne.

Aside from the shop, Adrienne sits on the board of the Patagonia Creative Arts Association, which focuses on providing art opportunities for youth in the community through performance and visual arts. They mentor writing and performing plays at the local arts center and screen films. They are also responsible for bringing a fall festival and an art walk to the town.

RESISTING THE URGE TO LEAVE

When asked how the community is encouraging Gen Z and millennials to leave for school and then come back to town to raise a family and preserve and work to protect the land, organizations like Borderlands Restoration Network share they are doing their best by partnering with youth ages sixteen to twenty-four "to grow a restorative economy by rebuilding healthy ecosystems, restoring habitat for plants and wildlife, and reconnecting our border communities to land through shared learning."

If this sounds like a familiar hurdle in your own small town or a problem you are working to combat, think about encouraging the future of your small towns by working with the middle and high school, 4-H Club, Boy and Girl Scouts of America, and continuing education classes that offer service classes where students discover ways to help their towns. Maybe it's a town facing food apartheid and students are taught how to garden, cook, and start a restaurant but also understand what food apartheid looks like and how to combat the issue in their own ways. Or maybe there's a push for restorative native plants and trees, educating students on the effects of native growth on the water and animals in the area. Or it could be like Patagonia, where students learn from organizations like Borderlands Restoration Network to rebuild the ecosystem around them.

When young people understand the problems and are trusted to be part of the solution, they gain a deeper understanding of their towns and what it means to come back and

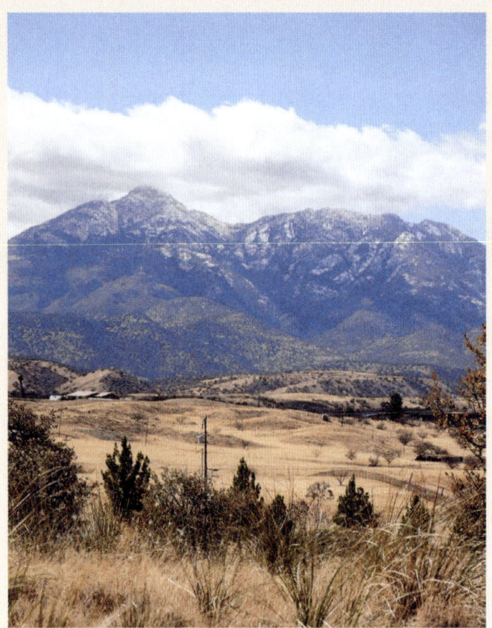

be a force in their communities. If we provide incentives to younger people to return and give them a place to care about, more and more will fight the urge to leave and never look back. Let the artsy child know they are welcome and support their ideas while helping them form new ones on how to live the life of an artist in a small town. Maybe they need to understand how to start an art education business or help creating their own website to sell their work. Or maybe it's the musician that doesn't know they could move back and be the one person in town that offers music lessons or the chef that dreams of opening a restaurant when their own town would welcome the type of food they are making. The ideas are endless, but it's important for the community that small towns are known for to step in and support the youth and their ideas.

HOW TO MAKE A SMALL TOWN WORK FOR YOU

If you are new to town, volunteer with the community. If you enjoy gardening, join the community garden to meet people. Serve food at the local senior center. Write an article for the local paper. Host a radio show. Start a bike club or lead nature hikes. See how you can turn your talent or passion into a way to enrich your community. Be a greeter at the visitors' center. Start a walking tour. Read to children at the local library or school. There are many ways to be involved and give back to your community.

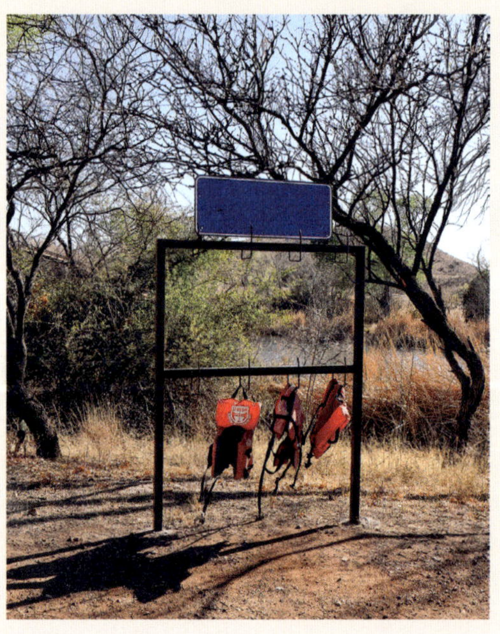

LOCAL ORGANIZATIONS DEDICATED TO PRESERVATION AROUND PATAGONIA

- Audubon Society's Paton Center for Hummingbirds
- Borderlands Restoration Network
- Circle Z Ranch
- Coalition for Sonoran Desert Protection
- The Nature Conservancy
- Patagonia Area Resource Alliance

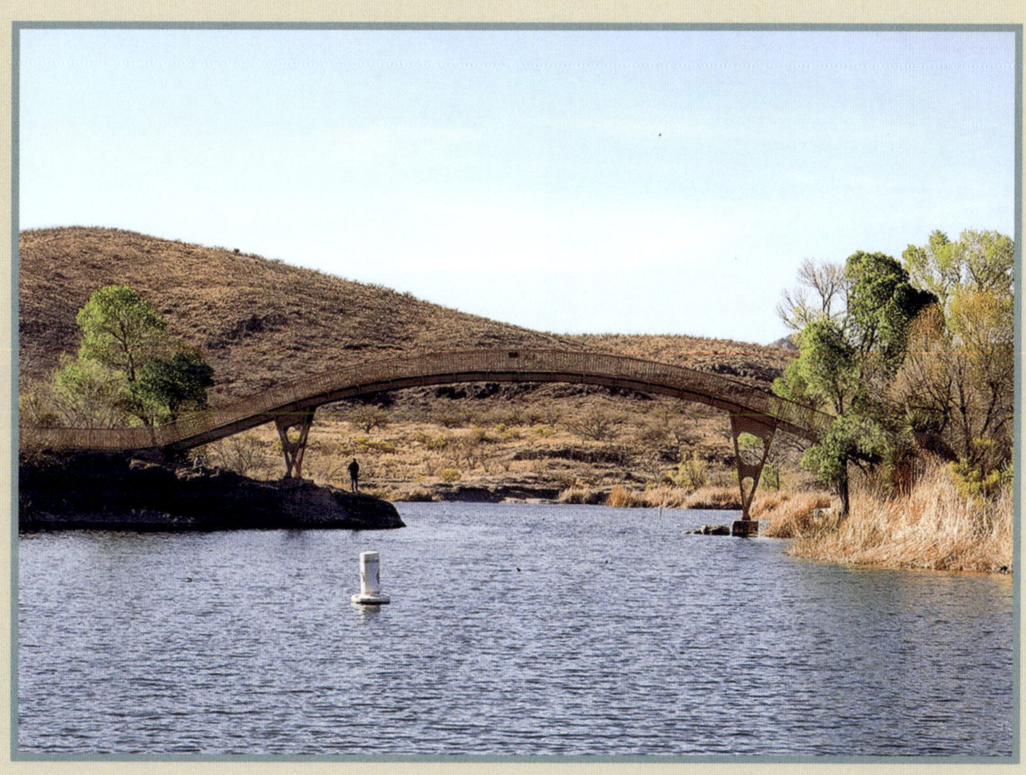

LEARNING FROM CITIES

Adrienne is a connector through and through. Whether traveling in cities or building relationships in Patagonia, making a connection with historic buildings and the natural world alike, she leans into the shared mindset we can all gravitate toward, even subconsciously. "I just love this connection between history and contemporary and how dynamic and resourceful and energized and committed people are to where they are, who they are, and what they are, or were [in the past]," shared Adrienne. "I want to affirm our shared humanity beyond language, place."

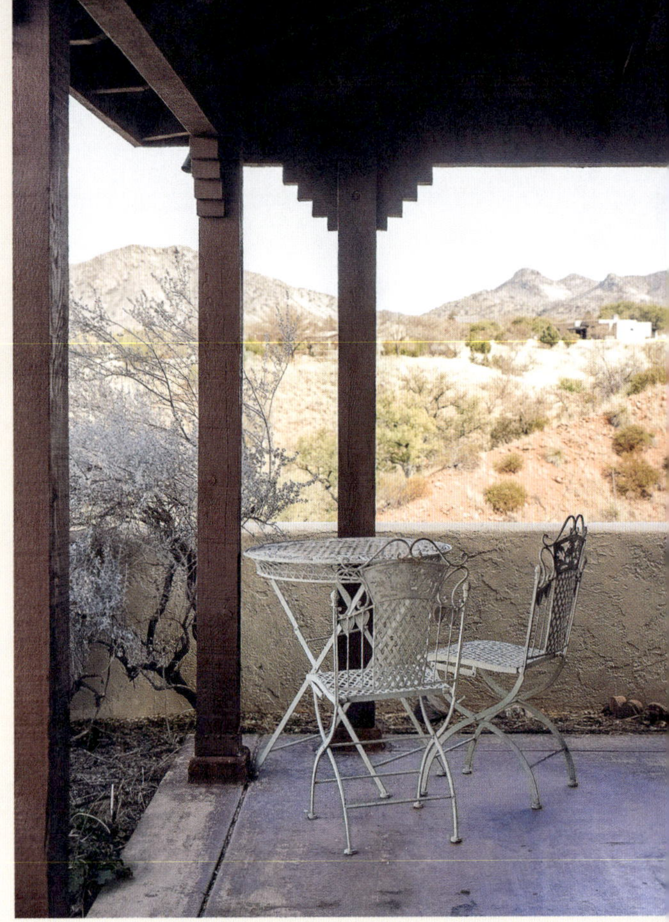

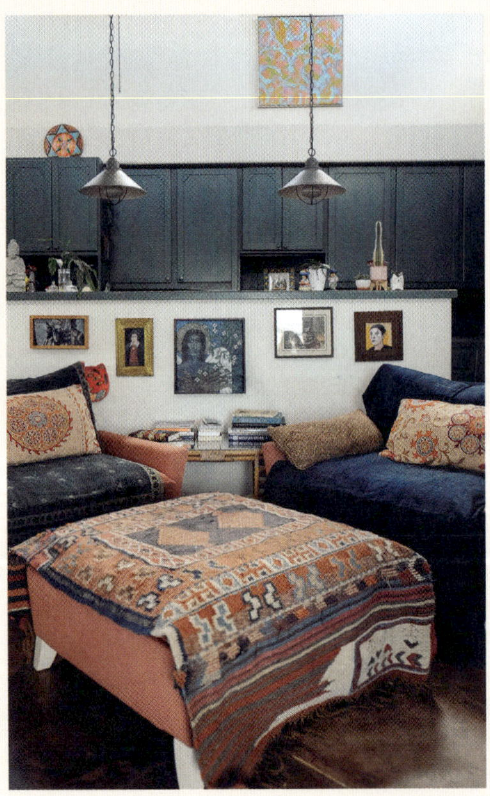

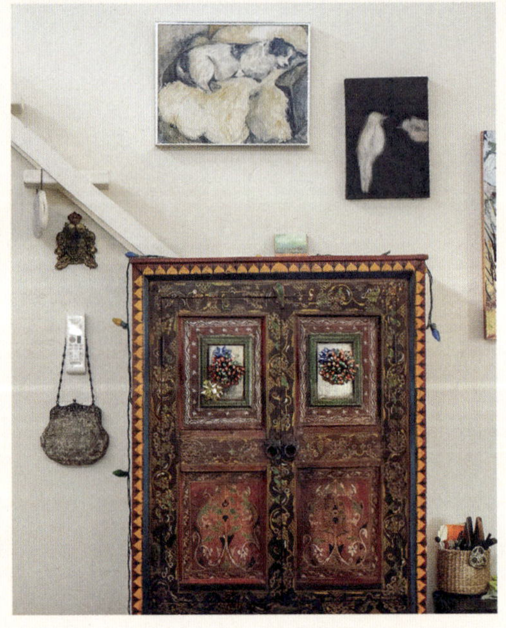

PATAGONIA, ARIZONA
POPULATION: 789 full-time residents in 2024
TOWN SIZE: 1.3 square miles
CLOSEST INTERNATIONAL AIRPORT: Tucson International Airport (55.4 miles)
CLOSEST REGIONAL AIRPORT: Marana Regional Airport (82 miles)
CLOSEST LARGE CITY: Tucson (64.1 miles)
BONUS TOWNS NEARBY: Sonoita, Nogales
BEST TIME TO BIRD-WATCH: March to September
TOWN FACTS: Patagonia is about fourteen miles from the Mexico–United States border. Welsh miners came to Patagonia from South America, and the mountains in Arizona reminded them of the Andes so they named them Patagonia. The town later also took that name. The elevation of the town is 4,058 feet. A few of the rarest birds to pass through Patagonia are the rose-throated becard and the elegant trogon.
SEASONS: Patagonia is a four-season town, with a monsoon season later in the summer.
WATER ACTIVITIES: swimming, kayaking, canoeing, paddleboarding, fishing, boating
WATER SPOTS TO VISIT: Patagonia-Sonoita Creek and Patagonia Lake

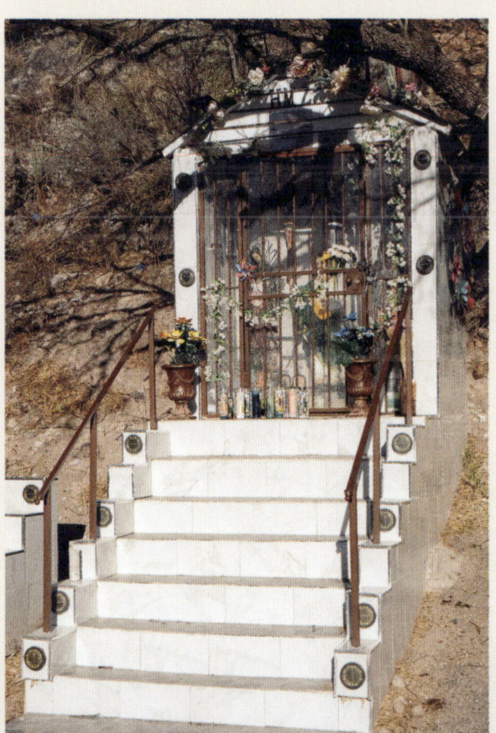

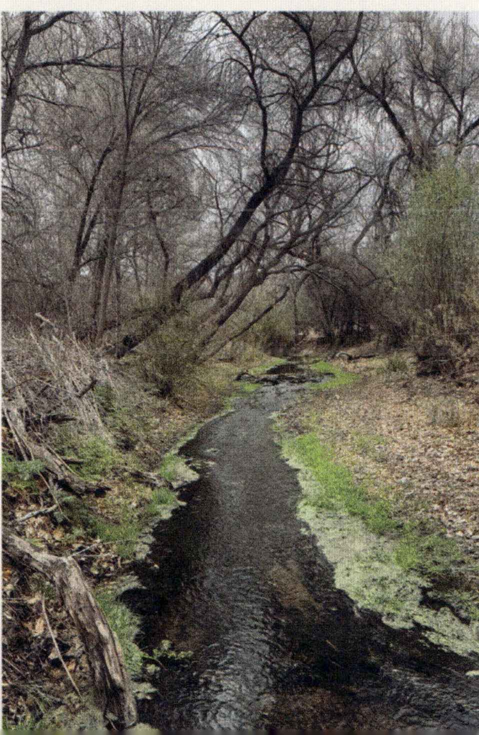

“Everything about living back in Sandpoint is like a fairy tale. It’s like living in *The Truman Show* because it’s just like, *How can this be real? How is everyone this nice?*”

—KATIE ADAMS

KATIE ADAMS

Restaurant Owner at Heart Bowls

SANDPOINT, IDAHO

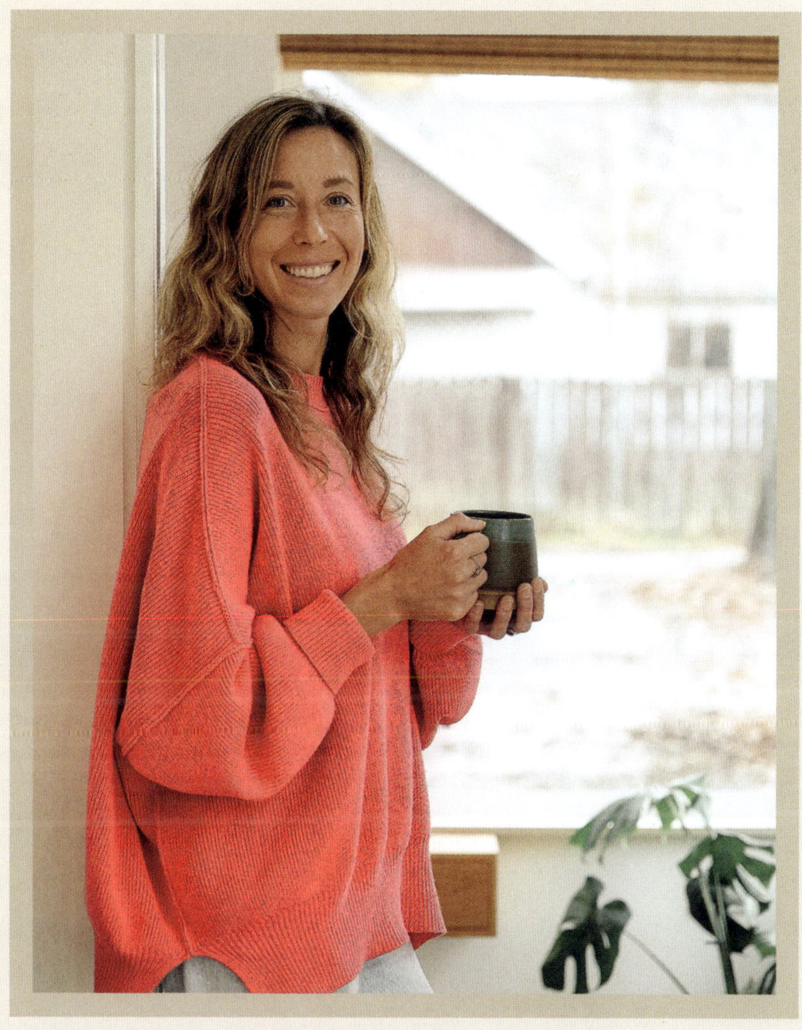

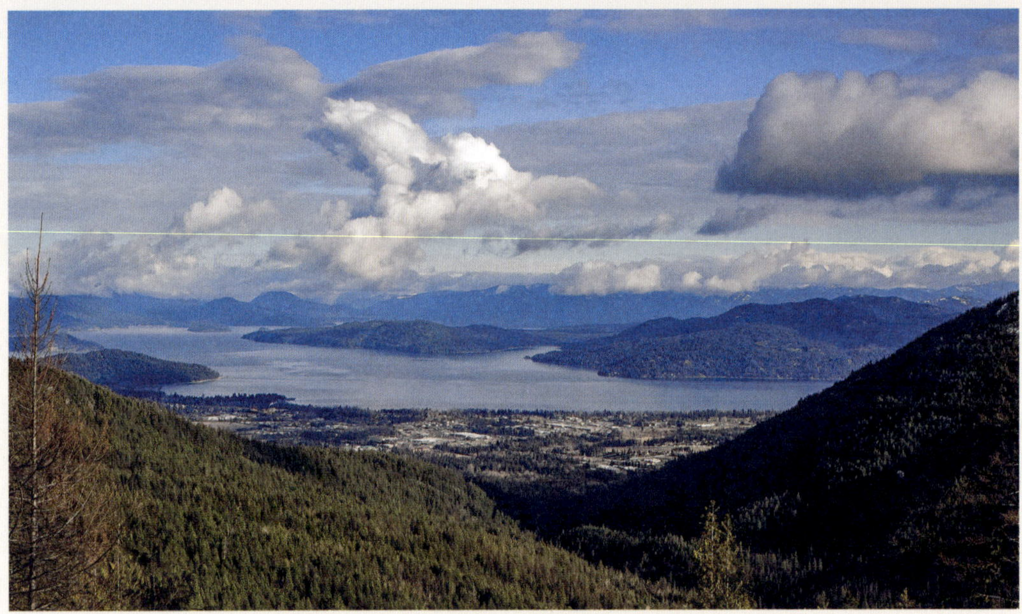

Katie Adams has always loved her hometown of Sandpoint, Idaho, but it didn't stop her from seeing the world. She traveled to Oregon for college and then spent time in San Diego, California, a little more time back in Oregon, and then took off to explore the world with the nonprofit group Sea Shepherd. Katie, an activist at heart, lived on a boat and went where help was needed before moving to Australia. There, she met her husband Gwen, a French professional hydrofoil surfer. In 2016, the couple decided to move back to Sandpoint and onto her family's land before building a home downtown.

A LIFE BUILT AROUND ACTIVISM

The move back home meant Katie could switch gears and slow down. Life on the Sea Shepherd boat for four years meant daily, nonstop work. It was high-adrenaline and fast-paced with no time to slow down. Now, she starts her day with a trail run, heads to work at her restaurant, and caps the workday with a swim in Lake Pend Oreille (pronounced Lake Pond-oh-ray) before heading home and picking vegetables from their garden for dinner. "It's such a simple life. But there's nothing else I want," expressed Katie.

When Katie and Gwen first moved back, they had plans to create a bed-and-breakfast experience on the family land up in the mountains surrounding Sandpoint, where they also put in massive gardens on the property. "The growing season in Sandpoint is pretty short, but it's really bountiful in those months," said Katie. Dedicated to a healthy lifestyle, Katie envisioned cooking plant-based meals for their guests while also guiding them on hikes and showing them all the wonders of Sandpoint.

"I center my life mostly around being outside and in nature—trail running, where I can go on day adventures with my friends and bring the dogs. That's why we chose Sandpoint out of all the places we could have gone. It's home," shared Katie. Sandpoint has given Katie and Gwen the nature they sought and the ability to share her passion for healthy eating. Early on in returning, she realized if she were to run a B&B on the mountain, she would be away from the community she was excited to be immersed in. They would meet tourists, yes, but not the locals of Sandpoint.

Shifting gears, Katie began taking shifts at a local coffee shop while working on bringing her restaurant, Heart Bowls, to life. Like many great businesses, Heart Bowls was started out of necessity, as Katie and Gwen could not eat out anywhere in town. She started first serving at the local farmers market and then moving into her own brick-and-mortar location. With a constant focus on both animal and human rights, Heart Bowls is dedicated to being a place for the LGBTQUIA+ community in town to feel safe and supported. Katie has made it her mission to advocate for and donate to everything from Pride events to the local animal shelter. Anything that works for equality, Katie is eager to help support.

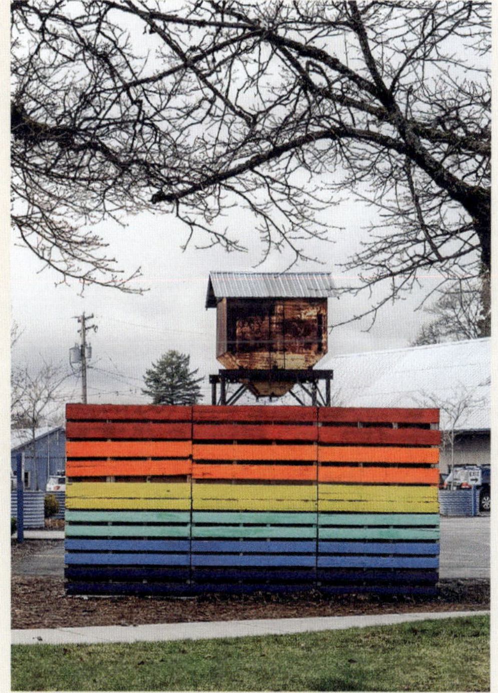

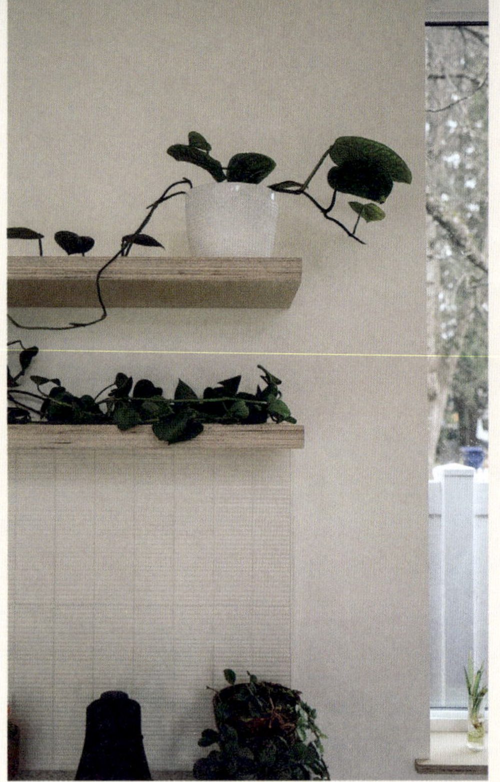

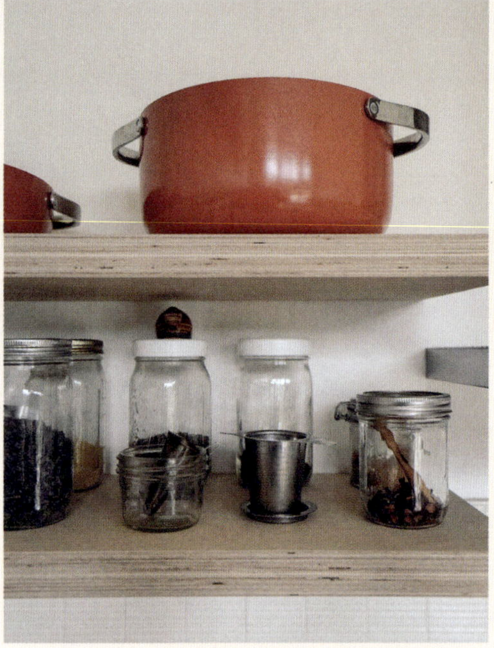

In 2019 and 2020, Sandpoint saw an influx of those opposing the historically liberal leanings of the town, which only pushed anyone actively working against oppression to be louder. The Pacific Northwest, which has lacked in diversity for a very long time, needs all voices to speak up, and Katie has made it her mission to be one of those voices. "If we had diversity in our community, they [racists in the area] would not be able to get away with it because they'd be facing the consequences and have to have a dialogue about what that means," expressed Katie. "I'm so happy to have Heart Bowls be one of the first businesses you see when you come into Sandpoint, and we have this massive equality flag hanging up." The support she's received has far outweighed any negativity, which has helped Katie to build a safe bubble for her customers and herself around Heart Bowls. "My business is my primary way of bringing my values into my community, and it's very effective because I serve so many people," shared Katie.

FINDING YOUR COMMUNITY IN A SMALL TOWN

"No matter where you are, you must do the things you love to find your people. Coffee, food, and trail running are my things. The more I did those things, the easier it was to find all the people. It came quickly," said Katie.

SEASONAL DYNAMICS IN A SMALL TOWN

Sandpoint is a resort town in several ways. The town is situated on Lake Pend Oreille, the largest lake in the state, making it an ideal summer location. In winter, the mountains that surround the town offer incredible skiing at Schweitzer Ski Resort—both downhill and cross-country—leaving it a more expensive place to live. Still, unlike other towns that rely on tourism and where many seasonal employees have to commute to work, many hospitality workers can live in Sandpoint. However, due to zoning laws in town, apartment buildings are very limited and ADUs (accessory dwelling units) are hard to get permits for with strict regulations.

Growing towns, especially resort towns, are facing the problem of pricing out the people needed to run their establishments. If these people can't afford to live where they work, a conversation needs to be had about the city code and how to accommodate them. "The Sandpoint Master Plan is working to develop our [town's] master plan for the next ten years. It's really a conversation of how to interact with tourism, with the locals, how to respect the locals in a way that people can afford to live here. And with the introduction of AI, are these jobs that people will have to go elsewhere for?" shared Katie.

WAYS TO HELP CHANGE AND BE PART OF THE SOLUTION IN YOUR SMALL TOWN

Be an example of what changes you want to see in your town.

Attend city planning meetings, town hall meetings, school board meetings, etc.

Advocate for those who can't advocate for themselves.

Approach each person you are working with to educate with kindness. Remember, they might not have ever had to think about the action you are advocating for before. You might be the first step in helping them address the problem. Kindness can go a long way.

Advocate for second homes to be allowed only outside of the city limits.

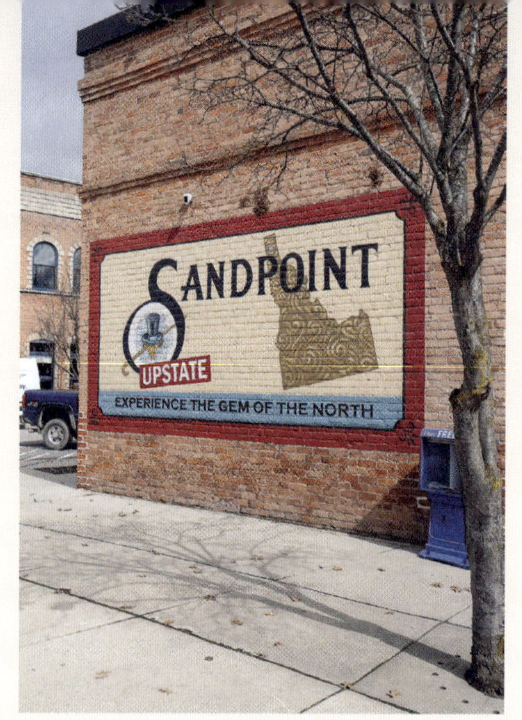

HOW TRAVEL CAN IMPACT YOUR SMALL TOWN

Travel gave Katie the courage to open her own business and believe in it. Without traveling, she would not have had the perspective or insight to know that places exist that are speaking up and speaking out. "Heart Bowls wouldn't be what it is without its commitment to equality. Traveling to bigger cities and seeing all the businesses that fly flags and believe in human rights showed what was missing in Sandpoint," said Katie.

When we travel, we learn early on what and who we might fear; people who look different than ourselves or are of a different religion, etc., aren't as scary as we might have previously anticipated. Travel works to break down those barriers. We quickly find we are a planet full of different opinions and views, but there's also so much beauty in the conversation and learning that can take place within those differences.

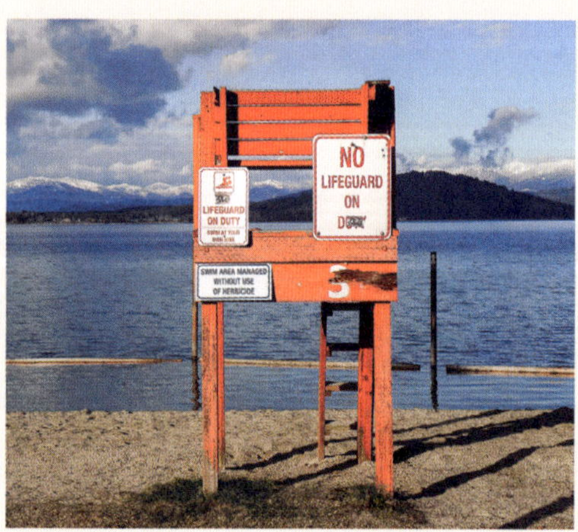

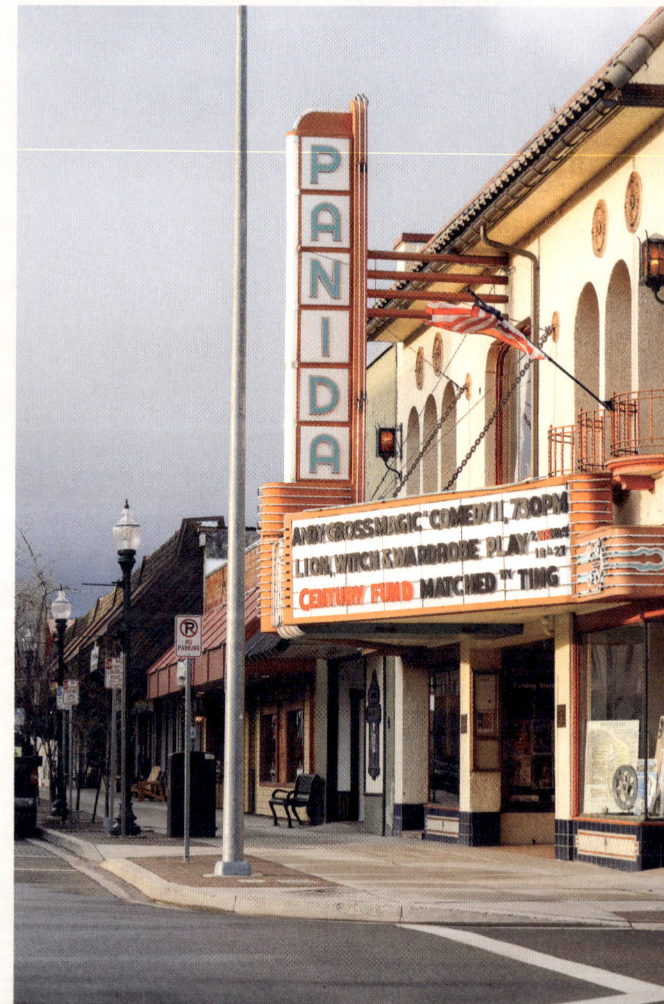

SANDPOINT, IDAHO

POPULATION: 10,024 full-time residents in 2024

TOWN SIZE: 4.8 square miles

CLOSEST INTERNATIONAL AIRPORT: Spokane International Airport, Washington (81.4 miles)

CLOSEST REGIONAL AIRPORT: Sandpoint Airport (0 miles)

CLOSEST LARGE CITY: Spokane, Washington (72.7 miles)

BONUS TOWNS NEARBY: Hayden, Hope, Dover

ANIMALS TO SPOT: moose, grizzly bears, caribou, bighorn sheep, bald eagles, river otters

TOWN FACTS: Sandpoint is part of a railroad funnel, meaning it's a junction for two intercontinental railways and two local railways meeting and going through the town. More than fifty trains a day pass through Sandpoint. The Panida Theater hosts several film festivals throughout the year. Sandpoint has a music conservatory that offers classes and outdoor concerts as well as in the concert hall. Sandpoint has a historical reputation for being a very progressive town in the state of Idaho. To the east, Lake Pend Oreille is surrounded by two national forests: Kaniksu National Forest and Idaho Panhandle National Forests. It's common to spot wild moose wandering the downtown and neighborhoods year-round.

SEASONS: Sandpoint has four distinct seasons.

WATER ACTIVITIES: shoreline hiking, boating, sailing, kayaking, fishing, windsurfing, swimming, hydrofoil surfing, Jet-Skiing, paddleboarding, guided boat tours

WATER SPOTS TO VISIT: Lake Pend Oreille and Pend Oreille River

A lot of Lake Pend Oreille is private land, but in the center of town is City Beach, providing public use of the lake, complete with a free boat launch. There's also a beach in the park, which gives free local access to the town.

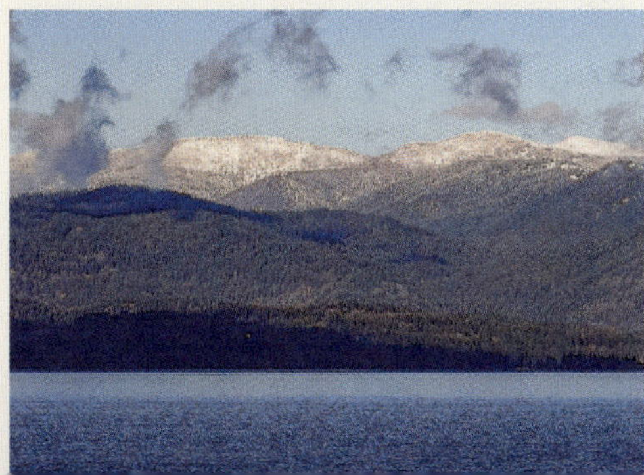

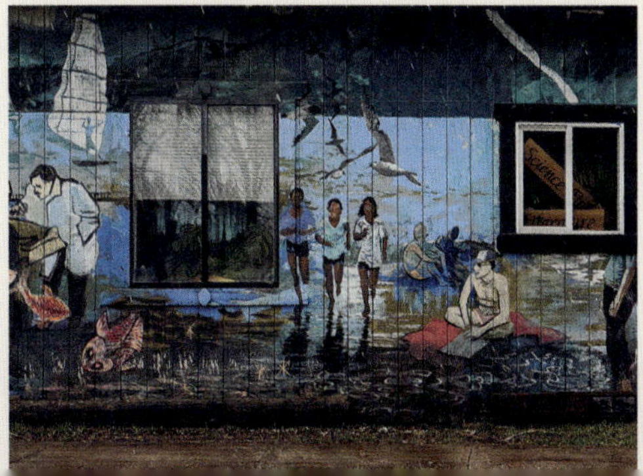

“We’ve been here three and a half years, and it’s changed even more of the fabric of our relationship, our kid’s relationship with us, what we think of as a community, and the things we care about. Our art and how we create are everything, and it’s given us so much more. I can’t imagine a better place to live.”

—KATIE JONES

KATIE AND TIM JONES

Film Festival Coordinator and Musician, Teacher

FRANKFORT, MICHIGAN

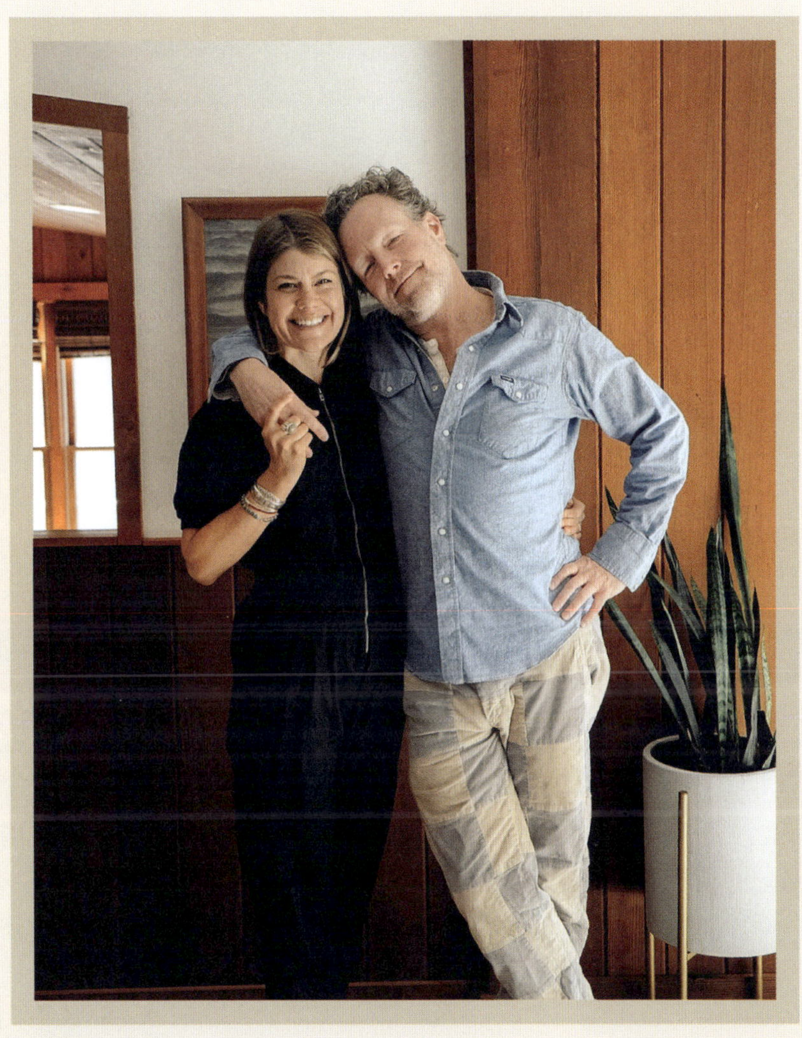

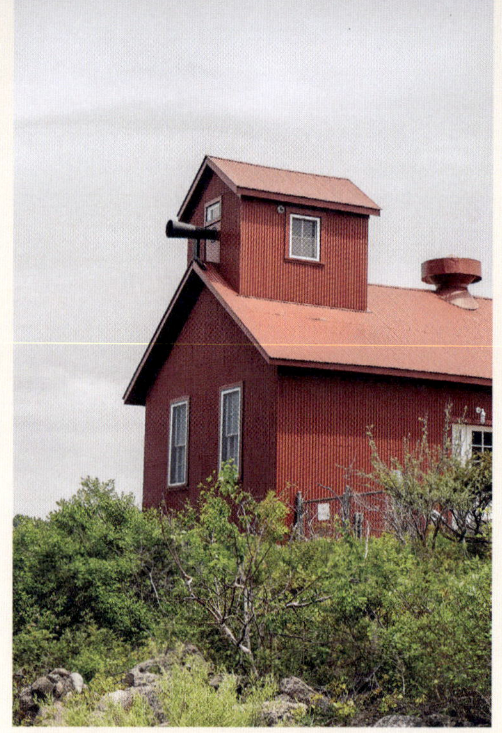

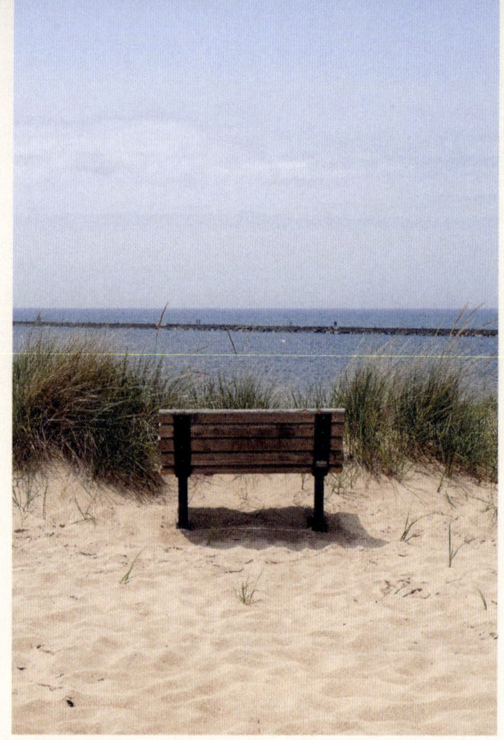

Once a filmmaker in Los Angeles, Katie Jones has taken a tour of the country in all the moves she's made throughout her life, hitting Ohio, Florida, Indiana, California, Illinois, and Tennessee before landing in the first small town where she lives with her family: Frankfort, Michigan. She was drawn in by childhood memories of summers spent in the town with her family. In 2020, while living in Nashville, Katie and her musician husband Tim found themselves, like most of the world, tethered to their home. Feeling confined and without a lot of space to spread out, the family began to look for alternatives to city living and for a place that helped to stretch their resources. And so they made their way to Frankfort full-time.

Tim had always fantasized about making their stays in Frankfort more permanent, while Katie wondered what she'd do for work in this small town she'd only known through summers as a child. With her background in film, it was kismet when she heard the 101-year-old local Garden Theater was looking to expand its offerings and switch to becoming a nonprofit. After a conversation with the owners, the couple moved two months later.

Frankfort is a town nestled between Crystal Lake to the north and Betsie Lake to the south and sits at the edge of Lake Michigan to the west. Everyone who lives in the town is connected to the water and lakes they are surrounded by daily. The lakes are vital to making Frankfort the town that it is.

BUILDING A LIFE AROUND COMMUNITY INVOLVEMENT

With big ideas for turning the Garden Theater into a focal point of the town, Katie knew more money would be needed. They had raised funds for a roof just as she was joining the team, but they still required infrastructure, lights, rigging, sound, etc., so more promotions got underway as soon as she began working. Leaning on her favorite movie of all time, *White Christmas*, she had the idea to do a holiday variety show. Katie turned to her husband to invite musicians from Nashville to perform, and the Holiday Gala was born. Now a tradition, over 1,200 people attend, and the event sells out in a few hours each year.

Along with the funds raised for infrastructure, Katie and her team also support music, dance, and theater alongside their operation as a movie house. Katie and Tim's merging of their creative work has been as rewarding for them as it has been for the people they serve. "We started this program: Stories That Heal. It's intergenerational, but we realize the real need is in the high school. It's healing through the arts, songwriting, process, and sharing," said Katie. She often jokes, "I'm not saving the world. I'm running a movie theater. But when you can make such a difference in the lives of these people that you care about, it's fun, and so when you can bring joy, like throwing a holiday gala, why not?"

Frankfort is primarily a vacation town, and its population balloons in the summer. With the seasonal crowd, though, comes a shortage of workforce housing. Tim joined the board of the Local Land Trust, and already they have been able to build four homes for workers. Tim and Katie are committed to seeing the good grow in the town they've become so attached to.

"We show movies every week, but we also collaborate with the schools. Tim and I are

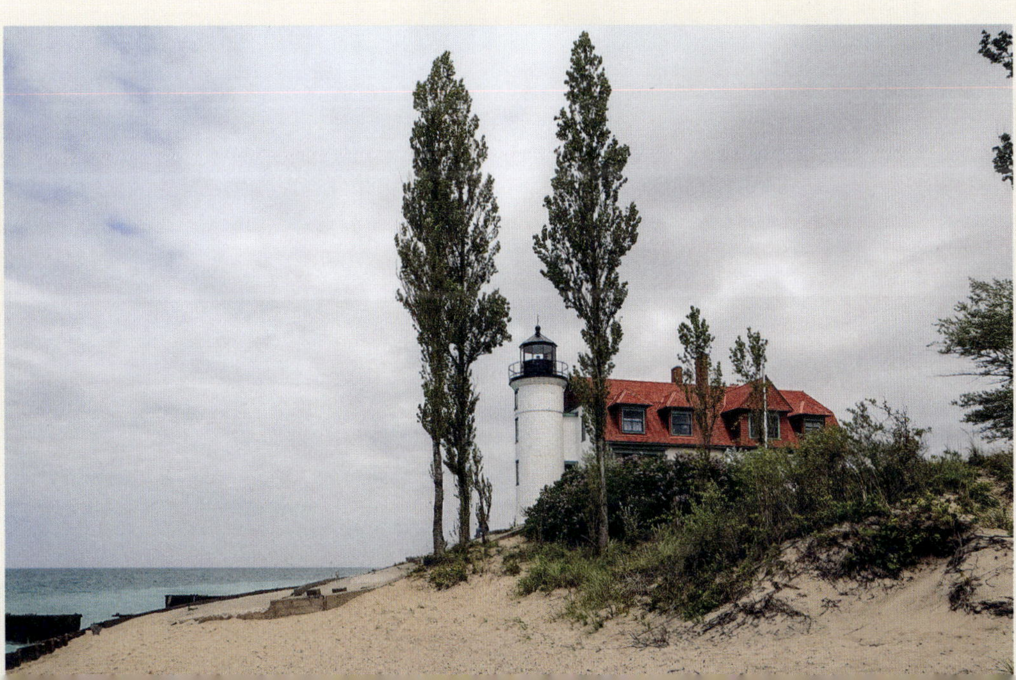

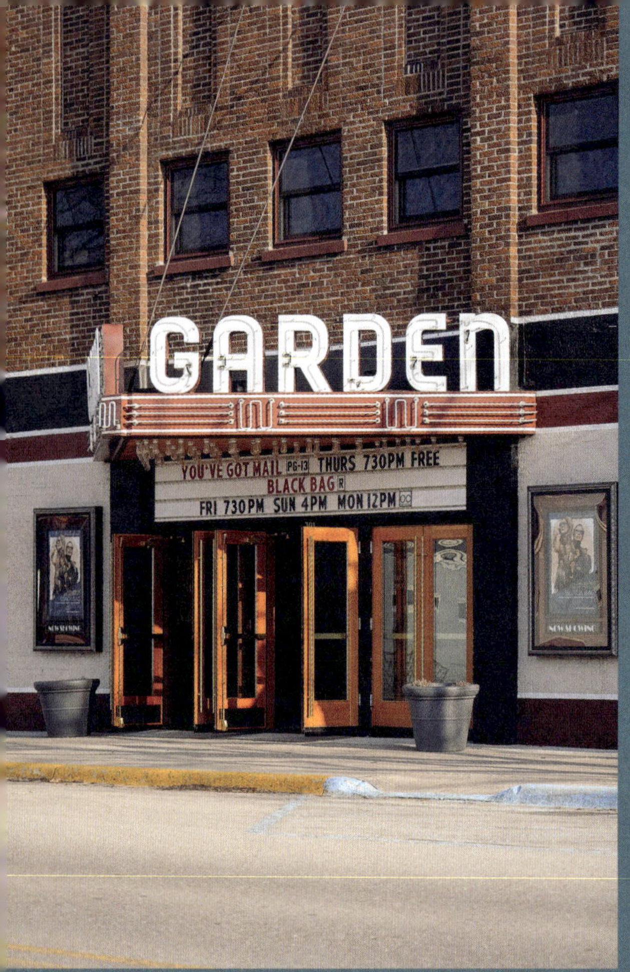
GARDEN
YOU'VE GOT MAIL PG-13 THURS 730PM FREE
BLACK BAG R
FRI 730PM SUN 4PM MON 12PM

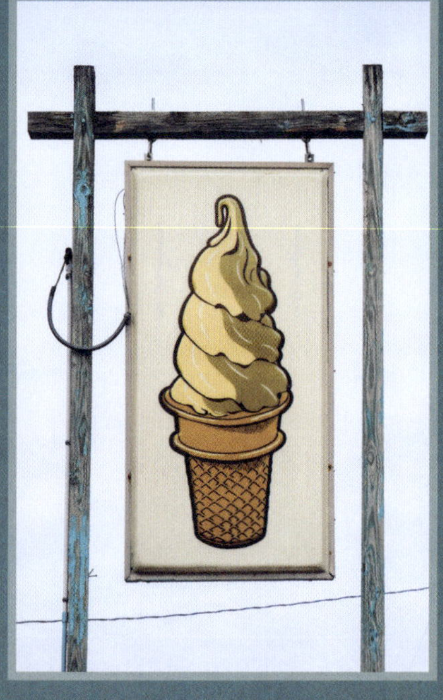

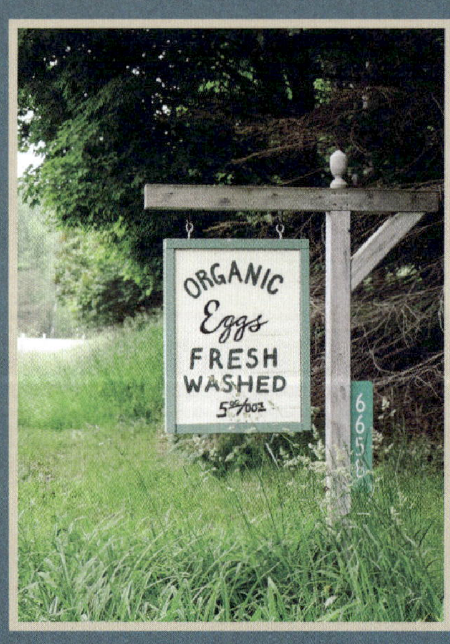
ORGANIC
Eggs
FRESH
WASHED

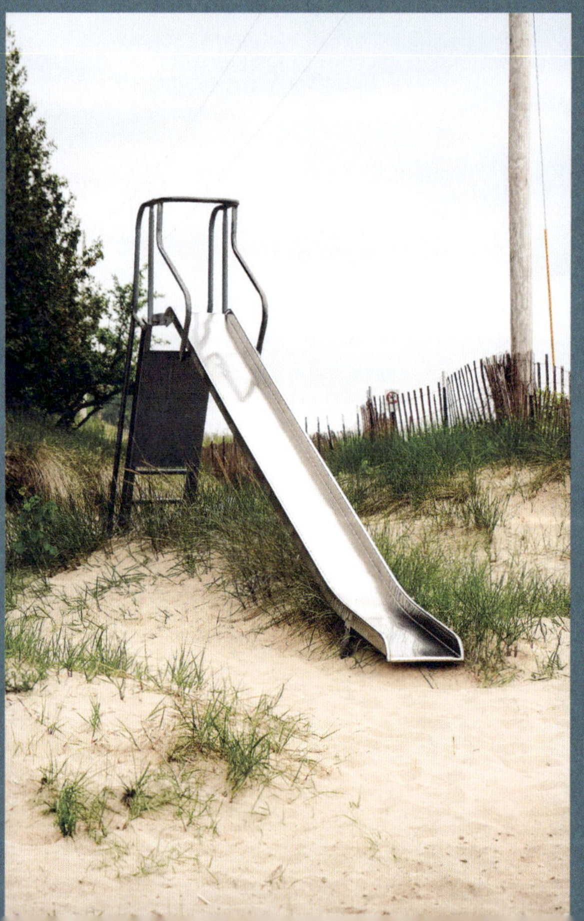

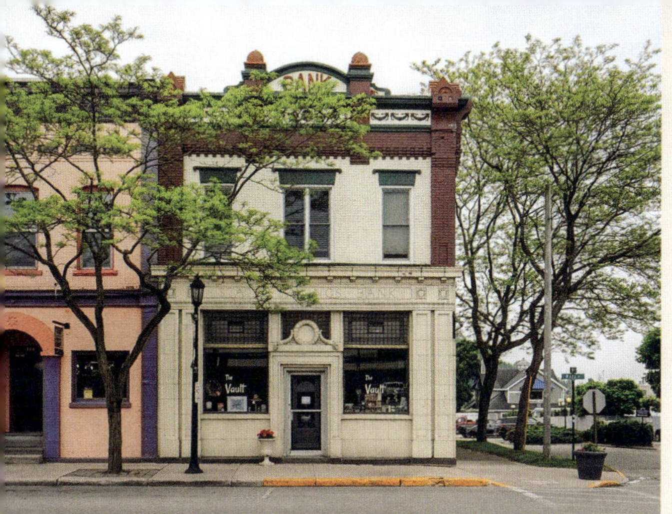

starting a theater program in the elementary that didn't have one before," shared Katie. A big part of the theater's mission is accessibility for the whole community. They put on as many free events as possible with that in mind. This singular goal combines the year-round community and the summer crowd, even if for just a bit. By offering free events, they give people living in the town and those passing through a place to converge and share space, regardless of age or socioeconomic standing. It allows for community members that might not otherwise cross paths to meet. They aren't interacting because their children are in the same class or they met on the playground. They aren't friends because they are coworkers. The bond is cemented over the love of community and film.

Something interesting that happens in small towns is intergenerational friendships. "The whole world right now needs connectivity, inclusivity, and acceptance," shared Katie, adding, "We are creating intergenerational events, asking ourselves: *Can somebody that is five enjoy this? Can somebody who's eighty-five enjoy this? Can somebody who's twenty-five enjoy this?*" From a scientific perspective, data shows the more you can foster intergenerational relationships, the better off a community will be.

EVENTS TO BRING INTERGENERATIONAL GROUPS TOGETHER

- Art shows
- Bird-watching neighborhood group walks
- Book clubs
- Community picnics
- Cooking classes
- Neighborhood block parties

BIG CITY VS. SMALL TOWN

"When somebody drops by or when I just can go get something easily, every little thing is a constant reminder of what was missing in our life before. It's not lost on me; it is present constantly," shared Katie when describing her feelings about the differences between living in a big city versus a small town. City life was all she'd known, and now, she has

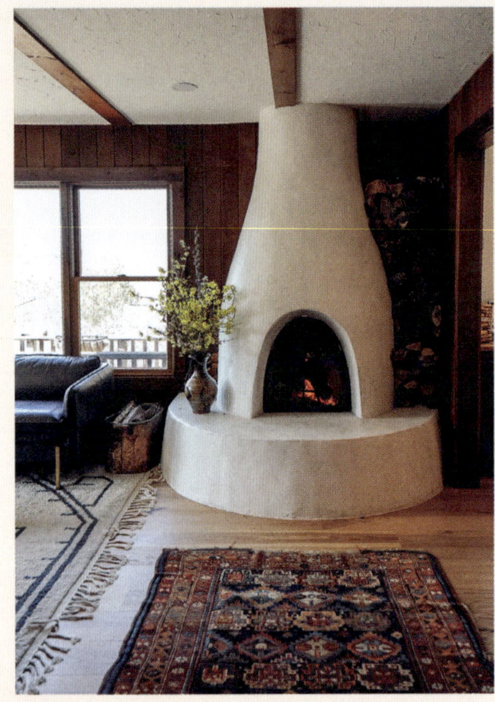

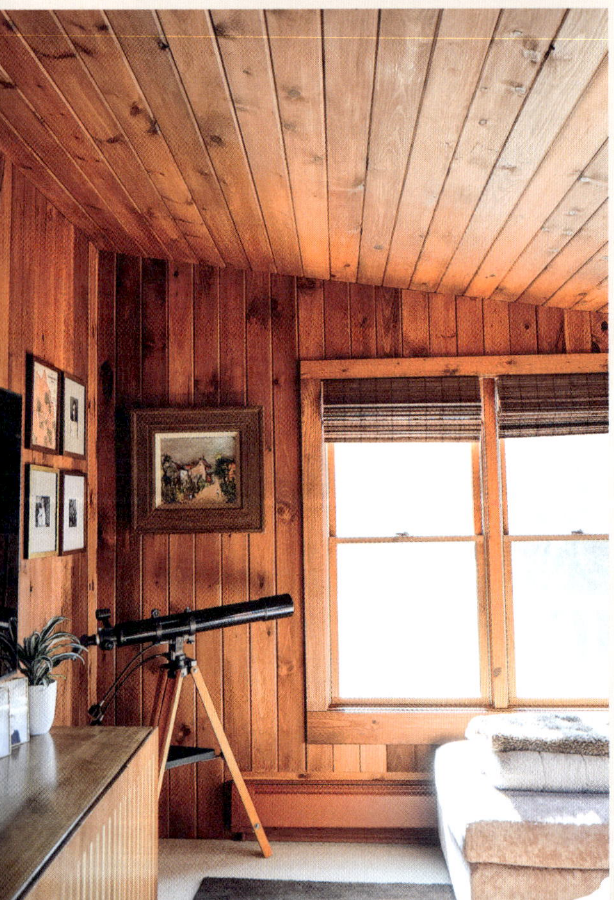

a hard time remembering what things were like before. Katie never felt settled as an artist in an artist-fueled town such as Nashville. She'd make friends with someone, and then they'd be gone on tour for several months or they'd move somewhere else.

On top of that, the need to constantly gig, line up your next job, play with multiple bands, and always look for your next project began to compound for the couple. Moving to Frankfort gave Katie and Tim permission to slow down and be mindful of what they were going to do next. Katie's job at the theater gave her direction and a routine she hadn't had in the city, while Tim was able to take a job teaching songwriting at the nearby Interlochen College for Creative Arts.

PROTECTING THE WATER

Lake conservation is important in Frankfort. With Lake Michigan's vastness, it feels more like an ocean when you look out over it. With a tremendous conservancy project, it's evident everyone feels indebted to the land and the lake. Much of the land around the lake has been donated to the conservancy, which is working to protect the beaches and water. "Lake Michigan is so unbelievably special. I don't think people understand until they arrive and go to the lake. It's so pure," shared Katie. "I always say at the theater that our number one competition is the sunset. It doesn't matter what time of year it is; if there is going to

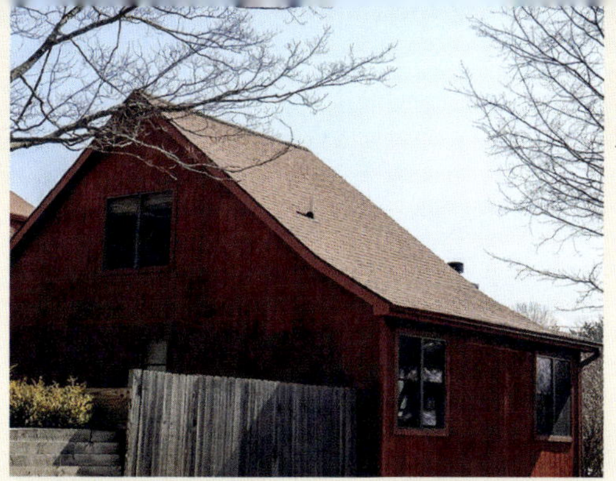

be a sunset, you can talk about it. If you don't know someone, you can always say, 'Oh, beautiful day, right?'" Weather is a universal connection with humans. For those in Michigan, you can always talk about the sunset.

RUNNING A SMALL TOWN FILM FESTIVAL

Years before Katie and Tim moved to Frankfort, before the theater had been restored, a few concerned citizens got together to pool their money and form an LLC to save the Garden Theater. "It's so indicative of this amazing community," remarked Katie. Two couples were running the theater at that time, and it was from their ingenuity that the film festival was born. What started as a casual idea became a great community event and their moneymaker, which funded the theater for the year.

If this sounds like the movie *Jerry & Marge Go Large*, you aren't off base. The real-life couple isn't from too far away, and the Hollywood version of their story was shown at the Garden Theater with the family all seeing it together for the first time in Frankfort. The community spirit of the movie continues to spill out into the streets of Frankfort every day, making it the number one thing Katie loves about her special town.

The summer lake crowd used to stay from Memorial Day to Labor Day, but the rise in popularity of the film festival, which is held in October each year, has changed their trajectory. Now they are sticking around to see the leaves change and only departing after the film festival each year, ushering in a new group of young people who might one day call Frankfort home year-round.

Katie noted, "It's not a huge festival—maybe fifteen or sixteen films—but it's on a quiet weekend when everybody just comes and watches together. All the films must have won some sort of award worldwide, a curated list of films that they wouldn't have seen elsewhere."

FAVORITE SMALL TOWN MOVIES

- *Dirty Dancing*
- *The Goonies*
- *It's a Wonderful Life*
- *Jerry & Marge Go Large*
- *Mystic Pizza*
- *White Christmas*

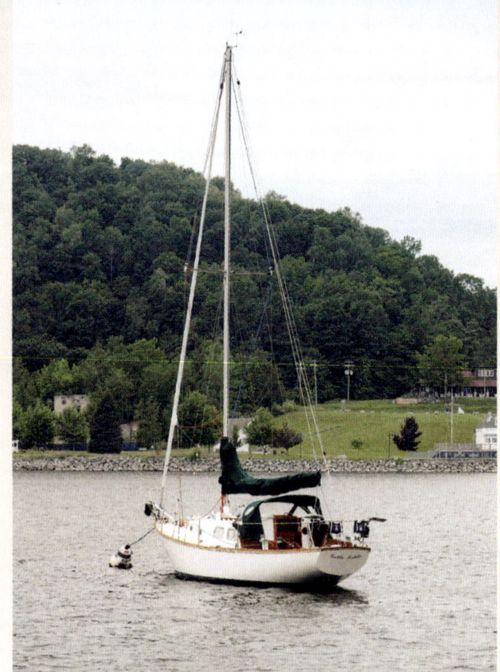

FRANKFORT, MICHIGAN

POPULATION: 1,277 full-time residents in 2024

TOWN SIZE: 1.6 square miles

CLOSEST INTERNATIONAL AIRPORT: Grand Rapids Gerald R. Ford International Airport (146 miles)

CLOSEST REGIONAL AIRPORT: Cherry Capital Airport—Traverse City (39.4 miles)

CLOSEST LARGE CITY: Traverse City (41.8 miles)

BONUS TOWNS NEARBY: Elberta, Benzonia, Empire

TOWN FACTS: Frankfort is the gateway to the Sleeping Bear Dunes National Lakeshore. The Point Betsie Lighthouse nearby has been in operation for 150 years and is considered one of Michigan's most photographed structures. Just outside of town is what's known as Gravity Hill. Some say it's an optical illusion, while others think it's a mystical anomaly.

SEASONS: Frankfort has four distinct seasons.

WATER ACTIVITIES: swimming, fishing, beachcombing, boating, skiing, sailing, paddleboarding, kayaking, tubing on the Platte River

WATER SPOTS TO VISIT: Lake Michigan, Betsie Lake, and Crystal Lake

"We're preservationists, first and foremost, and we're suckers for everything that we do at the camp. By every definition, we overinvest in every possible way to try to preserve, and then we resurrect the physical space we're in."

—TEREASA SURRATT

TEREASA SURRATT AND DAVID HERNANDEZ

Camp Owners and Preservationists at Camp Wandawega (pronounced One-da-wa-ga)

ELKHORN, WISCONSIN

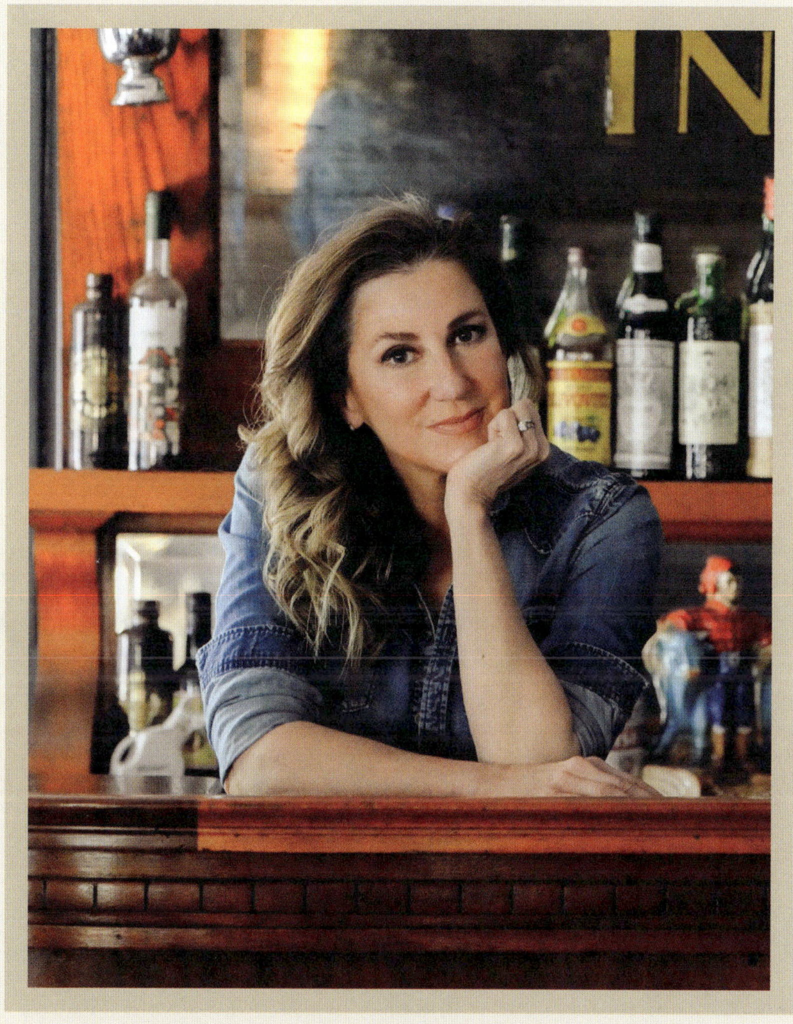

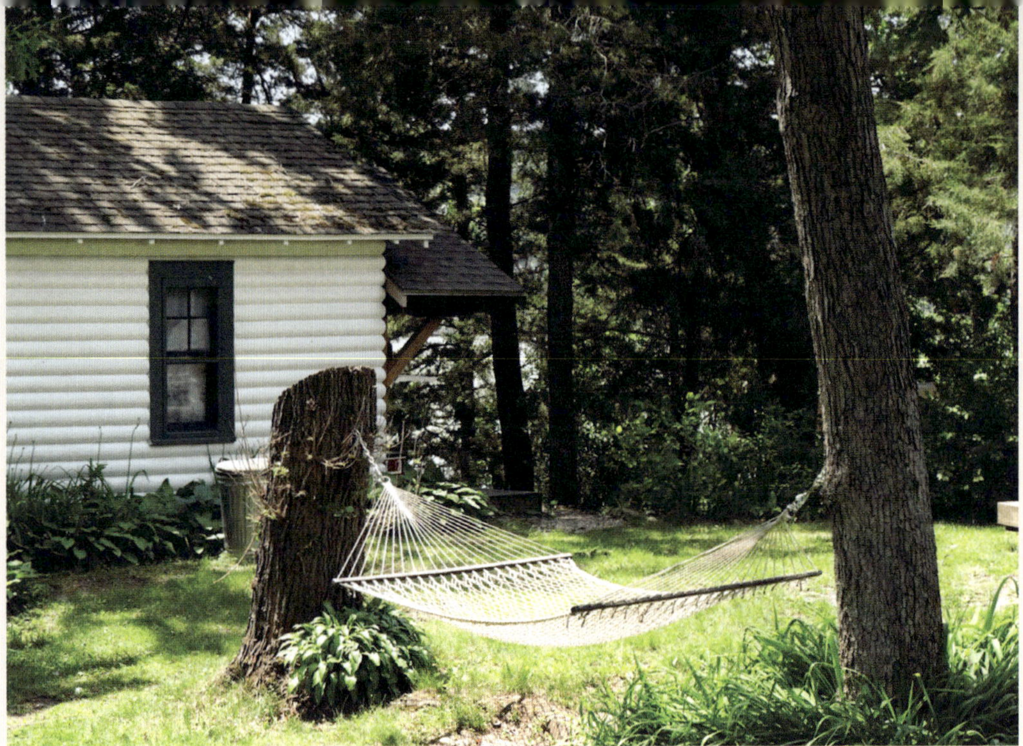

Camp Wandawega has a wild and fascinating history. David Hernandez's mother was a refugee from World War II who was born and grew up in a detention camp in Germany. She and her family lived there for three years before being paired with a host family in the United States. They were brought first to Ellis Island and then to North Carolina, where they lived for a few years before moving to Chicago to connect with other members of the Latvian refugee community who made that city home. As they were escaping to a safe zone, David's grandparents buried priceless family treasures in the ground of their homeland. They never imagined they wouldn't be able to return.

The Catholic Church supported charities for Latvian refugees, with David's mother being one of the recipients. "Starting in 1925, the Catholic Church let each of these Latvian families rent a tiny 10-by-10 room for around $300 a year, and it became a community space for them to practice their beliefs, music, and language and all the things they had to leave behind," said Tereasa.

David spent his summers at the Catholic Church camp with the women of his community, just ninety miles from his home in Chicago. They would live at Camp Wandawega, and the priest would visit on the weekends to hold mass at an outdoor community service. David repeatedly told the priest, "If you ever want to sell this place, let me know." "That's the voice of a ten-year-old," exclaimed Tereasa. And in a twist of fate, the priest called David when he was thirty-six, explaining he needed to move back to his homeland of Latvia and asking if David was still interested in buying the property.

Going up against a few other interested buyers, David and Tereasa won the private bidding war. While everyone else wanted to bulldoze it, David and Tereasa wanted to save it, preserve it, and bring it back to the glory of what David remembered as a child. Buildings were falling in at this point, but David with his wonderful childhood memories and Tereasa with her scrappy perseverance knew they needed to be the next generation to hold the keys. It was a difficult start. Interpol had to bust up an illegal car ring; hoarders were squatting in cabins; and a sixty-year-old Russian mobster would only leave when the priest called his mother to tell him to go. "It was a lot of work for David and me and sad to see in this beautiful place that for all those years was a place of community, where people were growing gardens and fixing up these buildings or maintaining them. But the good news is they never had the money to redecorate them. They didn't rip up the floors. They didn't tear down the walls. The poverty these Latvian refugees had is the very thing that preserved the property," said Tereasa. "We're preservationists, first and foremost, and we're suckers for everything that we do at the camp. By every definition, we overinvest in every possible way to try to preserve, and then we resurrect the physical space we're in."

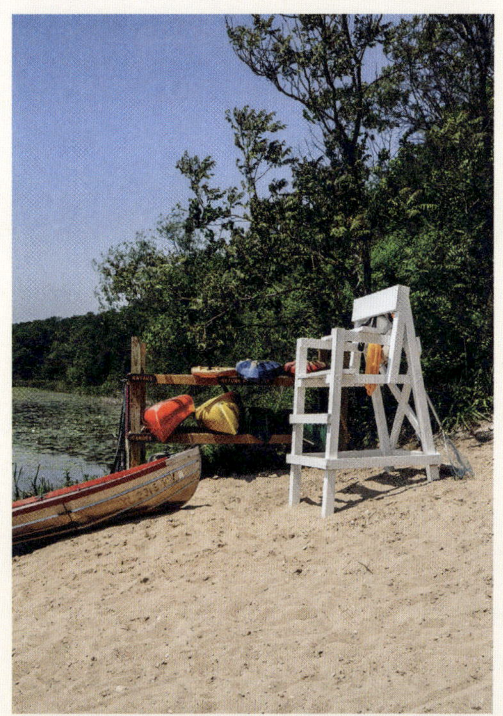

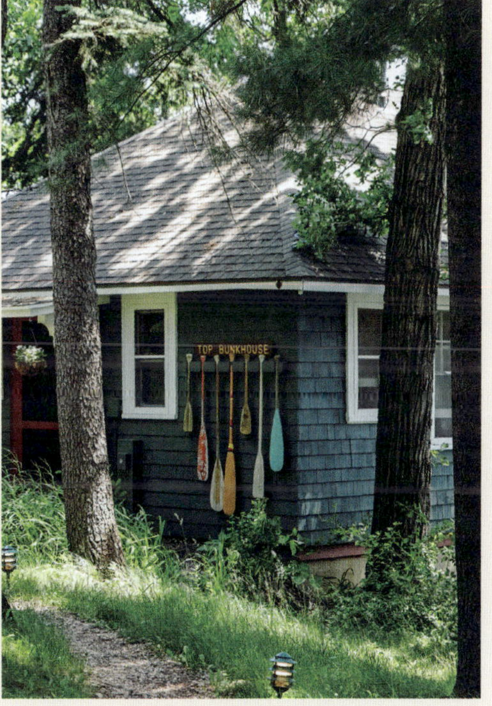

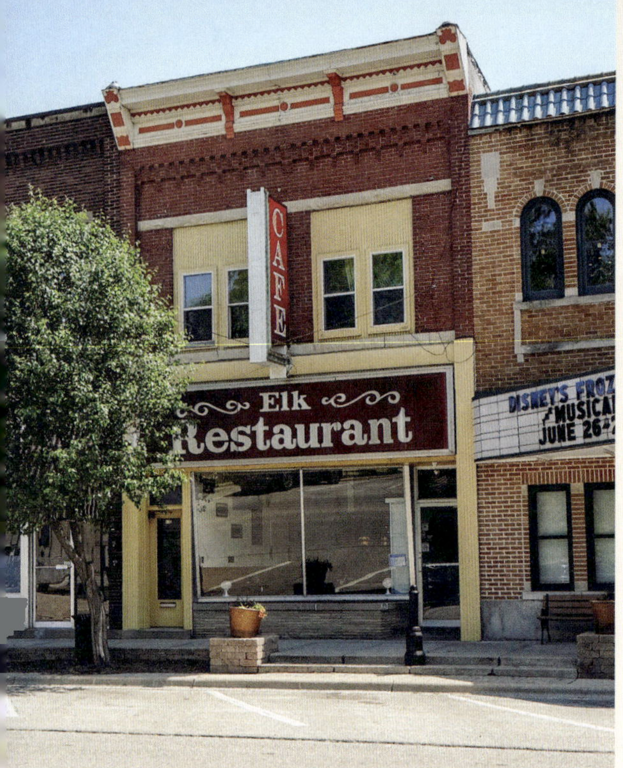

Going back further, before Camp Wandawega was owned by the Catholic Church, the 25-acre property was built by a Chicago architect during Prohibition as a brothel. “The state of Wisconsin wanted the camp to be listed on the National Register of Historic Places because it has significance—less architecturally but because of its history and the fact that it wasn't bastardized and it represents an era of America that is not discussed. But the truth is still a part of the American fabric, for better or worse,” shared Tereasa.

THE OFF-SEASON

Running an internationally known camp in Wisconsin requires a lot of systems. Bookings in the winter months account for only about 10 percent of the visitors, so Tereasa and David use that time as their building, repair, and new project season. For each season of refreshment, the couple adds a new house or cabin or new amenities from the farm stand to the offerings at Camp Wandawega. “We have twenty-five acres of century-old buildings. And every spring, there's going to be a new surprise. It will be broken waterlines, animals that moved in, broken windows, or structural things. . . . We start almost a month and a half into the season to just get set up. It takes us almost two months a year to set up and then a camp reset; mulch all the trails again and clear all the downed trees,” shared Tereasa. It sounds like a lot of work—and it is—but it's not anything Tereasa isn't used to. She grew up with soybeans on one side and corn on the other in a tiny rural town called Beardstown, a small farm community in central southern Illinois, which she still lovingly refers to as *home*.

The camp, technically in the township of Sugar Creek, is just seven miles outside of Elkhorn. Like many small towns, the communities fold in on one another, serving the joint

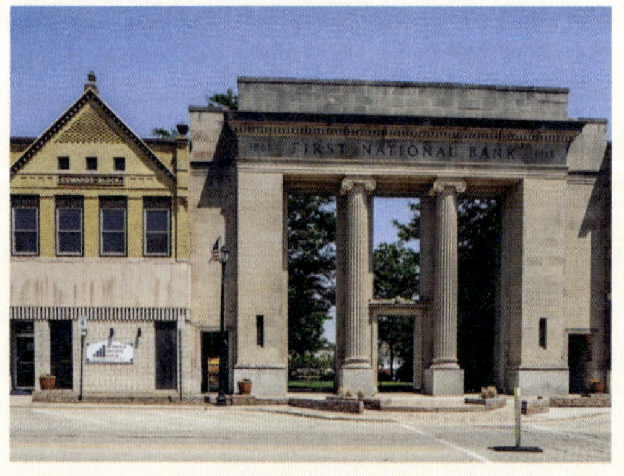

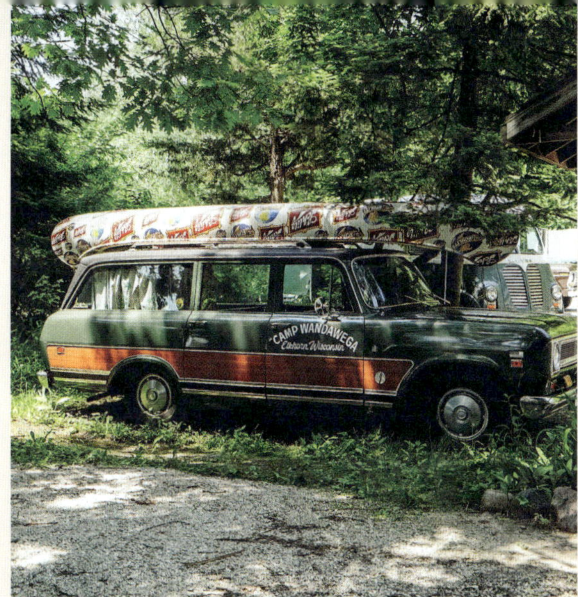

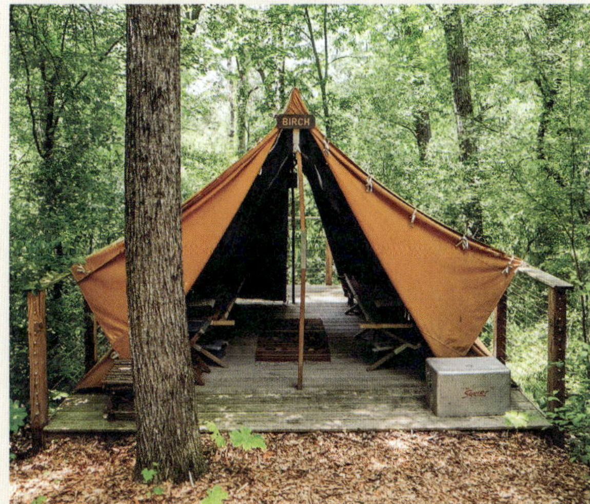

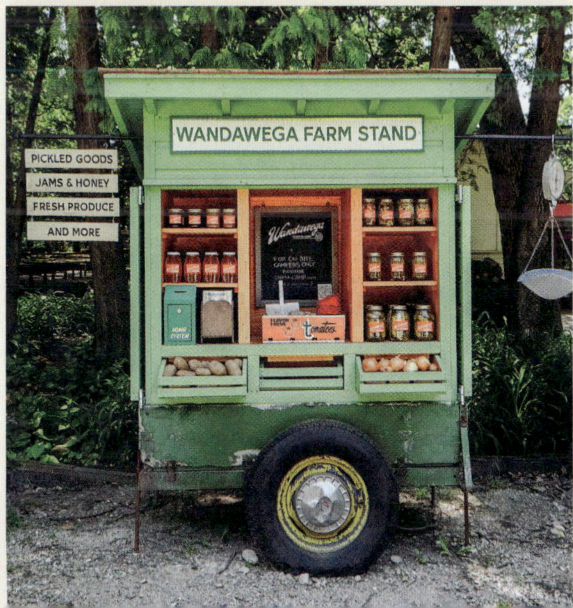

needs of the residents. Elkhorn still feels like a proper town to Tereasa, whose rural upbringing prepared her for this chapter in her life. On the flip side, David has lived in Chicago his whole life—a city kid through and through, who welcomes the break from the city to be in nature.

CITY KID, COUNTRY KID

David and Tereasa aren't the only ones on this camp journey. Their daughter has been with them at the camp since she was born, splitting her time between Chicago and Elkhorn with a foot in both worlds, a unique vantage point and access to the country and the city. "The older I get, the more I appreciate how I grew up because [the] things you learn growing up in a farm environment you can't learn that as you get older. Yes, you can leave the city and move to the country and teach yourself things, but the things that you gain growing up in that environment are the things that I apply in life, continually, always," shared Tereasa. Their daughter is navigating city life, surrounded by so many cultures. While at the camp, she's getting hands-on work experience learning to repair and host and understanding what it means to be a steward of the land. Raising a child with two vastly different perspectives becomes generational. Even though the family does not live in either place full-time, both communities carry over in sometimes subtle, yet often considerable, ways.

PRIDEFUL LABOR

Working the twenty-five acres of grounds at the camp is discussed earnestly. "We're hauling stuff, laying a patio, building bonfires, or dispersing firewood. If you are trying to run a property like we do, you get your hands dirty and keep them dirty from the beginning. I have pride in what I learned from my dad. The thing about growing up in the country is that, especially with farmers and machinists, you must know how to do everything by necessity," expressed Tereasa. She, her brothers, her brothers-in-law, and her dad built their own homes. David didn't build the camp, but they added about seven abandoned buildings to the property over the years, and each structure was painstakingly repaired and renovated. "When you invest in fixing something yourself, then it means more to you and more to the people that you host. They can see the effort that goes into it, and you appreciate the time you invest in it more. And I learned that growing up in the sticks," said Tereasa.

BRANDING A CAMP

Tereasa, previously a global group creative director at Ogilvy, bounced around to different titles within the advertising agency. She worked with brands to launch ad campaigns, created immersive experiences, and built museums. She worked in every form and medium worldwide for brands within the agency before stepping down to focus on their camp full-time. Now, through licensing ideas, events, and partnerships, she's helped to transform an over-100-year-old camp into a design haven of nostalgia and preserving a lost era. David, also with a background in advertising, helped brand the camp with items no longer part of the common vernacular, such as a tourist viewfinder or flocked felt patches, each piece connected to the last through both transportive designs. "Every product that we make allows us to share the story, or at least a piece of history," said Tereasa. They aren't just making a sweatshirt that says *Wandawega*; it's created with history, preservation, and design in mind, with complete intention, down to the color selected.

A FEW WAYS CAMP WANDAWEGA GIVES BACK

Donates the whole camp to inter-city youth for a camp experience

Has a bunkhouse reserved for an artist in residence, free of charge

Gives away 30 percent of the camp occupancy to different charity groups each year

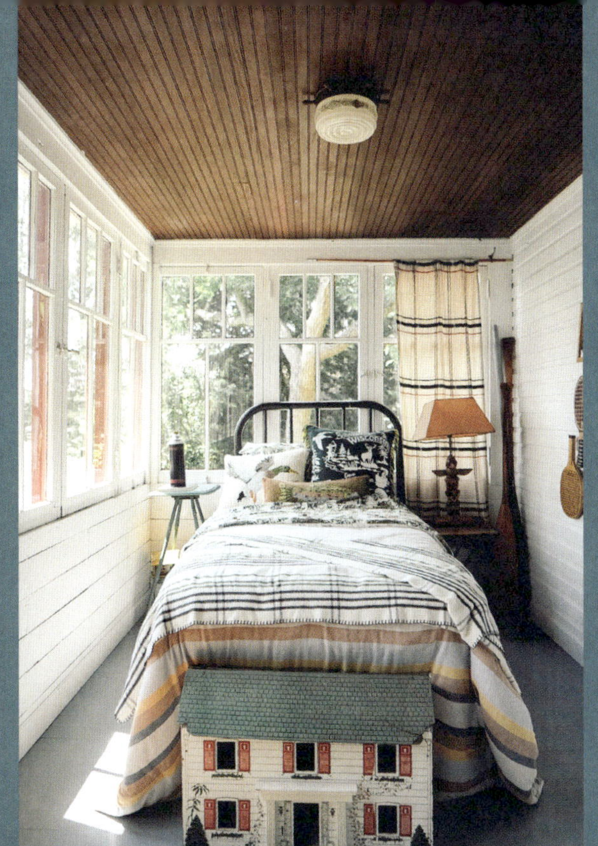

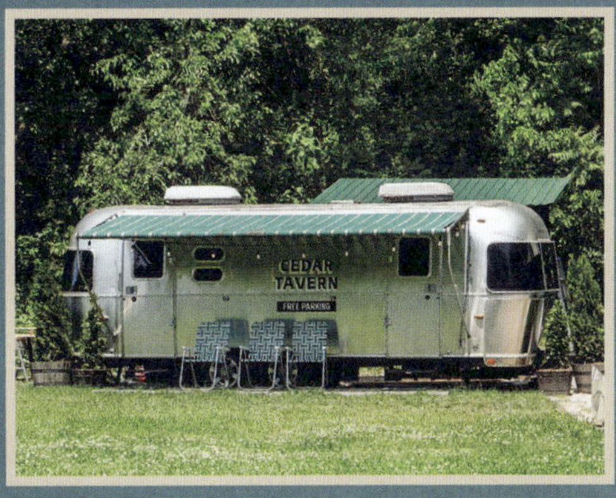
CEDAR
TAVERN
FREE PARKING

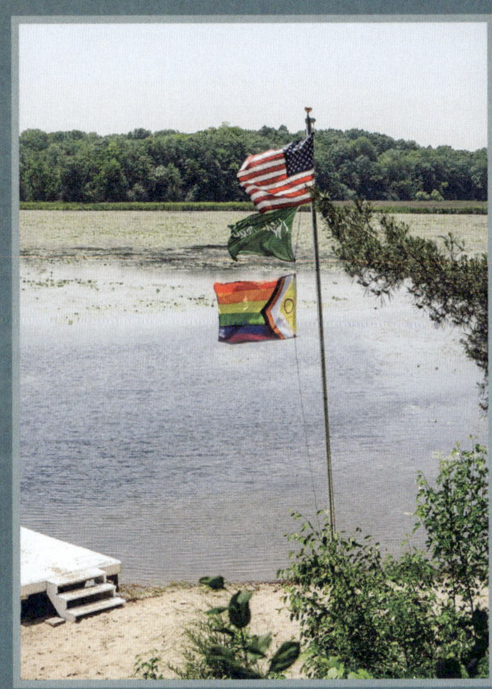

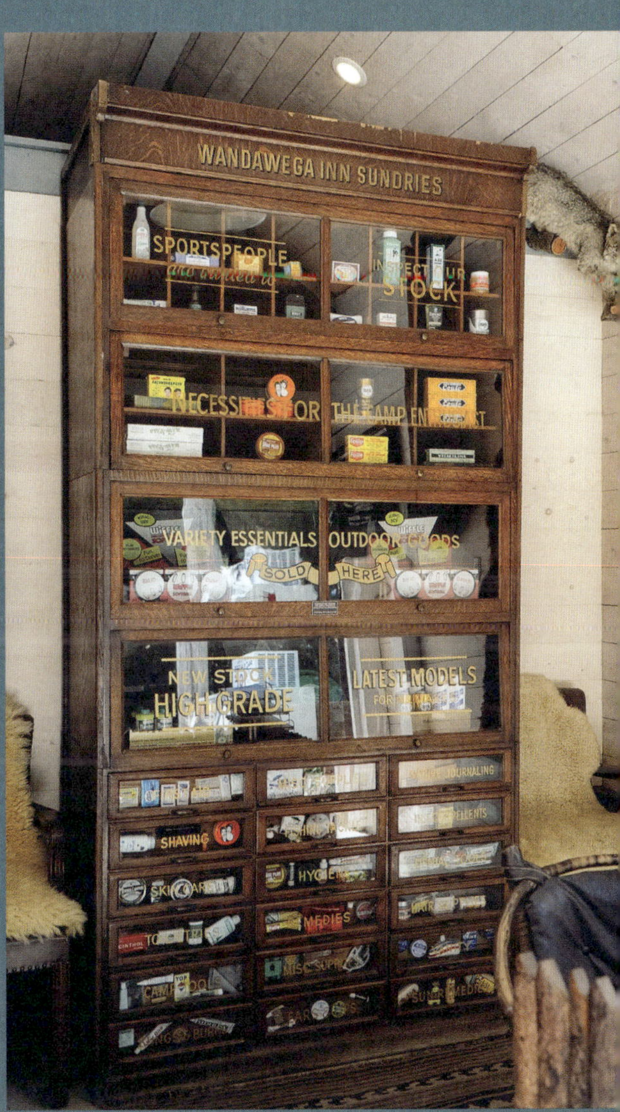
WANDAWEGA INN SUNDRIES
SPORTSPEOPLE
STOCK
VARIETY ESSENTIALS
SOLD
HERE
HIGH GRADE
LATEST MODELS
JOURNALING
SHAVING

ELKHORN, WISCONSIN

POPULATION: 10,230 full-time residents in 2024

TOWN SIZE: 8.1 square miles

CLOSEST INTERNATIONAL AIRPORT: Milwaukee Mitchell International Airport (42.9 miles)

CLOSEST REGIONAL AIRPORT: Dane County Regional Airport, Madison (63.4 miles)

CLOSEST LARGE CITY: Milwaukee (46 miles)

BONUS TOWNS NEARBY: Lake Geneva, East Troy, Whitewater, Delavan

ANIMALS TO SPOT: rattlesnakes, foxes, beavers, badgers

TOWN FACTS: Elkhorn was named after a pair of elk antlers spotted in a tree. Elkhorn has had the nickname "Christmas Card Town since before World War II." The town is home to the largest county fair in the state. You can listen to the full history of Camp Wandawega on the podcast *American Getaway*. Anna Pack sold whiskey out of an upright piano at the camp. There is a prop house full of vintage camp pieces used in photo shoots by brands that rent the camp. Elkhorn picks one place within the town to feature on their Christmas card each year; Camp Wandawega was selected for the 2024 Christmas card. *USA Today* listed Camp Wandawega as one of the best hotels in the world.

SEASONS: Elkhorn has four distinct seasons.

WATER ACTIVITIES: swimming, fishing, canoeing, kayaking, boating, waterskiing, sailing, ice fishing

WATER SPOTS TO VISIT: Lake Wandawega, Mill Lake, and Green Lake

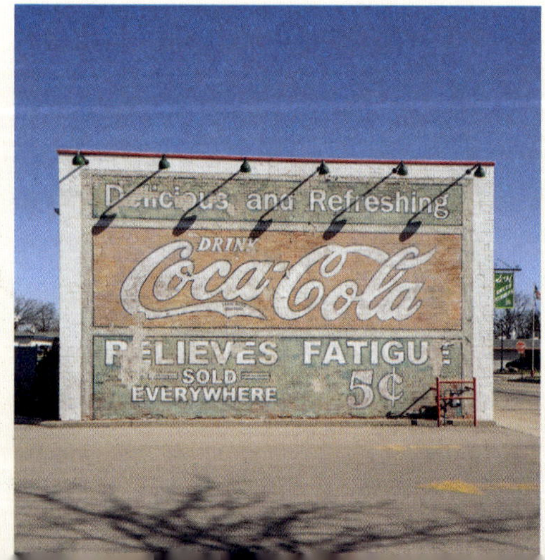

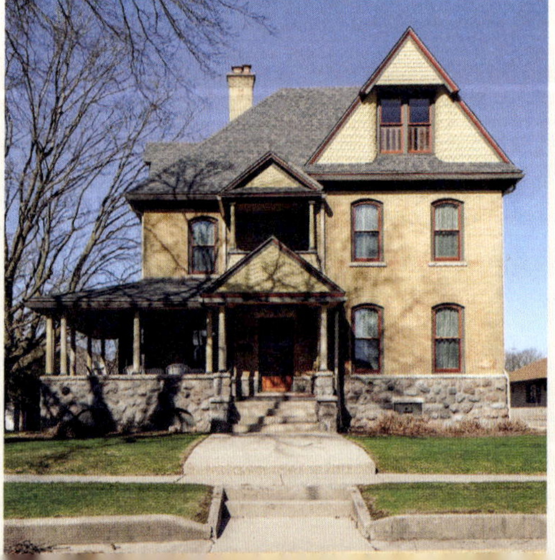

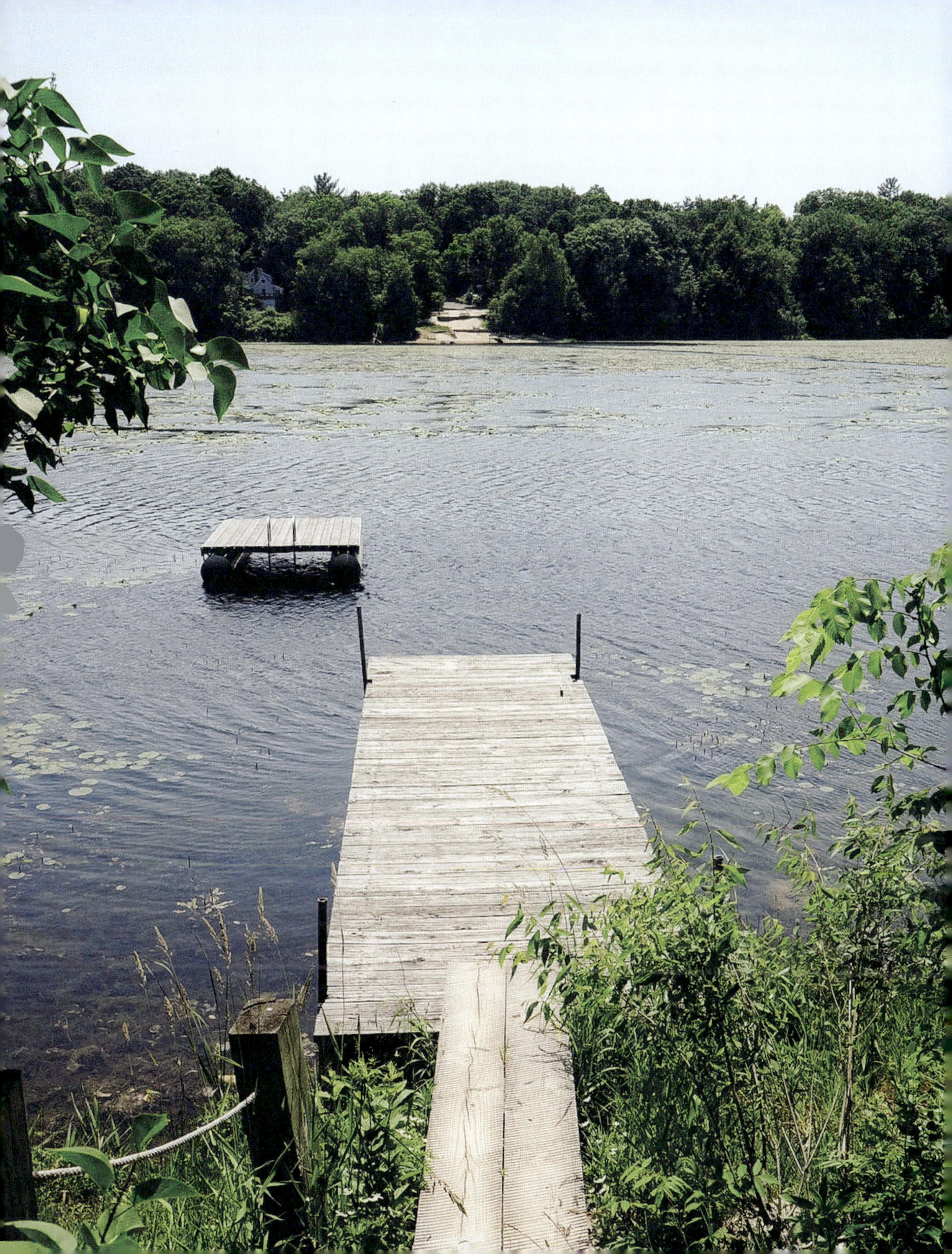

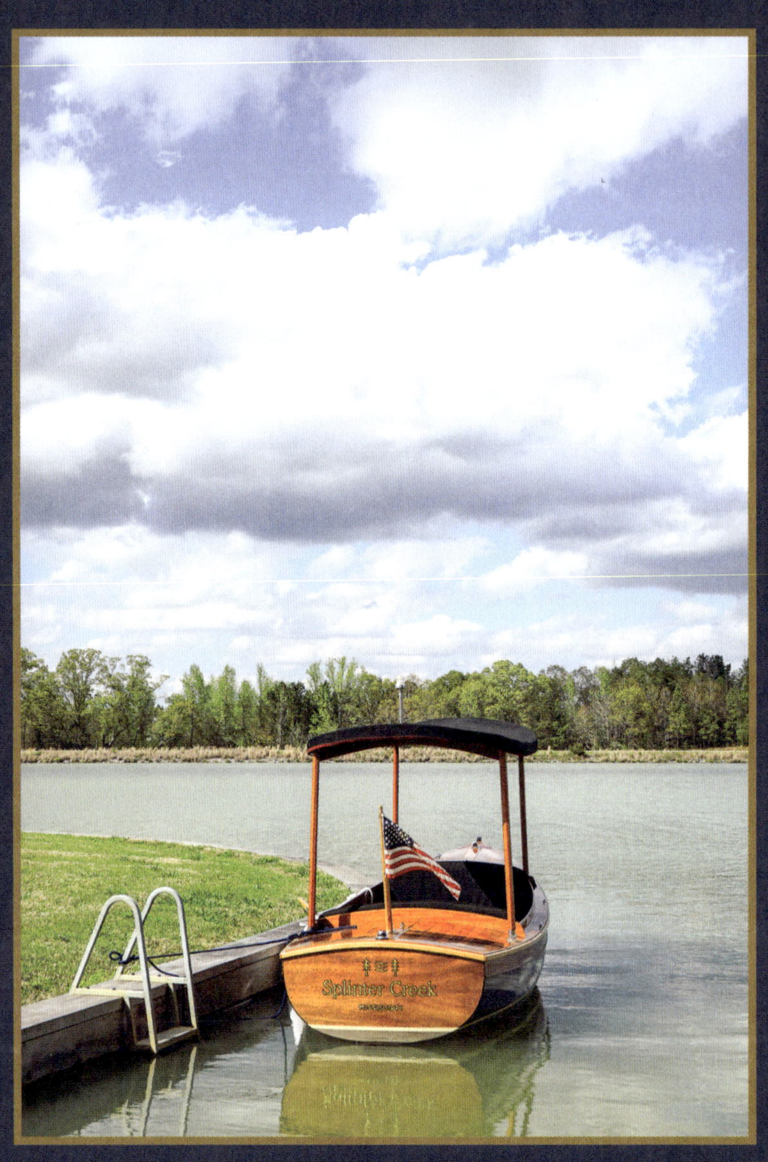
Splinter Creek

SPOTLIGHT

SPLINTER CREEK

Building a Lake Community

Anyone who's spent a summer in the South understands the sweltering humidity with the thickness of the air feeling like you are slicing through butter. Driving through the gates of Splinter Creek instantly cools you down, and you are brought to what one can only imagine a lakeshore of Sweden or Finland might be like, with a Nordic display of tree-lined lakes and oddly cool water coming from the cold springs below the surface.

Ellen and Eason Leake weren't planning to create a lake community in the hills of North Mississippi just outside of Taylor. But what was meant to be a timber investment of 750 acres became something entirely different over time. After walking the land and spending time among the trees, Ellen, Eason, and their two daughters, Elizabeth Keckler and Blair Wunderlich, had another idea. They got to work creating Splinter Creek, hoping to disrupt as little of the surrounding landscape as possible.

"We worked with the architectural firm Lake Flato to design Splinter Creek's overall plan. The firm has a reputation as a national leader in master planning and design of eco-conservation projects throughout the country. Their design process started with a comprehensive understanding of the environmental and cultural context and employed sustainable strategies unique to our region of the country. Together, we considered everything from the shape of the lakes to the entrance gates and road signs to the building materials. Great emphasis was placed on respecting the land's natural creeks and ridges. The roads follow the ridgelines, and the lakes, with multiple coves, feel like they have been there for a hundred years," shared Elizabeth.

The lakeside planning is forward-thinking, with modern homes juxtaposed on large lots surrounded by towering trees that must be approved for removal. "Splinter Creek envisions owners designing homes that will integrate with the natural features of the land, preserving mature trees and native plants and complementing the distinctive topography of the area. Where most developments today focus on clear-cutting trees for concrete slab foundations, we embrace the diverse topography and live 'lightly on the land,'" said Elizabeth. The three spring-fed lakes were built for swimming, boating, and fishing and serve as the "main streets" of the community, and each has a combination of docks, floating piers, a pavilion with firepits and an outdoor kitchen for use by neighbors, their families, and guests.

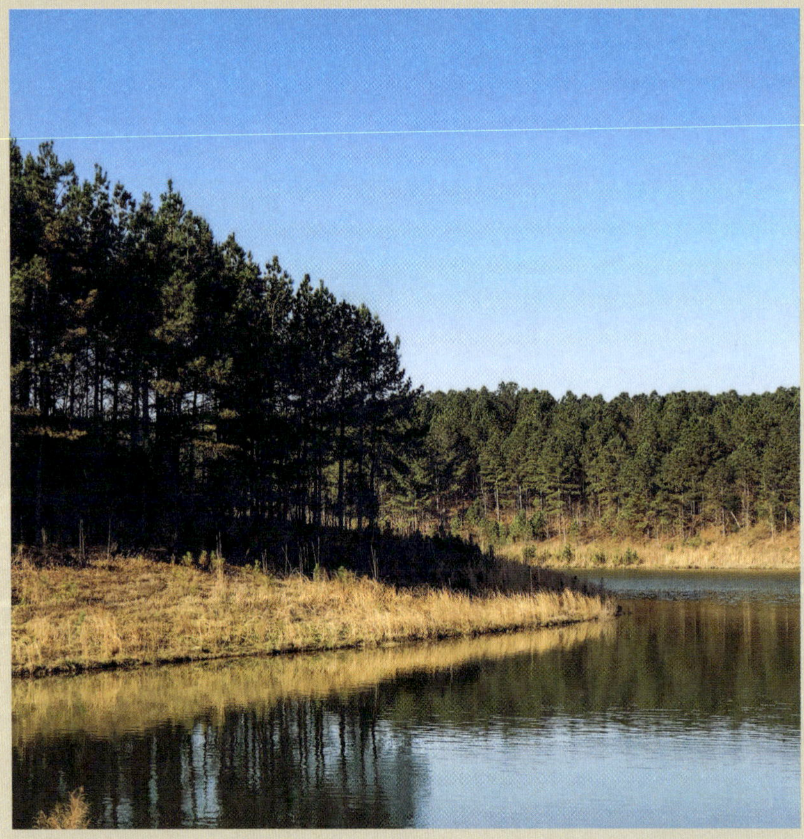

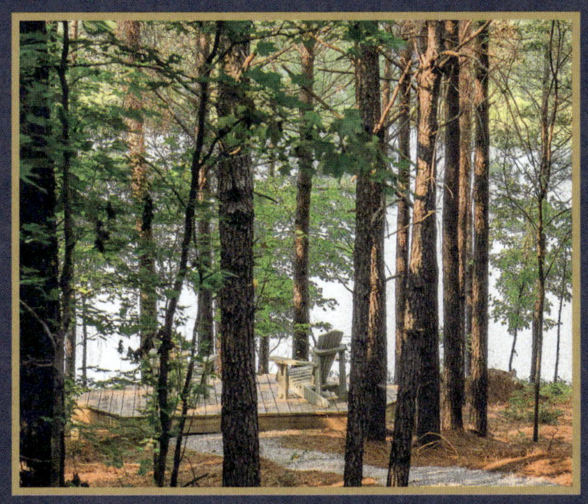
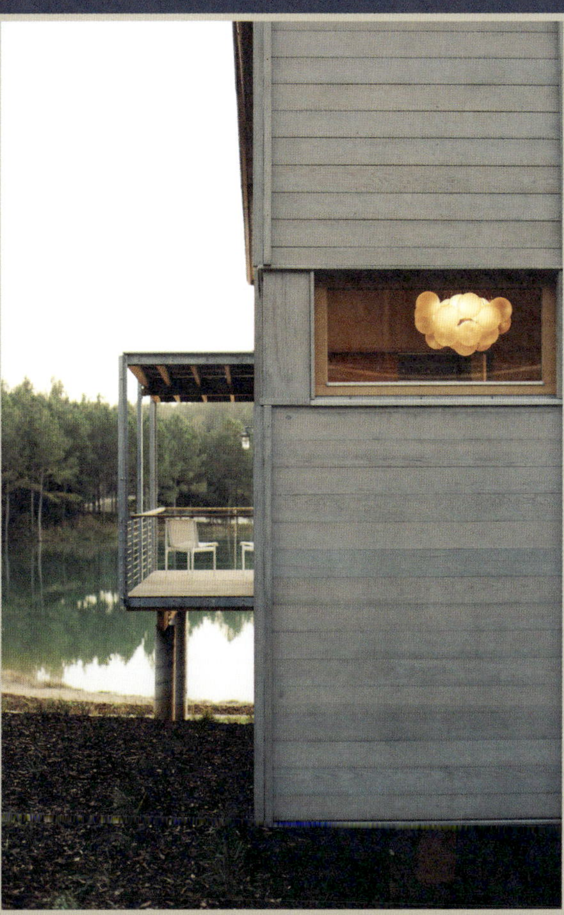
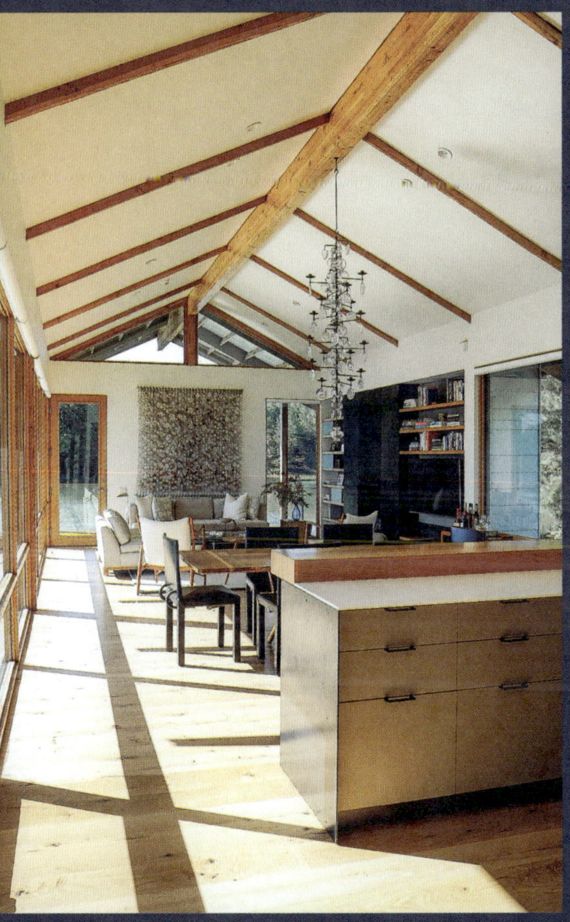
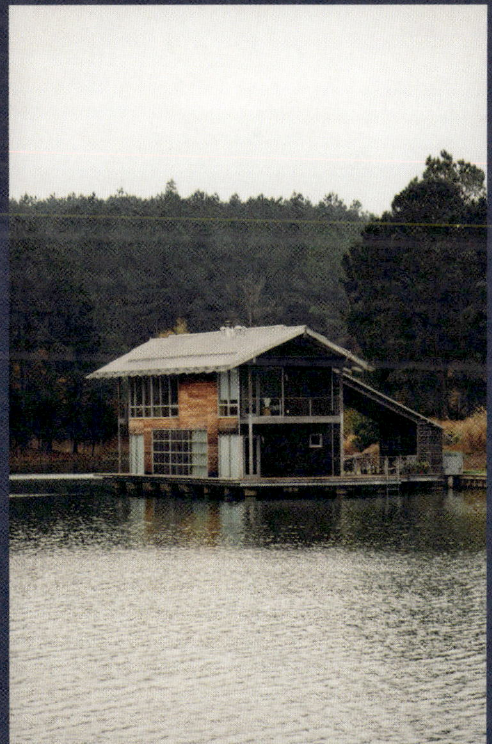

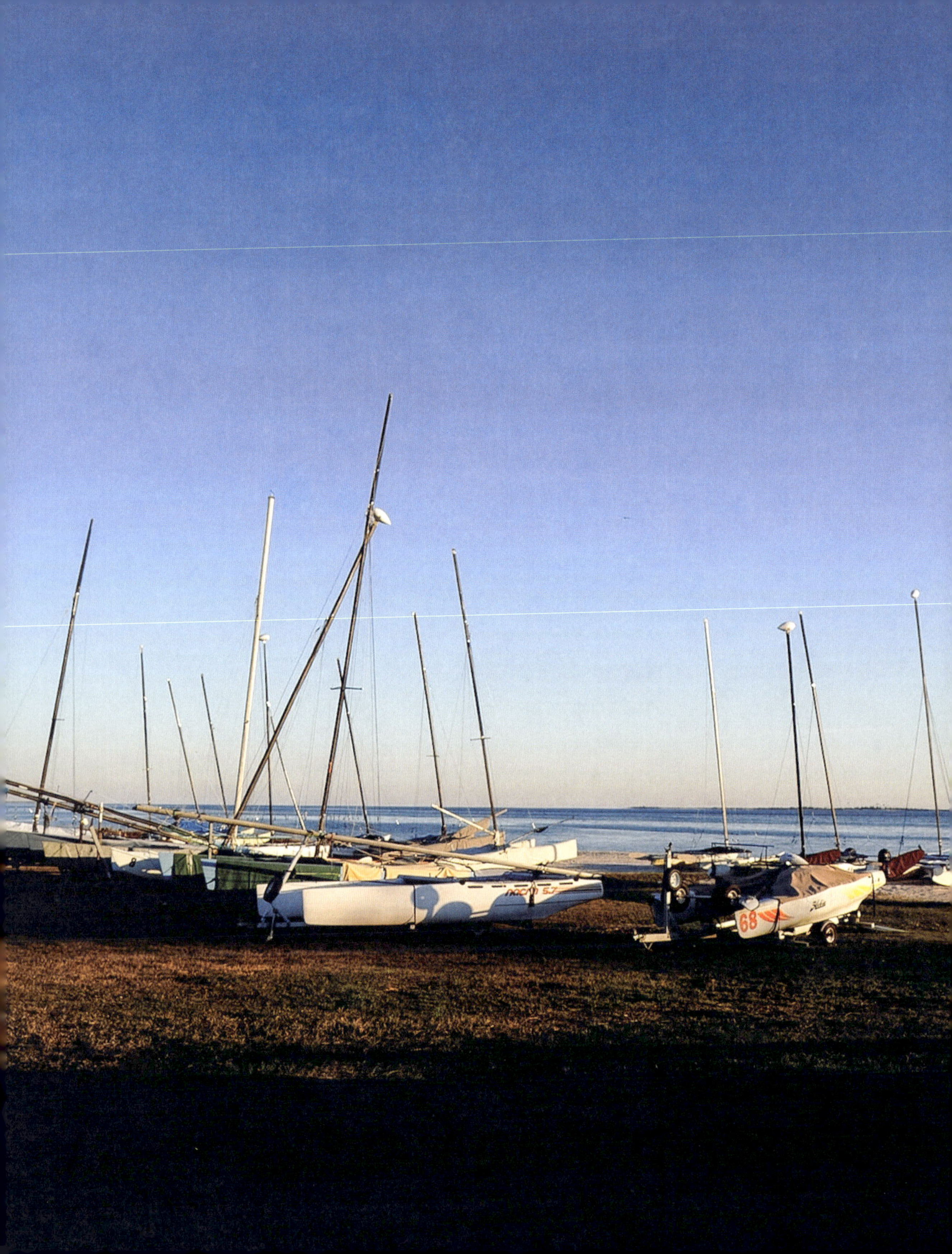
68

OCEANS, INLETS, SOUNDS, AND BAYS

"I knew I needed to be specifically in the houseboats because I'm from Brooklyn. I like a little bit of edge, and I'm not a suburban kind of girl, but I love nature. And so the houseboat community felt just kind of weird enough and its own specific universe that seemed like the perfect fit for my daughter and me."

—BLYTHE FRIEDMANN

BLYTHE FRIEDMANN

Interior Designer and Art Therapist

SAUSALITO, CALIFORNIA

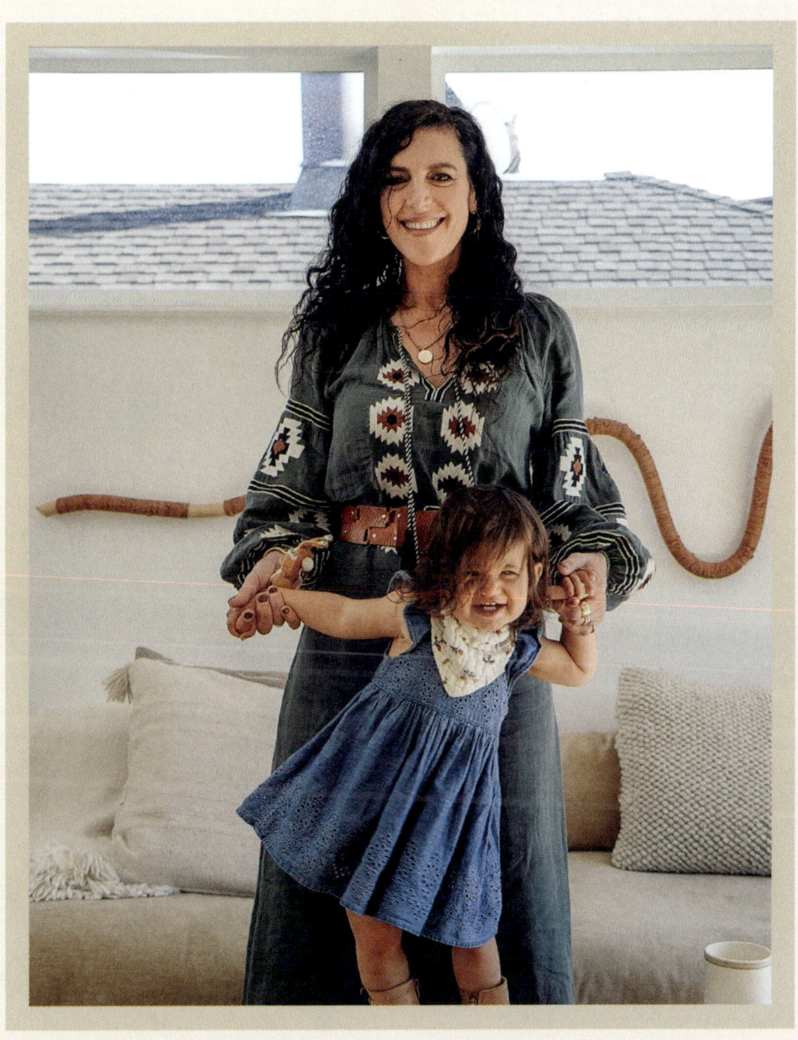

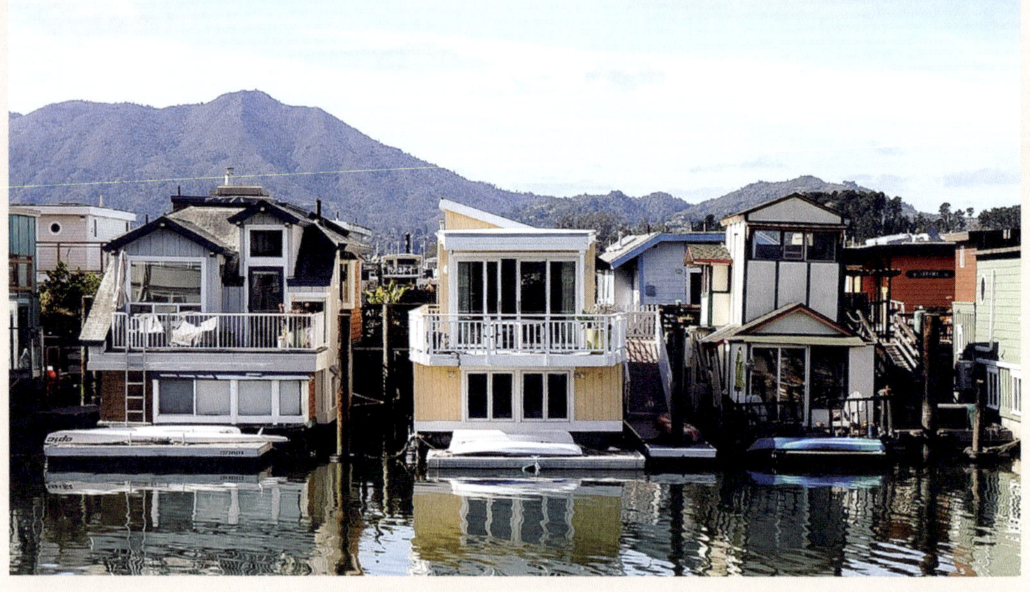

Sausalito sits tucked into the hills of Marin County, just over the Golden Gate Bridge from San Francisco, with houses stacked as you'd expect to see in parts of Italy. Along the boardwalk, you have sweeping views of both the San Francisco skyline and Alcatraz Island. Shops, restaurants, art galleries, and hotels fill the downtown, while on the other end of town sits a quiet houseboat or float house community dating back to World War II.

As World War II ended, Sausalito was left with discarded material and boats from the Marinship shipyards. Don Arques's family owned a lot of the shoreline, and Arques made a bid for the remaining barges used during the war to create homes for the burgeoning Beatnik era artists and musicians to live rent-free. They salvaged what they could find floating in the bay and in the salvage yards in San Francisco for materials to build the community. What started out as a structure that would likely be condemned by today's standards with no running water or electricity has transformed into a community of coveted, beautiful float homes. The transition wasn't without struggles. In 1971, the hillside community and the city wanted to wipe out the houseboats and create condominiums in their place. The community had to prove they were on a viable wetlands that would be destroyed with the construction of the condominiums. The houseboat wars continued until 1983 when an agreement was met.

The Galilee Harbor Community Association has grown to over 400 houseboats in

Richardson Bay today, including the home of interior designer and art therapist Blythe Friedmann. Originally from Brooklyn, Blythe moved across the country, first to Austin, then to Portland, San Francisco, and then Inverness, before moving full-time to Sausalito. In Inverness, she designed a 1973 A-frame right on the edge of Point Reyes National Seashore, surrounded by coastal oaks and bay trees. During the pandemic, she lived there full-time but now uses it as a rental where she also hosts wellness workshops and creative retreats.

COMMUNITY AND LIFESTYLE AMONG THE HOUSEBOATS

What led Blythe to the houseboats isn't exactly clear, but she had been searching for a few years for where to go next, knowing her time in San Francisco was ending. Waking in the middle of the night, she sat up with her eureka moment: "I'm going to have my baby on the houseboats," she shared. Having visited once before, she made her way to the docks to take a tour. It was a stormy day, but everyone was so warm and welcoming. "There were little kids and people in their eighties in this little village. I was really looking for a place where I felt comfortable having my daughter, Marigold, and where there are friendly neighbors," Blythe said. She found it tenfold in the houseboat community.

When there are storms, the community talks with each other, and they make sure everyone is prepared, lines are secured, ramps are on, and all the things you learn quickly when living on a boat. It's almost like a small town within a small town. Blythe shared, "The next morning, the rest of the town is at work and has electricity and heat and lights and is living its life. And we've been on an adventure. The boat has been rocking so much that we're off balance. We're really affected by the elements. And everybody in the parking lot is talking, *Oh, let's all go over here and make sure this person's okay.* It's just like almost an old-world feeling."

Living on the water isn't for everyone. When there is a storm and the power goes out, you also lose water. "It takes a certain type of scrappy and salty person to be affected by the

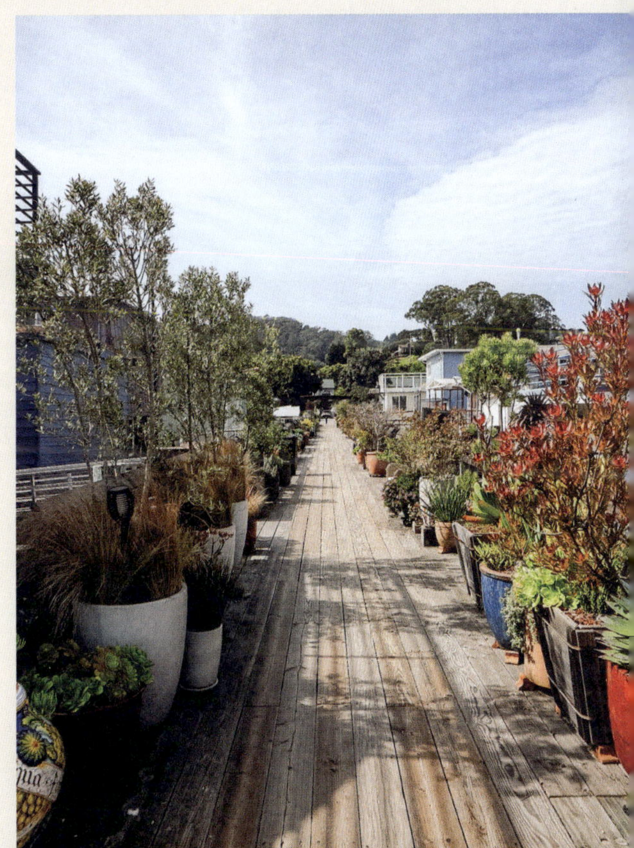

HOUSEBOAT COMMUNITY EVENTS

On the Fourth of July, folks paddle out to the lagoon to celebrate, and bands play from different boat docks while everyone paddles around to hear them.

The Holiday Lighted Boat Parade takes place one Saturday every December.

A Paddle Out Movies projects the film onto a boat, and folks paddle out to watch from their kayaks.

There are Pride Month gatherings.

tides this much. You have to be independent but focus on community," said Blythe. "I'm in a place where if it's high tide, I'm floating; if it's low tide, I'm in the mud. I experience being grounded in the earth and floating on the water. I'm aware of Mother Nature at all times." At the end of the day, it's the genuine caring that's involved in the process that lets Blythe know she made the right decision.

DESIGNING FOR HOUSEBOATS AND BEYOND

"The bay is such a great place to work because we've got all these pockets. There's Sonoma and Napa, and there's San Francisco and Marin. I've designed houses in Santa Cruz. There are diverse towns and neighborhoods that I get to experience all in this small place. It's a really great place to be a designer," shared Blythe, relishing in the ability to enjoy a neighboring town or a city neighborhood for the four or five months she's on a job, finding her favorite spots to grab lunch or have a coffee.

By 2025, Blythe had designed five houseboats in Sausalito, but it's not for everyone. Living on one herself sets her apart from other designers. She understands how the elements work, how the balance works with each design, and how items shift with the water, making use of the movement in very clever ways. As a longtime designer, doing a full gut remodel on her own boat gave her the experience to understand the scale of a houseboat remodel.

In houseboat construction, it's extremely important to consider the materials. Blythe commissioned a design partner of hers to create her front door, which was made of teak from a ship used during World War II. "It had already been out in the elements and was acclimated to the salt air," shared Blythe. "I

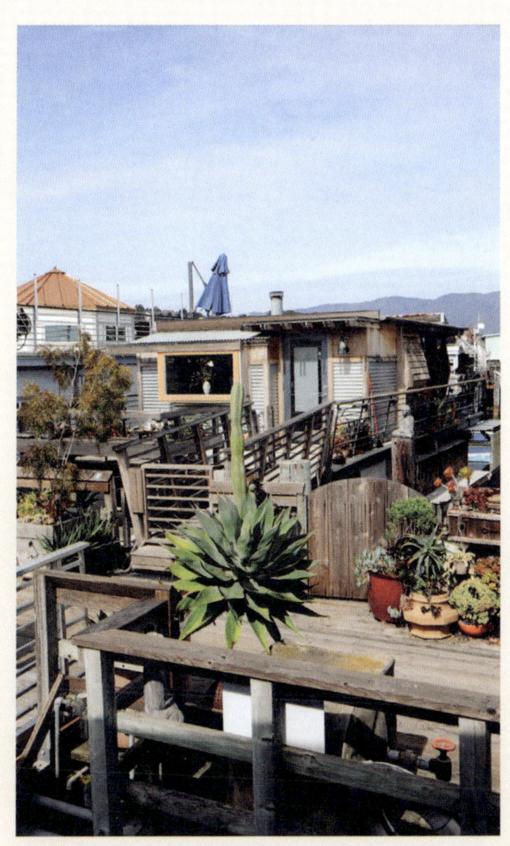

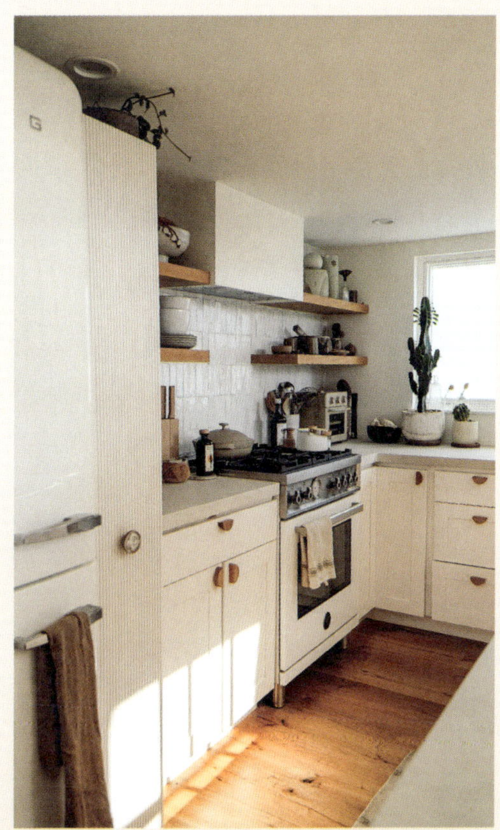

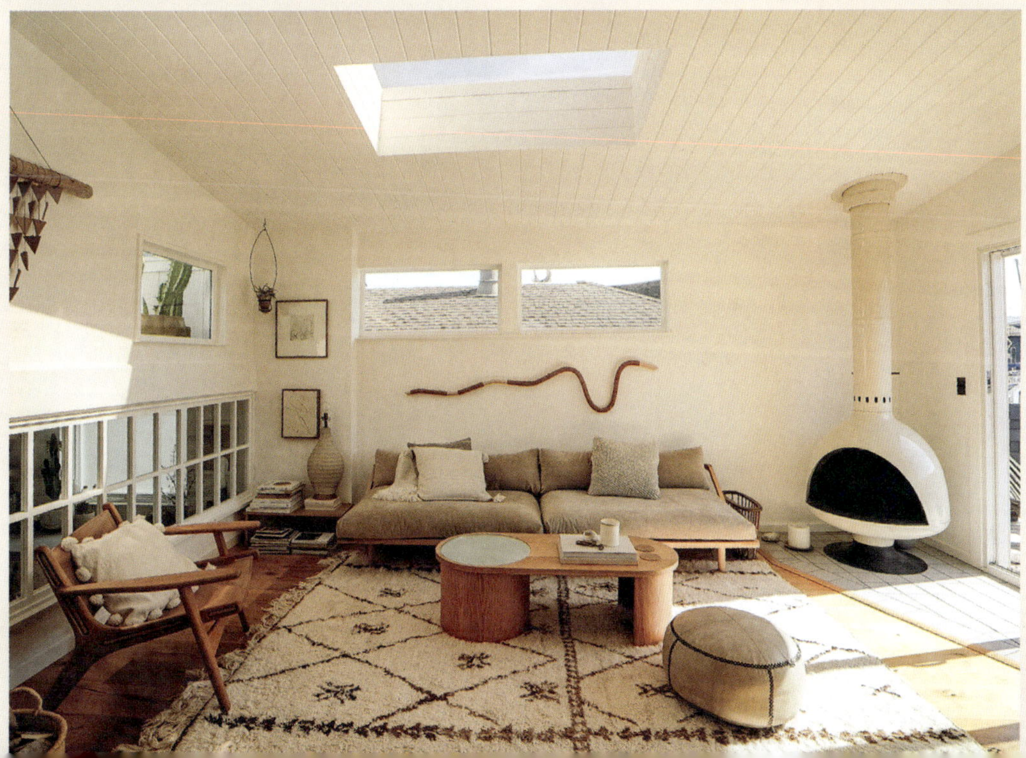

wanted to use both something with history, but also something that would patina over time." Looking for ways to use materials that don't need to stay perfect is a part of Blythe's design philosophy, while also asking how we are affected by Mother Nature and the Earth and then designing in that way. "I wanted something that would get weathered and show its sense of place and that it belongs here on the sea versus fighting with being on the sea. I want the human hand to be interacting with these materials. I want them to feel worn," said Blythe.

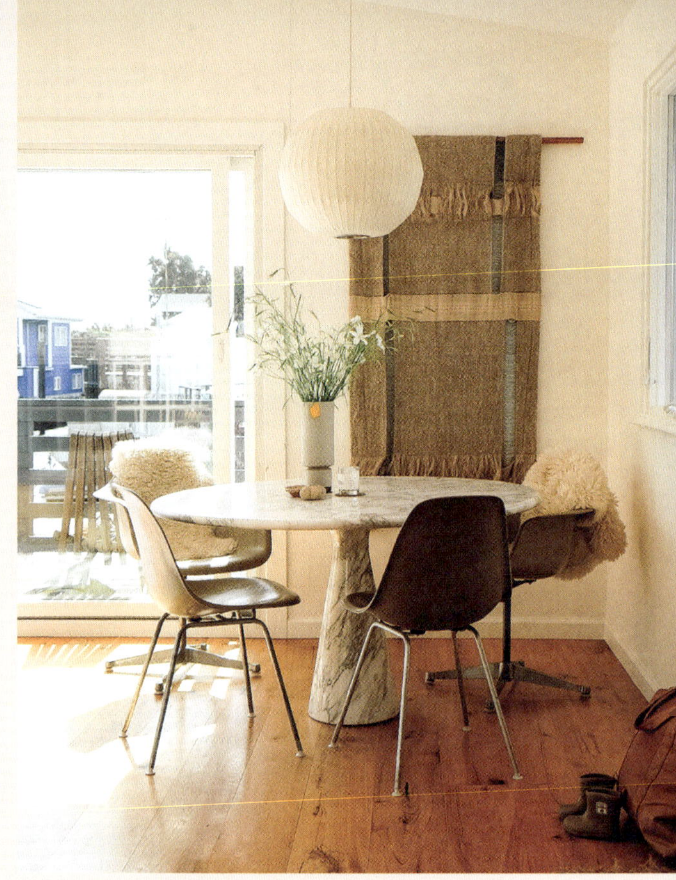

THINGS TO KNOW ABOUT BOAT LIVING BEFORE MOVING ONTO ONE

- Understand how the pump works.
- Know the lines for the boat.
- Recognize the noises a boat makes.
- Understand how you will be affected by the elements.
- Be ready for tsunami warnings.
- Adjust to your environment.
- Know how to read a tide chart.

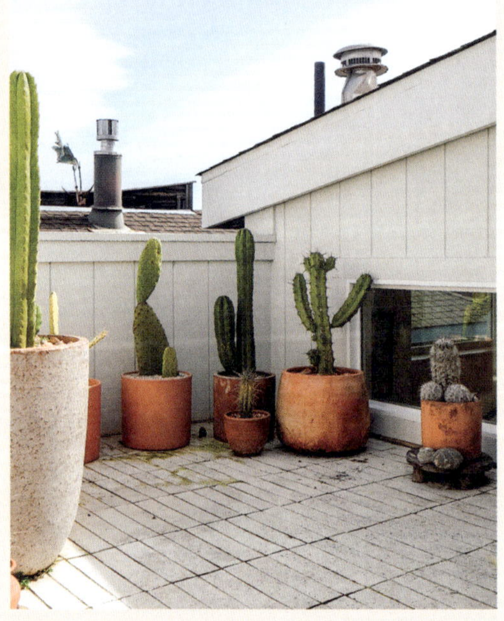

RAISING A CHILD IN A HOUSEBOAT COMMUNITY

Blythe's daughter Marigold has grown up living on a boat. Born on the sea and raised in an unconventional setting has been everything Blythe dreamed of for her. "It's idyllic. You see this group of seven- or eight-year-old boys in a rowboat, playing pirates in the bay. And there's kind of a throwback feel to our freedom as kids," shared Blythe. She also doesn't worry about raising a child surrounded by water. As someone who grew up in Brooklyn, Blythe understands the constraints of living on a boat and being raised in a small city apartment. "We didn't play in the street as children, the same way she's not falling into the water," shared Blythe. Marigold is already beginning to understand the safety involved. She wears a life jacket; she knows how to swim. There's a certain level of caution a child carries when it's all they've known that we will never possess.

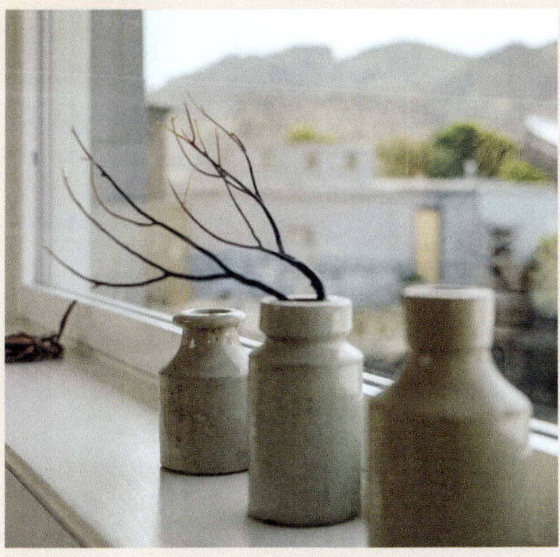

ECO-ORGANIZATIONS IN SAUSALITO

- The Marine Mammal Center
- NatureBridge
- Oceanic Society
- Open Space Sausalito

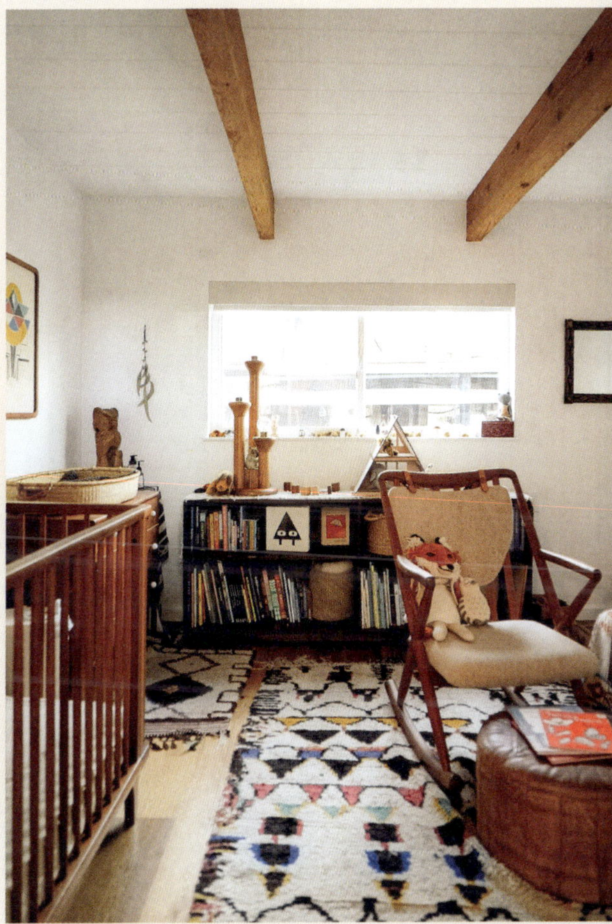

SAUSALITO, CALIFORNIA

POPULATION: 7,021 full-time residents in 2024

TOWN SIZE: 2.3 square miles

CLOSEST INTERNATIONAL AIRPORTS: San Francisco International Airport (23.5 miles), Oakland International Airport (27.8 miles)

CLOSEST REGIONAL AIRPORT: Charles M. Schulz Sonoma County Airport, Santa Rosa (54.9 miles)

CLOSEST LARGE CITY: San Francisco (9.3 miles)

BONUS TOWNS NEARBY: Mill Valley, Stinson Beach, Marin City

BEST TIME TO WHALE-WATCH: May to December

TOWN FACTS: You can take a ferry from Sausalito to San Francisco in just thirty minutes. You can also take the ferry to Angel Island State Park for a day of hiking and wilderness, with the city still in view. You can see Alcatraz and the city skyline from Sausalito. Otis Redding lived on a houseboat in Sausalito while writing "(Sittin' On) The Dock of the Bay," his first number one hit. Shel Silverstein lived on a houseboat in the town from 1967 to 1975. The largest marine mammal hospital in the world is in Sausalito: the Marine Mammal Center. Heath Ceramics was founded and still runs today in Sausalito. The Record Plant, a recording studio that produced the likes of Fleetwood Mac, Stevie Wonder, and Heart, to name a few, operated from 1972 to 2008. The town has been the backdrop in dozens of films, TV shows, books, and songs. Writer Amy Tan calls Sausalito home. Sausalito has one of the last working waterfronts left in the country.

SEASONS: Sausalito has two seasons.

WATER ACTIVITIES: sailing, kayaking, paddleboarding, canoeing, scuba diving, snorkeling, fishing, whale-watching, boat tours, swimming

WATER SPOTS TO VISIT: Richardson Bay and Pickleweed Inlet

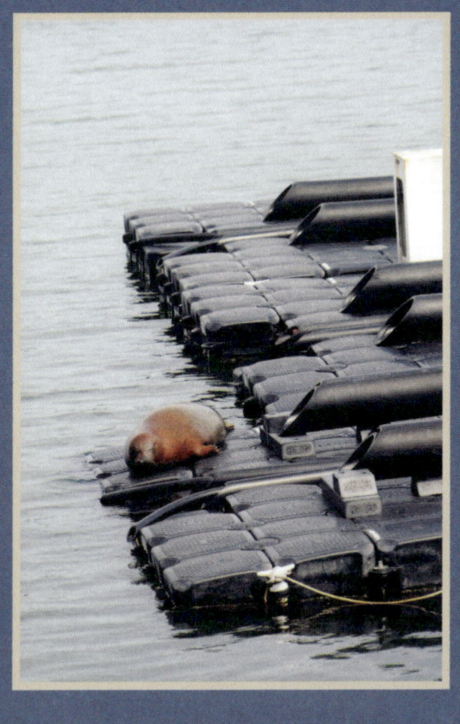

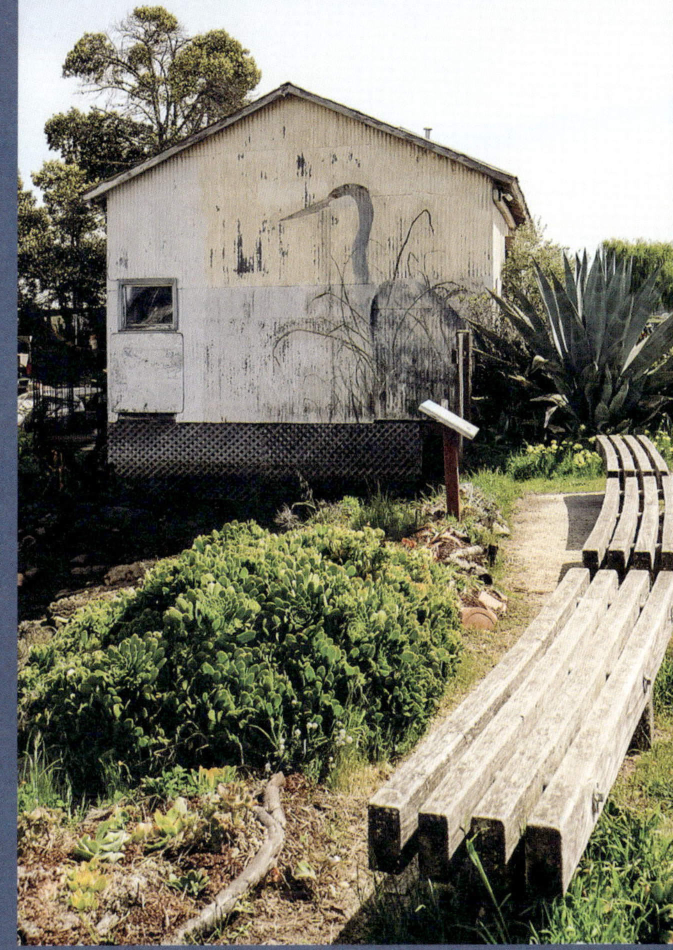

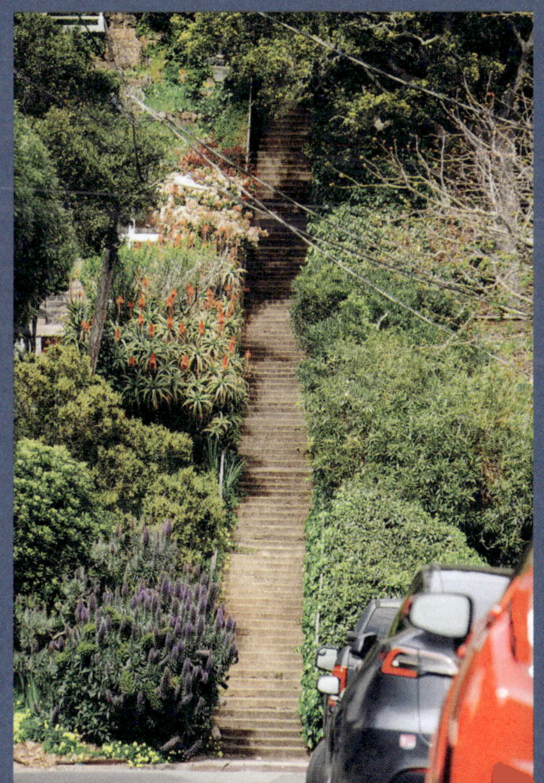

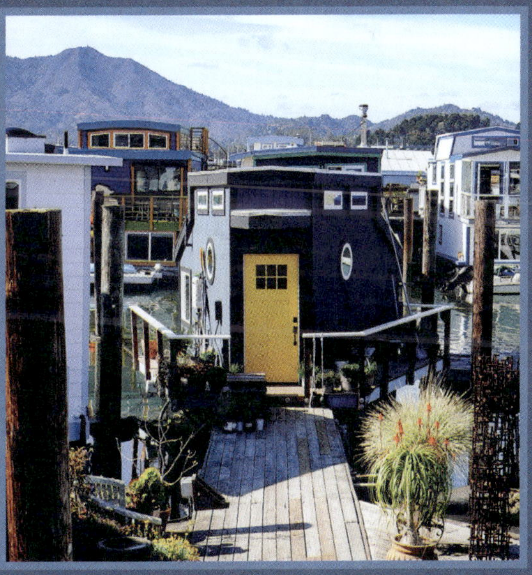

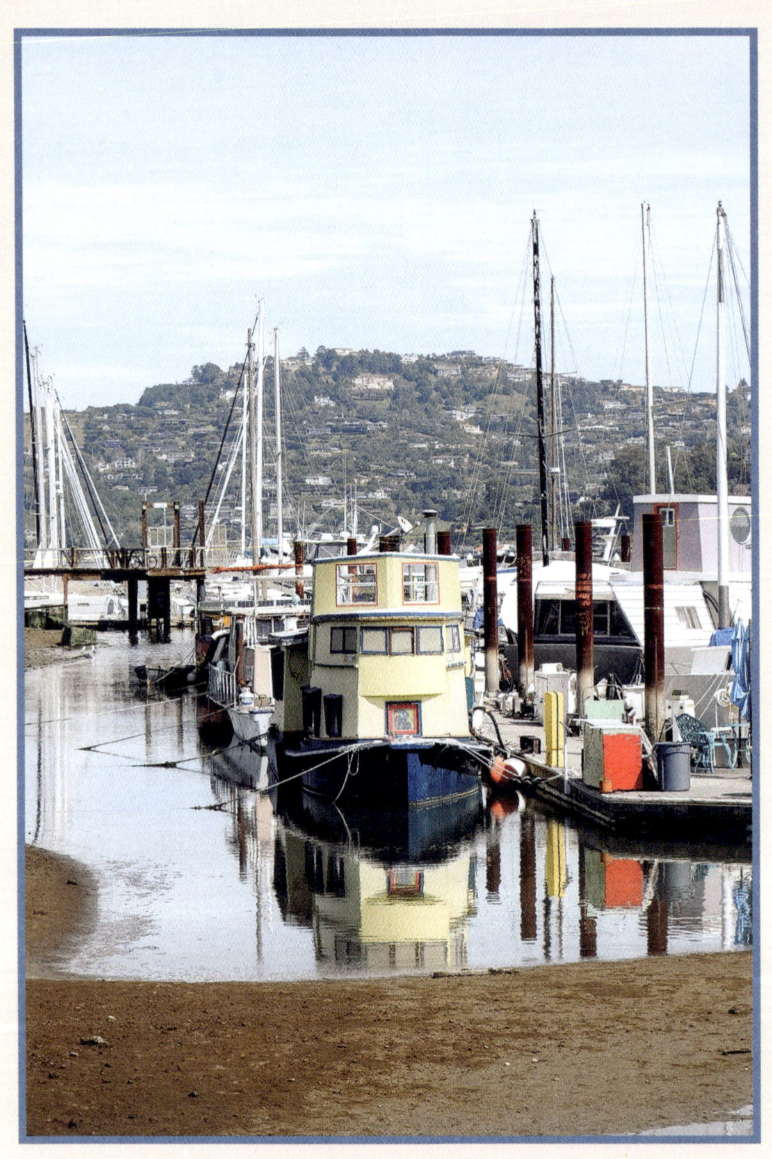

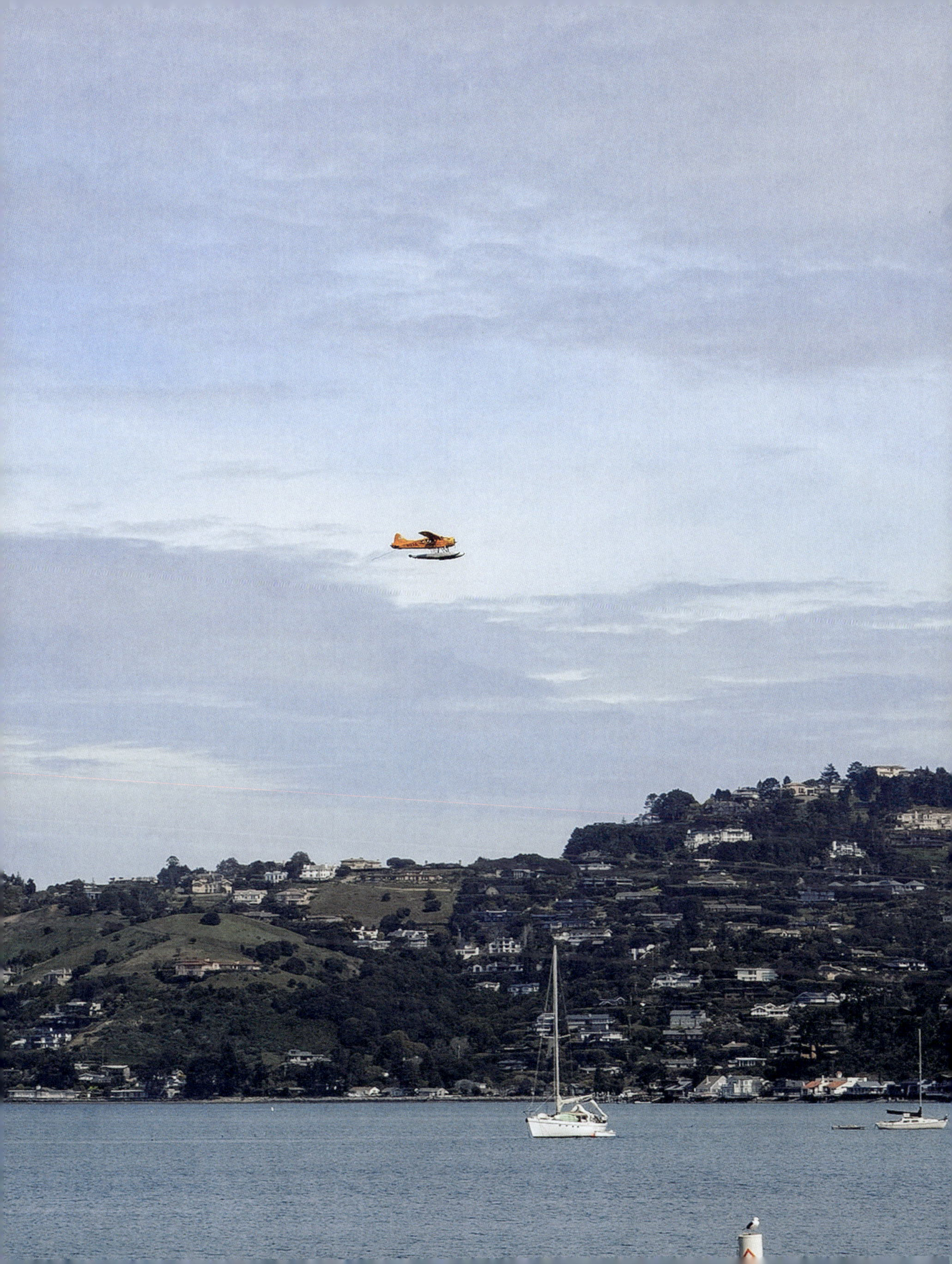

"I feel like when I am by the water and I'm able to tune out the noise of everything else and just be in my headspace, that it does help me dream or daydream a little about the direction I would like to steer in. When walking through nature or being in water, I'm always inspired by the colors, whether it's the bright green moss or the blue streams. I'm always looking at color palettes and textures in that way, and even the sand, shells, and crabs."

—RENEE TOUPONCE

RENEE TOUPONCE

Executive Chef and Partner at The Port of Call, Oyster Club, Dive Bar, and The Tree House

MYSTIC, STONINGTON, CONNECTICUT

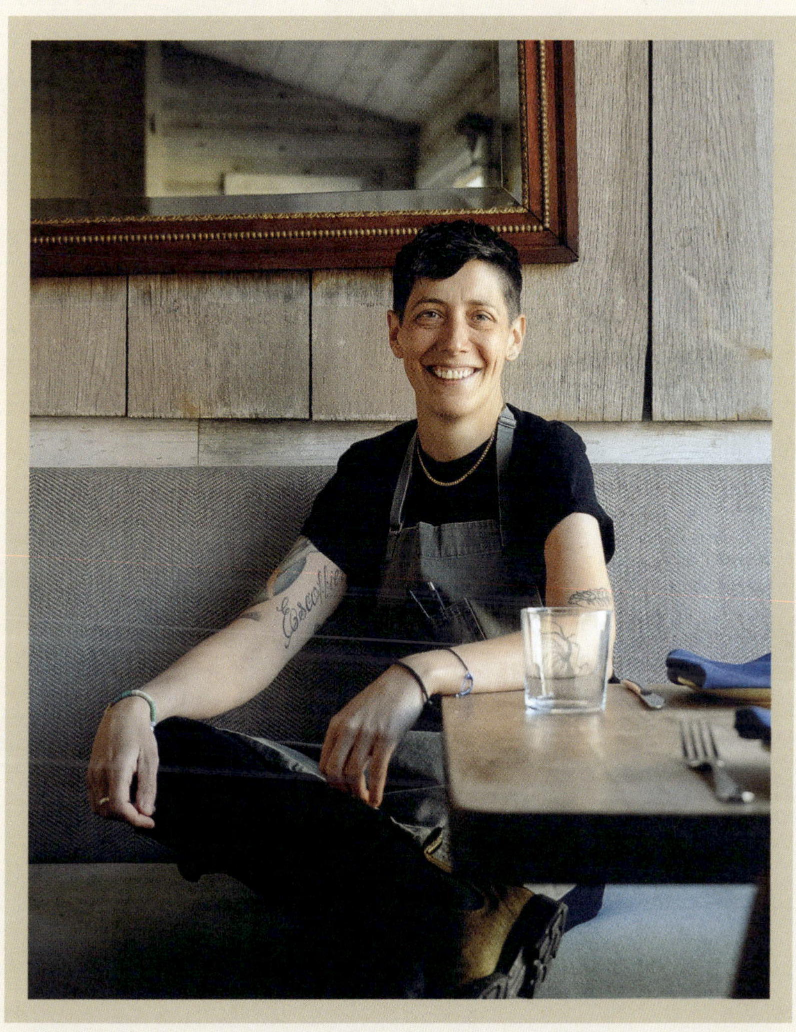

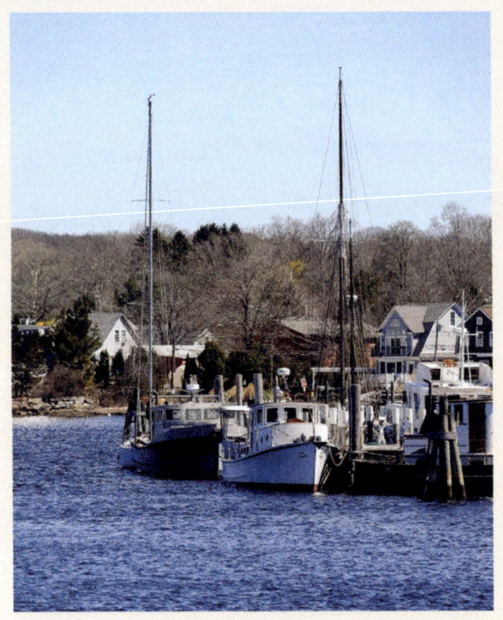

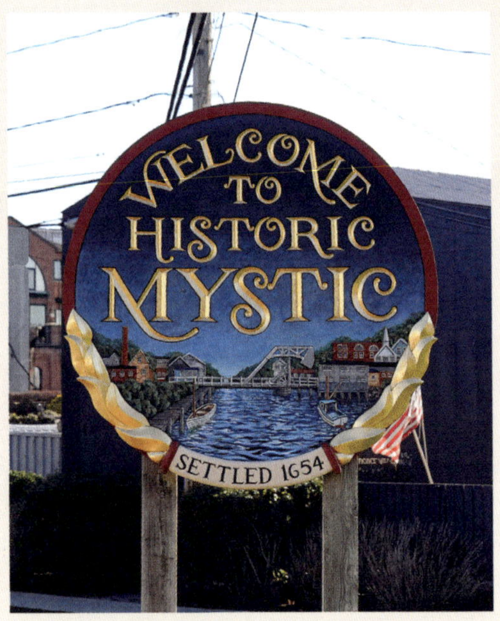

Connecticut-born Renee Touponce quickly knew the city wasn't for her. After leaving their hometown of Torrington, they moved to Burlington, Vermont, for college and then back to Connecticut, bouncing from Unionville, Farmington, and then Hartford before relocating to Westerly, Rhode Island, with their partner, Jade Ayala. Renee wanted the slower pace of a small town, and the area has been home ever since. The couple first lived in a multifamily home, which they both loved. When they heard the landlords wanted to sell and they would have to move, Jade thought quickly so she and Renee could buy it. The passive income then allowed the two of them to buy their own single-family home, an A-frame cabin in the rural area of North Stonington. They are still close to Westerly and their rental property and not far from where the couple both work: restaurants Port of Call and Oyster Club in Mystic, Stonington. Stonington is a small rural, coastal town on the Rhode Island border with several villages under its umbrella, including Mystic. Jade gets the city life they love, while Renee enjoys the calm of the woods surrounding their home.

FINDING YOUR SMALL TOWN AND YOUR PLACE IN THE TOWN

While living in Hartford, Renee and Jade would take day trip dates down to the sleepy seaport of Mystic. "It's so funny now, actively working here, to think of Mystic as the place we went to escape Hartford and be by the water. The water has always been very calming and Zen for me, so I'm very attracted to it," shared Renee. The two interviewed separately with Dan Meiser of 85th Day Restaurant Group—Renee as a chef and Jade for the beverage director role. Both were hired for the Mystic-based restaurant Oyster Club, serving fresh, local-caught seafood prepared with a forward-thinking approach to the water just outside the doors. Renee had previously worked as an executive chef in Hartford but saw the transition to a lower position as an important one, a time to learn from her peers and start fresh, connecting to the ethos of a new kitchen community. Working their way up, Renee began as the butcher, then sous-chef, and now is a James Beard Award–nominated executive chef and partner.

From there, Renee helped open The Port of Call just next door and works as the executive chef in the restaurant. The Port of Call has a completely unique spin: while dishes also use local ingredients, each represents different shipping ports around the world. You can travel the globe from one menu, which Renee creates. "I've been a part of this company since 2017. I really believe in it and love it. I'm happy about all the work that we do with our community, our farmers, and for queer advocacy. It's been a wild ride. I started from the bottom in this company and just absorbed and learned. I worked on the Stone Acres Farm and at all their restaurants and then became the chef. I had all the foundations I needed to feel secure in what I'm doing because I wanted to do it well," Renee expressed.

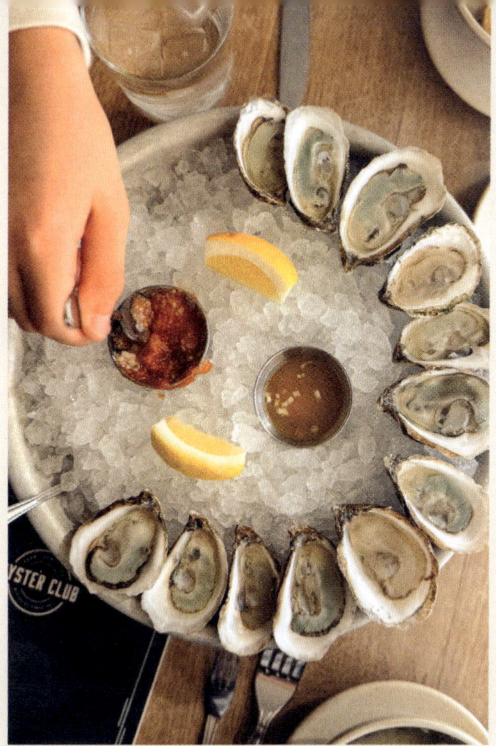

Working with the vendors by land and by sea just outside the doors of the restaurants is something Renee does not take lightly; it's a relationship she holds very dear. They first base each weekly menu on the ingredients available nearby, discussing the options with staff and ensuring everyone feels part of the conversation. Renee spends so much time in both locations the lines of each are blurred, and the staff spills over between the two as well. Chefs might move from one venue to the next just as the drink menus are created by Jade Ayala for either.

Because of the connection to her staff and the communication they have, Renee can treat each location with the same level of care, which translates to the customers.

Day in the Life of a Small Town, World-Recognized Chef

"I have meetings with the staff every day. I come in, and at Oyster Club, I'll look at all of our ingredients from our farmers and write a menu . . . talk it over with my chef . . . and then they'll talk to the rest of the staff. . . . Then we prep, get on the line, and cook. And then, for me, I'll go next door to The Port of Call and repeat the steps. . . . I'm in a world where I'll spend half of my time at Oyster Club physically cooking and then the other half at The Port of Call. And when it's slower, I have more time to not be the person physically on the line. When it's busy, it's like, all hands on deck, right? Asking: What can I do? How can I help?"

—RENEE

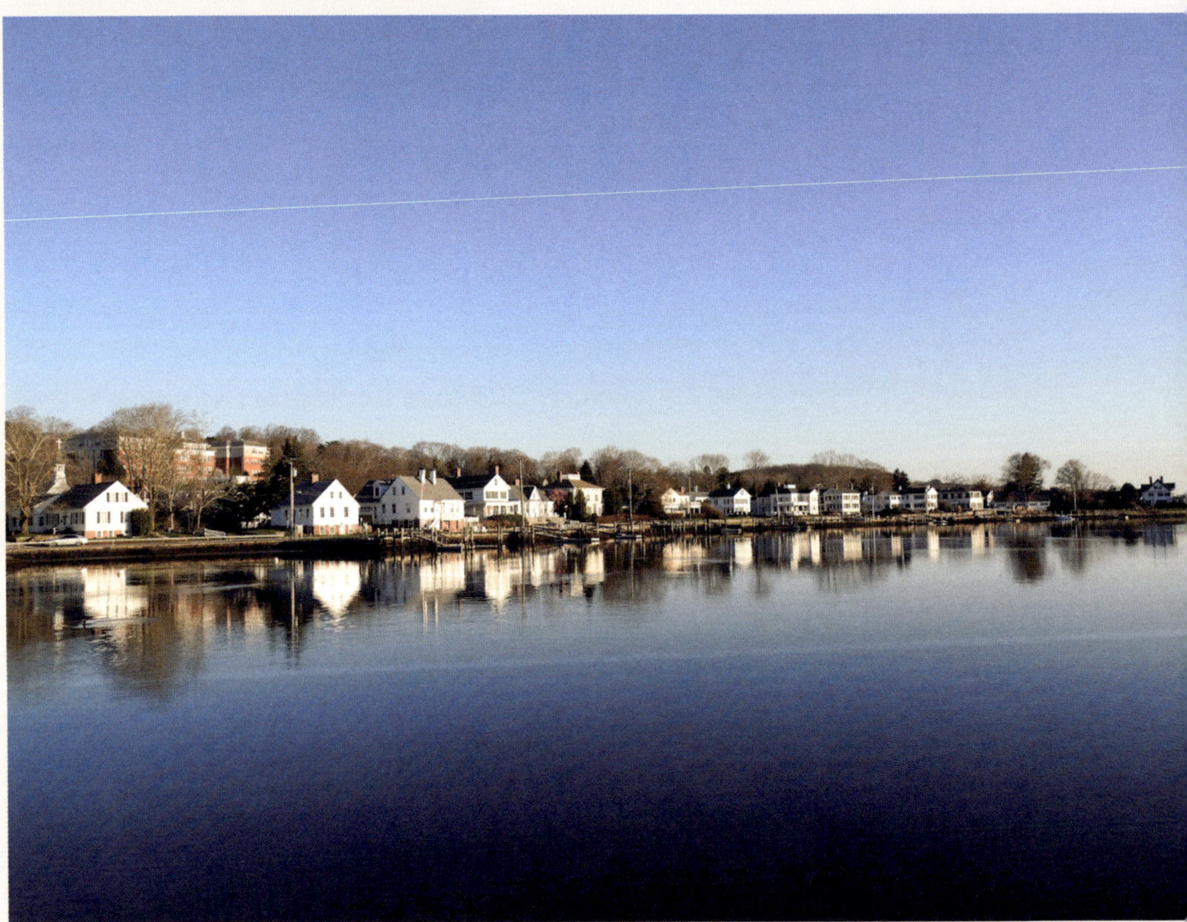

BALANCING WORK AND PERSONAL LIFE

Community is vital to Renee; they have built the two restaurants to feel connected. From the back of the house to the front, it is a simpatico union of the two locations, connected by a back alley where the staff can move seamlessly between the kitchens, all working in tandem. Being a hands-on leader in the space, Renee finds herself on the line, working alongside staff sometimes six or seven nights a week in the summer months. For this reason, bringing more balance to their life has been very important. "Because I am so involved and immersed in my food and staff, I never want to be the guy that's not present. I love it and care so deeply about it, but now I'm making a lot more dinners off-site. Things are shifting, which is new and exciting, and it's exciting for the people below me. They're able to excel and move forward in this world as well. We're all going through it."

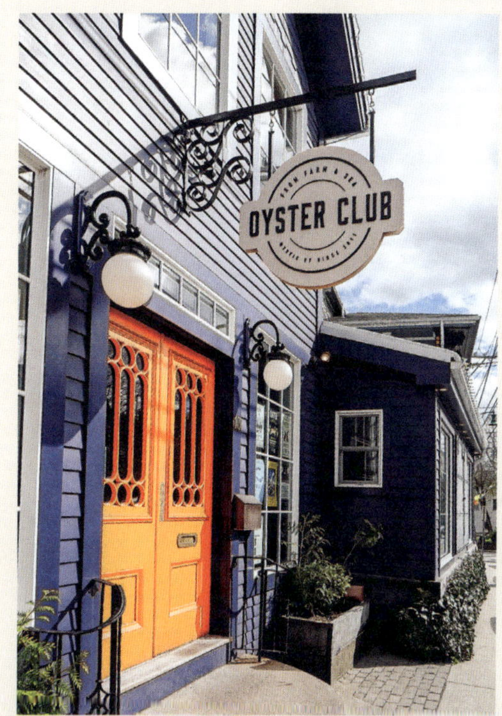

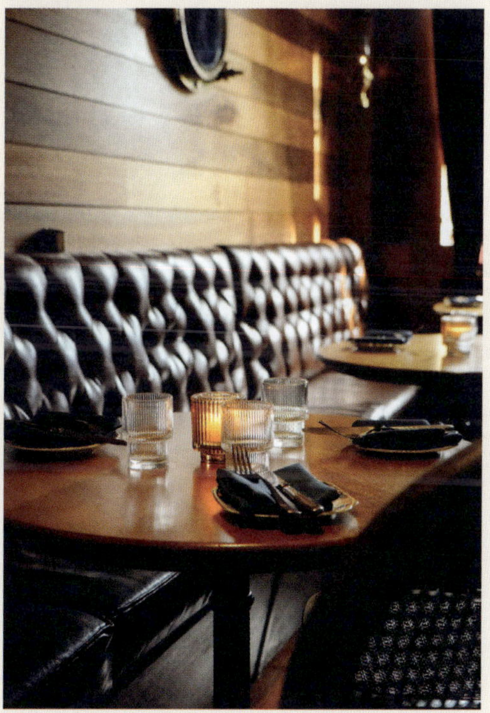

CONNECTION TO THE WATER AND LOCAL COMMUNITY

"On my days off, I try to spend some time at our restaurant farm or other farms in the area or on the water, harvesting oysters or farming kelp. Or I might go foraging in the woods." Renee is one to keep busy.

Dedicated to shining a light on the culinary arts, Renee spends time mentoring students at the local high school in their culinary program. She guides them in everything from

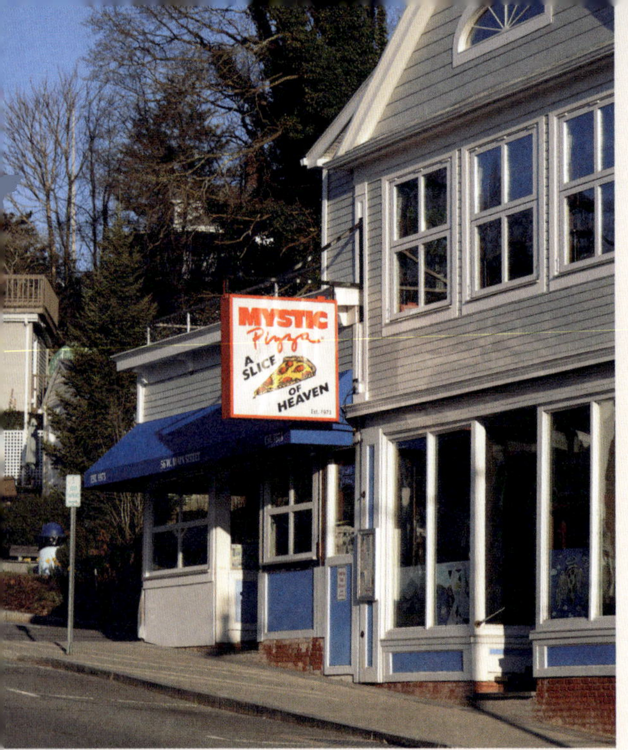

creating menus to executing their vision, while helping them in a cooking competition that is part of the program.

Aside from cooking, Renee is passionate about putting time and energy into advocacy for the LGBTQUIA+ community in the area, supporting drag shows and working with Stonington Pride. Ultimately, Renee wants to create a safe place for the queer community in Connecticut. "I just want to put on fun things for people to just be themselves and be free," expressed Renee. Dive, the dive bar below The Port of Call, hosts weekly drag and disco shows, serving as a light for the Pride community in the area. That involvement has expanded to the ongoing fundraiser at the restaurant, which is raising money to support groups like Q+CT, an organization working to uplift and empower queer youth.

WATER THAT HEALS AND SERVES

Renee has always connected with the water in such personal ways. She heads to the water when she's had a bad day or just needs to unwind. It's been a healing influence for them. "The water is a place that has always grounded me and made me feel calm and connected," shared Renee.

On days off in the summer, she and Jade like to make their way to the beach, relaxing near the water, although that doesn't sum up Renee's quest to be near the water. Working on the water is another facet Renee folded into their career. Renee spends time with oyster farmers, harvesting oysters for the restaurants and working with kelp farmers and fishers. "Learning that side is important and so much fun. It's not like work for me. It's just being out on the water, respecting the water, understanding it, and then being able to be connected to it in a way that I'm connected to my ingredients, and sharing the stories of the farmers, and then serving in our restaurant—and being able to put that out into the world is beautiful," said Renee.

TRANSITION FROM SLEEPY TOWN TO TOURIST DESTINATION

In the modern era, Mystic hasn't always been the bustling town it is today. In winter, everything has traditionally reverted to locals as the town's tourist season was limited to summer. In the last few years, however, Mystic has become more and more of a foodie destination, with people flocking to the small town and extending the season each year. Still, many places close or get creative in January and February and use those months to offer specials and work on new offerings—what they like to call Winter Warmers. Those in food service welcome the break, as it's their time to rest, replenish, and travel for themselves. We all need downtime, and those in places with a hectic high season find comfort in the slower months.

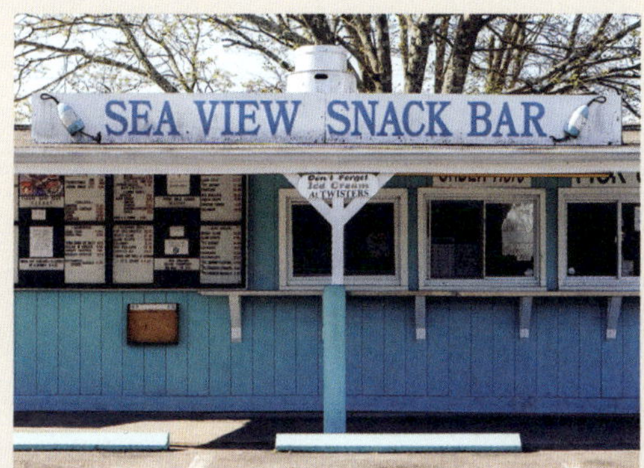

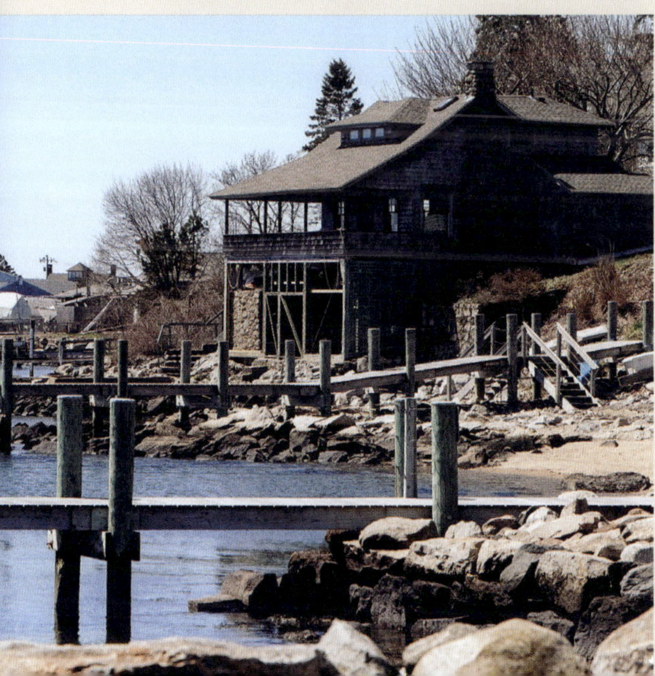

Renee acknowledged, "We work so closely with our farmers and fishers, and so at the peak of summer in Mystic we have all these ingredients to work with, which sparks your creativity because you're not limited. As chefs, we don't have much to work with in the winter. That's when I'm slowing down. It's a moment to reset. I get through a whole book, get inspired, and take a break. But for me, winter is when a lot of the things that I love doing, like preserving, curing, fermenting—taking all that larder from summer right before our break and saying, 'Okay, how can we preserve this, so we have a product to work with when we come back?' I love creating beautiful, raw dishes and getting creative in that way. But I also utilize waste, which is super-important to me. I get super-nerdy with fish and charcuterie, and preserving it is so important."

RENEE'S FAVORITE LOCAL INGREDIENTS TO COOK WITH

- Kelp
- Locally foraged mushrooms
- Oysters
- Stonington squid
- Tuna

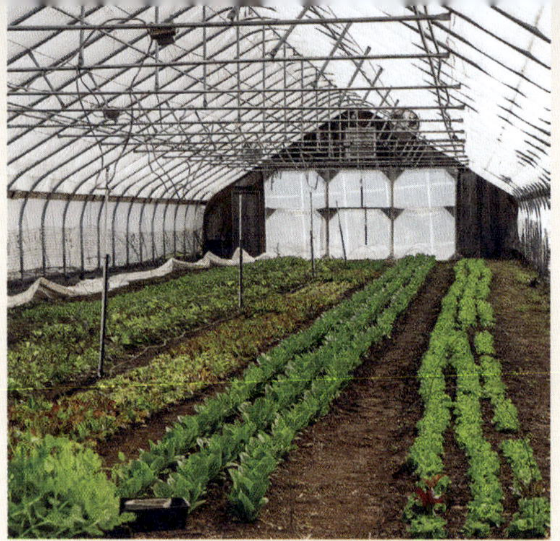

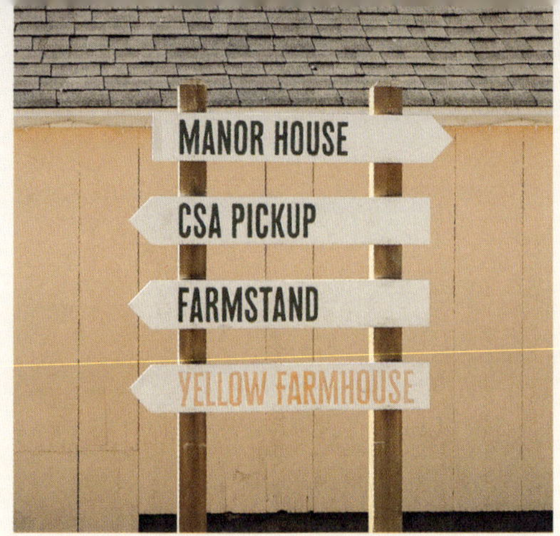

MYSTIC, STONINGTON, CONNECTICUT

STONINGTON POPULATION: 18,431 full-time residents in 2024

MYSTIC POPULATION: 4,417 full-time residents in 2024

STONINGTON SIZE: 42.7 square miles

MYSTIC SIZE: 4.1 square miles

CLOSEST INTERNATIONAL AIRPORTS: Rhode Island T.F. Green International Airport, Providence (42.2 miles); Bradley International Airport, Hartford (73.6 miles from Stonington, 68.2 miles from Mystic)

CLOSEST LARGE CITIES: Hartford (54.1–59.4 miles), New Haven (55.5–61 miles)

BONUS TOWNS NEARBY: Westerly, Rhode Island; Mason's Island, Noank

BEST TIME TO WHALE-WATCH: mid-May to October

TOWN FACTS: The movie *Mystic Pizza* was inspired by the actual Mystic Pizza restaurant in the town but was filmed primarily in neighboring communities. Previously, this was a shipbuilding seaport, and more than 600 ships were built in Mystic. The village of Mystic is not legally recognized as its own town; therefore, depending on what side of the river you reside on, you either are part of Mystic, Stonington, or Mystic, Groton.

SEASONS: Mystic, Stonington, has four distinct seasons.

WATER ACTIVITIES: visiting the beach, sailing, boating, fishing, clamming, kayaking, paddleboarding, whale-watching, lobster lessons

WATER SPOTS TO VISIT: Mystic River, Mystic Harbor, Beebe Cove, and Bass Strait

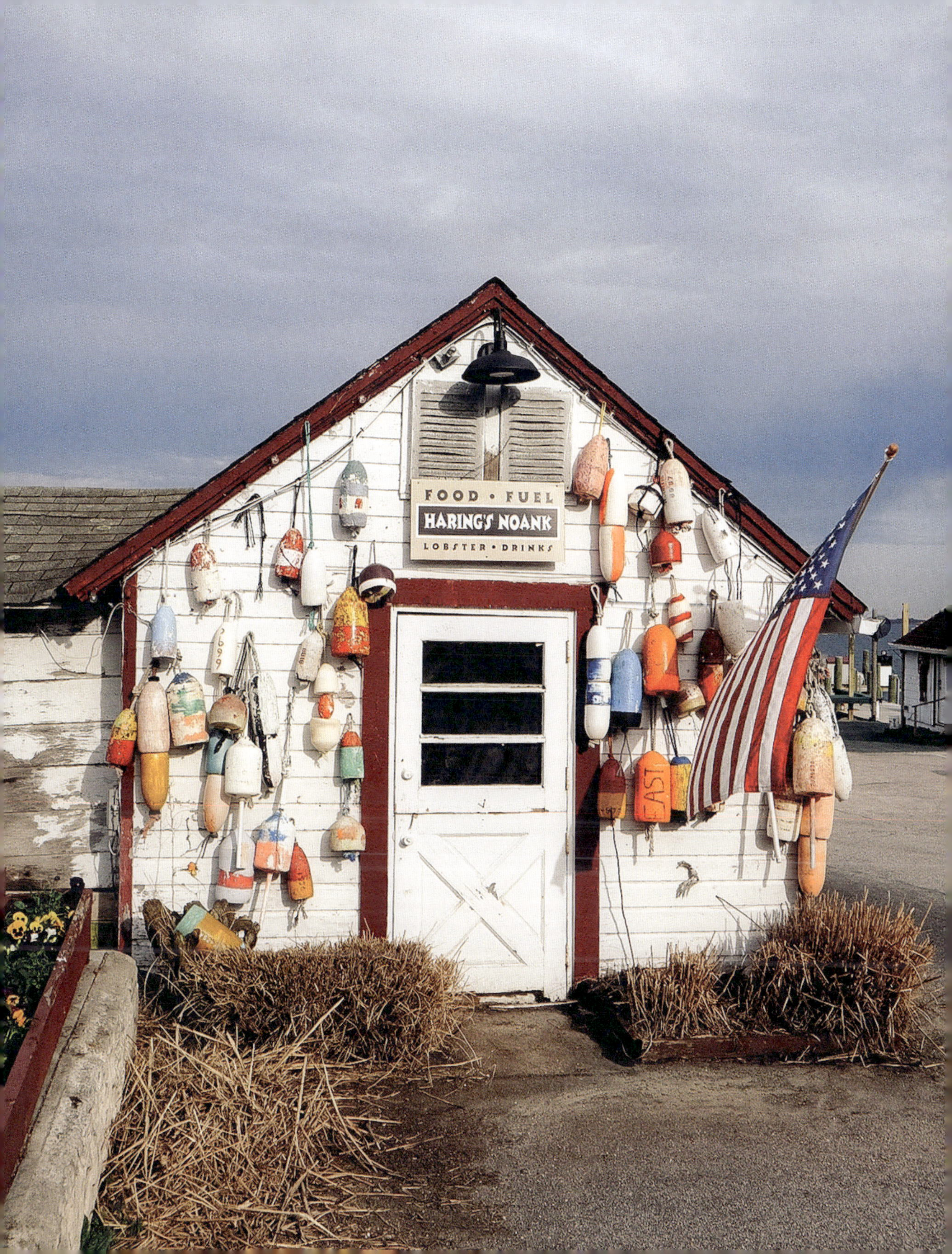
FOOD • FUEL
HARING'S NOANK
LOBSTER • DRINKS
EAST

"You can make waves if you're in a big city, but you can also get lost. There's a charm and a challenge to living and doing things here, but there's also more opportunity. There are fewer rules; fewer people are standing in the way; and that ultimately is what spurs creativity just as much as constraints can."

—JULIAN RANKIN

CAROLINE CROOM AND JULIAN RANKIN

Bookkeeper at Ground Zero Blues Club and Museum Director at Walter Anderson Museum of Art

OCEAN SPRINGS, MISSISSIPPI

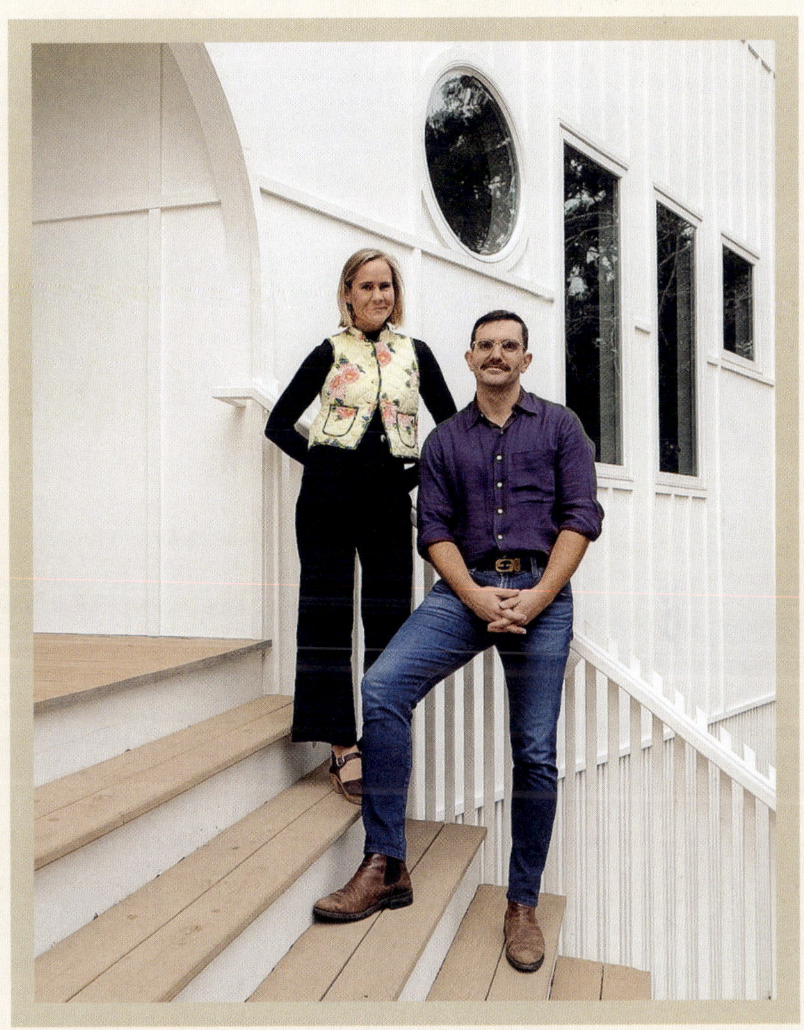

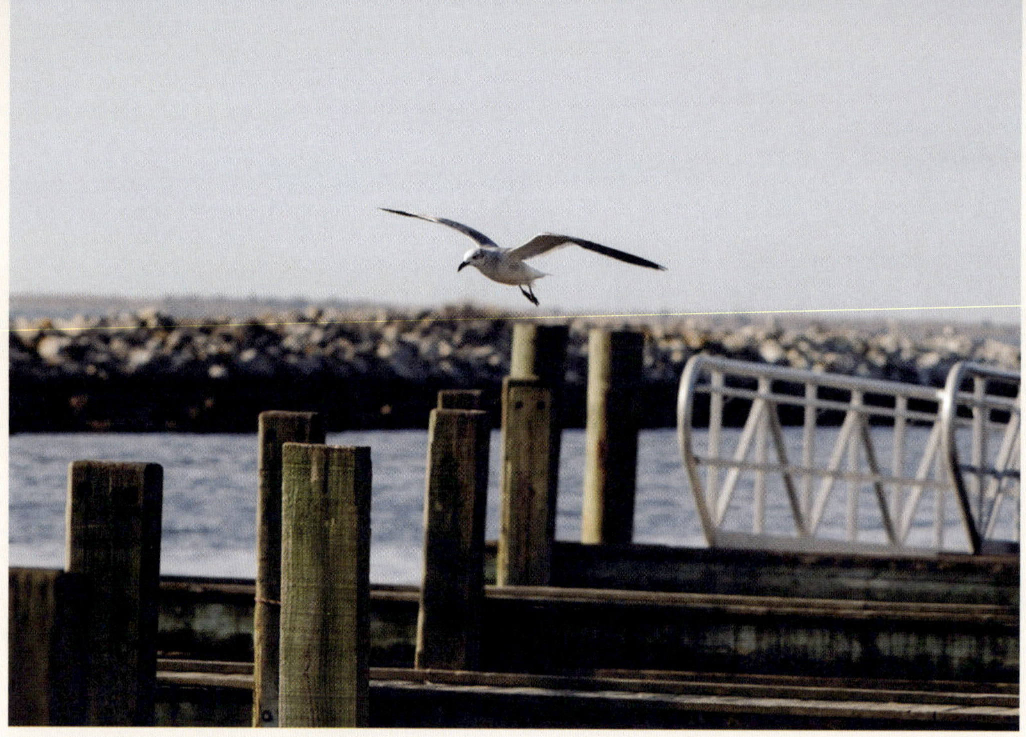

Caroline Croom and Julian Rankin have known each other since elementary school in Oxford, Mississippi, where they were in school together until the fifth grade. Julian moved with his family to North Carolina and stayed in Hillsborough until after college. He then moved to Washington, D.C., where Caroline also lived for a bit as well, separately from Julian. It wasn't until after college that the couple started dating and were later married. After going through the state from Oxford to Jackson, where Julian worked at the Mississippi Museum of Art from 2010 to 2018, they settled in Ocean Springs, Mississippi.

Ocean Springs is a small arts enclave along the Mississippi Gulf Coast. The downtown is lined with live oak trees, Spanish moss dripping from the branches, and you are reminded, at every turn, that the town was once home to famed painter Walter Anderson. And it was Anderson who brought Julian, Caroline, and their two boys to town in 2018. Julian serves as the director of the Walter Anderson Museum of Art in downtown Ocean Springs. While Julian is the face of the museum, both have been doing a lot of creative work behind the scenes.

Caroline has been there right alongside Julian by taking on a prominent role in designing The Traveler, a café that sits next to the Walter Anderson Museum of Art and serves as an extension to the mission of connecting art and the Ocean Springs community. The café adds to the art block neighborhood in the town, which is a node that includes the museum, hotels, restaurants, the library, and City Hall.

It's an area in town where you can visit and stay and eat, drink, and have the culture and curation all around you. "That's certainly been a big thing, especially because Walter Anderson culturally has so many touchpoints and fuels so much of even Ocean Springs itself," said Julian.

Caroline also had a significant role in designing the couple's home, which they built from the ground up with the famed Tall Architects. The house also has an Airbnb component, which Caroline manages.

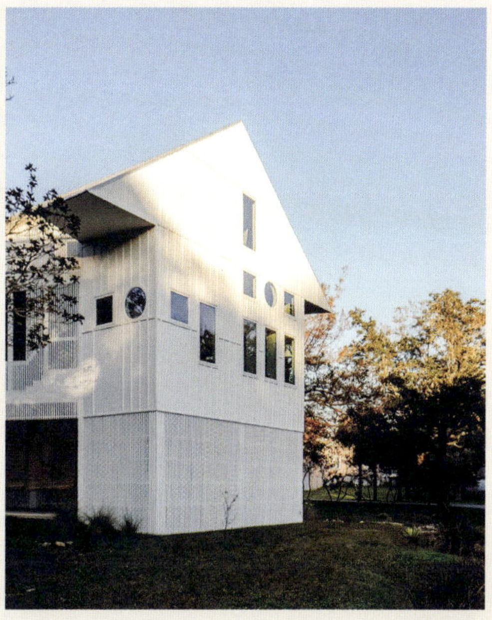

HISTORICALLY FORWARD BUILDING

"We are making a physical presence on the coast that we're rooted to, but we were also able to use local artists and architects, and it felt like a way to honor their work," said Caroline. In their collaboration with Tall Architects, Caroline and Julian wanted to intentionally reference a local style. Mississippi-born Carroll Ishee was a self-taught architect constructing midcentury modern homes along the Gulf Coast in the 1940s–1970s. At the time, his homes were like nothing anyone in the town had seen. Similar in aesthetic, Caroline and Julian's home was built upward, to respond to how homes on the coast are prone to storms and flooding. With a contemporary element, it still has an ode to the Southern farmhouse, much like an Ishee home.

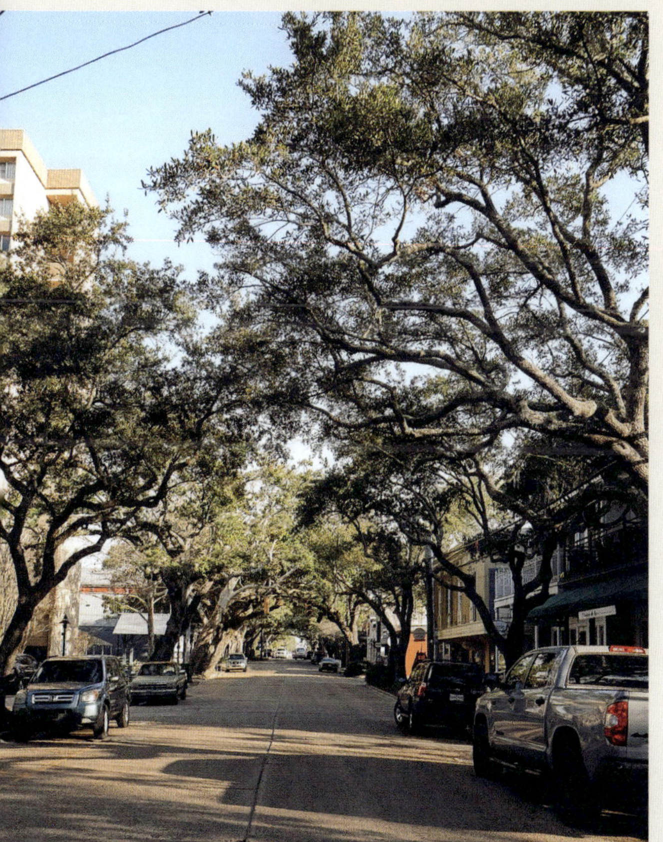

"The Ishee homes are beloved now, but if you think about when he was building them, they were avant-garde. They were built into wetlands and low-lying areas, with many porches, big open windows, and water around

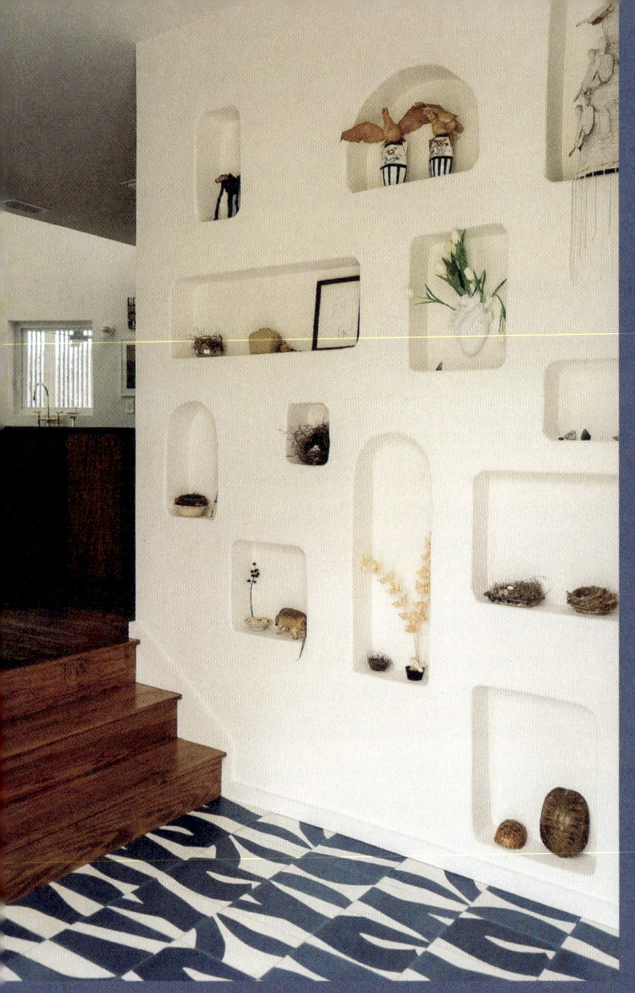

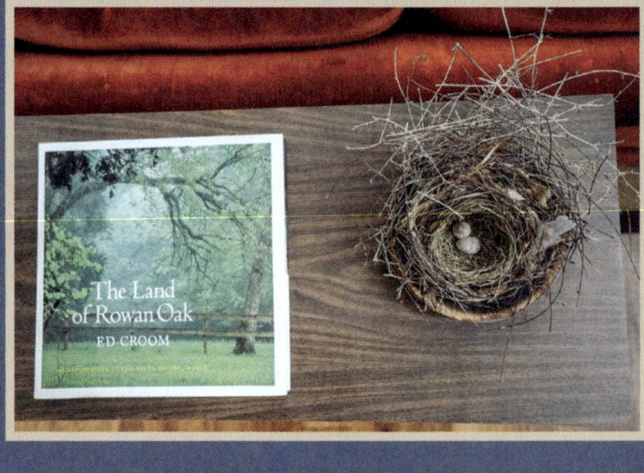
The Land
of Rowan Oak
ED CROOM

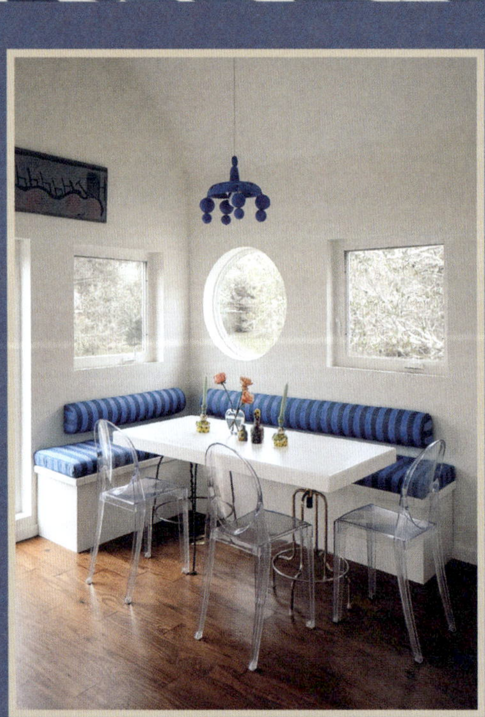

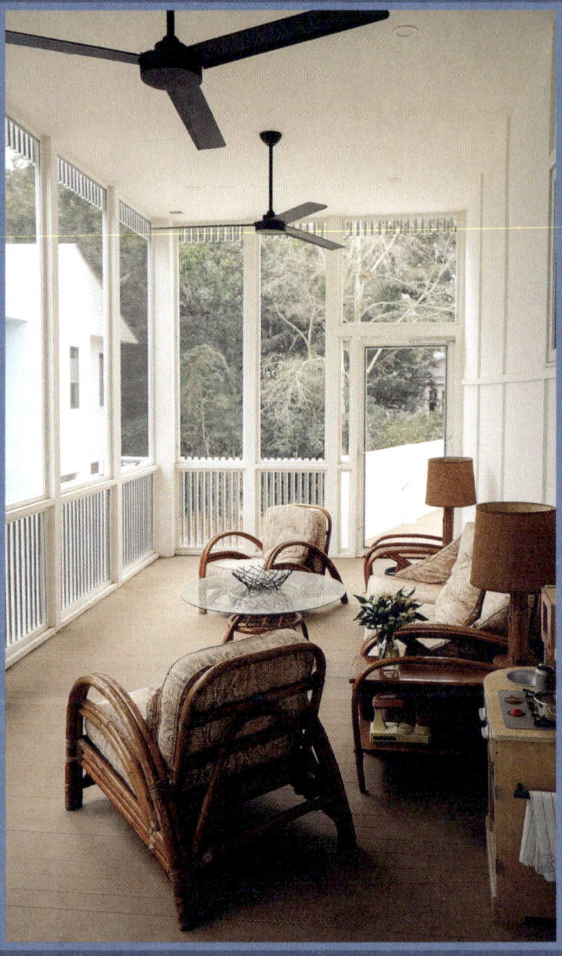

them. When building this house, we had to go in front of the Historic Preservation Commission. But this idea that the historicity of a place is not stuck in time, that the things you're making now become part of the history there, that's an interesting concept to talk about," shared Julian.

So much new construction isn't approached with the questions of how a structure will fit within a place's landscape ten, twenty, or even fifty years from when it's built. What's the easiest to establish is the forethought of the builders and homeowners alike. Equally important is how we educate city planners on how the permits they approve shape the future design of a town. We begin to see the connection between forward-thinking design and how it plays a part in how a town experiences and embraces growth.

CULTURAL AND ECONOMIC DEVELOPMENT IN OCEAN SPRINGS

"A lot of the things we [the museum] have tapped into [in Ocean Springs] have been creative economy and development and how culture can be infused into those private sector modalities and models. There's something powerful in that it empowers other creators, chefs, artists, woodworkers, and all the talented people who do different things, and knits that together into an experience. The museum has been building on our work in the past, Caroline's around Southern culture, and it's found

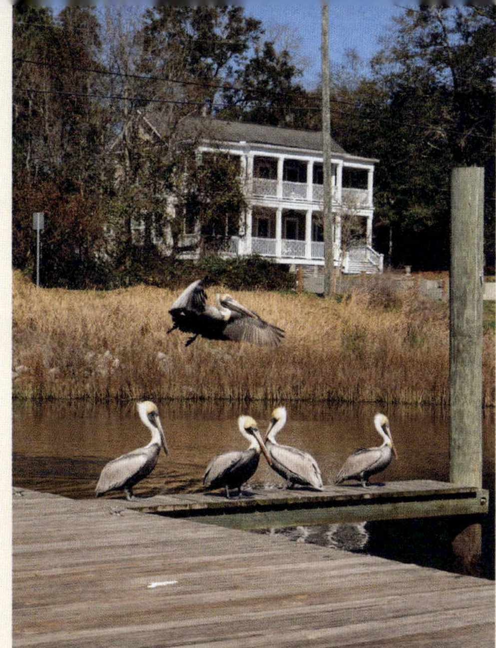

a physical home. This idea of resilience and sustainability is a reality because of the hurricanes, but it's also an ethos that I think is important when discussing developing, growing, or community-building in a small town. It's been a fun echo of some of the earlier cultural work we grew up in. I think down here on the coast, it has taken this kind of real estate and entrepreneurial flavor because of the opportunities here in the town, and with the growth is the need to do it responsibly," said Julian.

CHALLENGES AND BENEFITS OF SMALL TOWN LIVING

"Traditionally, Mississippi [has a] prodigious output of not just thinkers, but athletes and musicians and all the rest—so many people leave Mississippi, right? Mississippi travels the world, but Mississippi is also about small towns. I think bringing ideas back into

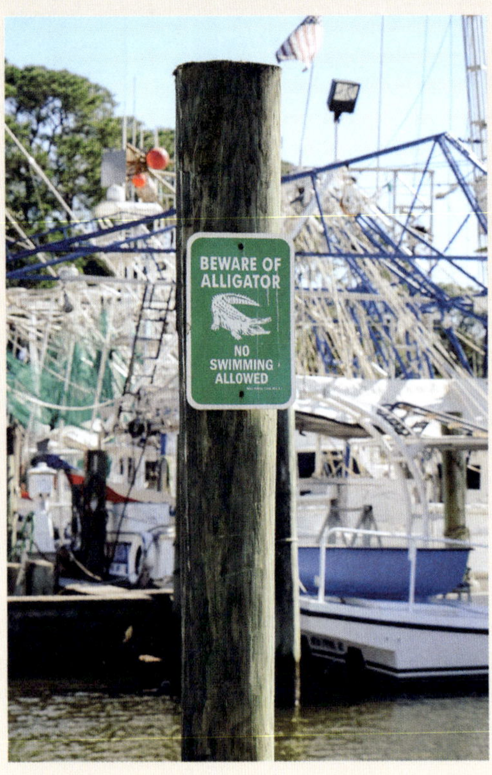

PLACES NEARBY OF SIGNIFICANCE TO VISIT, BOTH NATURE AND LOCATION

- Charnley-Norwood House
- Gulf Islands National Seashore
- Horn Island
- Mississippi Sandhill Crane National Wildlife Refuge
- Walter Anderson Museum of Art

Mississippi is inverting that notion. And bringing it to a small town, being local and wrapping your arms around something, can have a depth of impact rather than a scale of impact in touching people," said Julian.

Mississippi is the epitome of what community and small businesses are about. Chain stores and corporate America have become ubiquitous in larger communities, but where do you find the character? Small towns have managed to retain the charm that urban sprawl has lost.

There are a lot of small towns across the country and in the South that have retained the charm. Whether because of the economic footing of the town or the slow growth that happens in small towns, many of the classic, old buildings remain. There's not always a lot of new construction in a small town mixed with the historic preservation within a town. As things get more significant and more corporatized and globally multinational, there's a lack sometimes, or certainly less of a local flavor when we have so many big-box stores that are the same everywhere. Caroline remarked, "You can feel the town you're impacting, too. Whereas if you're in a city doing something on a scale, you may not ever feel all the various voices that are being impacted by it, here you are pretty aware." There's this idea of people wanting to return to their memories or nostalgia for what it means to grow up in a community. In many ways, the people doing things in

Diversity and Cultural Fusion in the Coastal Community

"Although we're not from here, we have learned and seen how the waterways connect, not just geographically, but with the identity of people. All the fishers have a direct connection to the multiculturalism of the place, and it's the reason we have such great Vietnamese food here, because of the influx of workers and families after the fall of Saigon, and that joined all these other families who had been here from the earlier twentieth century. Being on the coast and near the water, looking at the vista, doing the same kind of exploring that happened hundreds of years ago, I think there's an energy of pushing outward and trying to get away from the mainland, or what Walter Anderson called the dominant mode onshore, the status quo. There are a lot of renegades and enigmatic people who find their way to places like this because there's something about the water and the opportunities to escape the day-to-day that drives a lot of what we see."

—JULIAN

small towns fulfill the human urge to return to a time centered on entrepreneurs, mom-and-pop shops, and family.

THE ROLE OF WATER AND NATURE IN COMMUNITY LIFE

Ocean Springs is just ten or twelve miles from the barrier islands encompassing the Gulf Islands National Seashore. Traveling through silty water to get to the islands, you would not expect to find the crystal clear blue water, almost Caribbean-like, with dolphins swimming about that is there. "I think that's what attracted Walter Anderson, but also attracts all the people who go out there. To have a playground, so to speak, and a place to explore that is so compelling, evocative, and just beautiful, so close, is definitely a huge resource," said Julian.

HERITAGE AND TOURISM SIGNIFICANCE AND CONNECTION

Everyone wants to be a part of a remarkable story. Something Anderson and the Ocean Springs community have been able to do so well is talk about the stories happening in their town. "It's not just the art on the walls, but about the process of creation and iteration and collaboration, innovation, resilience, and that dovetails with everything from the oyster farmers, the charter fishermen, and the ecotourism to the artists who work here, the architects and all this," added Julian. "It's a connective tissue, and then that's rippled out. You see it in the boutique hotels that lean into the Anderson aesthetic." A local hotel, The Roost, named all their rooms after different Anderson block prints. The Springs is another boutique hotel based on the notion of wellness and the history of the healing springs of Ocean Springs. All their rooms are named after native Mississippi medicinal plants. These are private sector people reaching for inspiration and rootedness in a place. And they're reaching toward Anderson and nature.

"The museum itself is coming along as an engine of growth in its own right, collaborating with the town. We're helping put public art and big gateway sculptures at the entrances to town. We've been able to work as a conduit for good ideas and new ideas to come along. And hopefully, that means more opportunities for other people to find business, career, or employment," said Julian. Innovation is a process of bringing good and new ideas wherever you are. And in so doing, you're creating a story that other people care about.

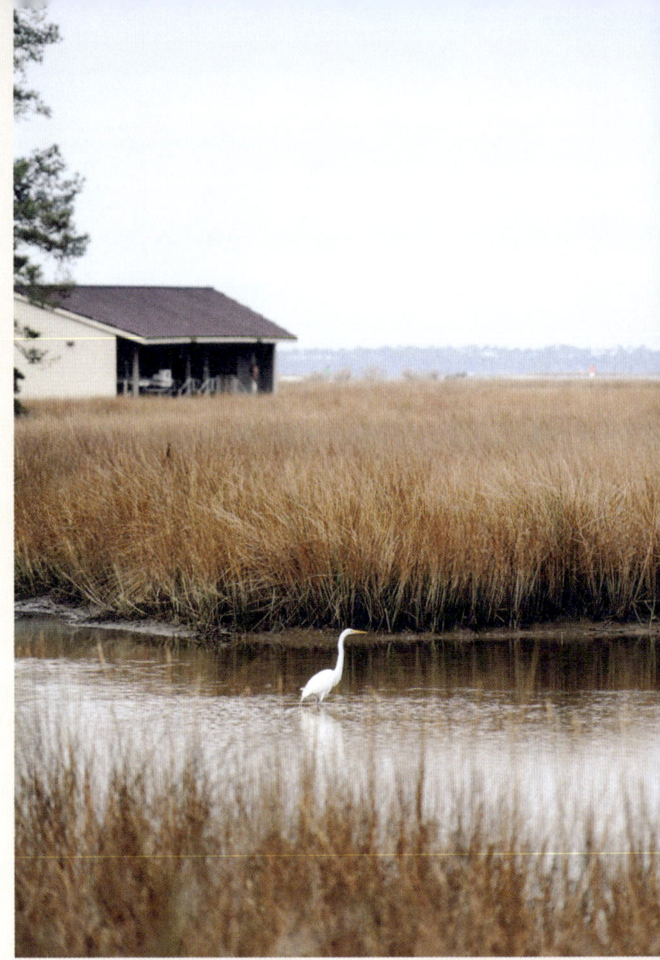

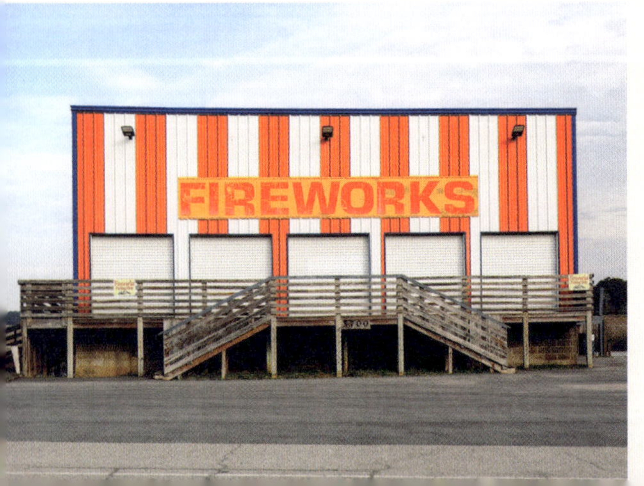

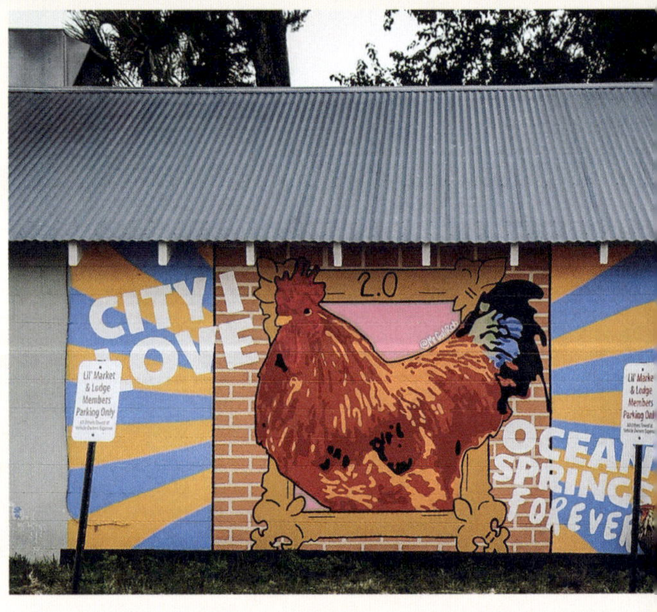

OCEAN SPRINGS, MISSISSIPPI

POPULATION: 18,997 full-time residents in 2024

TOWN SIZE: 15.2 square miles

CLOSEST INTERNATIONAL AIRPORT: Gulfport-Biloxi International Airport (21.4 miles)

CLOSEST LARGE CITY: Gulfport (17.1 miles)

BONUS TOWNS NEARBY: Long Beach, Pass Christian, Bay St. Louis

ANIMALS TO SPOT: alligators, otters, least bitterns, armadillos, dolphins, Perdido Key beach mice, ospreys, bald eagles

TOWN FACTS: Al Capone once lived in Ocean Springs. Walter Anderson made his life's work to include Ocean Springs. The town was hit by Hurricane Katrina in 2005. The Davis Bayou of Ocean Springs is part of the Gulf Islands National Seashore. Just off the coast of Ocean Springs, Horn Island is a boat-in primitive campsite also part of the national seashore. It was a place Anderson visited very regularly. Louis Sullivan, the father of the skyscraper, had a summer home in Ocean Springs: the Charnley-Norwood House. Frank Lloyd Wright was a draftsman for his mentor Sullivan and worked on this home. The Charnley-Norwood House was damaged during Hurricane Katrina and is now managed by the Mississippi Gulf Coast National Heritage Area. Wright designed the Louis Sullivan Bungalow, but it was also destroyed beyond repair in Katrina. Shearwater Pottery was started by the Anderson family in 1928 and is still in business today. Shearwater was an art colony bought by Annette McConnell Anderson in 1918 before becoming the family's pottery studio. The Peter Anderson Arts and Crafts Festival that began in 1978 in Ocean Springs was named for Walter Anderson's brother and the founder of Shearwater Pottery.

SEASONS: Ocean Springs has four seasons, but with its subtropical climate, it also has a monsoon season in spring and fall.

WATER ACTIVITIES: beach swimming, kayaking, paddleboarding, fishing, kiteboarding, aqua cycling, windsurfing, wind foiling, Jet-Skiing, boating, sailing

WATER SPOTS TO VISIT: Old Fort Bayou, Biloxi Bay, and the Gulf of Mexico

"We do a community cleanup each spring—collectively, in a way that gets lost in the sauce of a big city or feels a little more ambiguous. We live on an island, and it's not that big. So to be taking care of this physical space feels really special."

—BRIAN CHRISTOPHER

BRIAN CHRISTOPHER AND CARLA WEEKS

Furniture Maker at Bicyclette and Fine Art Painter

ARROWSIC, MAINE (PRONOUNCED AH-RAU-SIK)

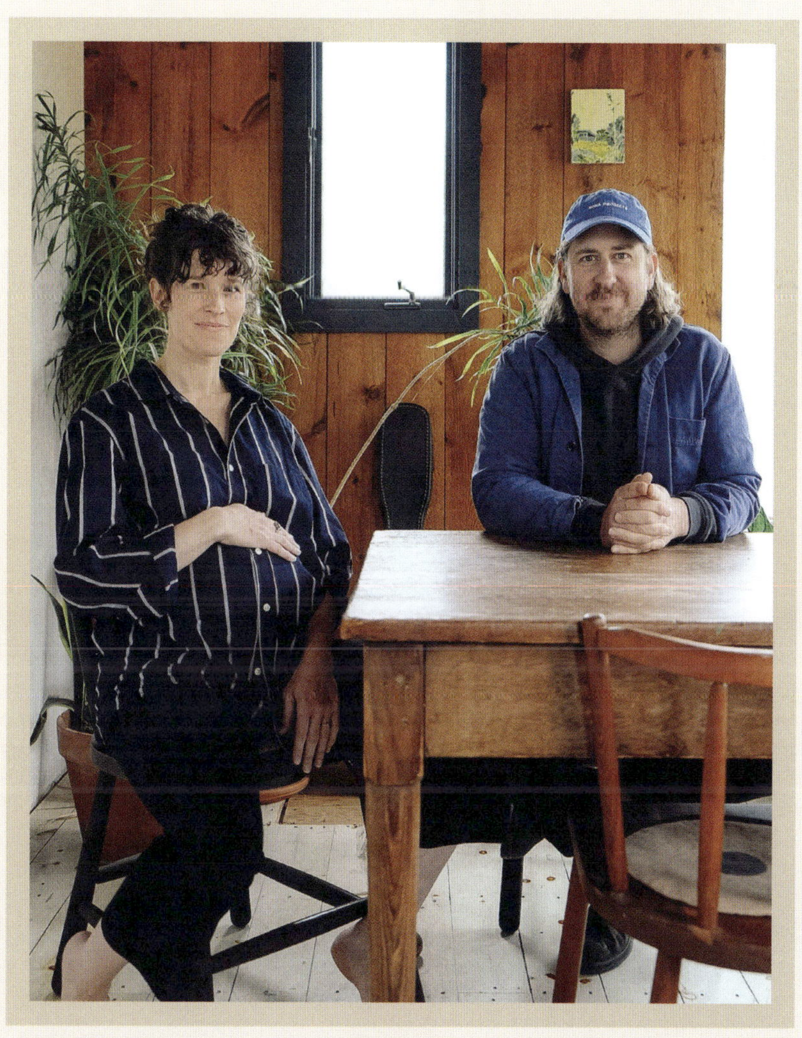

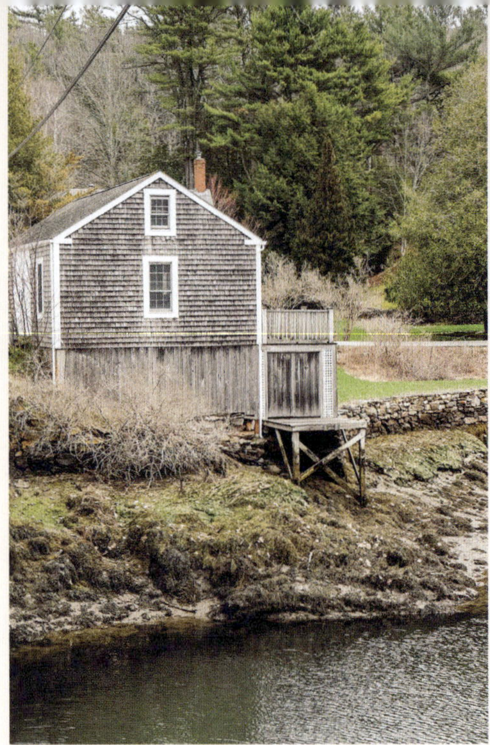

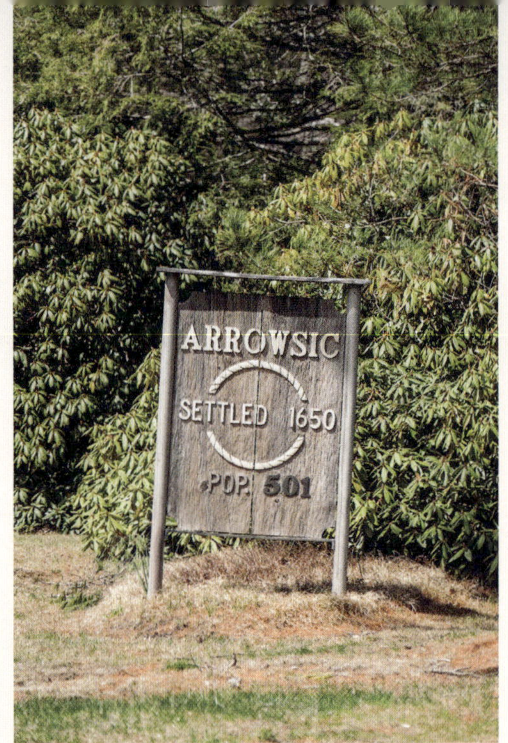

Originally from Philadelphia, Pennsylvania, Brian Christopher took quite the route to a town with a population of under 500 on a small island in Maine. It's not your typical island setting, however, as once you are there you barely know you have left the mainland as the transition is so subtle. After college in Baltimore, Maryland, he hiked the Appalachian Trail for six months and found his way to San Diego, California; New York City; Hoboken, New Jersey; and back to Philadelphia, where he met his wife, fine art painter Carla Weeks, before moving to Maine.

"For a long time, I daydreamed about moving somewhere more open and rural. I envisioned myself living there and growing my business in a place like that. It was open-ended as to where that place was. Then I met my wife, and we got to know one another and told each other about our dreams. We both had similar aspirations to move somewhere more open and rural, have some land, or live near the water. And then COVID pushed that into the conversation realistically," said Brian.

With unknowing forethought, the couple had a long-planned trip to a tiny cabin in the middle of nowhere in March of 2020. They had taken the month off from work to experiment with living in a small town, out of the city and away from people. When the pandemic hit, they were eight days into their trip. Staying longer than planned, they sorted out their next move and attempted to wait out the shutdown of the world. It was time to decide if small town or rural living was for them.

FINDING YOUR SMALL TOWN

"We got out a map, started looking, and poked around Upstate New York, Vermont, and New Hampshire. I grew up always going to New Hampshire, which has a special place in my heart, but I ultimately landed in Maine for a few reasons. I had some friends here that I already knew and had been visiting over the years, and I just fell in love with Maine in that way. But also it was the access to water. My wife was adamant that she wanted to live near the ocean or some big body of water," shared Brian. Carla was originally from Surrey, England, an hour south of London, before she and her family moved stateside to Atlanta, Georgia. She had had a career as a mural and fine art painter for almost ten years when she and Brian met.

Drawn to Portland, Maine, but knowing a city wasn't what they were looking for, they got out a map, drew a one-hour radius, and started the hunt. Brian and Carla didn't know Arrowsic was even a place before they started looking. They knew of nearby Bath and liked that Portland was just forty-five minutes away. Arrowsic is a small community surrounded by three different waterways on all sides: the Kennebec River to the west, which connects to the eastern side; Back River in the south of the island; and the Sasanoa River, which runs north of the island. With water being such a factor in the move and a built-in community in the area, Brian and Carla relocated to Arrowsic in 2023. They found their home near the ocean and a pond across the street that checked all their boxes.

Brian and Carla had feared they wouldn't find community while living in a place where they couldn't even see another house from theirs. But in true small town fashion, they've found more community in Arrowsic than previous places. "People have just been so open and extended themselves. There's always something going on, and people follow through in this amazing small town way where if they say they're going to do something for you, they do, or if they say they're going to invite you to a thing, it happens," explained Brian.

MOVING YOUR BUSINESS TO A SMALL TOWN

Brian's furniture-making adventure started while living in New York before he jumped over the river to Hoboken, where his first shop space was for his company Bicyclette, still in its infancy at that time. Brian was also working

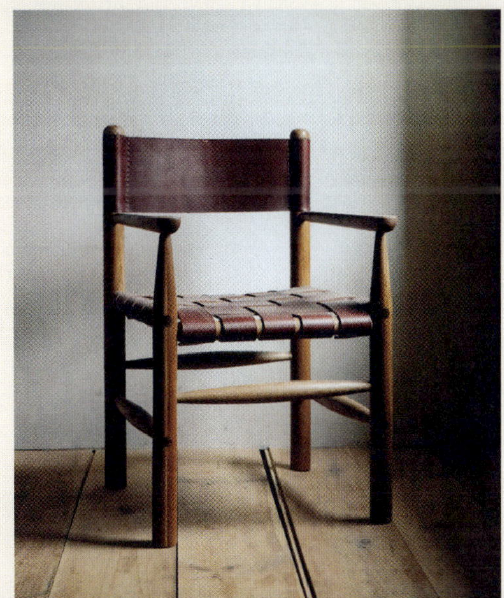

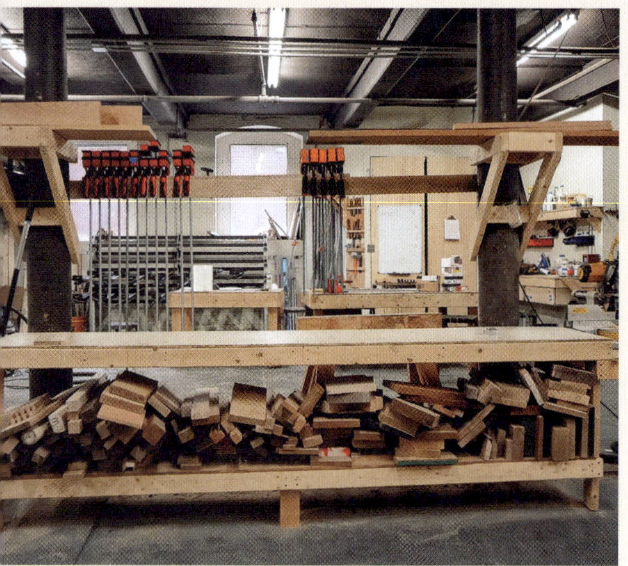

other jobs while learning and building furniture for friends. With strong roots to friends and family in Philadelphia, he made the move back, taking his new business with him. Keeping costs lower than New York City offered was just the beginning for Bicyclette. "I ended up having a full-time employee toward the end of my time in Philly, and then we moved to Maine. I came up here alone in my business and was prepared to be a one-man show for as long as I needed to be, and I was content with that," said Brian.

The pandemic of 2020 spurred a lot of growth for a lot of people with small businesses. It was a time to reflect on what's working, what's not, what to cut, what to increase within the business, and so forth. Brian felt he had to push himself into his business, and the rewards have been plenty. He's now busier than he's ever been, with a client base not tied to Maine specifically. Branching outward has given Brian the security to know his business is not going to collapse. Because so much of his business ships out of Maine and he felt the pull to keep more of his work within the state, Brian opened a showroom in the neighboring town of Wiscasset (pronounced Wi-ska-suht).

"I have fallen in love with some brands and companies that have really cool spaces where people can go and meet the people that make the furniture and experience the whole brand in its entirety," shared Brian about his showroom. Having that in Maine was much more possible with overhead being four to five times lower than what he'd been paying in much larger cities, without sacrificing his client base with his move.

Maine is a summer destination for so many people. Brain has welcomed people from almost every state and all the corners of the world. Living in a place that attracts so many has been wonderful for brand awareness, and the shorter tourist season leaves him with time throughout the rest of the year to focus on creating more. Planning the year out and knowing when the highs and lows in business are coming have helped him grow Bicyclette in ways he might not have otherwise.

THE EFFECTS OF WATER

When Brian and Carla moved from Philadelphia to Arrowsic, they were quite literally grounded: they weren't walking on concrete

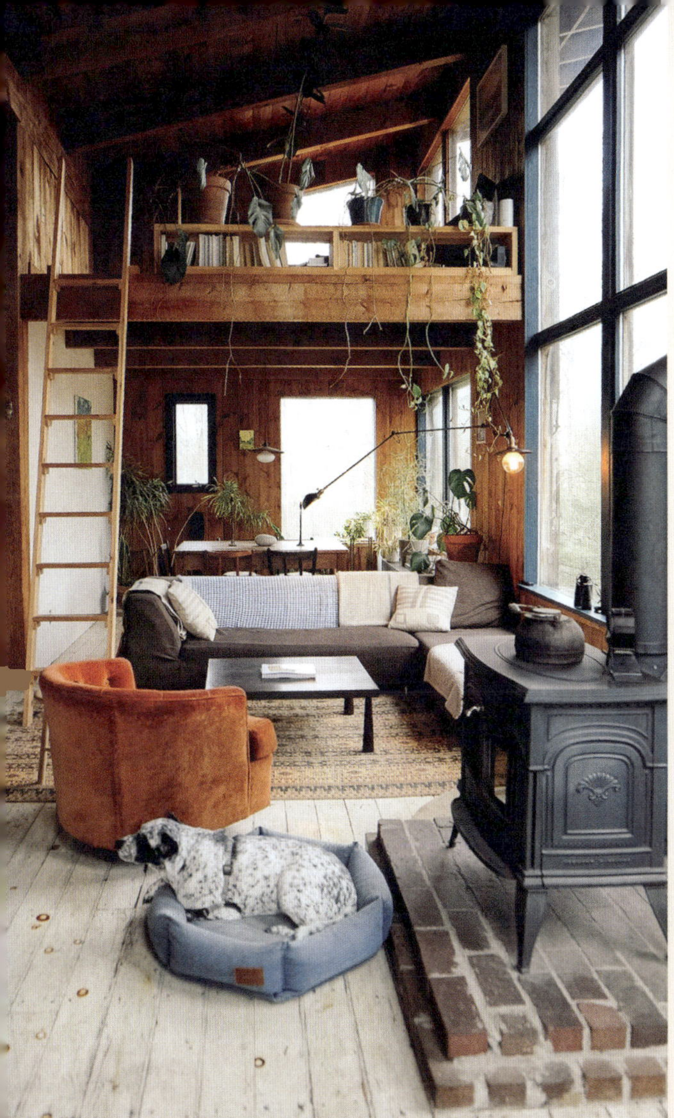

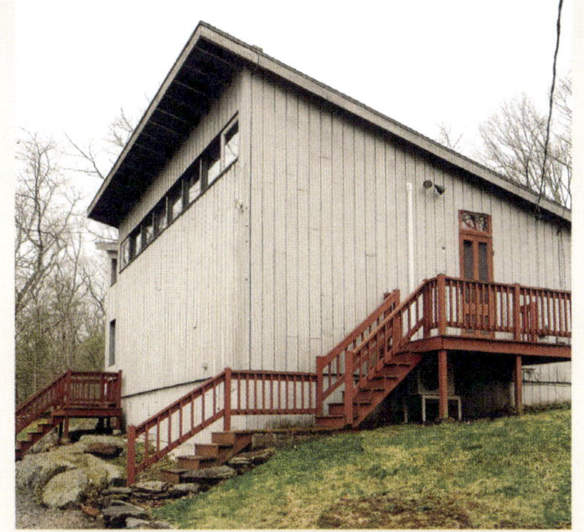

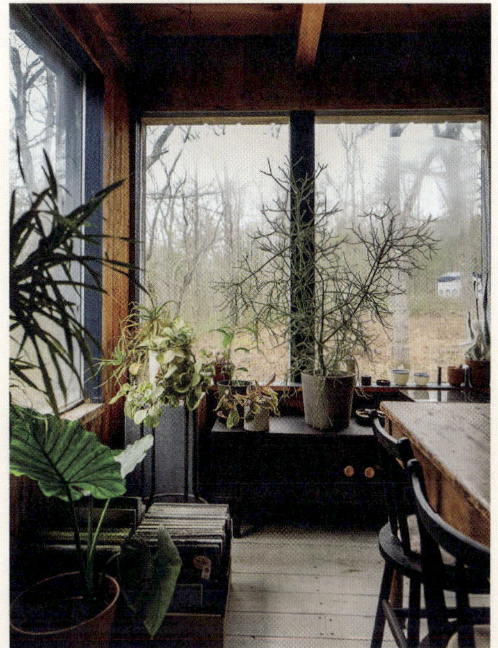

The Beauty in Staying Small

"Maine is a little stuck in time in this totally wonderful way. And you would hate to suggest something that would start to chip away at that. You know, we've seen that happen to places around the country that are just the right amount of time away from a big city. A train line and a couple hotels later, and that place has lost its magic. So I don't really wish for anything to change up here."

—BRIAN, SHARING ABOUT PRESERVING THE SMALL TOWN FEELING VERSUS INCORPORATING BIG-CITY IDEAS INTO HIS TOWN

day in and day out. They could feel the water's fluidity and wander among the trees in the woods. For Carla, she began to see water and the surrounding land more and more in her paintings, while Brian has seen more playfulness in his work. "Maybe that's a result of where we live. And getting to be outside, in water more and in the woods, is a special thing for me. You can be a kid in those spaces and play again. Water is such a playful material, and to be in an open space and able to play—that must influence you on what you're thinking creatively," said Brian.

Brain and Carla can't get away from water working its way into their day-to-day. They live on an island while also welcoming the views just across the street from their home of Sewell Pond, a local gathering spot for the community to both picnic and swim in the warmer months. When they found their house, they weren't thinking so much about the pond access across the street, but it's been something they have loved getting to enjoy. Carla is actively testing the water each year to ensure it continues to be a healthy body of water for the community. The surrounding waters of Arrowsic are mostly private land, without a lot of public access to use the water. So the town purchased land from a family selling waterfront property and turned it into a pocket park, complete with a composting toilet and a floating dock, giving the public a place to launch their canoes and kayaks, swim, and be on the water.

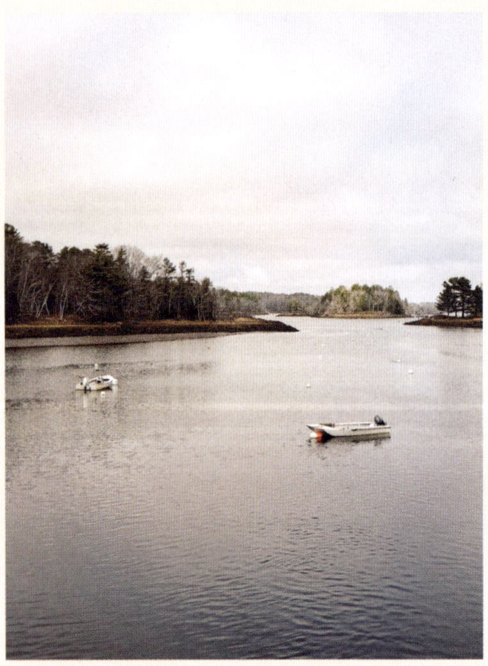

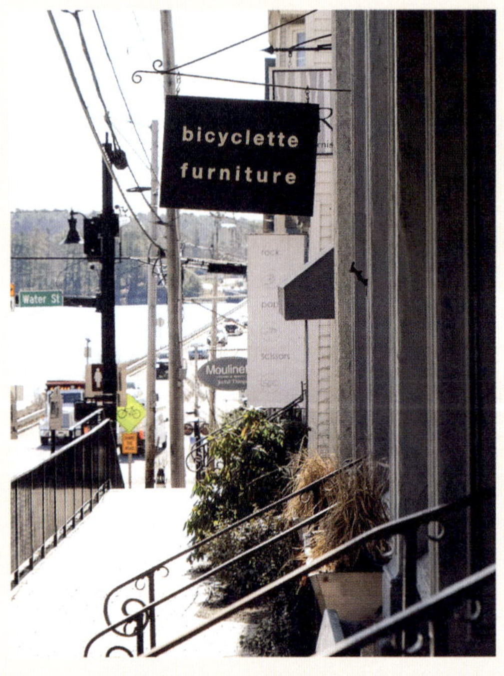

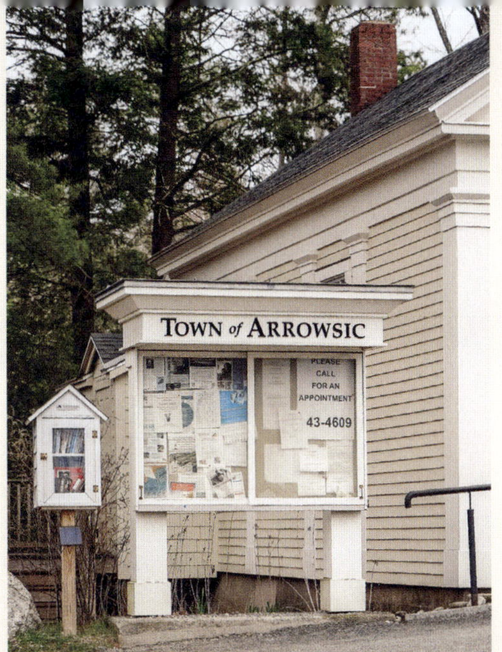

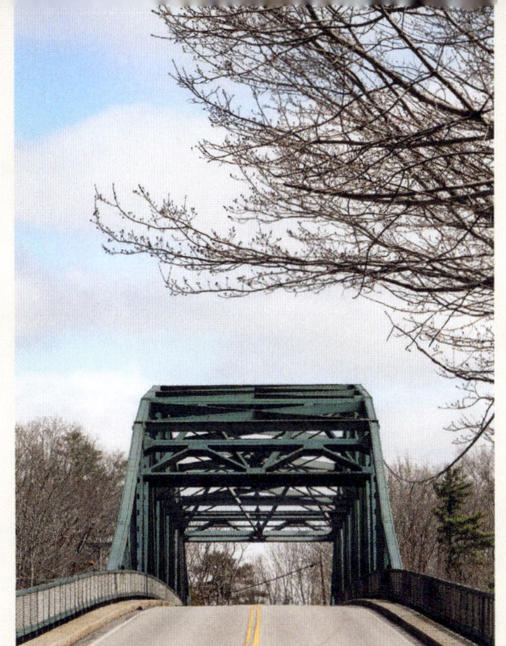

ARROWSIC, MAINE

POPULATION: 477 full-time residents in 2024

TOWN SIZE: 10.8 square miles (7.8 land and 3 water)

CLOSEST INTERNATIONAL AIRPORT: Portland International Airport (42.9 miles)

CLOSEST REGIONAL AIRPORT: Brunswick Executive Airport (12.4 miles)

CLOSEST LARGE CITY: Portland (39.8 miles)

BONUS TOWNS NEARBY: Bath, Woolwich, Wiscasset

BEST TIME TO WHALE-WATCH: May to October

TOWN FACTS: Arrowsic has several lighthouses on the island. The Arrowsic Conservation Commission has taken the guesswork out of a rising tide by installing wooden posts to more easily identify water height during high-water events.

SEASONS: Arrowsic has four distinct seasons.

WATER ACTIVITIES: kayaking, swimming, whale-watching, fishing, boating, sailing, paddleboarding, canoeing

WATER SPOTS TO VISIT: Kennebec River, Back River, Sasanoa River, Sewell Creek, and Sewell Pond

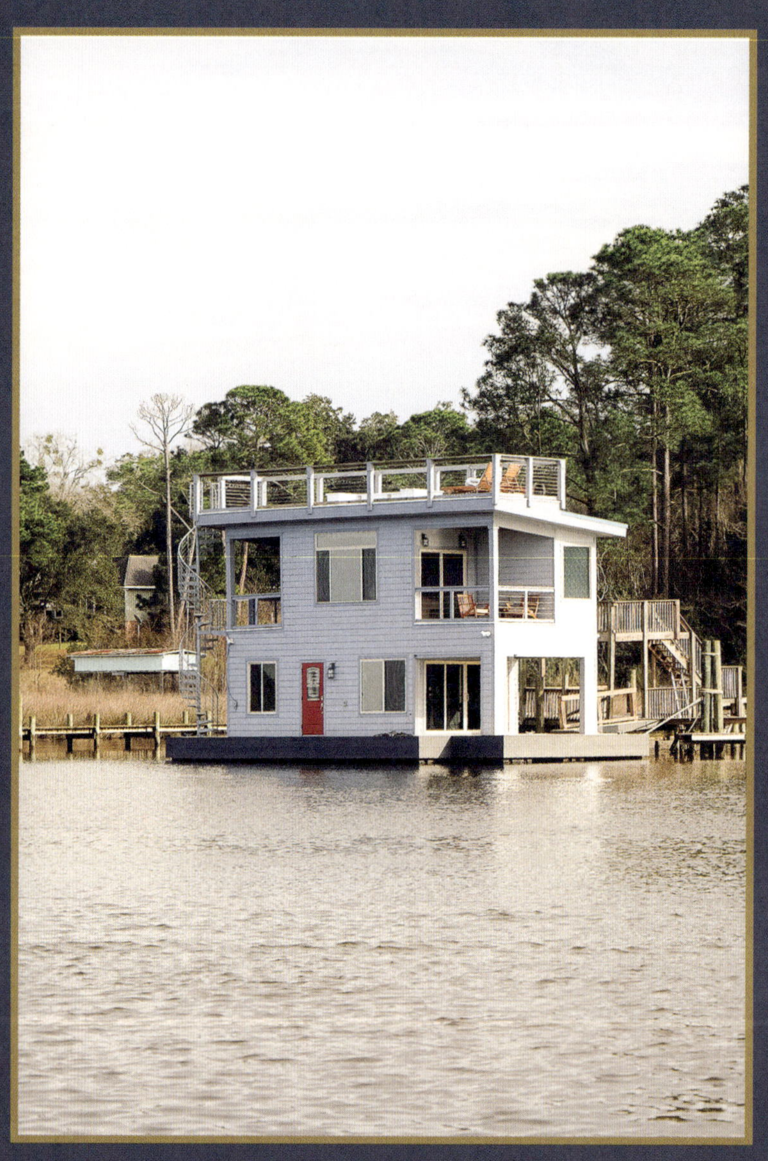

SPOTLIGHT

HOUSEBOAT AND FLOAT HOUSE COMMUNITIES IN SMALL TOWNS

There are float house and houseboat communities in both cities—such as Seattle, Portland, and Wilmington—and small towns alike. If you are wondering what the difference is between the two, one can move through the water, and the other is stationary within the confines of the water. A houseboat is a boat that also serves as a house, whereas a float house is more like a real home constructed on a platform in the water. A few float house and houseboat communities in small towns are in these locations:

- **Branson, Missouri**
- **Brunswick, Georgia**
- **Demopolis, Alabama**
- **Fort Washington, Maryland**
- **Friday Harbor, Washington**
- **Page, Arizona**
- **Piermont, New York**
- **Sausalito, California**
- **Shasta Lake, California**
- **Winona, Minnesota**

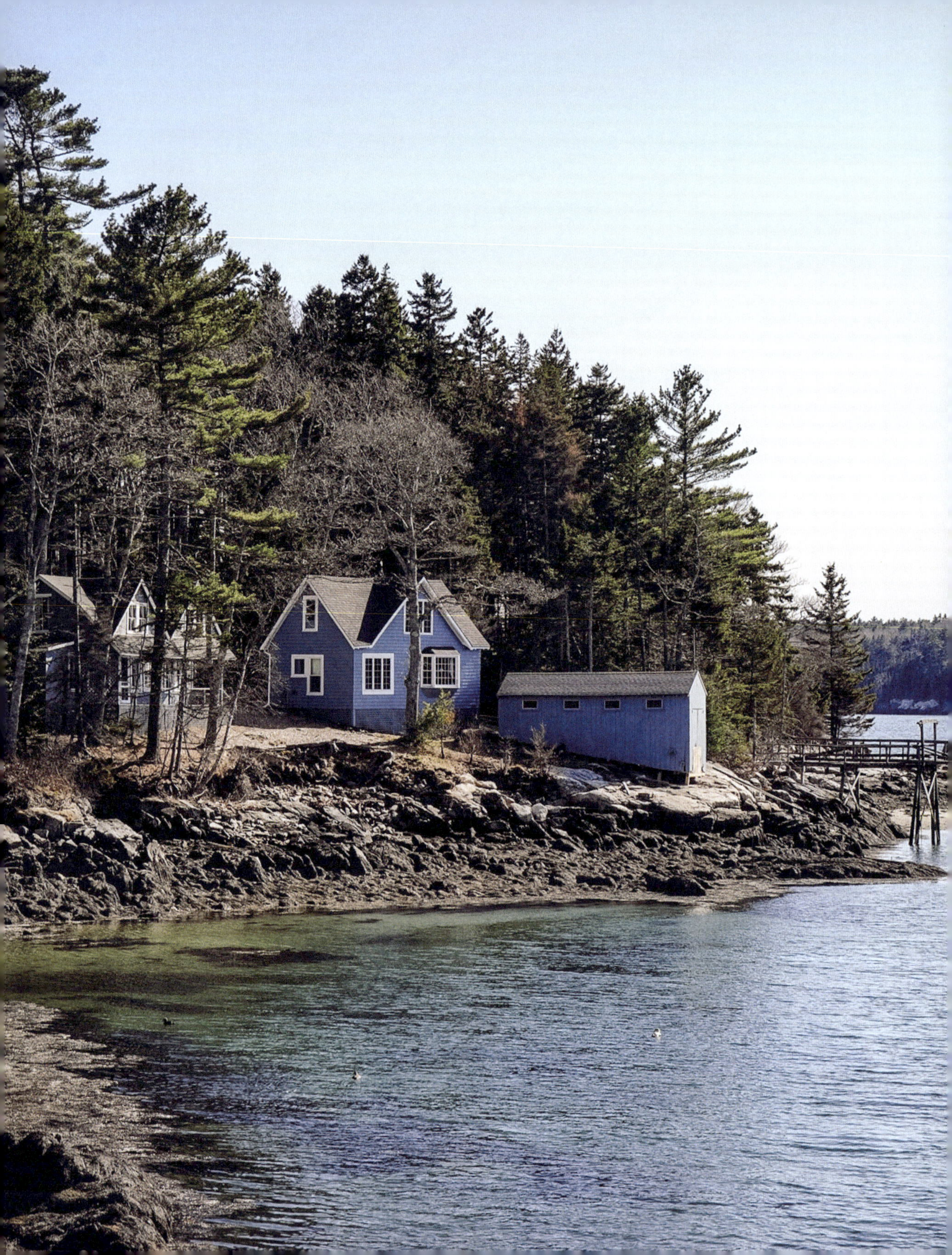

ISLANDS

"Maine, to me, is being rooted deeply and securely in a familial community. It is being restored, internally, by the wonder of creation. It is sharing the love of this rocky shoreline and sea air with the next generation."

—ASHLEIGH COLEMAN

ASHLEIGH COLEMAN

Photographer

RUTHERFORD ISLAND, SOUTH BRISTOL, MAINE

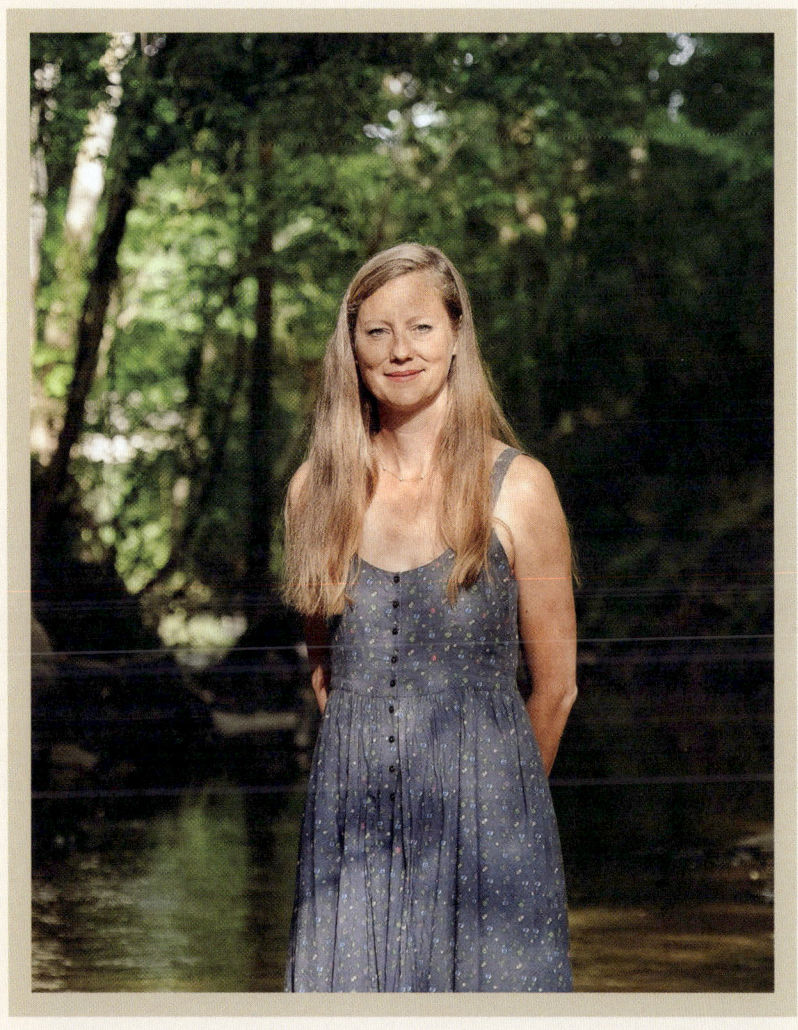

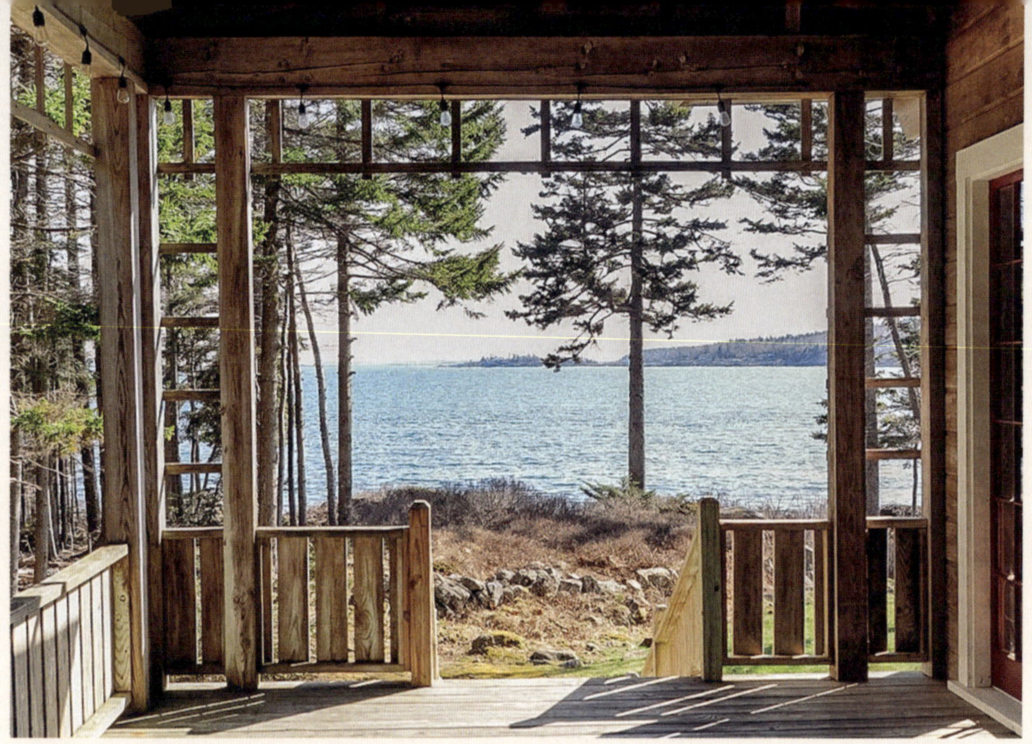

Ashleigh Coleman, originally from Columbia, South Carolina, has been splitting her time with Maine for most of her life. Swapping South Carolina for rural land outside of Ackerman, Mississippi, and Rutherford Island, Maine, part of South Bristol, remained a constant for her and her family. With the flexibility in her work as a photographer, Ashleigh often makes the long drive a few times a year with her three children in tow, stopping along the way to take pictures. Her children, often the subjects of her photography, share their mom's old haunts with her on the long drives, photographed in recurring familiar locations at different times of the year. Spending her time in both places has given Ashleigh the ability to build bodies of work in both places that she calls home—both of which are surrounded by nature. In Maine, she's posed in a home surrounded by both a river and a bay, while in Mississippi, she's afforded use of the adjacent land owned by her in-laws. A large creek runs through the property, large enough to feel like a river at times. This gives her children year-round access to wilderness in some form.

Rutherford Island has a long history of people spending their summers there. In the 1800s, it was so busy that the small island could support four hotels, with people disembarking from steamships to spend their long, lazy days there. In 1911, Ashleigh's grandmother's best friend's family built a home on a point of the island. Her grandmother was invited to visit, and for the past twenty-nine years, the family has returned each year. She and her extended family of parents, siblings, their spouses, nieces, and nephews all piled into the home, spending the summer jumping into the water at the edge of the property, cooking together, and bonding over card games. For Ashleigh, she was also creating a community of friends outside of her family and making visits to her favorite shops and restaurants. She's only missed one summer in all those years, which is not an easy feat for someone who left for college and then started a family. Her parents now own part of the summer home, sharing it with the original family who built it all those years ago.

When a beloved location she had dreamed of owning since she was thirteen went on the market, Ashleigh and her husband Josiah jumped at the chance to make an offer. The home, positioned between the Damariscotta River and Johns Bay, both opening up to the Atlantic Ocean, was once an old store and overlooks the only way on and off the island: the drawbridge. Her children have made watching the boats moving through the channel a favorite pastime and one very different from their past years spent on the island.

Their 1880s three-season, two-story clapboard-style home isn't for everyone, with no heat and a cistern that needs to be drained in the winter. Because the house is so close to the water, it's built with an overboard discharge system for its septic tank, much like what you would experience living on a boat. Ashleigh

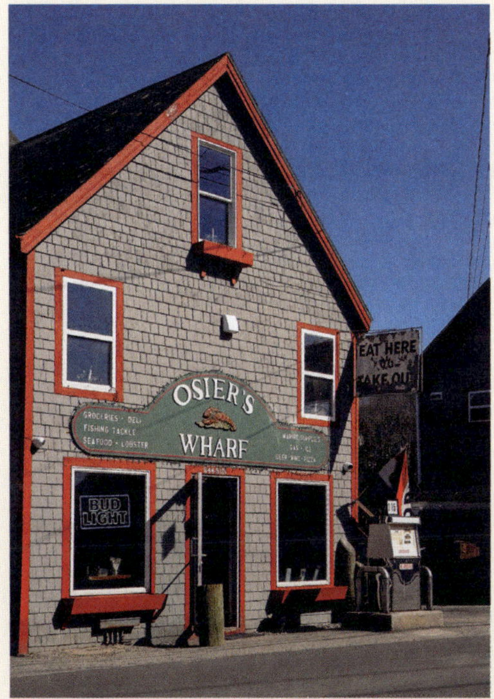

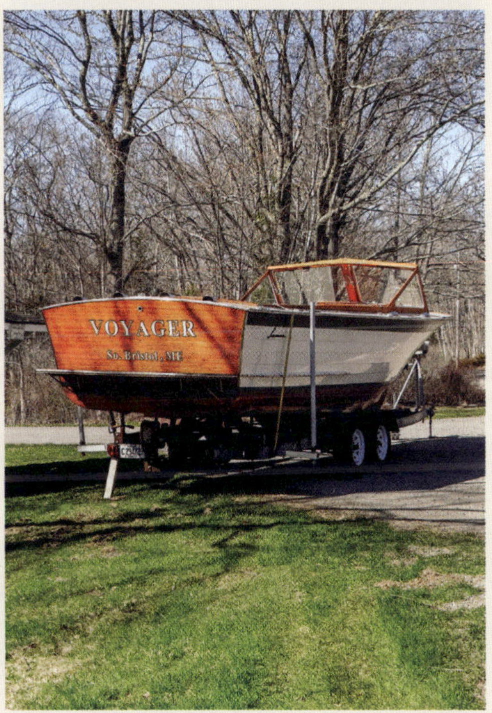

PLACES TO MAKE FRIENDS IN A SMALL TOWN

Attend a church in the community.

Join a local sports team for adults.

Join a book club through the library.

Work remotely from the local coffee shop a few days a week.

Make friends with your postal worker; they usually know everyone.

Volunteer.

Befriend the shopkeeper of your favorite shop.

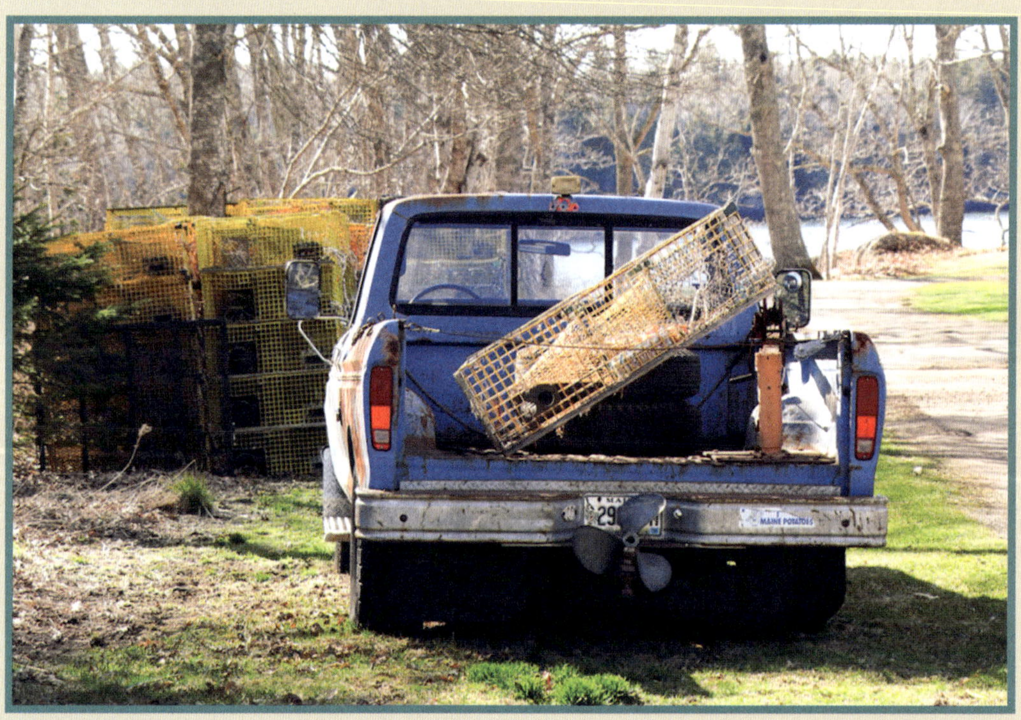

and her family try to get to the house three times a year, school schedules and weather being the biggest factors to consider. As the children get older and she and her husband retire, they hope to spend more and more time in their Maine home. They aren't there yet, but the long-term goal is on her mind.

ASSIMILATING IN A SMALL TOWN

Letting your brain settle when dividing your time between two places can seem daunting, but Ashleigh makes it look easy since she has been in the practice for most of her life. She's branched out and been able to do some photography in Maine, trying to generate a body of work that encompasses the Maine culture she's so fond of. Her children have started to make friends there, and so has Ashleigh.

"Life continues. I still must make dinner. Some of my routines stay the same, but being on the water is also so different. It's very refreshing. And it's different than Mississippi because we are so close to the harbor. We get to watch the boats, watch the lobstermen. We talk to the bridgemaster, who stays and sleeps in the bridge house and oversees the raising and lowering of the bridge. That's a twenty-four-hour job, seven days a week. I run into the ladies at the thrift store. We meet our neighbors when the drawbridge gets stuck outside our home. We open our home to new friends and visit with our neighbors," shared Ashleigh.

Creating a community for yourself, even when it's not your full-time home, means you must work a bit harder to blend in and feel like you have a seat at the table. When you immerse yourself in the town, you allow yourself to positively participate in the transformation. Smile at the locals and say hi when you see a new face. Wear your graciousness on your sleeve. "Being a good neighbor goes a long way—being kind to people and listening to them and smiling at them," shared Ashleigh. "I'm genuinely interested in what it's like to be a fisherman in South Bristol or what it's like to be a contractor on an island and in an area that has a shortage of contractors. I feel like being interested in other people goes a long way in assimilating."

LIVING IN DIFFERENT RURAL REGIONS AND COMPARING EXPERIENCES

"The fishermen in Maine are a lot like farmers in Mississippi. I feel like there's a very strong connection between the people working on the water and boats and the people in Mississippi working on the land. That feels very familiar as I go back and forth between the two places," shared Ashleigh. Maine and Mississippi have many similarities as mostly rural states with a large working-class population. Often locals work on the same land or waterway as their family did before them, holding strong to the same values and beliefs passed down to them through the generations. Both states also have wariness toward people who are not from each place. Ashleigh, knowing this and addressing

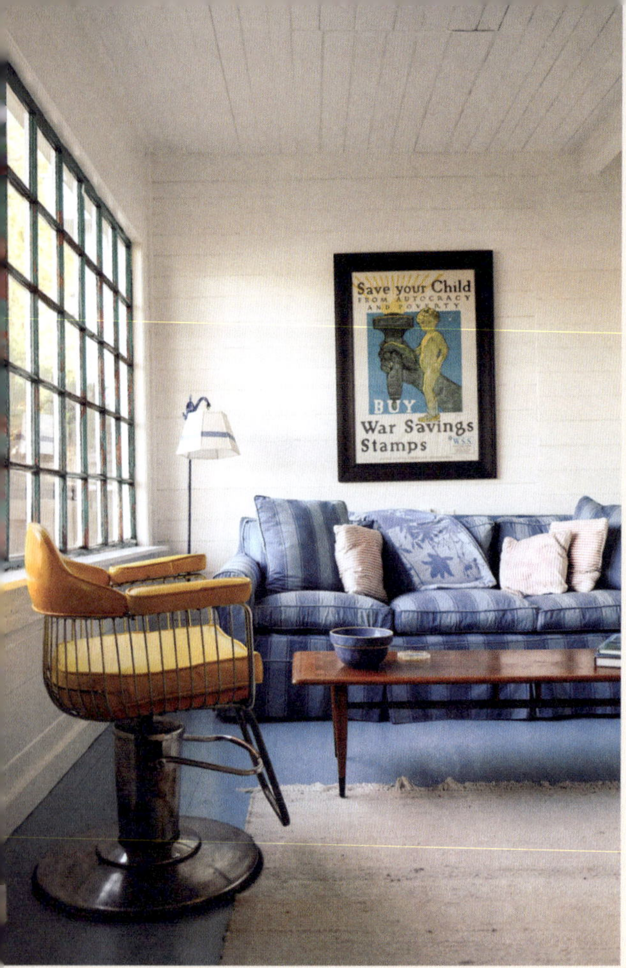

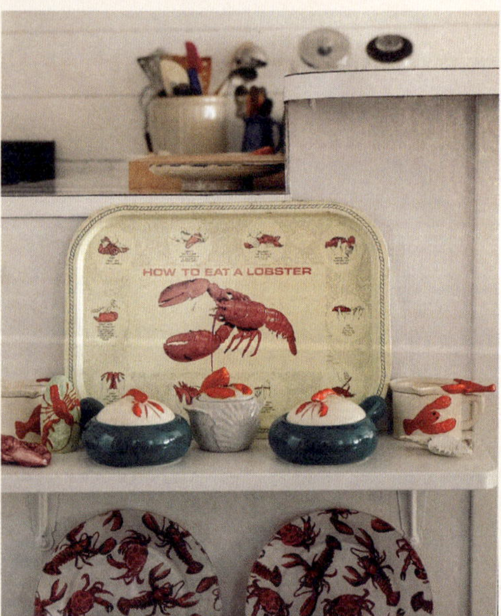

it head-on, is quick to acknowledge she's not living her day in and day out in one place, paying her dues, but it's a mindset she can understand. She is neither a farmer nor a fisher, but she can pick up on the conversations and relate in small ways; there's an affinity. "When talking to the fishermen, I can relate in small ways. I can track with the conversation a bit more because I've listened to men talk about farming in Mississippi," Ashleigh shared.

BUILDING TWO BODIES OF WORK

"I think the thread between Maine and Mississippi is looking for ways to photograph that will either help me frame things in a new light and see them differently or help other people do that. I look for subjects that make me curious and make me ask questions. So how do we photograph what is common in a way that will make you stop and look at it again?" asked Ashleigh.

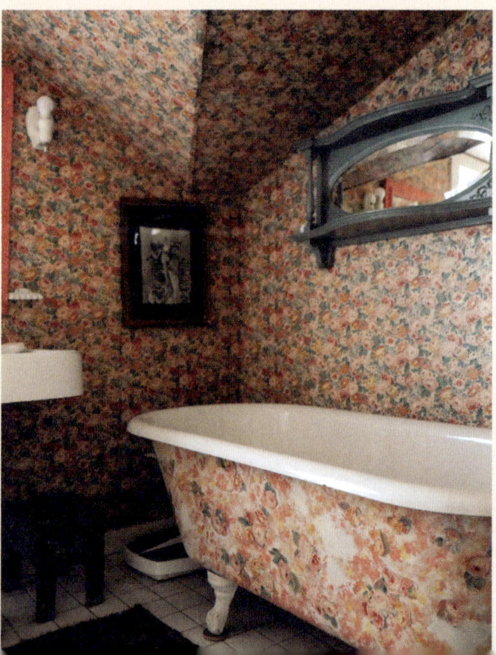

Fluctuating from one rural community to another, Ashleigh has built her work around sharing a look into the two worlds. "I found some photographs that someone made in the seventies of South Bristol and the people who lived in the village, and they're amazing. I would love to be able to document life in the village similarly, but in this era, for the historical society. I think doing what I do in Mississippi and trying to find the value and beauty of everyday life in places it can be easy to overlook is something to continue up there," said Ashleigh.

Living in a smaller town can certainly affect creatives in a very positive way. Ashleigh shared, "Small communities allow me the leisure of working slowly, which I think is important. It marries my work time to figuring out what I'm trying to say with a photograph or a series."

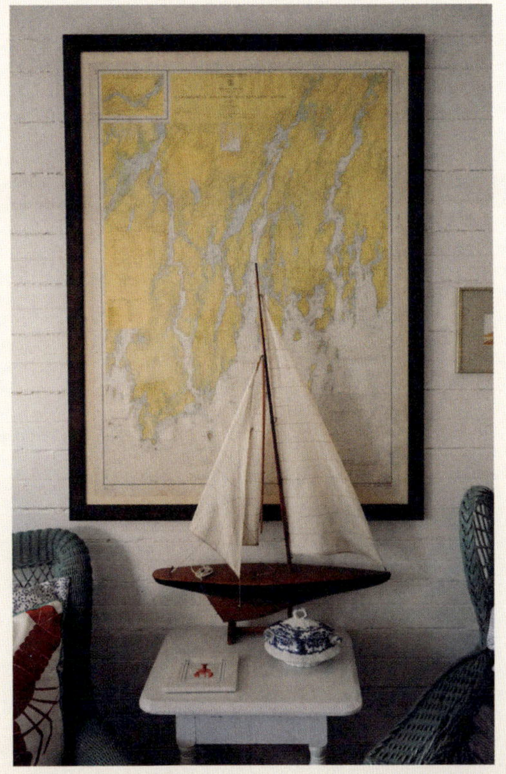

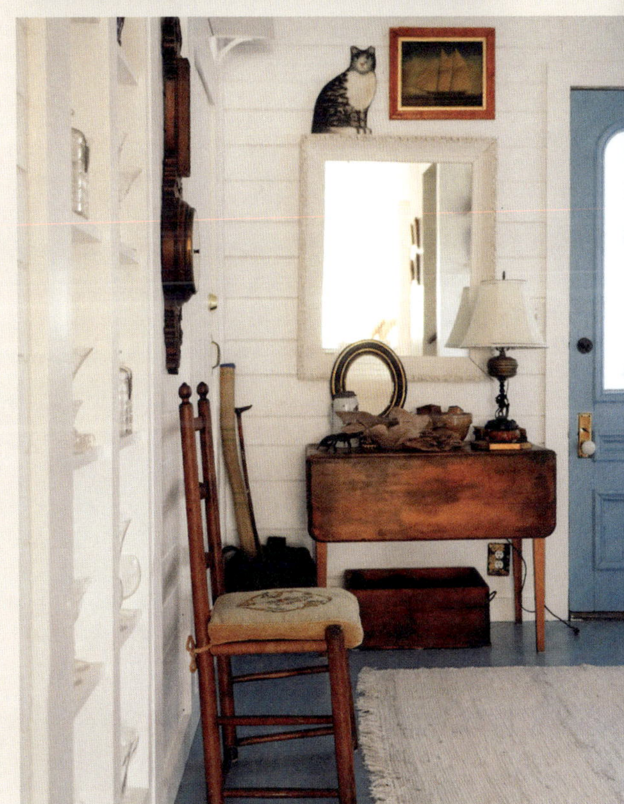

LIVING NEAR THE WATER

Ashleigh expressed that living so close to nature is her favorite thing about spending time on Rutherford Island. "I love to watch the birds and the seals. I love watching the tides change. And the swimming. It's stimulating, and it wakes you up to be there," she shared. In any direction you look from Ashleigh's home, you see water. It's all-encompassing, pulling you in like the moon pulls the water in and out; you can't help but fixate on the water, watching the boats move from the cove to the bay, adjusting as they pass from lobster trap to lobster trap. The birds glide through the sky, waiting to dip into the water for a fish just below. The water in the bay creates its own bustling community, one where those on the shore are merely spectators, simply curious when the next performance starts.

UNEXPECTED THINGS THAT COME WITH LIVING ON RUTHERFORD ISLAND IN SOUTH BRISTOL

There's no town water because you can't run pipes when you live on an island made of rock. Some houses have a well, and some have a cistern. Time is taken learning about collecting rainwater. The lack of water will make you more conscientious at home, and the number of new wells that are dug on newly constructed homes can impact the island's water table. Yes, you are surrounded by water, but it's salt water. Everyone's actions affect everyone else on the island as well.

FUTURE OF THE COMMUNITY AND FISHERS' LIVELIHOODS

The current practices of the fishers have come under question in the last few years, leaving them to buy more expensive traps and different ropes to ensure the trap will disconnect and not tangle on any creature. Many older fishers, who learned one way, aren't ready to embrace the new modes of operation. They are opting to retire or look for other work because, between new technology and stricter regulations, it's not the same work they once knew the ins and outs of.

Lobster fishing in Maine is a job passed down from generation to generation, and it's a job that not just anyone can set up and start doing. If the lobster fishing goes away, so will many of these small towns that depend on the lobster. Ashleigh added, "I really hope the fisherman's way of life is protected and valued. I think they feel marginalized, but it's [lobster trapping] very much like it is a small town, so if that dies off, that's really the heart of the community, right? And because they're here year-round, I think it's important for the work to be protected. And by protected, I mean we value the work that they're doing." Protecting their work also means protecting a large portion of the surrounding area from an unrecognizable transformation. Without the fishers, the industry will dissolve, with their land running the risk of being sold off because of rising costs and the charm that we know Maine for fading away. It sounds dramatic, but it speaks to the magnitude of importance an industry can present to an environment.

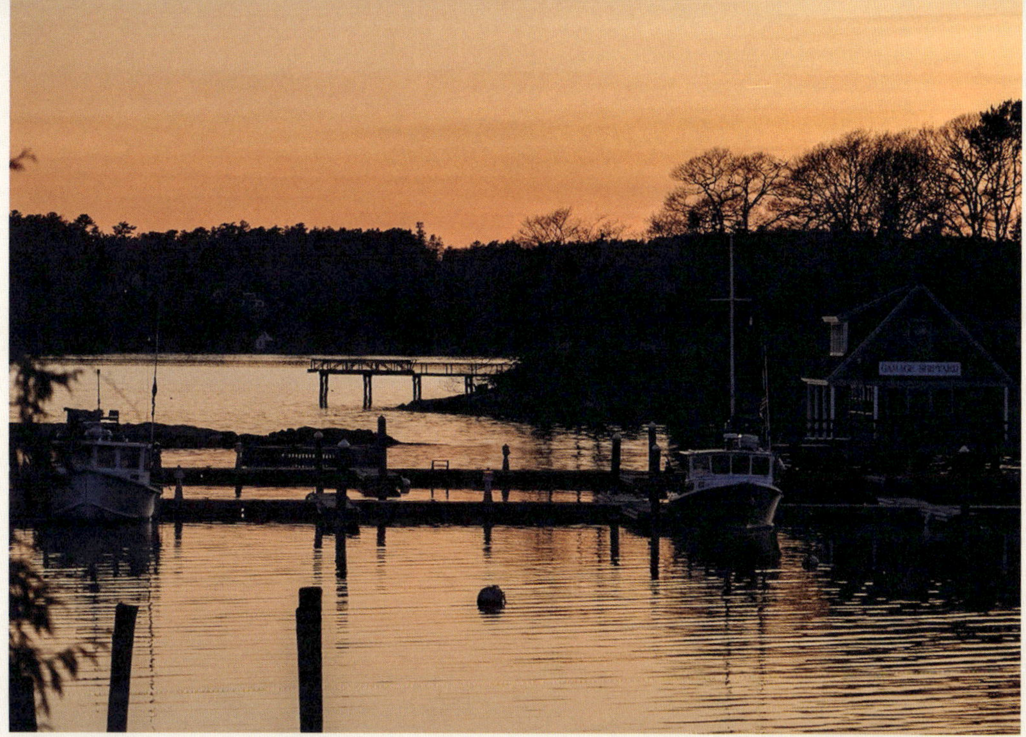

SOUTH BRISTOL, RUTHERFORD ISLAND, MAINE

POPULATION: 1,127 full-time residents in 2024

TOWN SIZE: 29.7 square miles, of which 16.6 is water

CLOSEST INTERNATIONAL AIRPORT: Portland International Airport (68.5 miles)

CLOSEST REGIONAL AIRPORT: Brunswick Landing (38.3 miles)

CLOSEST LARGE CITY: Portland (65.6 miles)

BONUS TOWNS NEARBY: Damariscotta, Boothbay, Walpole

TOWN FACTS: The town has six nature preserves. Rutherford Island has approximately 100 year-round residents. The Thompson Ice House Museum uses harvested ice each summer to make ice cream for an ice cream social.

SEASONS: South Bristol, Rutherford Island, has four distinct seasons.

WATER ACTIVITIES: lobstering and fishing, taking cold dips, paddleboarding, birding, boating, kayaking, canoeing, sailing

WATER SPOTS TO VISIT: Christmas Cove, Damariscotta River, Jones Cove, and Johns River

"It's a delight to walk on the island because of the cadence. First, when you get on the ferryboat, which is the only way to access the island, it immediately calms your nervous system. Then you arrive, and it's prolonged. It's beautiful for walking, and about 30 percent of the island is forever wild."

—REBECCA BLAIR

REBECCA BLAIR AND WATT BISHOP

Fashion Consultant and Retired Orthodontist

SHELTER ISLAND, NEW YORK

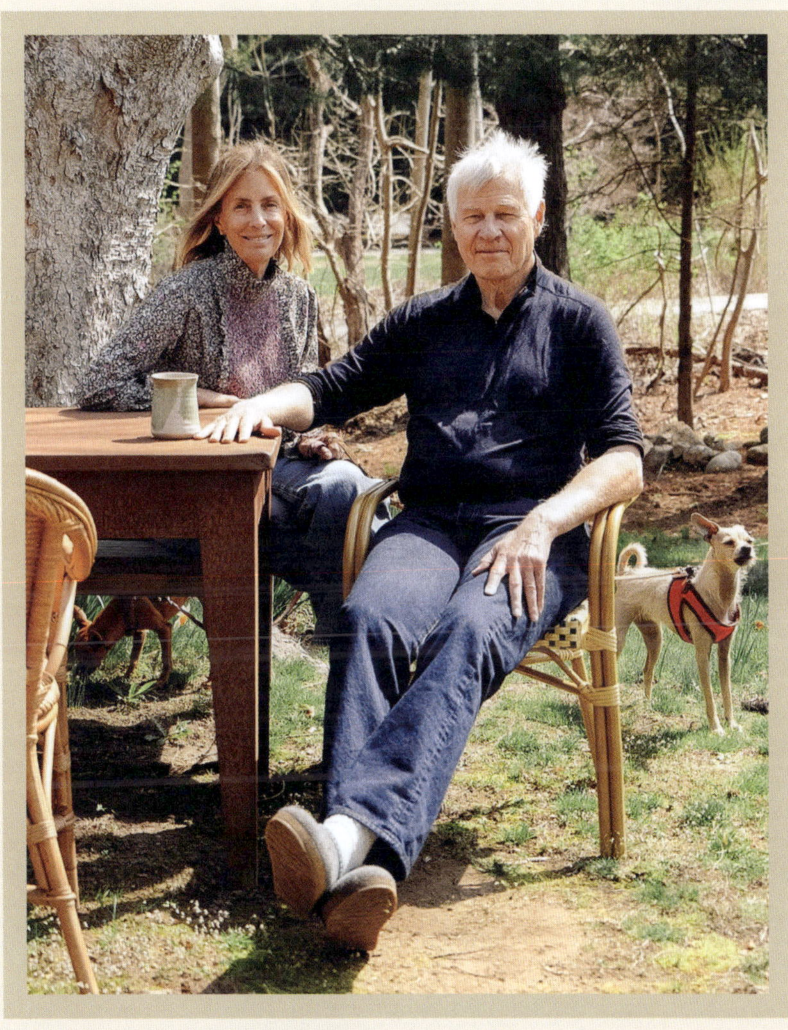

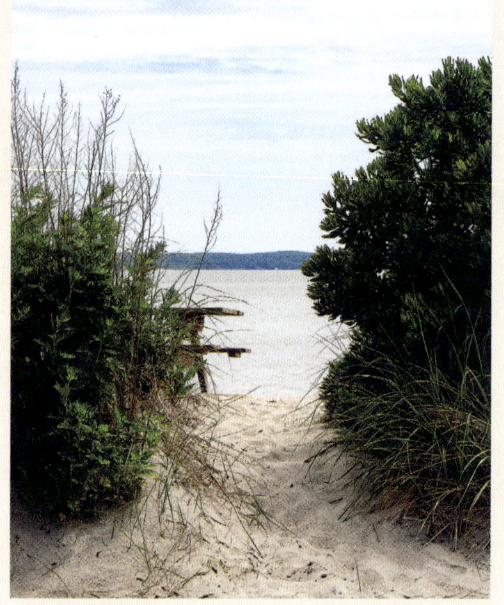

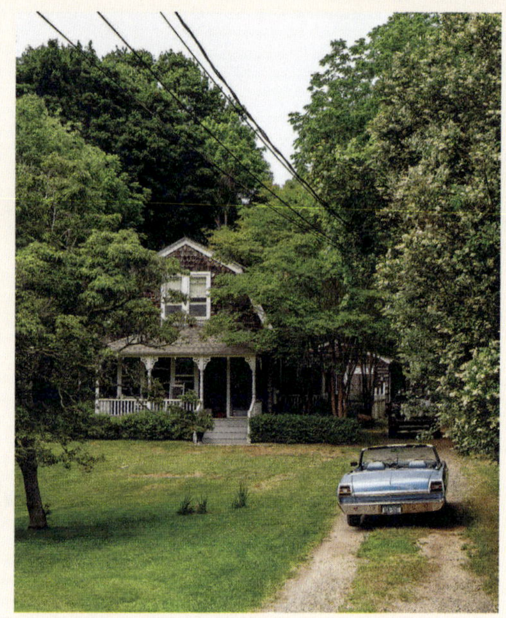

How Rebecca Blair ended up on Shelter Island, New York, was fate. Originally from a town called Canandaigua in the Finger Lakes region of Western New York, Rebecca was drawn to a more solo adventure and the New England charm of the North Fork of Long Island after college. While her friends were all renting homes together for the summer in the Hamptons, she chose a little guesthouse alone and made her way over to Shelter Island for dinner one evening. "Just getting on that ferry, there was something that I just couldn't get out of my system," recalled Rebecca. The following spring, she and a friend returned to Shelter Island to look at the rentals available in the local paper. They found a small cottage to rent for the long season, from May to October, for just $1,500 each for the entire term of their stay. Thirty-five years later, Rebecca is still as in love with the island as she was that first evening when she took the ferry over for dinner. Her partner, Watt Bishop, originally from the Mississippi Delta, is no stranger to remote areas steeping in long days and quiet nights. The island brings much solace to both Rebecca and Watt. The couple splits their time with another small town—Oxford, Mississippi—where Watt has lived for many years and where two of his children and grandchildren live.

LIFE AND WORK ON SHELTER ISLAND

Rebecca spent her early years on Shelter Island as a seasonal resident, bouncing from rentals and seasonal homes, until 2004 when she bought her house from a German photographer after instantly falling in love with the property. Primarily based in New York City, Rebecca has always seen her time on the island as a means to find a calm from the grind and hustle of a career in fashion in the city. Compared to her small studio apartment in New York City, the home on Shelter Island, while also smaller, allows her a little more space to spread out and highlight some of the creatives she's made a career out of supporting.

Rebecca spent many years in the fashion industry, working for brands such as Chanel, Prada, and Gucci. In 2013, she went out on her own and set up a consulting firm for brands just starting out and existing brands looking to improve their vision.

Currently, time is Rebecca's biggest luxury as she enjoys working with notable creatives, such as Alejandra Alonso Rojas and Gabriela Hurst, while also allowing for the flexibility to split her time between Shelter Island and Oxford. Spending time with Watt's children and grandchildren has been a priority for the couple, especially in the last few years after Watt broke his femur. Her experience working in fashion has left Rebecca with her own ideas percolating too. And with her own desire to be in one place as she ages, time will tell where the couple decides to put down more permanent roots. "I think I would be happy in Oxford [full-time], but I think the big miss for me would be nature. You know, just like what it is being around the water, the light on the island. It's just remarkable," shared Rebecca.

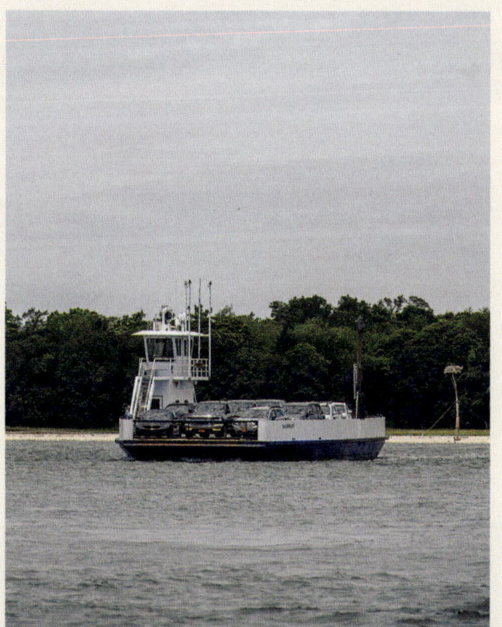

SMALL TOWN DYNAMICS AND TOURISM

The island is home to just over 2,000 people year-round, with the population ballooning to 8,000 in the summer months as people, mostly from New York City, look for a reprieve from the heat. This leaves the town with very seasonal amenities that include a few restaurants, a grocery store, a school, and two operating farms. One is Sylvester Manor, a working organic farm. The Historical Society hosts a weekly market every Saturday as well. "We love the off-season. We love it there in the spring, and I love it in the fall. September, October, and November are my favorite times on the island," shared Rebecca.

A shift on the island happened in 1997, when hotelier André Balazs opened Sunset Beach, a beautiful boutique hotel overlooking the water where a local scallop shack had been previously. People who typically only went to

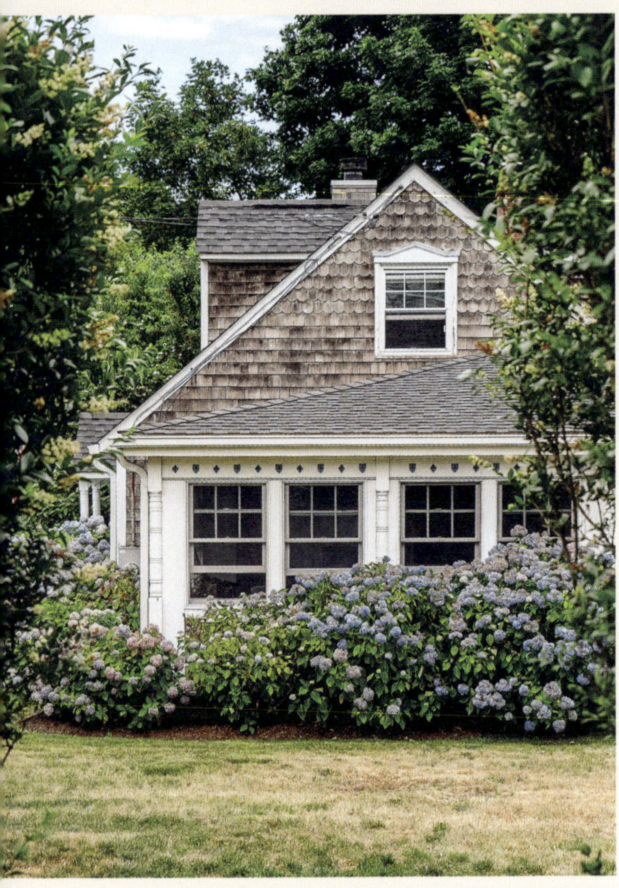

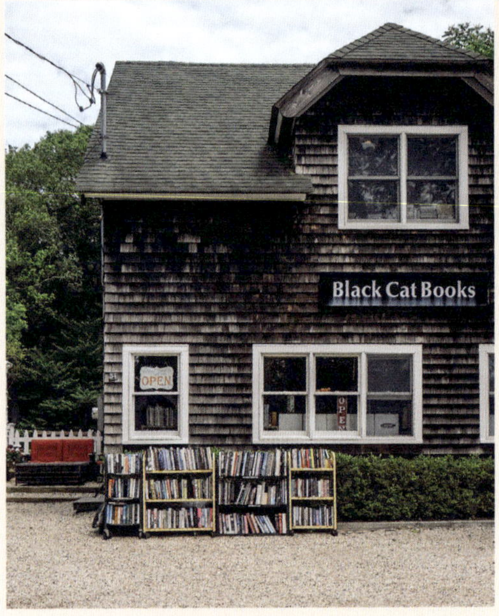

the Hamptons began to frequent Shelter Island. Around this time, property values soared, and what was once a more affordable, off-the-beaten-path location started to gain more traction with the summer people and European travelers. "I never get the sense that it's too crowded. The grocery store or farmers market might be busier, or if you plan to go to Sunset Beach, which I do enjoy, you just go during the week," said Rebecca. There are still ways to plan your days around the influx of summer traffic and tucked away are spots only the locals frequent.

As in many places in North America, housing is an issue on Shelter Island, but the fact that most of the land on the island is protected also means the preservation of the land and the nature surrounding the island. Due to stringent zoning laws, much of Shelter Island will never be developed, with nearly 8,000 acres of land and over 27.1 square miles of marsh. When discussing the internal struggles of the town, the push and pull from the locals and the tourists, Rebecca described, "There's a good rapport and appreciation [from the locals] of the fact that if these tourists didn't come here, the economy would be a completely different situation. The people who visit support the economy in such an important way, many of whom are small business owners. They wouldn't be able to thrive if we didn't have the tourist business, right?"

SHELTER ISLAND'S CHARM AND COMMUNITY

With its quiet calmness, the island has become an enclave for writers, creatives, and the like over the years. It's a place that gives your mind time to rest and focus without the distractions of a larger place. At night, when the lights are dim, you can hear nature come alive, grounding you to the island in a way you might not experience in other surrounding areas.

"It draws a lot of writers and artists; it's considered kind of like the un-Hamptons, even though you're right next door to the Hamptons," Rebecca noted. There has been some growth, and some larger homes have been approved for construction, but overall, the island still feels like a place from another era.

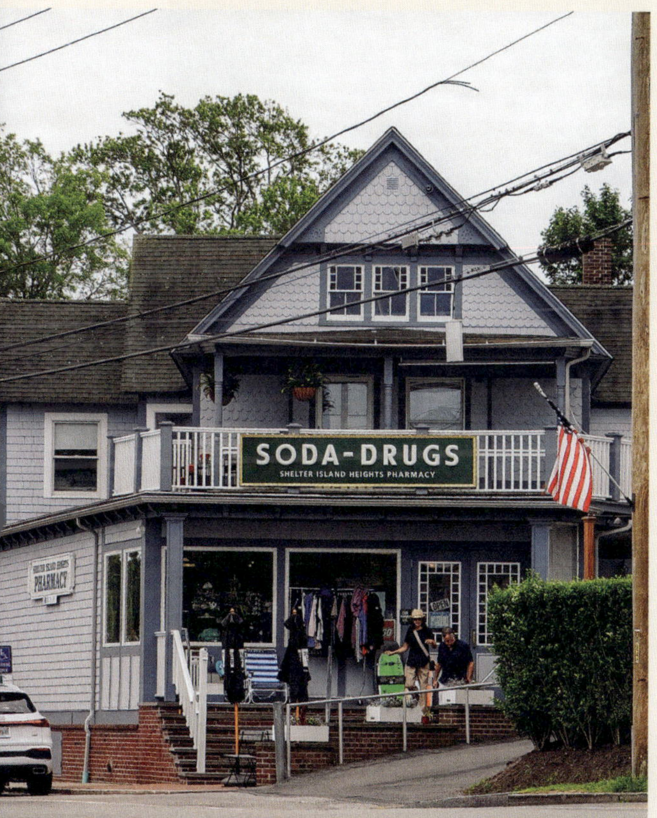

ENVIRONMENTAL EFFORTS ON THE ISLAND

The Nature Conservancy has a stronghold on Shelter Island with 2,350 acres protected and forever wild. With abundant trails and a beautiful nature preserve, the Mashomack Preserve makes for an incredible wonderland surrounded by water. As for the water itself, the Peconic Land Trust is working to protect the land and water across Long Island, including efforts to serve Shelter Island. They are also actively protecting the island's drinking water.

THE EFFECTS OF THE WATER

Because of where Shelter Island sits tucked into the Peconic Bay, the water is amazingly calm, almost like a lake. That calmness can add so much to a person's general creativity. For Rebecca, she finds herself in constant awe of the nature around her. "Getting outside of yourself and having a sense of peace, really looking around you, and being in awe of how beautiful life is and when you can connect with nature, that can be a big part of your life," shared Rebecca.

BUILDING A CREATIVE LIFE WITHIN THE PARAMETERS OF AN ISLAND

When you're living in a bigger city, it's just you and your interfacing, traveling and running from place to place, but for Rebecca and Watt, Shelter Island offers such a respite. "It's peaceful, and there's a lot of solitary, recharging time, which I love," shared Rebecca. "I have these secret places all over where you can walk and collect the most beautiful shells or have time to reflect. That's what Shelter Island represents to me. And I think the water does help connect you more with your intuition. If I lived in a hectic place, I don't think I'd be as connected."

Being in a small community like Shelter Island can be the biggest asset to the small business owner because commerce is only small business-minded and the island doesn't have chain stores and larger companies. Rebecca said, "In a small town, think about what you know, how you could contribute to the community, and add something your passion might be missing."

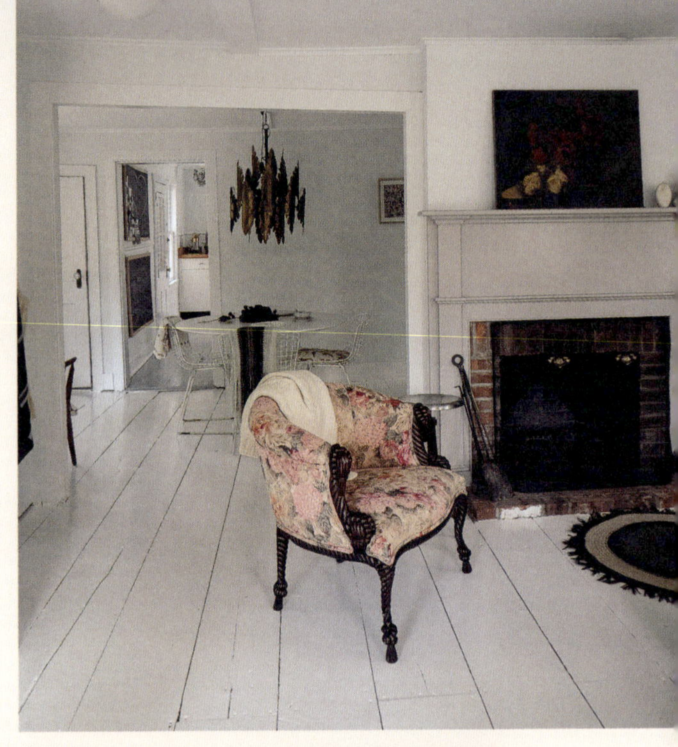

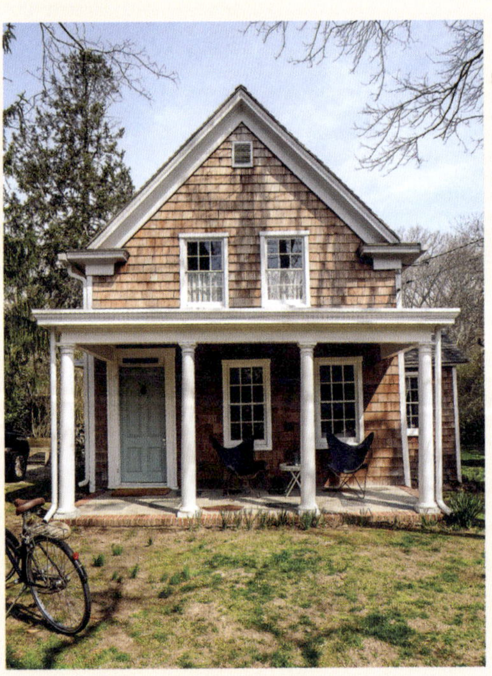

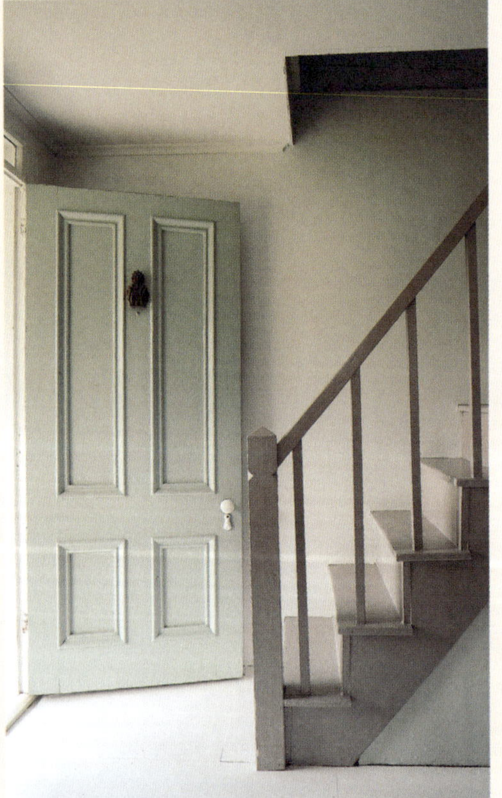

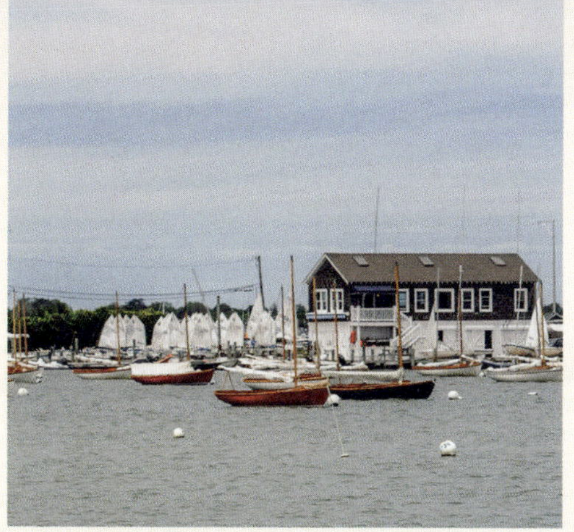

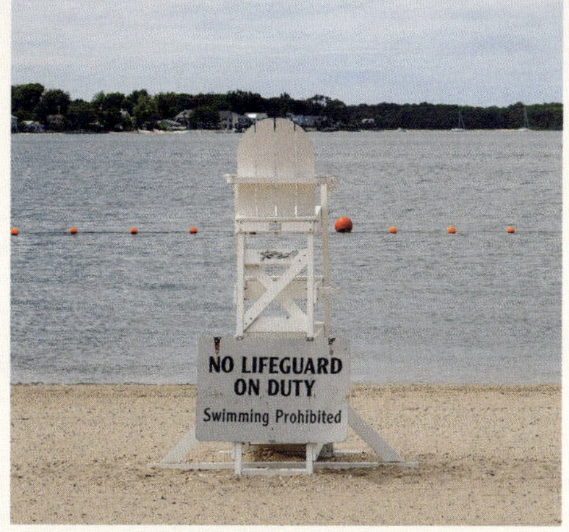

SHELTER ISLAND, NEW YORK

POPULATION: 3,292 full-time residents in 2024

TOWN SIZE: 27.1 square miles

CLOSEST INTERNATIONAL AIRPORTS: JFK International Airport (94.4 miles); New York LaGuardia Airport (95 miles); Bradley International Airport, Hartford, Connecticut (96.2 miles)

CLOSEST REGIONAL AIRPORT: Long Island MacArthur Airport (54.4 miles)

CLOSEST LARGE CITIES: New Haven, Connecticut (78.6 miles with a ferry); New York City (106 miles)

BONUS TOWNS NEARBY: Greenport, North Haven, Sag Harbor

BEST TIME TO WHALE-WATCH: June to mid-September to spot humpback whales

ISLAND FACTS: Before the name was changed to Shelter Island, it was called "Manhansack Aha Quash A Womak" by the first settlers, the Manhansets, which means "Island Sheltered by Islands." British troops stripped the island of its goods during the American Revolution. You can access the island from Greenport or North Haven using two different ferries. It's a wonderful place for bird-watching.

SEASONS: Shelter Island has four distinct seasons.

WATER ACTIVITIES: fishing, sunset cruises, paddleboarding, kayaking, swimming, canoeing, beach visits, boating, parasailing, surfing, kiteboarding, sailing, whale-watching

WATER SPOTS TO VISIT: Shelter Island Sound, Coecles Harbor, West Neck Harbor, Dickerson Creek, Menantic Creek, and Gardiners Bay

"I learned that as a surfer, if I really wanted to be good at it and learn to surf in my thirties, I needed to be able to go whenever I wanted because the waves are unpredictable."

—BROOKE ROSELL

BROOKE AND JERRY ROSELL

Surfer and Photographer; Entrepreneur and Fisherman

FRISCO, HATTERAS ISLAND, NORTH CAROLINA

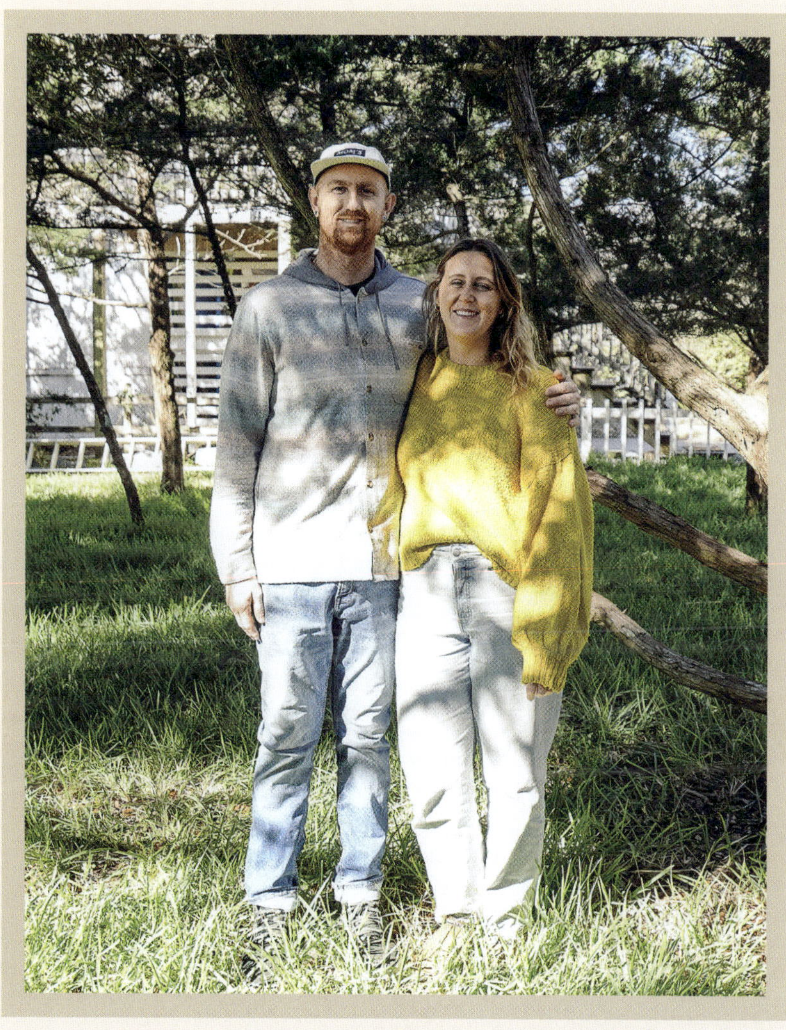

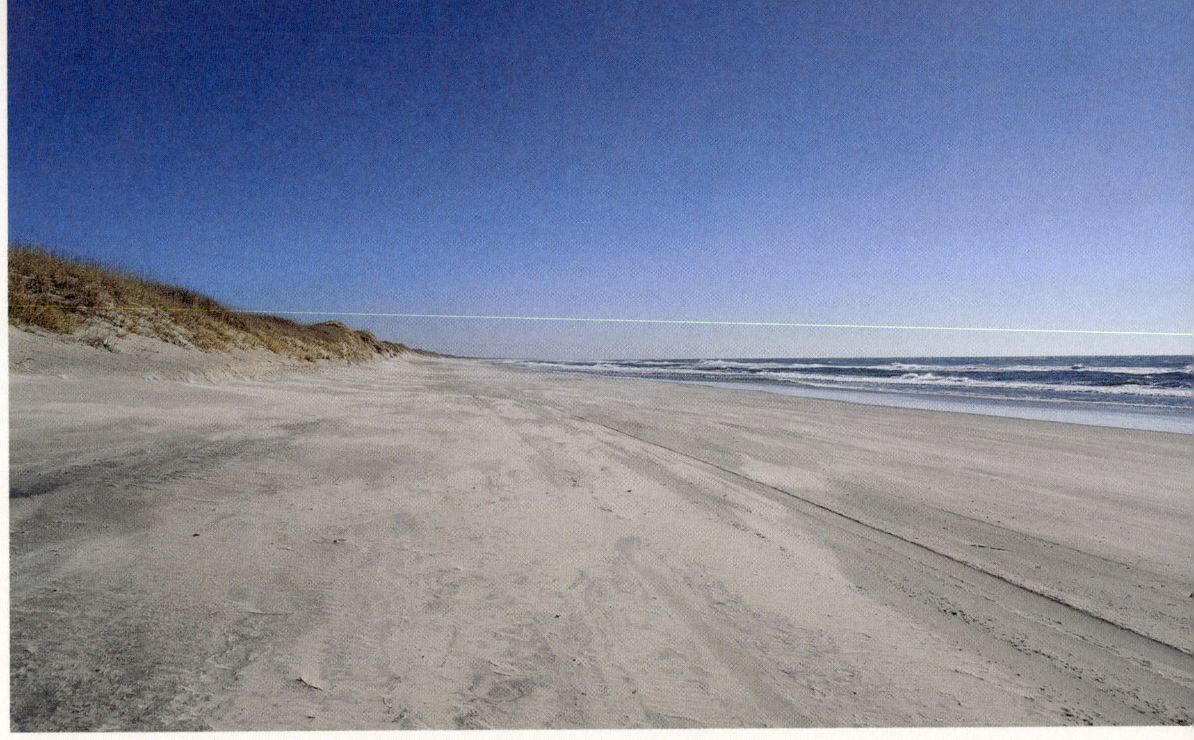

Brooke Rosell, originally from Farmville, North Carolina, studied abroad in Spain during college at Appalachian State before moving to Hatteras Island after college. What was supposed to be a temporary landing point while she figured out her next move turned into a life change, and now she can't envision herself anywhere else.

Brooke isn't a skateboarder but was drawn to Hatteras Island by the skate culture. The indoor skate park in town is a haven for teenagers, creating a safe place for them in the community. She saw moving to Hatteras as a fun way to spend the summer at the beach, working at the skate park. "I moved here in 2012, which was special for me. It was the first place postgrad that I really loved. And then I met Jerry, my husband. I knew him in college, but he was born and raised in Hatteras and volunteered at the skate park," shared Brooke. When the summer was up, she applied for different jobs, but the idea of leaving Hatteras gave her a pit in her stomach. Brooke decided to stick around into the fall and help Jerry coach middle school soccer. She didn't know a thing about soccer, but she knew she didn't want to leave the island. The two started dating shortly after the soccer season, and she's lived in the Outer Banks ever since.

CAREER SHIFT AND PERSONAL GROWTH

Brooke was never a planner; she wasn't sure what her next steps would be after college. She considered moving to Texas or going back to Spain. "I would still love to live abroad part of the year, but I knew I wasn't returning to the Greenville area. And I felt like my time in my college town had ended. Hatteras kind of presented itself to me when I needed it to," said Brooke.

Hatteras Island is a very seasonal place, with most of the residents working hard for three months of the year followed by nine months when it's slow and quiet. Moving to Hatteras as an outsider differed from other places Brooke had lived. Brooke, who studied Spanish, public relations, and photography in school, bounced from job to job in her first year in town—a sandwich shop and the hardware store—just trying to figure out what she wanted to be doing. Then she got her teaching license and taught middle school Spanish for several years.

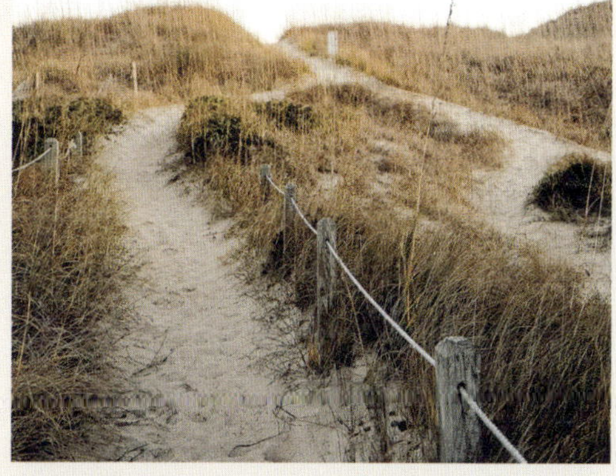

"I loved teaching in a small town. I wouldn't have loved teaching the same way in a bigger city. The school here is amazing because it is such a small town; everything revolves around the school, sports, and community. I feel like when I stepped into a classroom, that's when Hatteras became my home," said Brooke. She got to know the children, and they got to know her. Through her teaching career, Brooke became a greater part of the community and started to make friends.

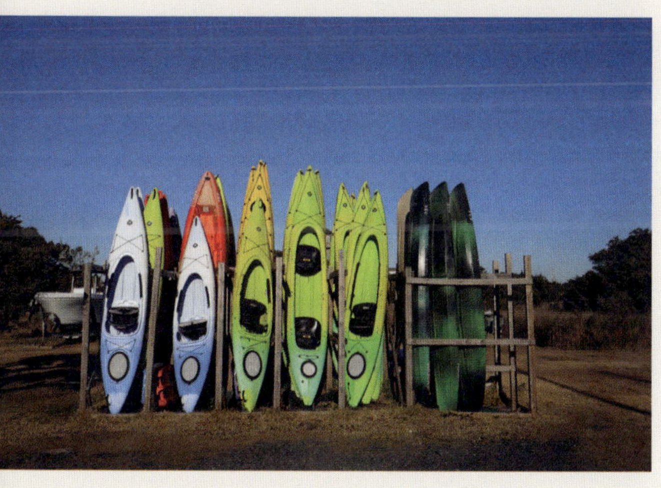

In 2020, when she began teaching remotely as a residual from the COVID pandemic, Brooke saw it as an opportunity to do something for herself when she wasn't teaching. She took up surfing, which has a strong culture on the Outer Banks. "I learned that as a surfer if I really wanted to be good at it and learn to surf in my thirties, I needed to be able to go whenever I wanted because the waves are unpredictable," shared Brooke. She

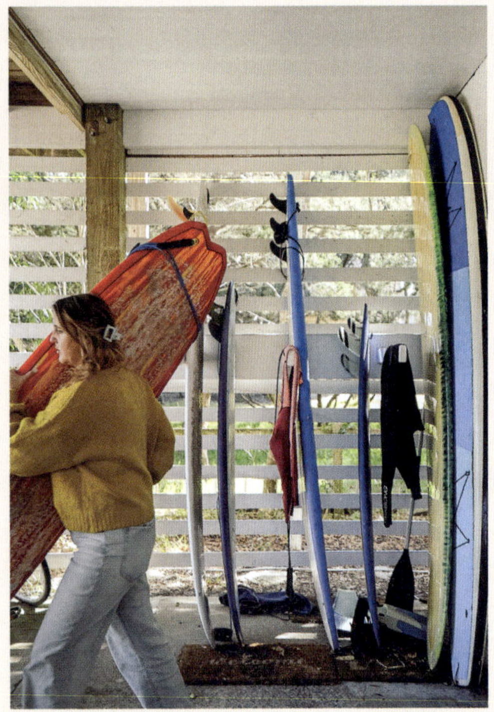

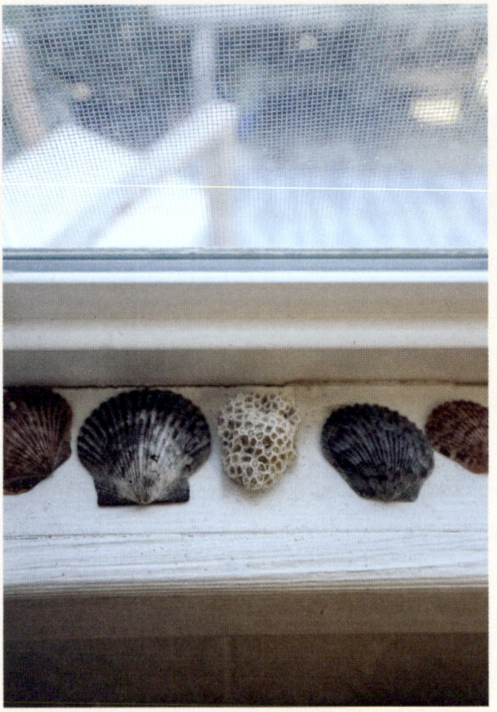

WHAT TO EXPECT WHEN MOVING TO A SMALL TOWN

Level your expectations. Not every town is going to have the amenities you are used to.

Be okay with making your own fun.

Learn to live with less.

Think of places like coffee shops or cute shops as a treat, not something you must have.

Slow and steady. You don't need to talk about what the town doesn't have. Focus on what drew you in to begin with, and if you need to work on growing the town, slow growth is best.

took the downtime on the island as a sign and went where she could surf every day, where the weather wouldn't be an issue, and she could still teach her classes. Brooke and Jerry moved down to Costa Rica for a bit so Brooke could train. It was a life-changing trip for Brooke because it clarified what she wanted to be doing with her life. She had lost her mom early in 2020, and throwing herself into doing what she loved became her way to make the most of life.

In the summer of 2021, Brooke decided to resign from teaching and fall back on an art she had been doing for many years: photography. Working for herself gave her the much-needed time to continue surfing and the added luxury to veer into photographing the female surfers of Hatteras Island and beyond, along with offering marketing and storytelling for local businesses. She's been back to Costa Rica to shoot for several surf retreats and plans to continue folding that into her story. Hatteras is so quiet for part of the year that having the flexibility to get out and explore new places, make new connections, and surf has been vital for Brooke's wanderlust.

ECOTOURISM AND ENVIRONMENTAL CONCERNS

Hatteras Island has had some help in preserving its town, island, and region for many years to come after much-needed restoration and support from the National Park Service, which

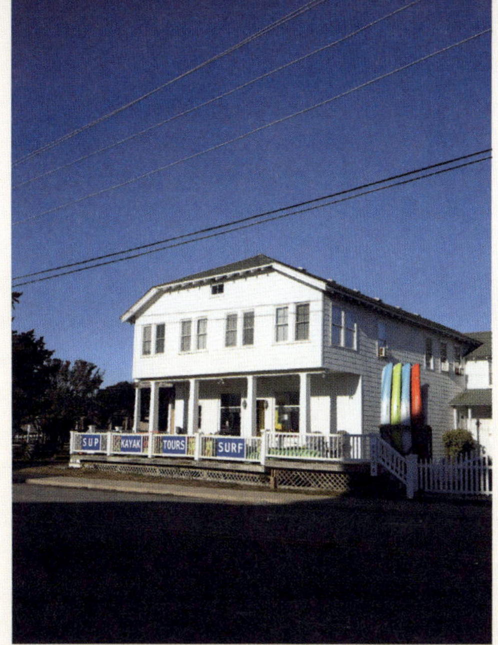

created the Cape Hatteras National Seashore. It was authorized by Congress in 1937 but wasn't established until 1953. Many threatened and endangered animals have found refuge through the protection of the land on the barrier islands of Hatteras, Bodie, and Ocracoke. Because it's a national seashore, it also protects the town's size and limits unwanted growth.

Without protection, it's not just the shorebirds and sea turtles who would suffer. Due to erosion, homes have fallen into the ocean, crumbling into the water. If not for the park service, there would likely be more destruction and unlivable conditions. "I want people to have a nonpolitical conversation about what we're going to do about our island floating away," said Brooke. "And I wish they would have these conversations with people who know how barrier islands work. But a lot of litigation is happening in D.C. offices from people who aren't aware of our community."

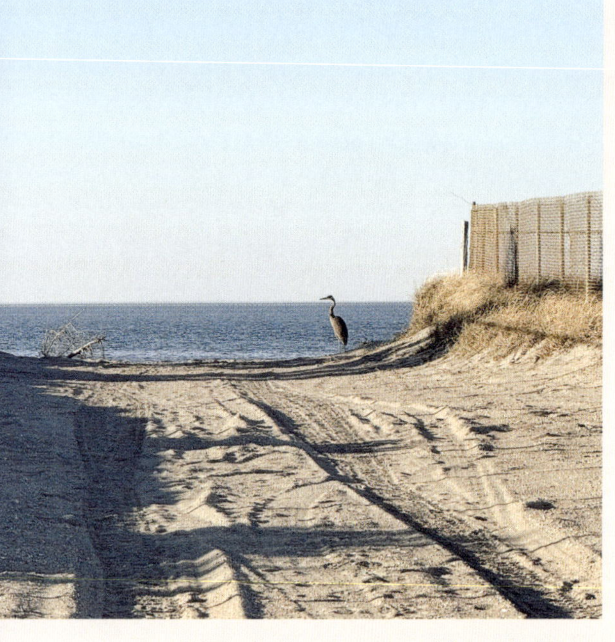

With the hurricanes and low winds that come through the area and the possibility of the main road in and out of the island getting washed away, Brooke has refined her abilities to read wind charts and the weather radar. Being in a small town where the closest channel reporting on the weather in Hatteras is in Virginia Beach, three hours away and with a very different climate and conditions at any given time, it's common for Hatteras to manage on its own. Although becoming a weather expert is not something you always think about when you are considering a move to a small town, "I have to look at the information and interpret it myself because we are not a part of everyone's weather prediction," confirmed Brooke.

SMALL TOWN DYNAMICS AND THE FUTURE OF HATTERAS ISLAND

"Locals get passionate talking about tourists and new people to town. There are people whose families shipwrecked here and have been here for generations," shared Brooke when discussing the generations some families go back on the island. Still untouched, Hatteras could keep under the radar. The tourist season is so short, so big-box stores can't thrive there. Remote islands are hard to get to, so most tourists don't make it as far out as Hatteras and many people don't leave. Being an island, there's no new land to develop, so it can remain very similar to what it's looked like for many, many years.

It's an even split regarding community for Brooke on Hatteras. She craves a community of other like-minded, thirtysomething self-employed women with whom she can share, but she also loves her community, which lacks some of what she seeks. She loves running into former students in different parts of her day. "That's beautiful and fulfilling. It's just so personable. I love being able to go to the store and talk to people. You know, not be a stranger in the town where I live," shared Brooke.

What the next twenty years will look like on the island depends on the continued activism of the townspeople and on having people in office who care about the community, too.

HATTERAS ISLAND, NORTH CAROLINA

POPULATION: 4,000 full-time residents in 2024 on Hatteras; 659 residents in Frisco, within the island

TOWN SIZE: 33 square miles

CLOSEST INTERNATIONAL AIRPORT: Norfolk International Airport, Virginia (140 miles)

CLOSEST REGIONAL AIRPORT: Coastal Carolina Regional Airport, New Bern (190 miles)

CLOSEST LARGE CITIES: Chesapeake, Virginia (130 miles); Norfolk, Virginia (134 miles); Virginia Beach, Virginia (148 miles)

BONUS TOWNS NEARBY: Avon, Roanoke Island, Kitty Hawk, Ocracoke Island (by ferry)

ANIMALS TO SPOT: sea turtles, marsh rabbits, many species of birds throughout the year

TOWN FACTS: There have been over 3,000 shipwrecks off the coast of Hatteras Island. Hatteras is part of the first national seashore in the country. All the beach access is public land. Five different types of sea turtles nest on Outer Banks beaches. Over 250 species of birds pass through Cape Hatteras National Seashore throughout the year. The elevation of Frisco is 3 feet.

SEASONS: Hatteras Island has four seasons.

WATER ACTIVITIES: surfing, paddleboarding, sea kayaking, beachcombing, kitesurfing, windsurfing, boating, sailing, parasailing, Jet-Skiing, fishing

WATER SPOTS TO VISIT: Hatteras Bight and Pamlico Sound

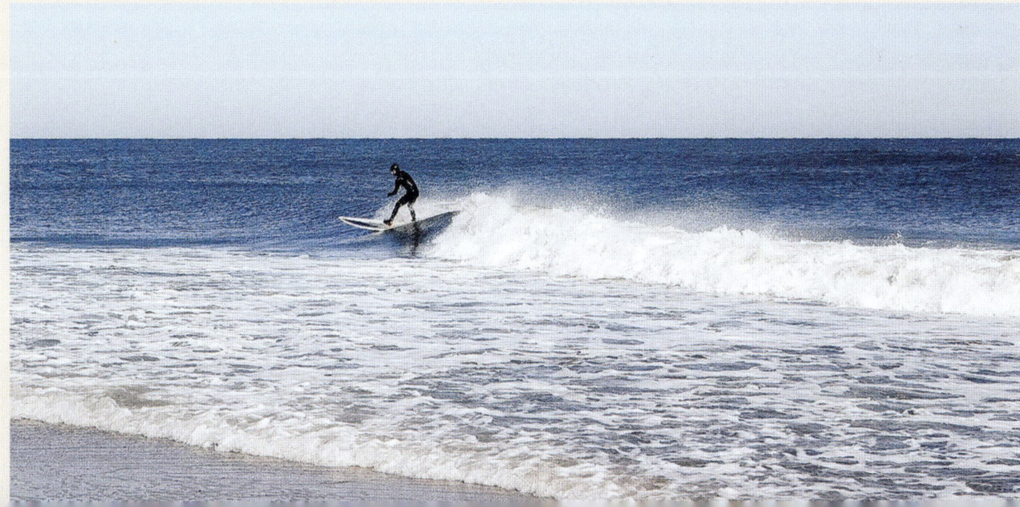

"The environment keeps me feeling creative. I can chill and focus on the project [I'm working on]. I put my headphones on and play music, but I look outside. It's calm, even when it's raining or snowing. It's so cool to be here."

—SHOGO OTA

SHOGO OTA

Artist

CAMANO ISLAND, WASHINGTON
(PRONOUNCED CA-MAY-NO)

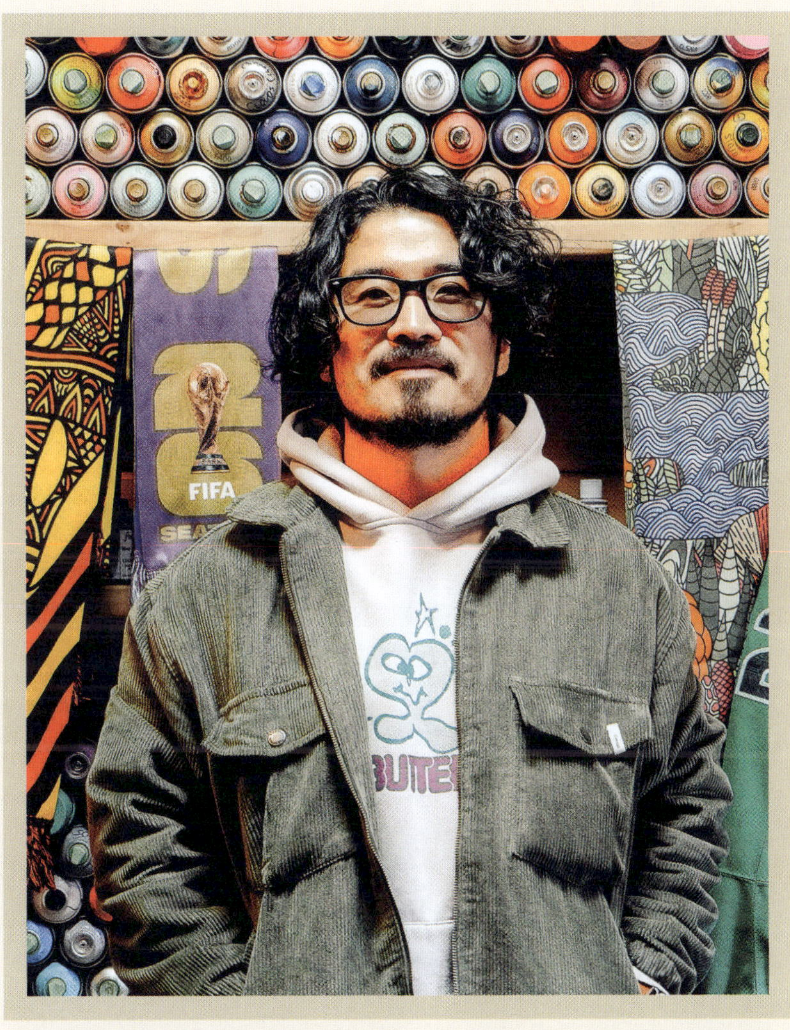

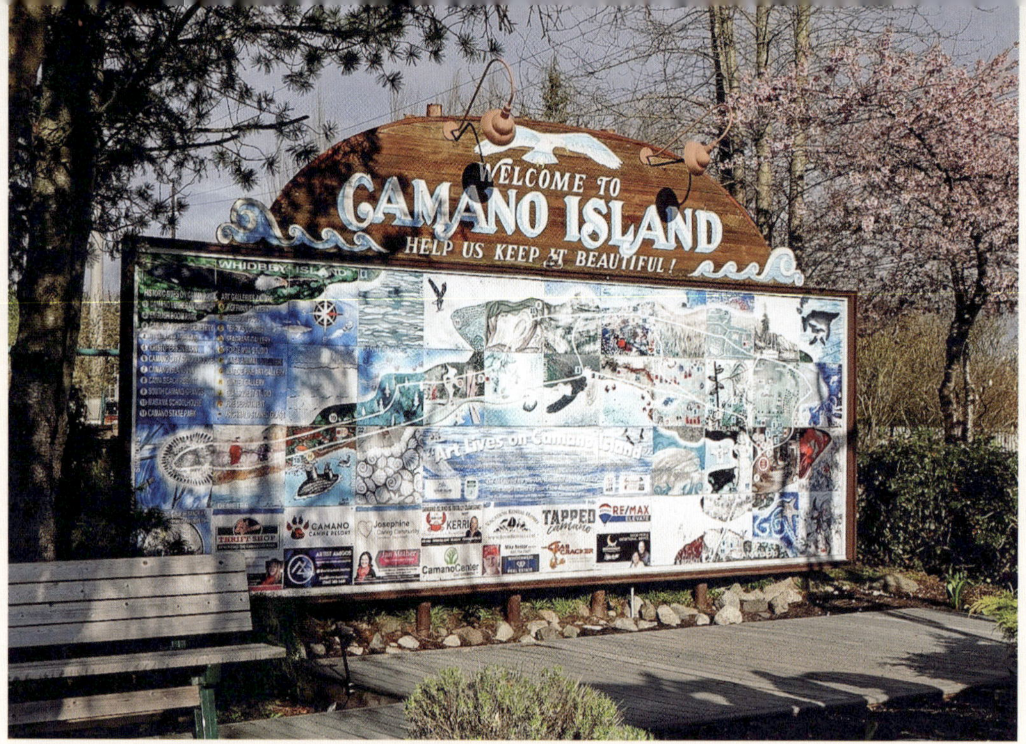

With the rising costs of the Seattle housing market and the growing Ota family, Shogo and his wife Taurean recalled the cute area they visited on Camano Island for a wedding a few years earlier. Seeking more space, an in-home studio for Shogo's art career, a slower pace to raise their three children, and an easy commute to the city, they began looking to move to the island. After touring multiple homes, they returned to the first one they visited: a modified 1974 A-frame, meaning it has a flat top rather than the usual pointy one. "This cool, old, funky house sort of backs up my art career. It's not brand-new or anything, which is how we like it," shared Shogo.

Early into their residence on a day trip to the beach, the couple made a new friend who had taken over his dad's construction business. With this friend's help, Shogo and Taurean have remodeled their bathroom, replaced the roof, put in the septic and French drains, and built a deck. When the handy friend is too busy, he's kind enough to let Shogo use his tools to independently create or fix things the home needs.

Unlike many islands in Washington state, Camano Island has no ferry system. The one main road through the island connects it to the mainland via a bridge to another small town, Stanwood, so Shogo doesn't have to plan around ferry schedules to get to meetings or evening art events. So much of their lives are still connected to Seattle, which made accessibility to land off the island essential.

BRINGING YOUR PASSION TO YOUR SMALL TOWN

Shogo saw a need to grow the creative community on his island. Funding for the arts is so often slashed in schools, so with the hopes that his three children wouldn't lack exposure to art, Shogo joined the grassroots efforts of SCAAC (Stanwood Camano Arts Advocacy Commission) to help generate art events and after-school classes for children on the island and in Stanwood. Through SCAAC, Shogo has been involved in block parties, children's painting classes, live art events, and more. He has also teamed up with his children's school to come in as a visiting artist and engage the children in a group art project.

Camano is known for the artists who reside there, making it a natural transition for Shogo. The artists on the island open their doors each summer and host a studio art tour. You can follow a map to visit each location and see how the artists operate from home to create their work.

Shogo's advice for someone moving to a small town wondering how to integrate their creativity into the community is to try out your ideas. He gave the example of an art show he wanted to do: He wasn't sure if people would come, but he did it anyway. And now, community members often ask him to continue doing it and look forward to the next one. That seemingly small event has led to mural and logo work. "You never know what it will lead to," Shogo shared. The beauty of living in a small town is that you can take more risks and create the cool things you want to see in your community.

HOW THE QUIETNESS OF A SMALL TOWN CAN INSPIRE A CREATIVE LIFE

When asked what inspired him to create on Camano Island—whether it is that the place

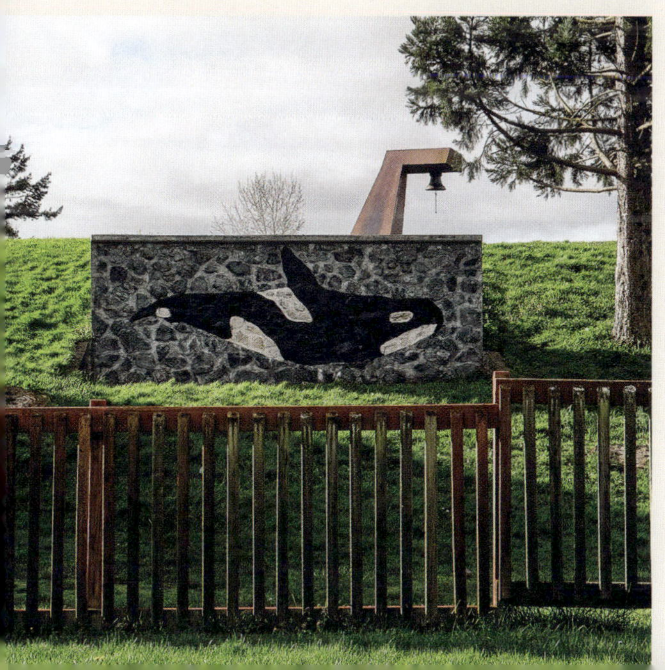

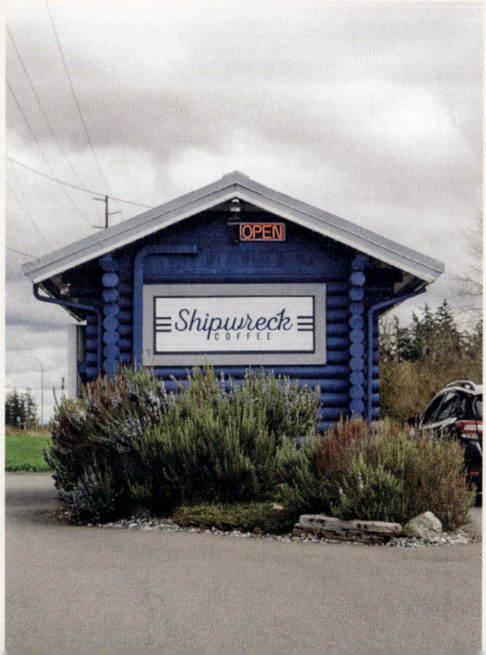

reminds him of his small community in Japan, the water that surrounds him, or the quietness and stillness of the place that was the most inspiring—Shogo reflected on the last reason. "When I lived in West Seattle, I would walk or bike to Alki Beach to get inspired or empty my mind and think of new ideas or projects," shared Shogo.

When talking about the nature he can see from his in-home lofted studio, Shogo shared the story of an owl family who returns to this view regularly. He can see them flying by from his window, and now his children are on the lookout for the family of four that return to the Ota yard each year.

"The environment keeps me feeling creative. I can chill and focus on the project [I'm working on]. I put my headphones on and play music, but I look outside. It's calm, even when it's raining or snowing. It's so cool to be here," said Shogo.

REFLECTING ON A CHILDHOOD SPENT BY THE WATER

Growing up in rural Japan, in Gujo in Gifu Prefecture along the Nagara River, Shogo reflected on warm summers before the family got air-conditioning spent with friends swimming in the river, pausing only to eat ice cream, and then jumping back into the water. He and his wife now share that mindset in raising their three children, who know nothing but a life surrounded by water with Skagit Bay to the north and Port Susan to the south within the Whidbey Basin portion of Puget Sound. Shogo shared that being near the water now and raising his own three children makes him nostalgic at times. "Camano is safe and calm, and it's cool that we can go to the beach and just hang out and be together," said Shogo, thinking back on the simple childhood he had in Japan, riding bikes with friends, gone from home all day in the summer, out exploring.

LIVING ON A RURAL ISLAND

When we talk about living in a small town, with it comes looking to other places to find goods and services not readily available in our own communities. You might need to head to the city for certain groceries or one town over to get to the drugstore. We must consider these things when thinking about where we might call home. Imagine a world without relying on the internet to bring you things as quickly.

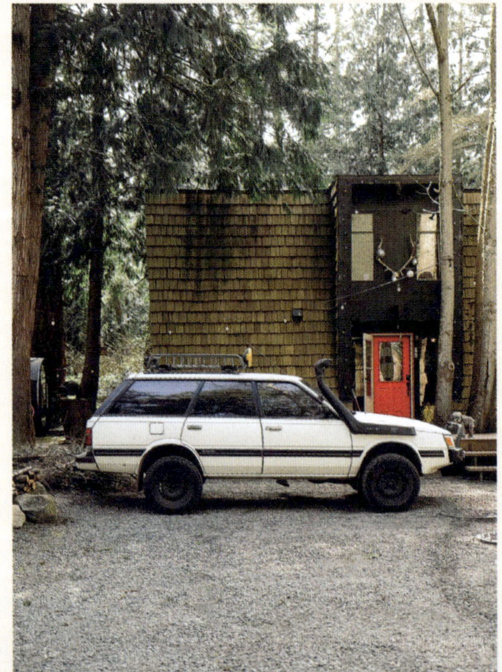

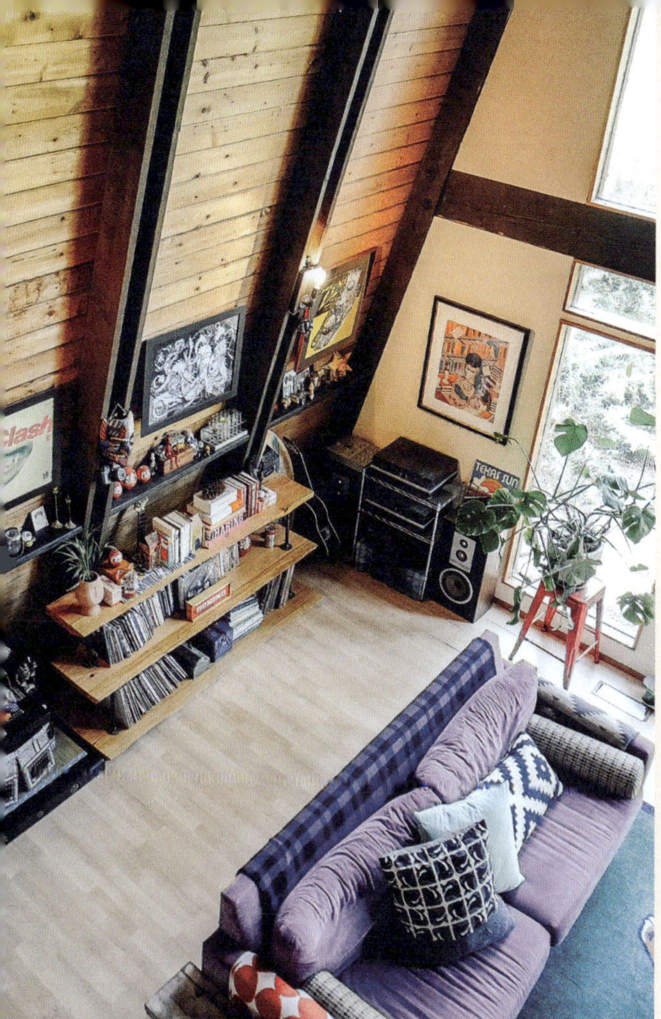

Think about how you can support your local communities for your everyday needs. Maybe it's only shopping for local, in-season vegetables from the town farmers market or farm stand or setting up visits to your rural health clinic, making the local doctor your primary care provider, or leaving specialized doctor's visits for the closest city if your town doesn't have one. Support the local feedstore for pet supplies. If they don't carry the brand you are used to, it doesn't hurt to ask them to pick up the one you like.

WHEN DECIDING TO MOVE TO A SMALL TOWN CONSIDER HOW FAR YOU WILL HAVE TO GO FOR:

- Airports
- Car repairs
- Doctors/emergency care
- Gas
- Groceries
- Pet supplies
- Restaurants
- Recycling
- Schools
- Work supplies and meetings

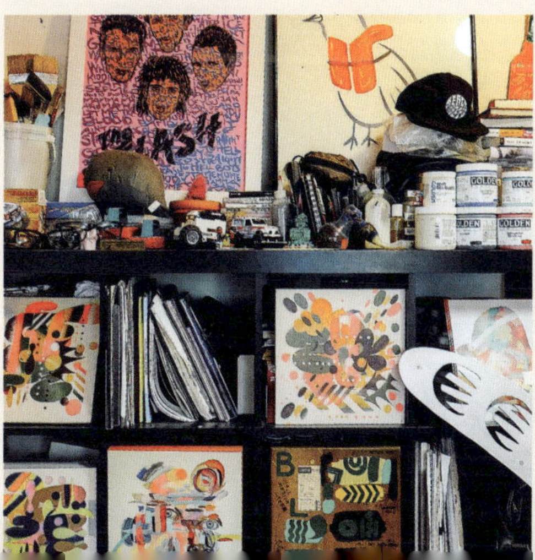

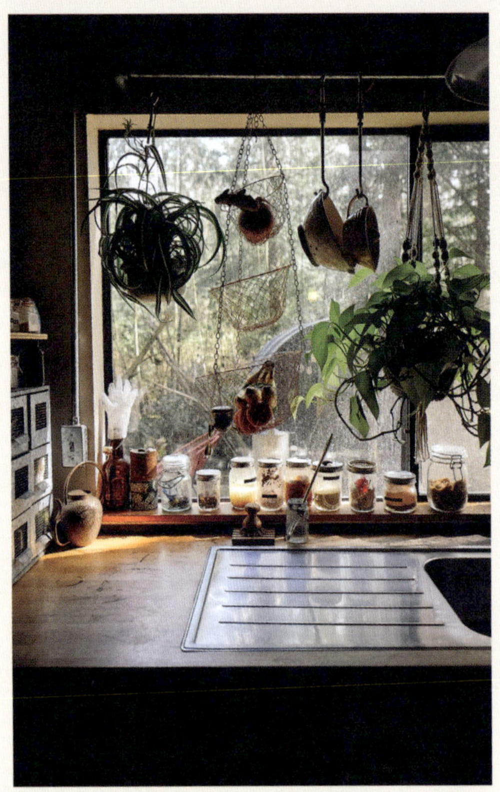

ADAPTING TO A NEW LIFESTYLE

When Shogo and Taurean moved to the island from Seattle, there was an adjustment period for scheduling work and family. With an hour-long commute added to the mix, what had been an evening out with a new client, running to the local art supply store on a whim, or stopping into their favorite Japanese grocery now needed to be planned far in advance, correlating with family needs and drive time. Making it all work isn't always the easiest. Shogo shared that the most challenging part about living on an island is when Seattle clients need to meet in person. "Meeting clients in person is more dynamic and we can discuss details a bit more, but there's just more scheduling involved when you live on an island," shared Shogo, adding, "I still love going to Seattle to check out food, music, and the culture." Seattle is just an hour away, and living on a small town island with close proximity to a large city is blending the best of both worlds.

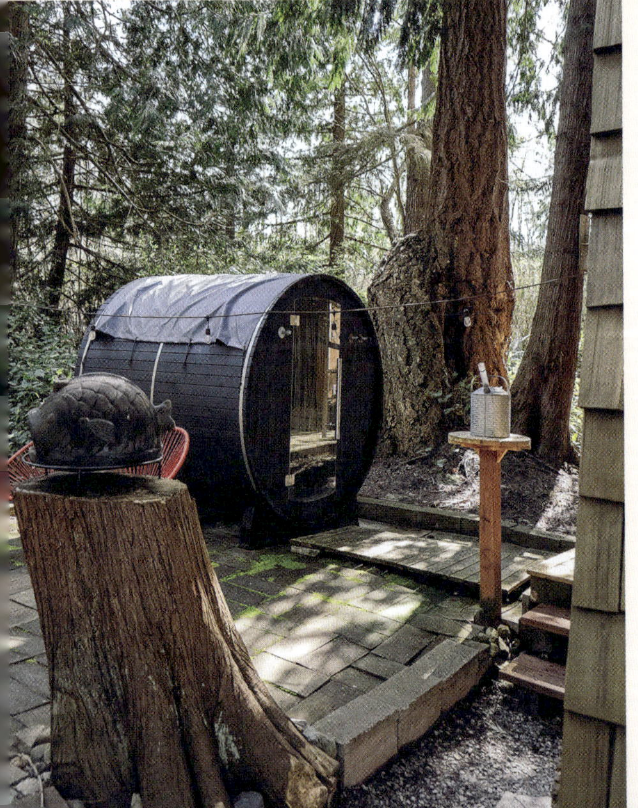

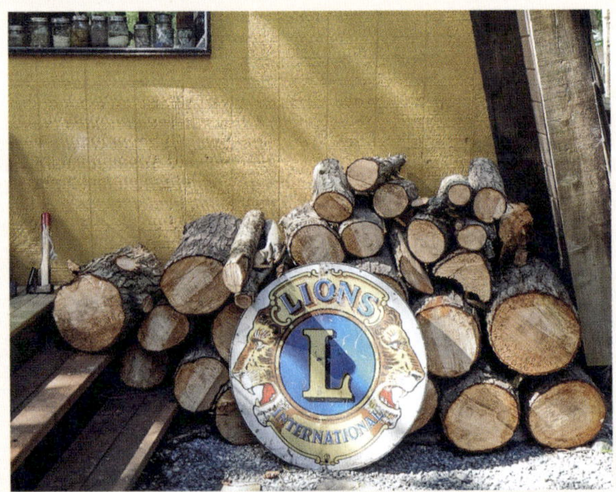

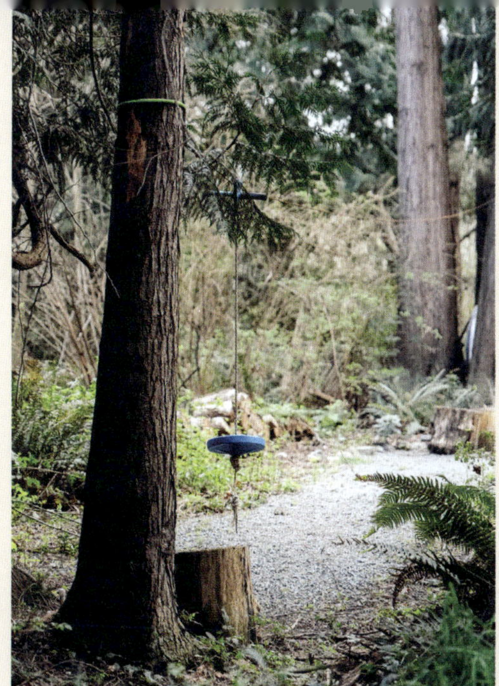

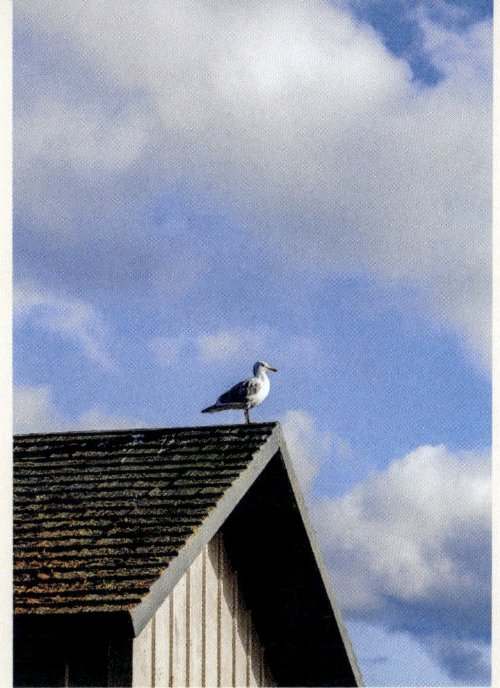

CAMANO ISLAND, WASHINGTON

POPULATION: 17,642 full-time residents in 2024

TOWN SIZE: 39.8 square miles

CLOSEST INTERNATIONAL AIRPORT: Sea-Tac International Airport (76.3 miles)

CLOSEST REGIONAL AIRPORTS: Arlington Municipal Airport (23.8 miles), Paine Field (42.3 miles)

CLOSEST LARGE CITY: Seattle (62.2 miles)

BONUS TOWNS NEARBY: Stanwood, Mt. Vernon

BEST TIME TO WHALE-WATCH: March through May and October through December

TOWN FACTS: Camano Island is home to two state parks where you can camp. Camano Island is one of the largest islands in Washington state.

SEASONS: Camano Island has two seasons: summer and winter.

WATER ACTIVITIES: crabbing, fishing, clamming, kayaking, paddleboarding, sailing, beachcombing, whale-watching, boating, sailing

WATER SPOTS TO VISIT: Skagit Bay, Port Susan, Whidbey Basin, and Puget Sound

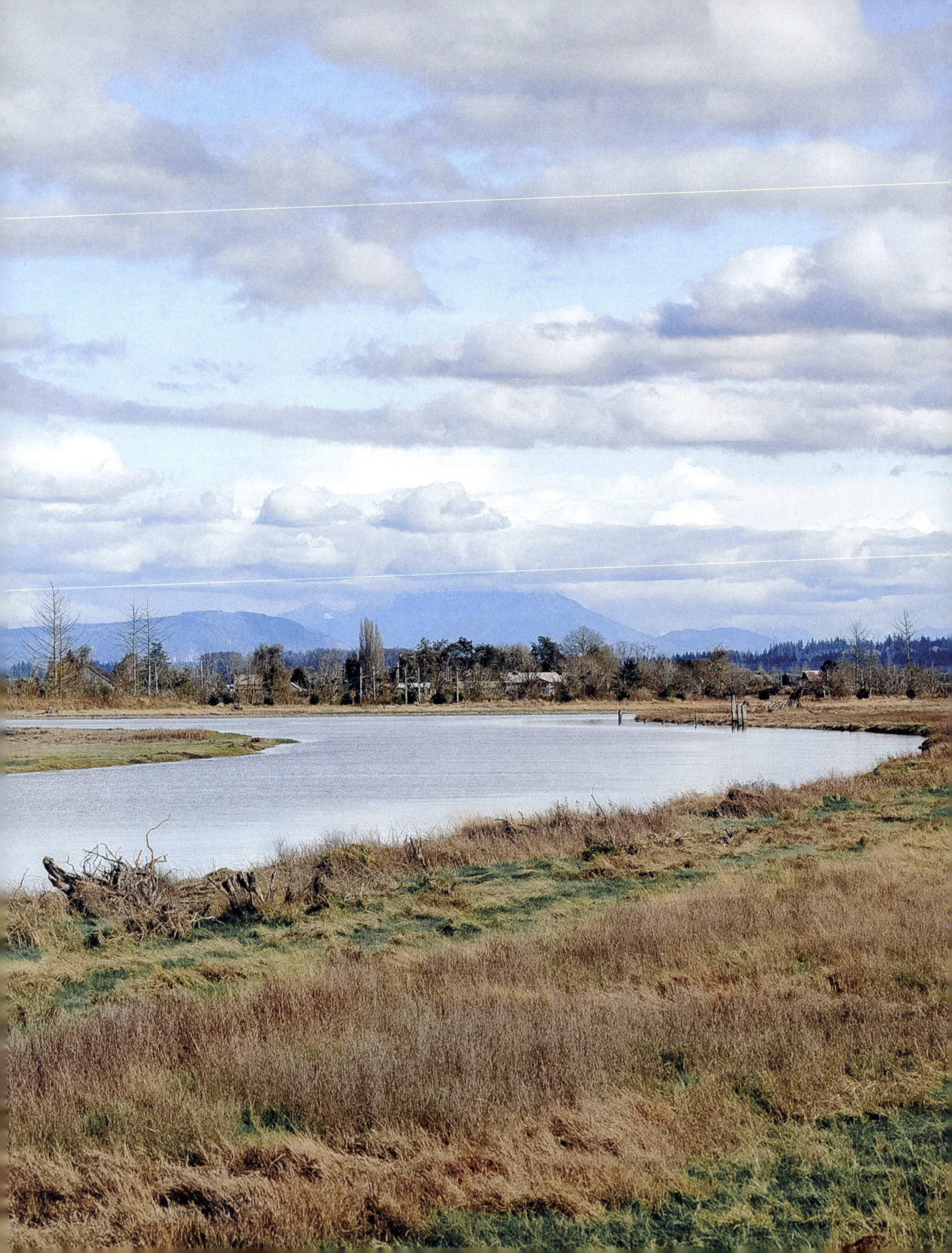

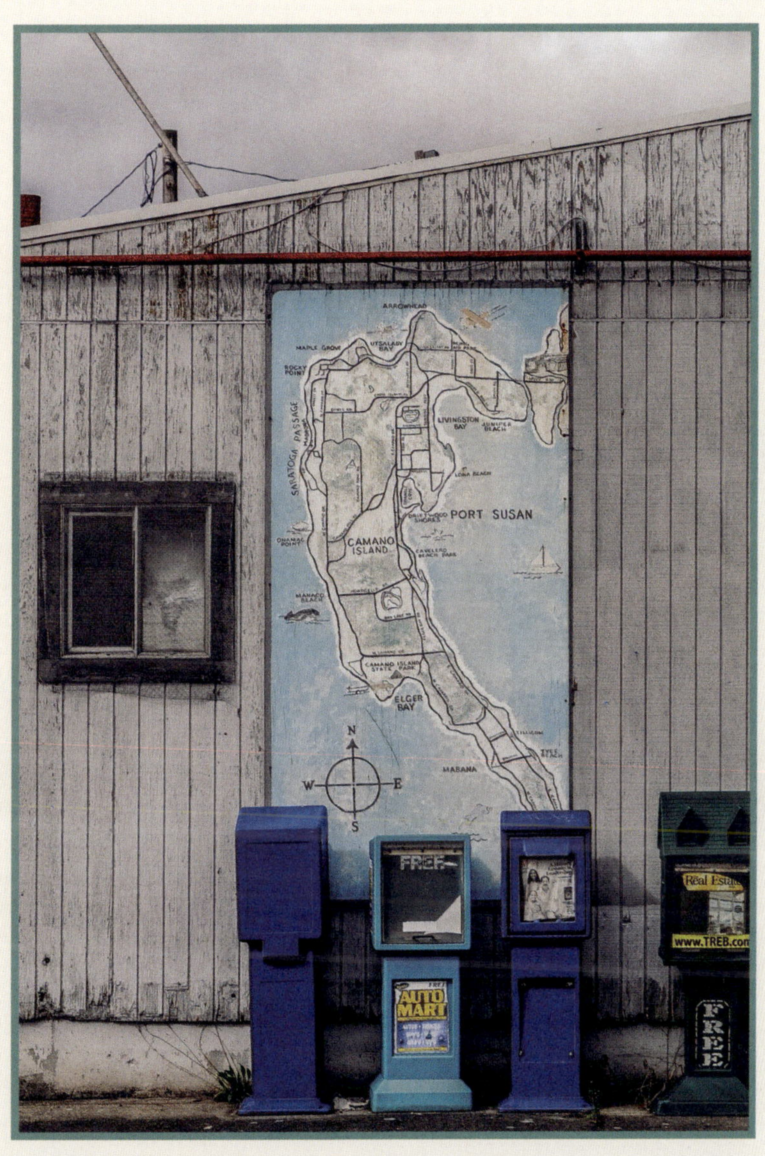

ARROWHEAD
MAPLE GROVE
UTSALADY BAY
ROCKY POINT
SARATOGA PASSAGE
LIVINGSTON BAY
JUNIPER BEACH
LONA BEACH
PORT SUSAN
DRIFTWOOD SHORES
CAMANO ISLAND
CAMANO ISLAND STATE PARK
ELGER BAY
MABANA
N
W
E
S
AUTO MART
FREE

"An important part is remembering that you're called to move to a space for certain reasons. Take the time to slow down and find the system that replaces what you've missed instead of trying to change something; remember, you moved there because it was going to be slower. You need to embrace the town and embrace the system."

—KYLE WATERMAN

KYLE WATERMAN

Nonprofit Fundraiser for Nonprofits and Shop Owner at Princess & Buck

GREENBANK, WHIDBEY ISLAND, WASHINGTON

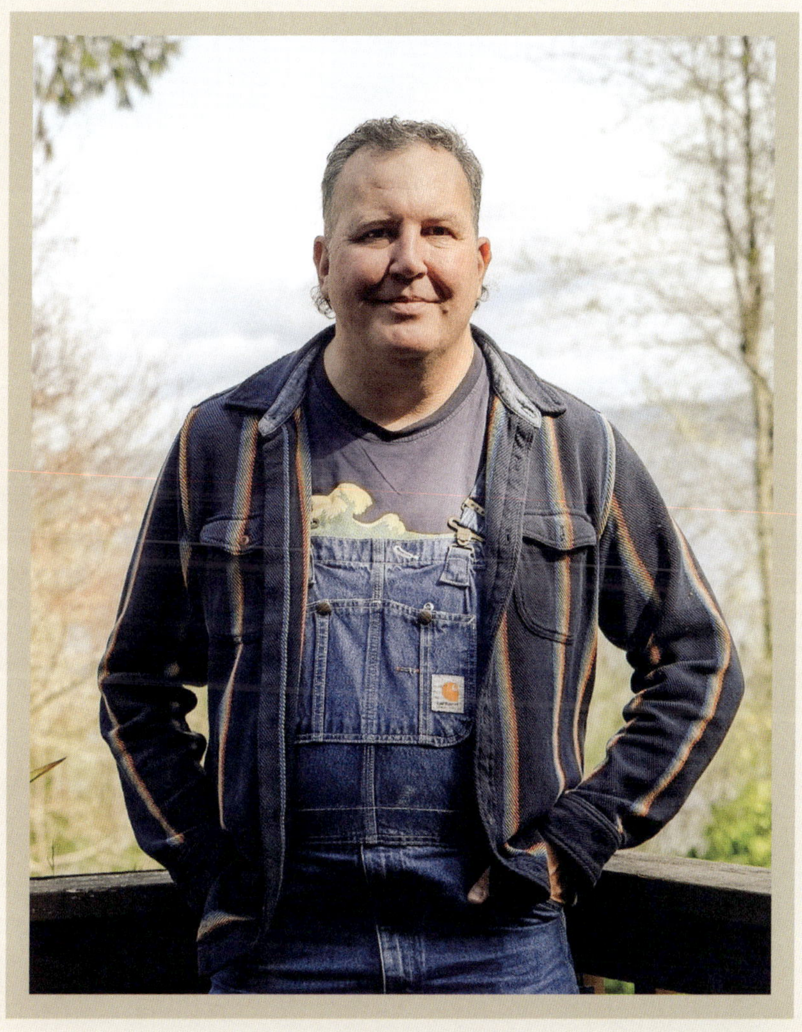

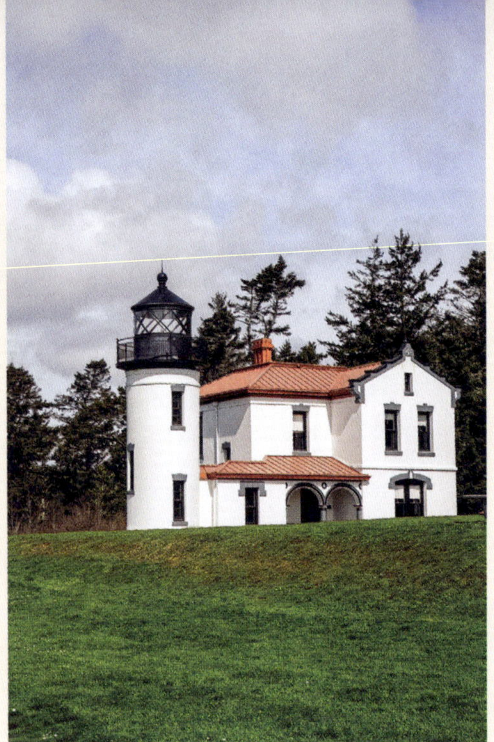

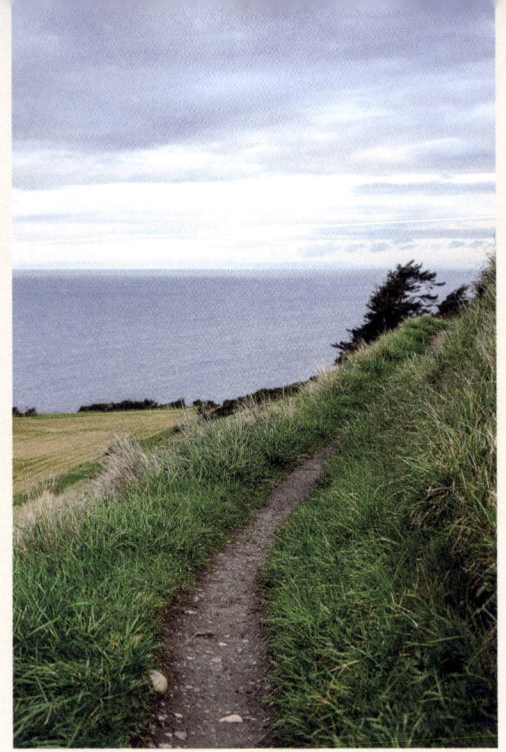

Kyle Waterman has been on island time for the last ten years. Growing up in Montana, he felt the need to push past the town limits and get out and explore. College took him to Evergreen College in Olympia, Washington. From there, he went east to New York and then started the slow move back west with a few years in Chicago.

Kyle met his husband Steve in 2007. At the time, Kyle was still living in Chicago and the long-distance relationship had them splitting time between the Midwest and Seattle. Tired of the back-and-forth travel and different time zones, Kyle returned to the Pacific Northwest, this time to Bellingham, before the couple moved full-time to Whidbey Island and the small, unincorporated area of Greenbank, Washington.

NAVIGATING SMALL TOWN LIFE AND COMMUNITY DYNAMICS

Living in a small town, you are constantly navigating community dynamics, and how you approach encounters with those around you differs in many ways than in a city. This includes dinner parties, town events, church, etc. You know your neighbors when you live in a small town, and in knowing your neighbors, you might not always see eye to eye with them. How we navigate small town communities differs significantly from how we navigate when we live in a city. "There's a luxury in the city because you are around so many different people; it doesn't really matter if you don't get along with someone. You can be anonymous in a lot of ways," shared Kyle. You might also connect with someone in a small town you might not otherwise know because of the proximity to other people. Your neighbor might be your best friend because no one is around for miles. Not wanting to destabilize that relationship becomes your top priority, and you begin to tiptoe around specific subjects or stay on the surface so as not to offend. It can be tricky if you are new to town and don't understand the dynamics of your small town yet. How do you share enough of yourself, retaining your authenticity, while also making sure you don't end up in a friendship that doesn't align with your core beliefs?

Get involved with organizations that do align with your beliefs. "My mom always taught me to volunteer or go to church, and you'll meet anybody," shared Kyle. If you like to hike, find your hiking friends. If you are interested in books, join a book club. If something doesn't exist already in your town, don't be afraid to start it. Even if you can't agree on everything, you will find people who share the same love as you on specific topics.

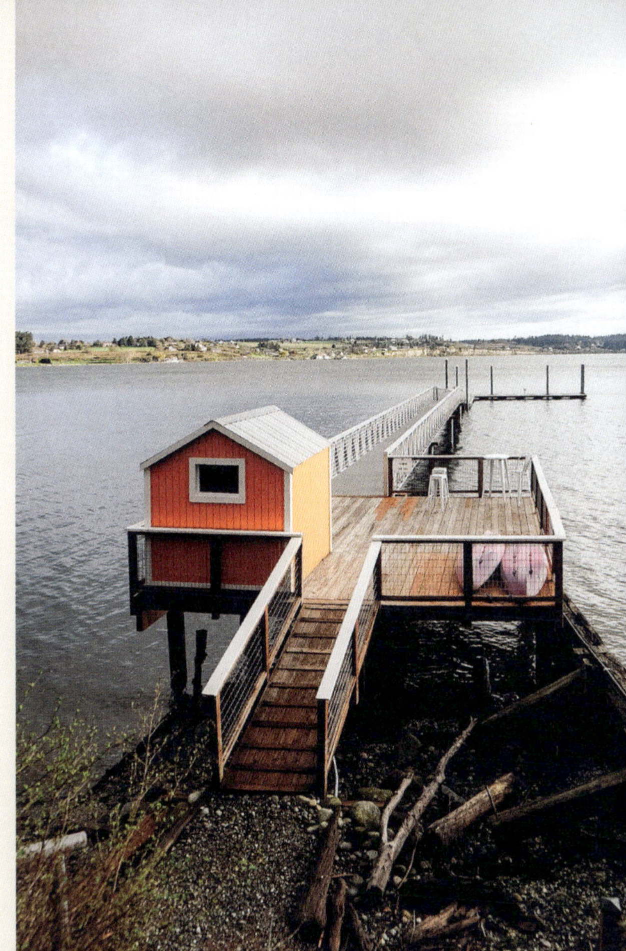

COUNTRY MOUSE OR CITY MOUSE

Steve, who dreamed of living on Whidbey Island, asked the age-old question, "Do you want to be a city mouse or a country mouse?" Without hesitation, Kyle said, "Country mouse!" And with that, the couple found a home on Whidbey Island north of Seattle.

Being on Whidbey Island full-time became more difficult as Kyle's father in

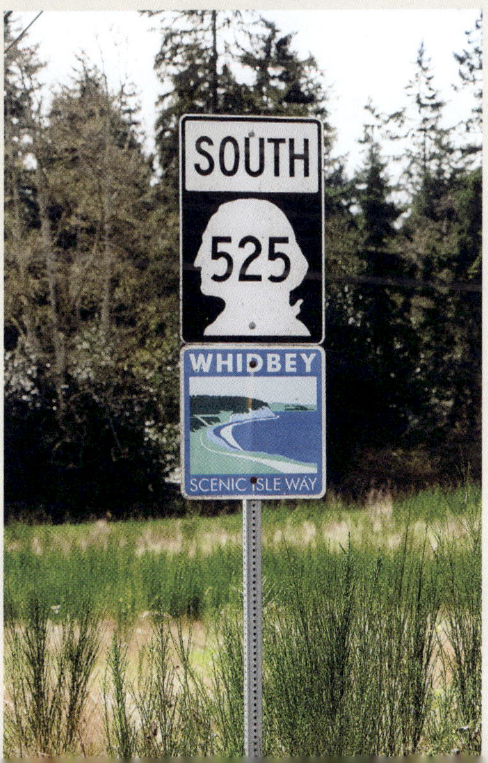

Montana got older, and Steve, a rural doctor, wanted to be able to provide more to his patients. The couple decided to keep their home and move back and forth, spending part of the year in either place, while Steve could work in both locations. "As we age, I think we're more likely to probably move back to Whidbey full-time. I think about our health care; as we age, living close to the city is a little bit easier—and the moderate temperatures," shared Kyle.

SMALL TOWN POLITICS

Doing nonprofit work can be challenging, but Kyle has always flourished. He loves networking and meeting people, which makes up most of his work with the various nonprofits he has been a part of. Kyle loves to dive into how that's done in two locations and with two vastly different groups of people and thrives in the constant back-and-forth between the two homes.

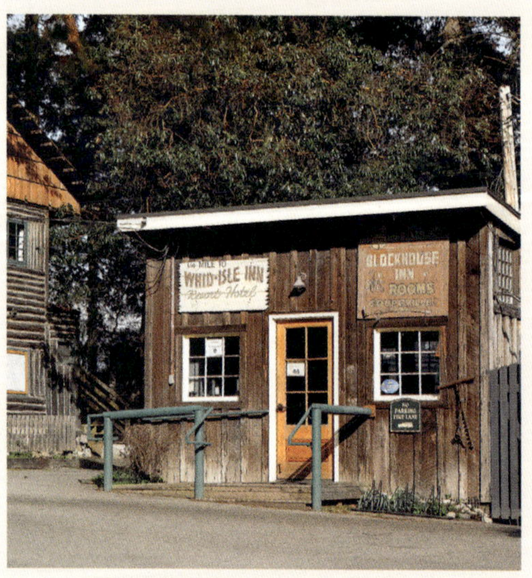

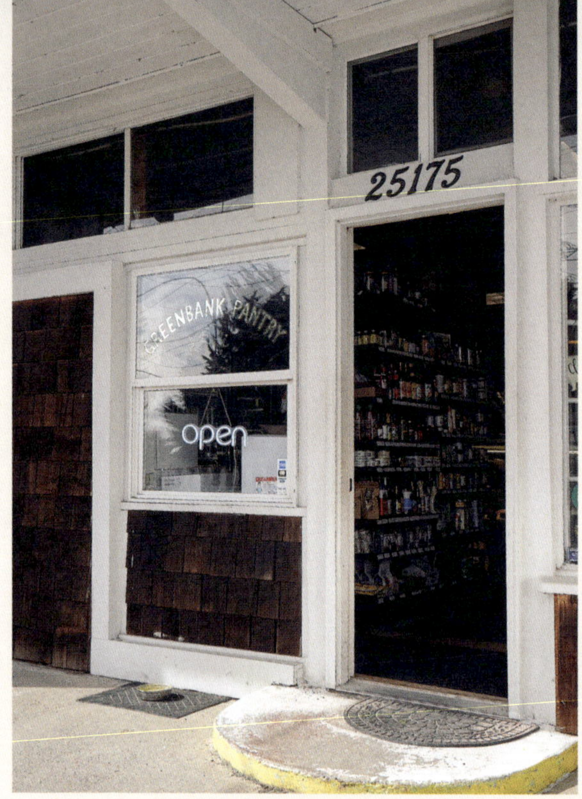

THINGS YOU DIDN'T KNOW YOU NEEDED BEFORE LIVING SMALL: KITCHEN EDITION

Cooler bags that live in your car

Deep freezer

Learning how to preserve

A pantry of canned goods and dry beans

An understanding of what can be frozen for later use (It's more than you'd think.)

Small Town Life Lessons

"Learn new habits. For example, the biggest thing about living in a rural setting is closing the gate after yourself. If the gate was closed when you arrived and you didn't think there were any cows or anything in the field, you could just blow through it. But just know that somebody thinks that the gate is closed. So take the time to learn and be much more mindful of those around you, and close the gate after yourself. I think many people blow past those gates or move to change things or try to keep their city life in their rural life. That's where you're going to fail."

—KYLE

Kyle had felt strongly about dipping his toes into politics for years, and he decided to run for city council—and won. He chose to run in Montana over Washington for several reasons. "I know Montana politics a little bit better. Effecting change takes much more work in a rural setting, but once you make the change for something, you think, *I did that,*" he shared.

CHALLENGES OF ISLAND LIVING AND ADAPTING TO PREPPING LIKE A LOCAL

"There's a different isolation living on an island. Part of the reason I wanted to return to Montana is a little more connectivity. Montana gives us big-city life, and Whidbey Island is our small town. It's the concept of 'on island time' and 'off island time,'" said Kyle. Planning is part of everyday life on an island. Prepared with a list of errands, Kyle saves everything up to do all at once—go to the bigger or bulk grocery, get gas, recycle, etc.—to live a more sustainable life. He or Steve can't easily run to the grocery store when out of something. It takes meal planning and staying organized to run like a tight ship. We take for granted the ease of errands in a larger city. If you are out of something, you can simply pop into the corner bodega, but it's often searching for substitutes or doing without in a small town. "It's rural living; we've always had two fridges. During the pandemic, I felt like my grandmother: let's go; we've got this!" laughed Kyle, adding, "If you're not going to find it on the island, you're not going to find it."

This way of thinking has resulted in Kyle and Steve recognizing the true value in the things they bring into their home and finding peace in a simpler, more sustainable lifestyle.

Slowing down and thinking about what you carry into the home makes you aware of the things you can live without. Maybe you don't need as many internet purchases or can find the same items at a local level or in

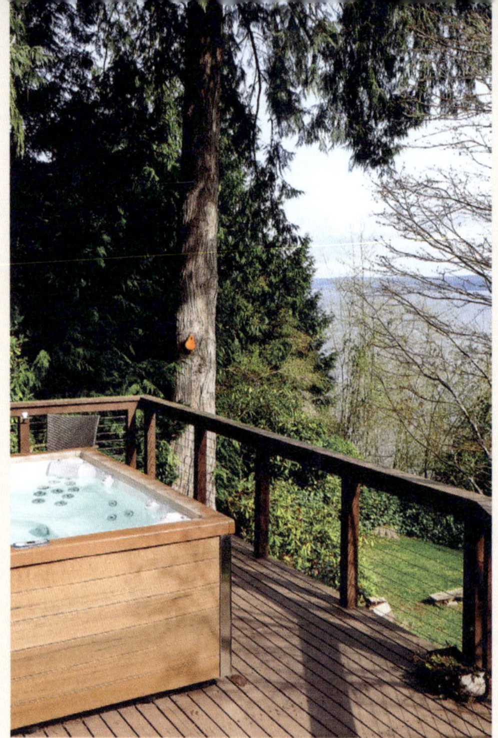

a secondhand shop nearby. As you distance yourself from "stuff," you begin to really see the items you do surround yourself with as well as what you find actual value in. We can live with a lot less than what we've been taught to believe.

SHOPPING LOCAL

Kyle saw a need to shop locally after living in a rural setting. It's easy to shop online or in big-box stores, and without a healthy assortment of places to shop nearby, it's sometimes harder to do locally. You can't always find what you need or haven't learned how to reframe the idea of your needs. "I want to meet with the chamber director to discuss how we should teach people to shop locally. What does shopping locally look like? Where do you start? You must have the diversity of enough shops to do it because it's convenient to go to Costco, Target, etc.," said Kyle.

Some ideas for towns to think about could be giving incentives to open a shop. It takes a lot of money to start, but being prepared with information about grants and small business loans is a good beginning. Landlords really benefit from having a long-term tenant. Negotiate a small rent for the first six months in exchange for signing a long-term lease. These price breaks for small businesses are vital to the growth of a community. Yes, it falls on the landlord as they are losing that rental money, but if a town could offer some incentive to landlords, such as a stipend, to make up for that break for tenants, it could be fantastic for the growth of a small town community. It's ideas like these that make organizations

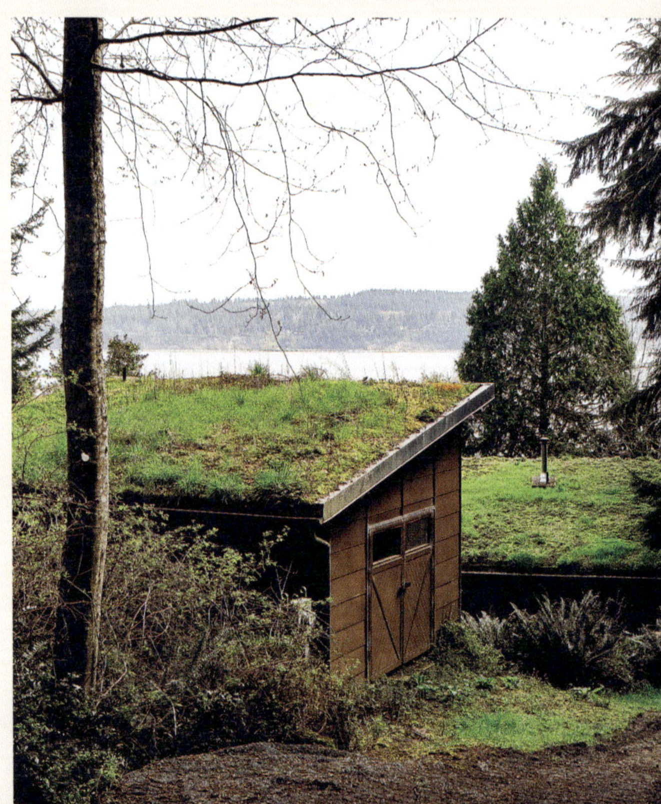

HOW TO PRACTICE A MORE SUSTAINABLE LIFESTYLE

Shop locally.

Look for local meat, vegetables, and dairy when possible.

Learn to grow simple items like tomatoes, berries, and herbs if you have the space.

Utilize your windows and screen doors in the fall and spring.

Have one day a week where you try to use less energy within your home.

Compost.

Invest in a house water filter rather than bringing in single-use plastic water bottles.

Meal plan and cook at home most nights.

With most needs farther away, invest in a hybrid or electric vehicle.

Keep a running list of needs and plan those visits together on one day.

like a Main Street Association and a Chamber of Commerce vital to a small community. It's a built-in network of resources, grants, and community that a town and shop owners need. These organizations can become your liaison to a more efficiently run community while also helping to bring the community together through neighborhood-led events, such as art crawls, shop local events, and progressive restaurant dinners.

ISLAND WATER

"I grew up as a land lover. My grandmother is from eastern Montana and always said when we'd go somewhere, 'Don't drown.' And I don't know if it was a deep proof of sarcasm or if I was more worried about flooding," said Kyle. Riding the ferry, as you often do when living on an island in the Pacific Northwest or being around the water, it has taken Kyle some time to get his grandmother's voice out of his head and be comfortable on boats. "If you are in and around boats and nicely reading a book on a boat, you're calmed, but you're stuck. It's not a good thing. You should be active and at risk of always falling into the water," laughed Kyle.

He and Steve have made crabbing with neighbors and seeking out fresh mussels from the local mussel farmer part of their island life. They've also learned to read a tide chart, plan for the tide's movement, and prepare for king tide. Living by the water has been an adjustment for Kyle, but one he finds enjoyable.

GREENBANK, WASHINGTON

POPULATION: 1,892 full-time residents in 2024

TOWN SIZE: 12.4 square miles

ISLAND SIZE: 168.7 square miles

CLOSEST INTERNATIONAL AIRPORT: Sea-Tac International Airport (58.8 miles including ferry)

CLOSEST REGIONAL AIRPORT: Paine Field (24.6 miles including ferry)

CLOSEST LARGE CITY: Seattle (46 miles including ferry)

BONUS TOWNS NEARBY: Langley, Clinton, Freeland

BEST TIME TO WHALE-WATCH: You can see orcas year-round and gray whales from March to May and October to January.

TOWN FACTS: Greenbank Farm is the largest producer in town of loganberries, a cross between a blackberry and a raspberry. The Whidbey Audubon Society built a viewing platform at the marsh at Greenbank Farm for the observation of many types of birds. The Meerkerk Rhododendron Gardens are a must-visit. People who live on Whidbey Island frequently call going to the mainland "going to America" because they feel so far removed from the rest of the world.

SEASONS: Greenbank has four seasons, with winters mild but longer, while spring is shorter.

WATER ACTIVITIES: crabbing, fishing, clamming, kayaking, paddleboarding, sailing, beachcombing, whale-watching, boating

WATER SPOTS TO VISIT: Lagoon Point County Park, Hidden Beach, and South Whidbey State Park

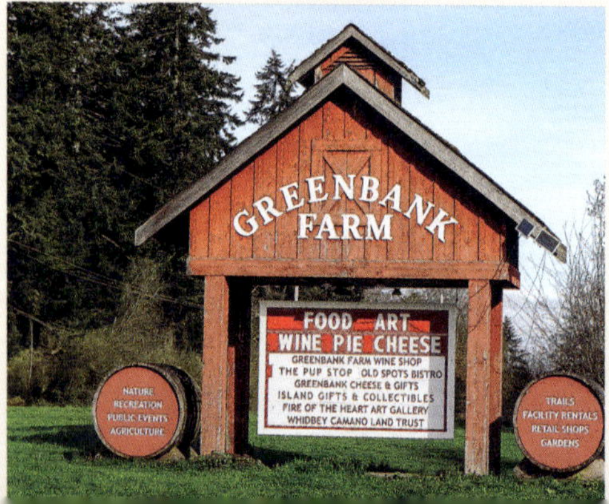

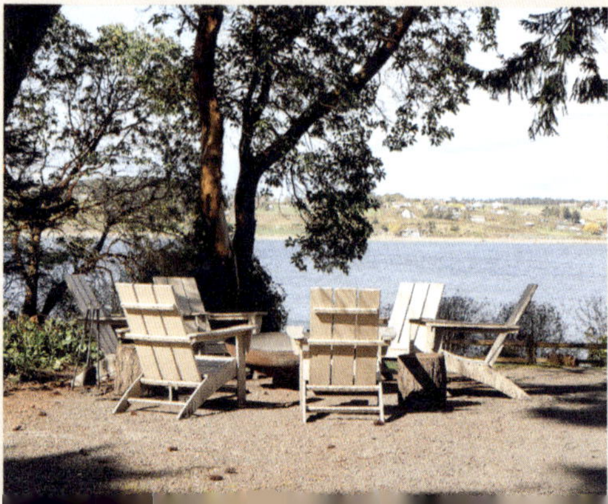

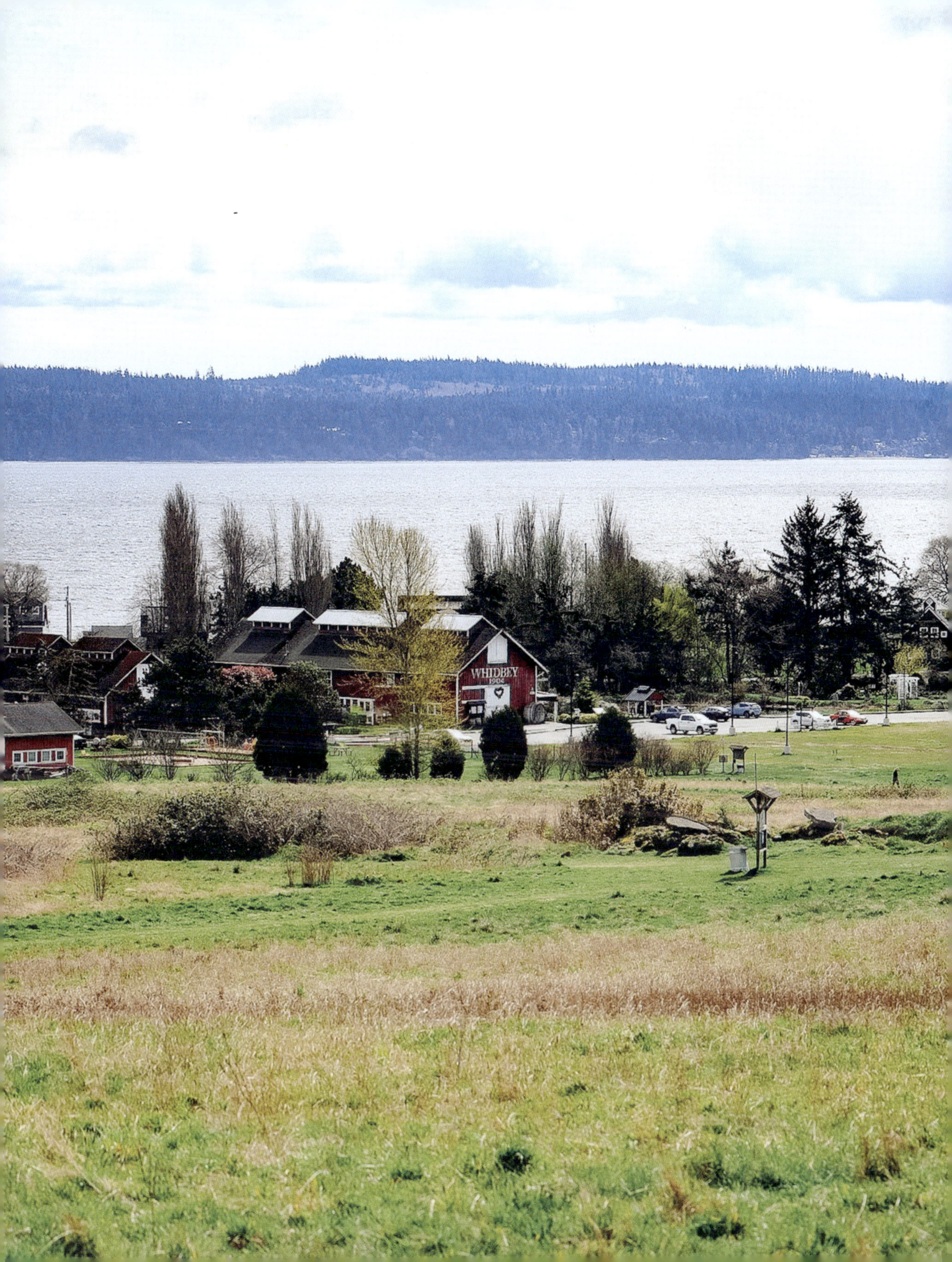
WHIDBEY

"My idea would be to find that creative enclave, and brainstorm how we can make a small, but possibly snowballing impact in the community."

—JASON GRUBE

JASON AND SHANNON GRUBE

Graphic Designer and Registered Dietitian

OAK HARBOR, WHIDBEY ISLAND, WASHINGTON

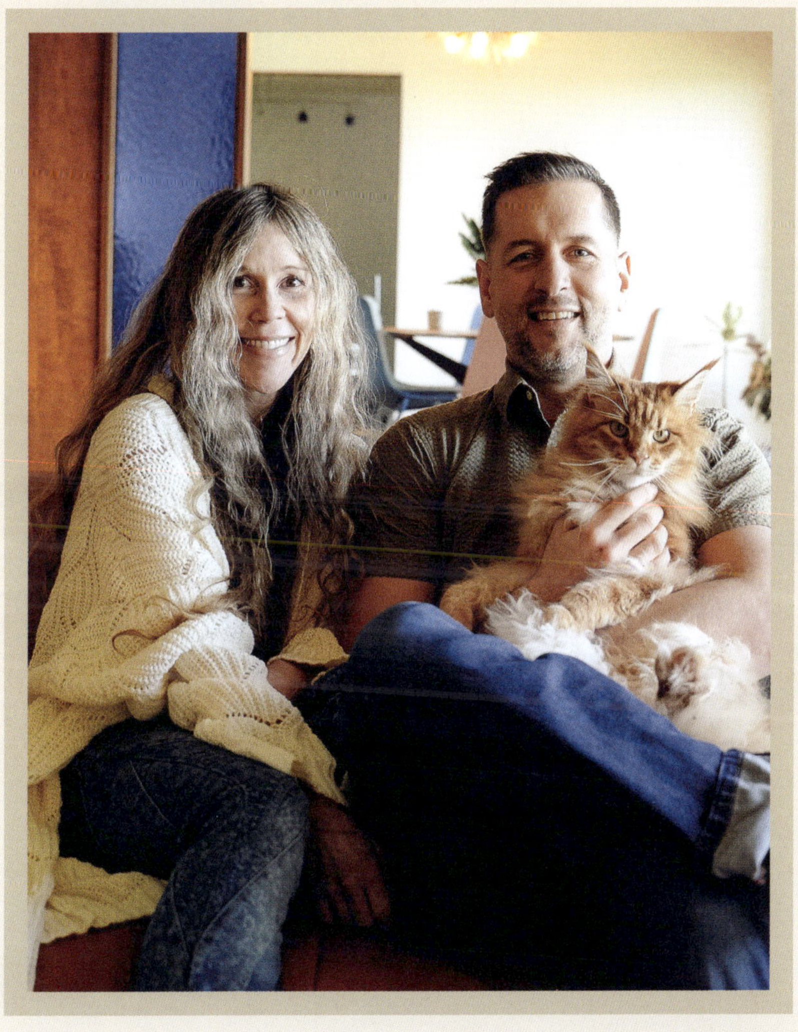

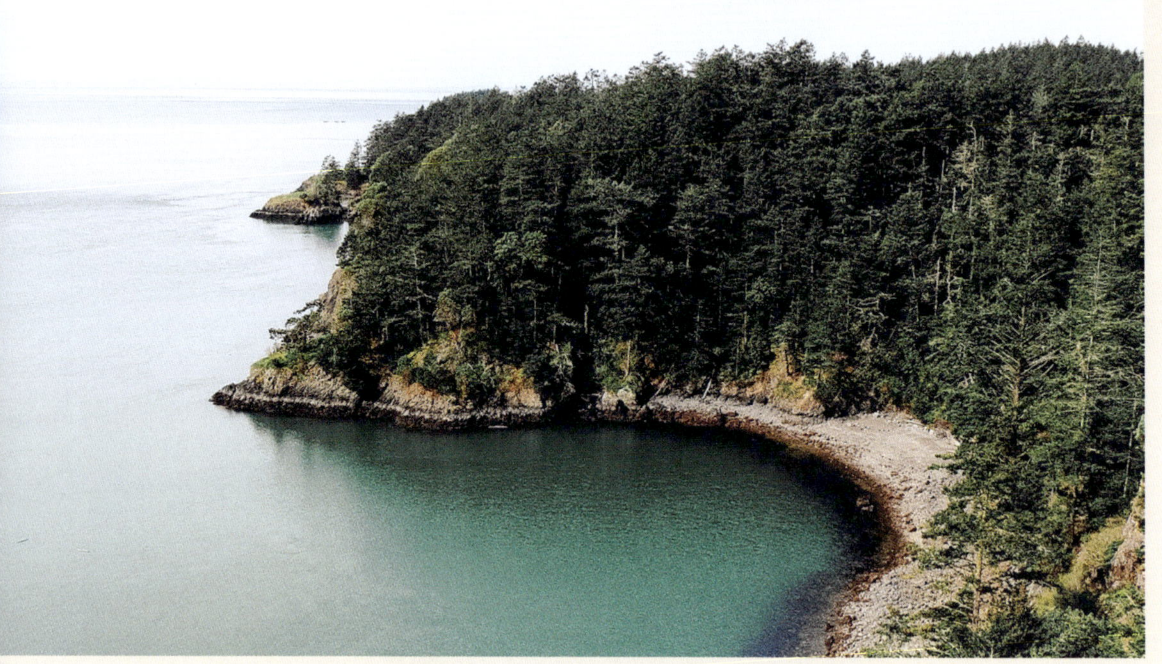

Fighting layoffs and watching agencies fold, former Seattle-based graphic designer Jason Grube made the leap to the world of freelancing. Welcoming the flexibility it gave him to spend time with his family, Jason preferred the new pace. It also allowed him to move out of the city to Oak Harbor on Whidbey Island north of Seattle. "I've always made more money when I freelanced, and I really liked the flexibility and the fact that I didn't have to be afraid of my job. I wasn't stuck under someone I may not always respect," shared Jason. The family of five looked at neighboring islands, such as Vashon and Bainbridge, and the peninsula in towns like Kingston and Port Townsend. They lived in Suquamish for a bit, but the faulty power grid left them continuing their search, landing the family on Whidbey Island in the town of Oak Harbor.

Originally from Wisconsin, Jason bounced around from his home state to New York and Minnesota before moving to Washington. His wife Shannon moved from Alabama to Hawaii to Minneapolis, where she and Jason met, before the couple relocated to Washington. Always on the hunt to move to another island, she found Whidbey checked almost all the boxes for her—minus the warmth from her previous stints in the South and tropical states. Being surrounded by water and mountain views on Whidbey helps her look past the often-cold months.

COMPARING CITY AND ISLAND LIFE

"Every two years, we seemed to be moving.

We had a house in Tacoma for a couple years, and we bought it on a bubble. We were first-time homeowners. The economy turned; I lost my job; we had our first kid; we were getting burglarized quite a bit; I was commuting to Seattle and riding the bus four-plus hours a day; and we were so upside down," expressed Jason. The couple moved to Alabama with his in-laws for a bit while they figured out their next plan. Drawing circles on a map to expand out of the city of Seattle, the couple had a few needs to meet: good schools for the children, a nice place to live, and a midcentury modern home with mountain views. So the circles kept getting larger and larger. Losing bid after bid would have been discouraging for most, but Jason and his family continued searching.

It was a complete mystery to the couple how they uncovered a home meeting all their wants and needs. They found a complete fixer-upper was a challenge they were willing to endure. They realized their home wasn't listed as having mountain views, but after clearing the bushes in the back, they quickly learned it has sunrise vistas over the Cascades.

Another challenge for Jason and Shannon has been living with one car. As a one-car family in Seattle, they only drove an average of 1,000 miles a year because the city was so walkable. On Whidbey Island, it's been hard to maintain the same dedication to having a single car. Sure, small towns can be walkable, but it's a misconception to assume they always are.

RAISING CHILDREN ON WHIDBEY ISLAND

"The house is unbelievable, and there is potential to make it more. I can't see leaving. However, as the kids get older, my passion for building this great house for them and their friends is slowly waning because they may move somewhere else in the country. I like the quiet island life. It's a lot like my hometown,

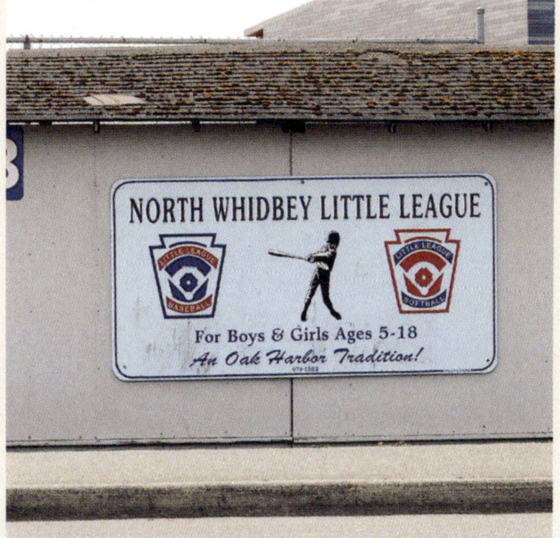

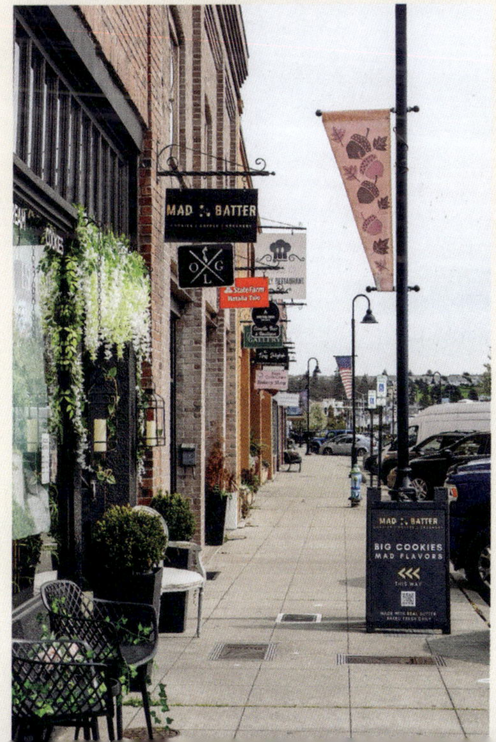

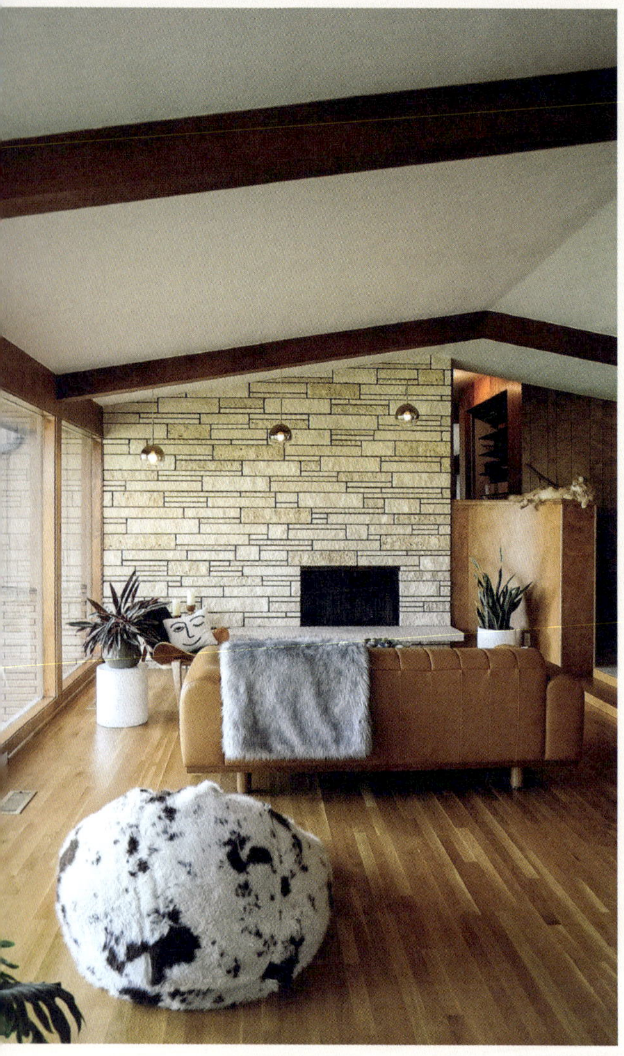

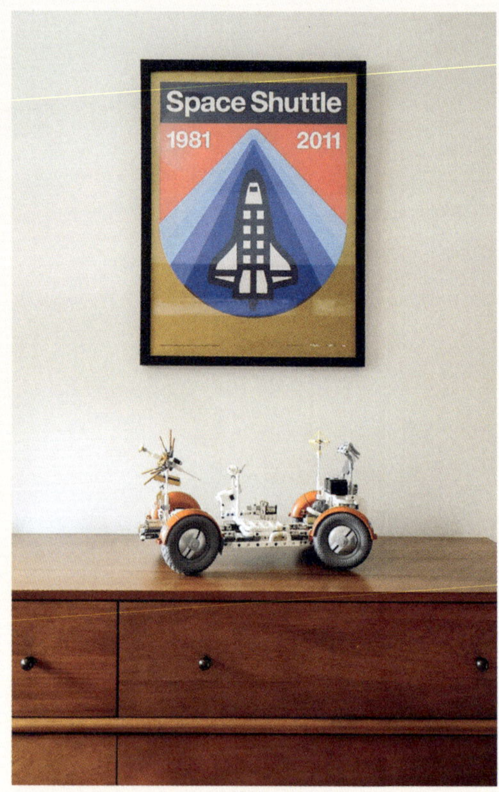

which is ironic because I couldn't wait to escape," shared Jason. With three boys ranging in age from preteen to teen, life on the island can vary so much from the city. Jason's oldest son was involved in School of Rock in Seattle and still remembers vividly what city life was like and misses it often. He doesn't have the same outlets on Whidbey that he was once afforded. Oak Harbor is a sleepy town and doesn't offer as many things for children and teens to do. Not all children will be as inspired by the island, but that's not the case for Jason's middle son, who's thriving with a steady stream of sports to play or with visits to the neighboring Navy base.

DIVERSITY AND CULTURAL EXPERIENCES IN OAK HARBOR

Washington state hasn't always been seen as a cultural melting pot, which Jason was worried about when moving farther away from the city. He wanted his boys to have a different experience than he had had in Wisconsin. Jason tried introducing them to other types of food

HOW TO BUILD AN INCLUSIVE COMMUNITY IN A SMALL TOWN

Create inclusive events.

Address inequality.

Support local businesses.

Attend town hall meetings to allow for your voice to be heard.

Welcome everyone, breaking down the walls of any misconceptions.

Run for local political positions, like school board member or alderperson.

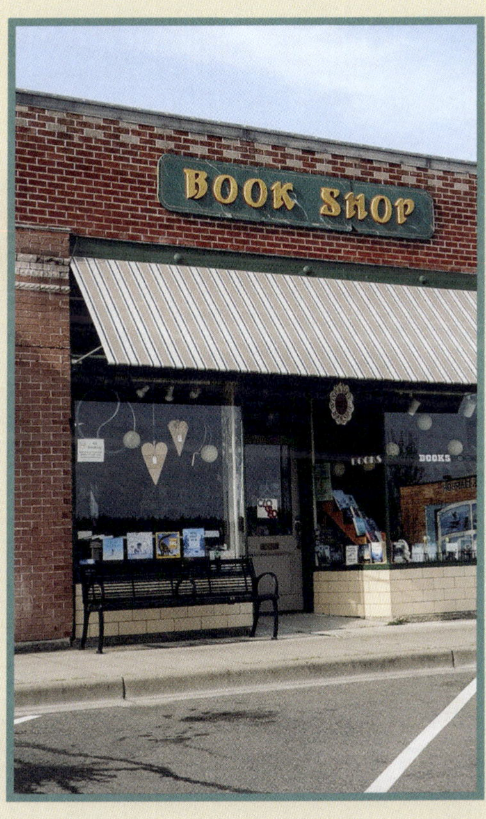

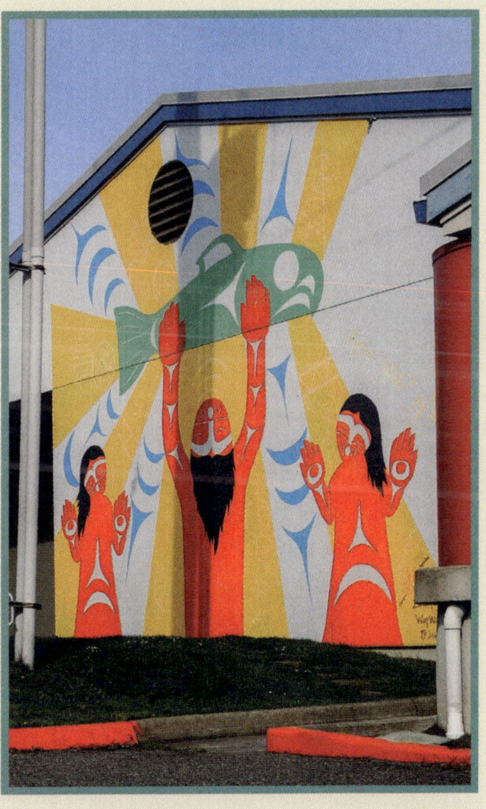

and ethnic enclaves than how he was raised. He and his wife were pleasantly surprised to see how much more diversity his children are now exposed to living in a small town on an island in Washington than in Seattle or Tacoma. Due to the neighboring Navy base, Oak Harbor splits its diversity across white, Black, and Indigenous American, Alaskan, Native Hawaiian, and Asian cultures.

CHALLENGES AND OPPORTUNITIES IN COMMUNITY-BUILDING

Whidbey has a highway that runs the length of the island, and as it veers through Oak Harbor, it takes you around the historic downtown. Because of this, people often overlook the town and make their way to nearby but smaller Coupeville. It's not that people shouldn't visit both, but simply because of the diversion of the road, the town of Oak Harbor has had to work harder to encourage people passing through to make a stop.

Jason saw the need for a good coffee shop or a few more good stores but understood that the clientele might not be there to support those businesses. He asked himself, *What can I do to make an impact here?* Jason hoped to get a holiday cycling group started with a big group ride to share his love of cycling. He put energy into getting to know the people at the bike shop and the barbershop and worked to build relationships within his community and to see how it went from there.

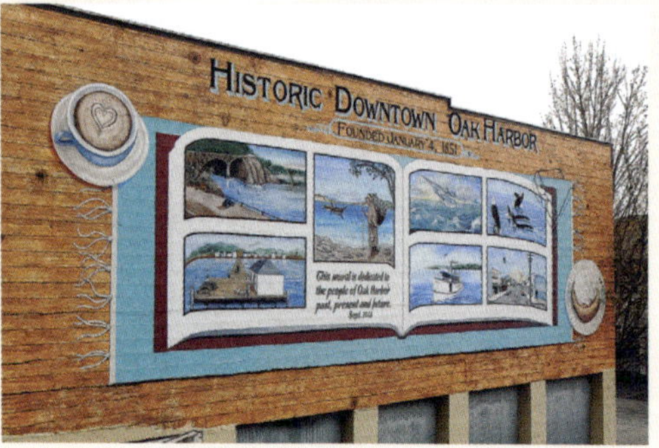

MINDFULNESS INSPIRED BY THE ENVIRONMENT

"Water is emotionally, unbelievably calming. If I'm worked up, I'll bike or drive down to the beach and walk with super-low tides. We'll go as a family to the long flats on the beach. Or I'll go for a run. I can run a 10k on a beach down here when it's super-low tide and just go barefoot," shared Jason.

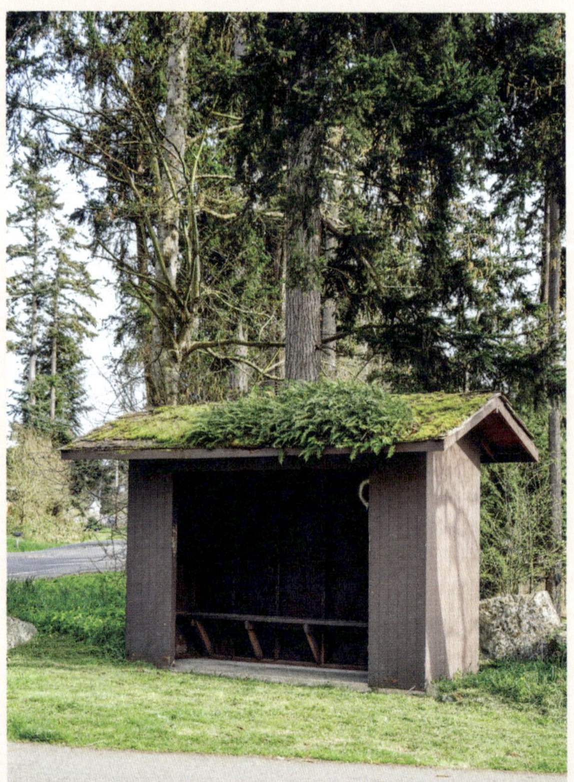

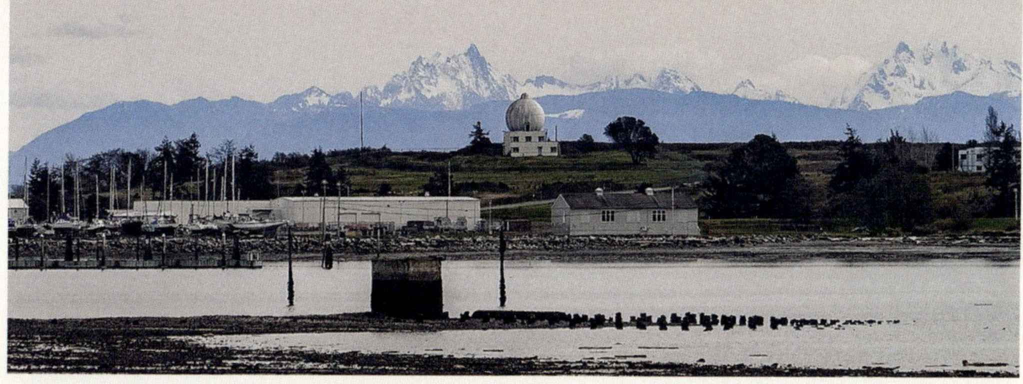

OAK HARBOR, WASHINGTON

POPULATION: 23,813 full-time residents in 2024

TOWN SIZE: 9.5 square miles

ISLAND SIZE: 168.7 square miles

CLOSEST INTERNATIONAL AIRPORT: Sea-Tac International Airport (104 miles)

CLOSEST REGIONAL AIRPORT: Anacortes Airport (19.1 miles)

CLOSEST LARGE CITY: Seattle (92.9 miles)

BONUS TOWNS NEARBY: Coupeville, Anacortes, Burlington, Port Townsend (via a ferry)

BEST TIME TO WHALE-WATCH: March to May and October to January for gray whales, but you can see orcas year-round.

TOWN FACTS: People call themselves Northenders or Southenders based on which end of the island they live on. Whidbey is home to Deception Pass State Park. The island is in a rain shadow because of the Olympic Mountains, meaning it gets half the yearly rainfall of Seattle just an hour away. You can access Whidbey Island by ferry or bridge. There are six Whale Trail sites on the island.

SEASONS: Oak Harbor has four seasons, with winters mild but longer, while spring is shorter.

WATER ACTIVITIES: crabbing, fishing, clamming, kayaking, paddleboarding, sailing, beachcombing, whale-watching

WATER SPOTS TO VISIT: Oak Harbor, Penn Cove, Deception Pass, Cornet Bay, Cranberry Lake, West Beach, and Ebey's Landing National Historical Reserve

"Hedgebrook is a global community of women writers and people who seek extraordinary books, poetry, plays, films, and music by women. A literary nonprofit, our mission is to support visionary women writers whose stories and ideas shape our culture now and for generations to come. We offer writing residencies, Radical Craft Retreats, and convenings at our retreat on Whidbey Island, as well as public programs that connect writers with readers and audiences around the world."

—HEDGEBROOK

SPOTLIGHT

HEDGEBROOK—FREELAND, WASHINGTON

Founded in 1988 by Nancy Nordhoff, Hedgebrook was built down an unassuming road on a quiet island in the middle of Puget Sound and has come to be known as one of the most remarkable writers' retreat spaces, dedicated to the art of women and assuring they are given the gift of time. "Nancy understood the space was for something else and was also super-practical. She talked to many kinds of artists and eventually settled on writers because we're easy and all we need is a desk. She was inspired by *A Room of One's Own* by Virginia Woolf. And so we provide the space; we provide the time; we provide what we call radical hospitality, which is really caring for caretakers; and that formula works well to give women what they need to be able to just do the work that the world doesn't make space for," shared Kimberly A.C. Wilson, executive director of Hedgebrook since 2020.

Kimberly spent her life moving throughout the East Coast and France before landing on the West Coast, first in Oregon and then Washington. As a journalist, she bounced around from place to place before finding the island. When the world shut down, Kimberly used her new adventure of island living to explore the nature around her, making daily walks in the woods part of her routine.

As for the writers making their way to Whidbey Island, they come from all over the world to practice their craft at Hedgebrook, landing at Sea-Tac, and then being shuttled through Seattle traffic to the ferry dock. "They get on the ferryboat, and they're transported. It feels like you're going to a different dimension. Then you come over to this rural island that, as the crow flies, is thirty-five miles away from Seattle. But it's two hours to travel here," added Kimberly. "It is so far removed that you really do get a sense that you've left behind some of the pressures and concerns of our modern lives and are in a space that is intentionally created for women."

CREATING SPACE FOR ALL WOMEN

Many of the writers who come to Hedgebrook are LGBTQUIA+ and writers of color. It's a space made to embrace them instead of being an afterthought. People from all kinds of identities and experiences can connect with each other. "Being in the middle of nowhere gives you the opportunity to go deeper into yourselves as writers and also with each other as writers," shared Kimberly.

CONNECTING WITH THE LOCALS

"As in any small, rural place, you can either be rural or you can be deeply creative and appreciate the arts. And so we have that good relationship with our community," shared Kimberly about the local love for the Hedgebrook showcase of one act and scene that the writers put on for the people of Langley.

WATER IS ALWAYS IN SIGHT

Hedgebrook is just across from Useless Bay, always in sight for the residents. The pull to the water begins with the first ferry ride and continues each day. You can see the water from anywhere on the property, and you are always aware of the weather, as it's constantly changing. "There's something primal about being this close to the water. The whales are a constant presence," shared Kimberly, and you feel the connection.

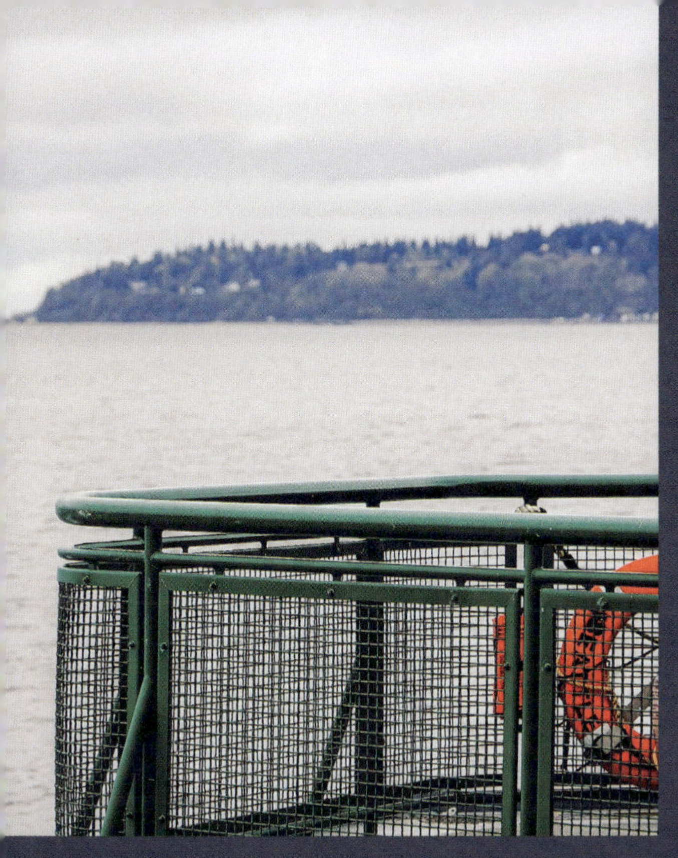

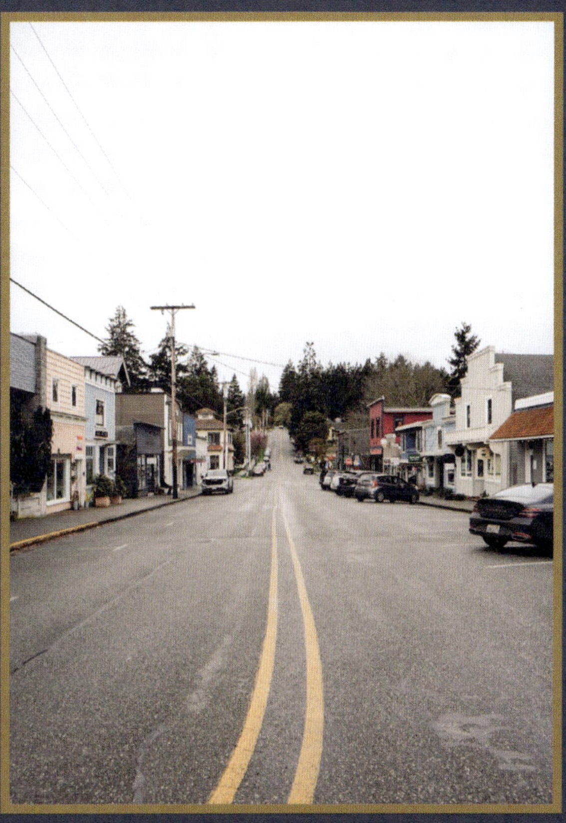

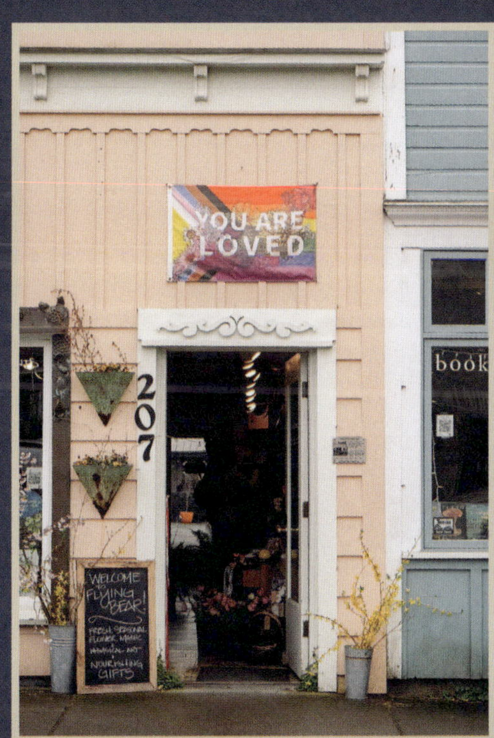
YOU ARE LOVED
207
book

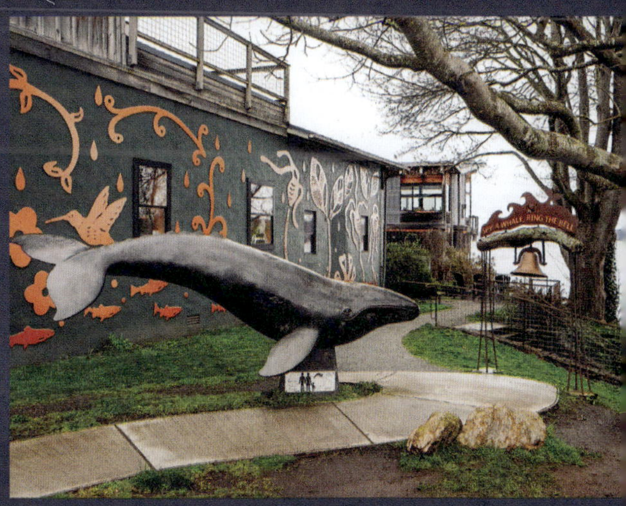

"I get the same small town vibe between Incline, Truckee, and Saint Michaels. All are a very close-knit community for the folks who are there full-time. There are a lot of second homes, so all the folks have a bond among the full-time residents of Saint Michaels, the full-time residents in Incline, and the full-time residents in Truckee. You also see an emphasis on water-related activities. On the Truckee River, there's a ton of fly-fishing. And in the summers, people float down it in tubes. In Tahoe and Saint Michaels, it's boating, kayaking, and rafting."

—ALLIE BALIN

BONUS SECTION: BICOASTAL LIVING

Allie Balin, Incline Village, Nevada—Wine Distributor and Co-Owner of The Wildset Hotel and Restaurant and Ruse
K.C. Lager, Truckee, California—Interior Designer at the Kathryn Lager Design Studio and Co-Owner of The Wildset Hotel and Restaurant and Ruse

ST. MICHAELS, MARYLAND; TRUCKEE, CALIFORNIA; AND INCLINE VILLAGE, NEVADA

Sisters Allie Balin and K.C. Lager grew up outside of Washington, D.C., in Northern Virginia, spending their summers at the family home of K.C.'s husband in the small coastal town of Saint Michaels, Maryland. As the years passed, the sisters moved around, Allie bouncing from New York City to Pennsylvania, Denver, Buenos Aires, Nashville, and then Incline Village, Nevada. K.C. moved to Philadelphia for college before returning to D.C. for a bit, moving west to Los Angeles, and settling in Truckee, California. Allie has worked in the food industry for many years, from creating restaurants like Nashville's Henrietta Red to working as a sommelier, while K.C. established Kathryn Lager Design Studio, her interior design business.

Feeling a pull to be closer to family, both sisters found their way to the Lake Tahoe area. "When I started working for myself and not working for another designer, it made the move possible," shared K.C. Truckee was an ideal location for K.C., her husband, and their two boys with the ability to be outside and active most of the year. The small town also made driving from school to soccer much more doable for the busy family. Fearing winters would be more of a slog, K.C. was nervous going into the season, but early into her time in the mountain river town, they experienced the biggest winter in 100 years. She quickly realized she loved it! Spending cozy days at home and active days skiing, they knew they'd made the right choice to leave Los Angeles.

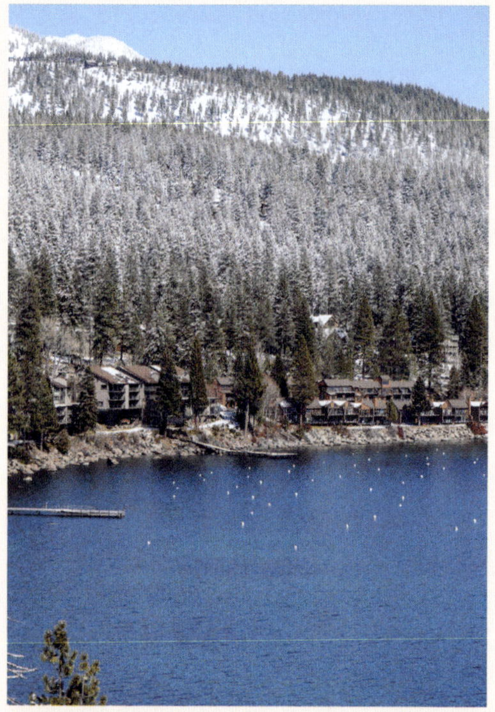

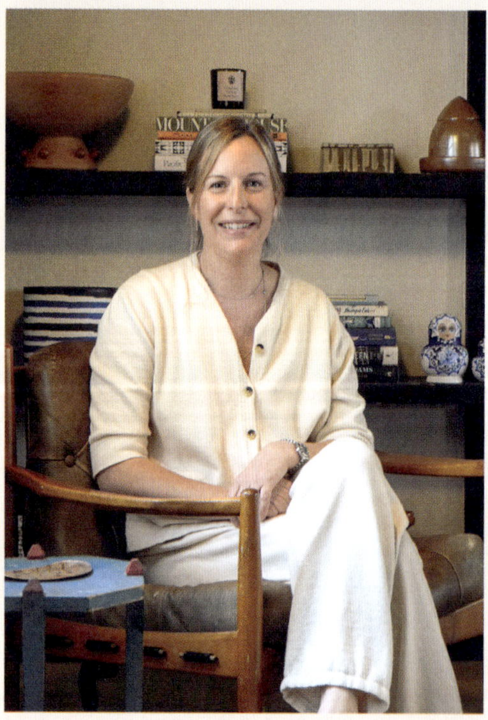

Incline Village, Nevada, is like Truckee in many ways, the pace being the biggest, but at about half the size. As nicknamed by the locals, Incline sits right on Lake Tahoe's lakeside. Generally, more retirees reside in Incline, but with the pandemic the town experienced younger families with small children flocking to the area looking to have more space, a slower environment, and a smaller location.

RAISING CHILDREN IN YOUR CHILDHOOD DREAM LOCATION

"I moved out here in January of 2020, when I had been living in Nashville. I had a restaurant there, and we had always dreamed of moving to Tahoe. It felt like if I continued on my path, I would never do it. I could have immersed myself more in the community in Nashville, which would have been fine, but it was always our dream to be out here," shared Allie. Raising her daughter in Incline has been everything she'd hoped it would be. Like K.C., Allie loves to be outside amid nature and is in awe of what children in the area are exposed to. The children go skiing, kayaking, whitewater rafting, and many more fun and engaging outdoor activities in gym class. "I think it's so fun and awesome for my daughter and K.C.'s boys to grow up in a community where there's such an emphasis on being outside," expressed Allie. K.C. added, "Many activities engage you in the town and make you feel really happy."

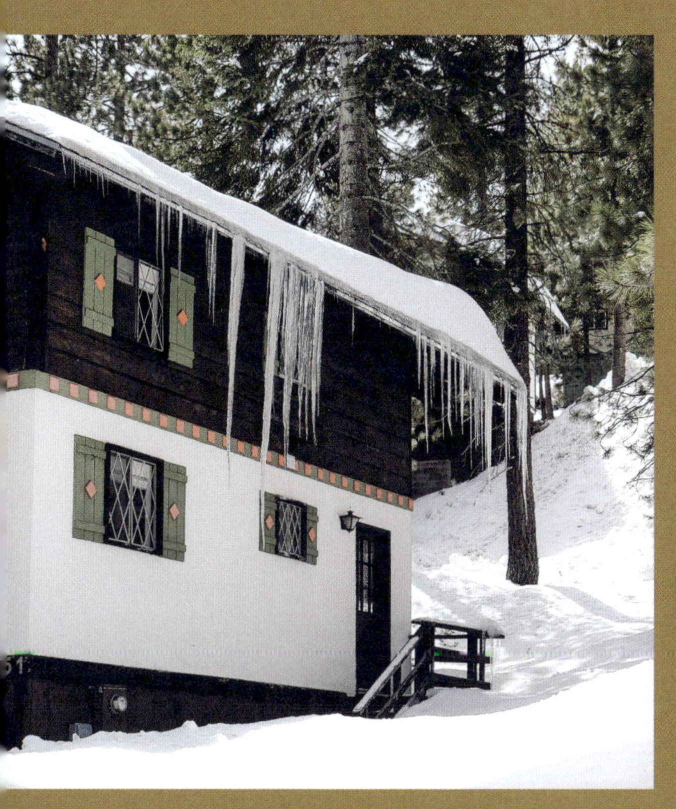

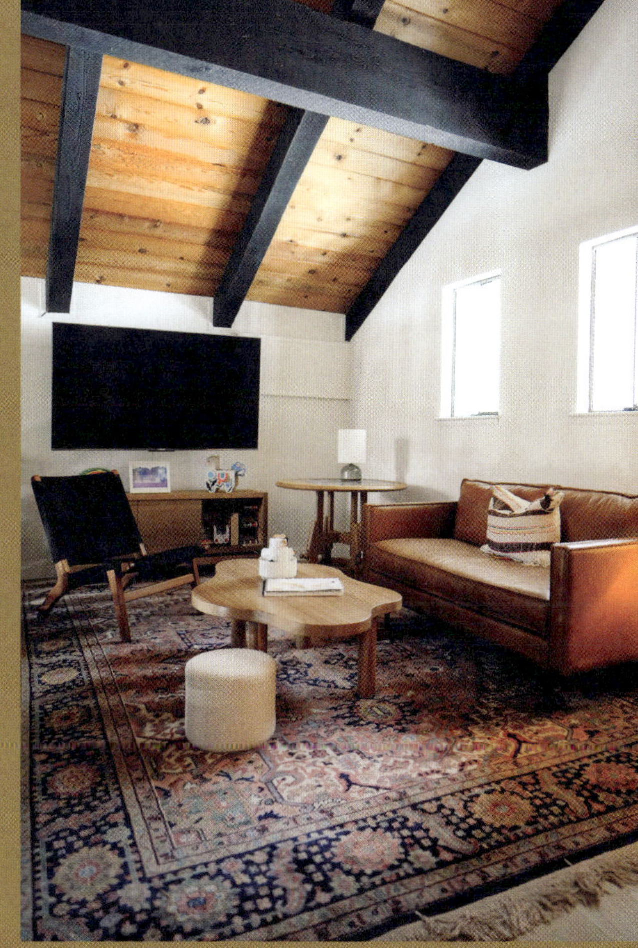

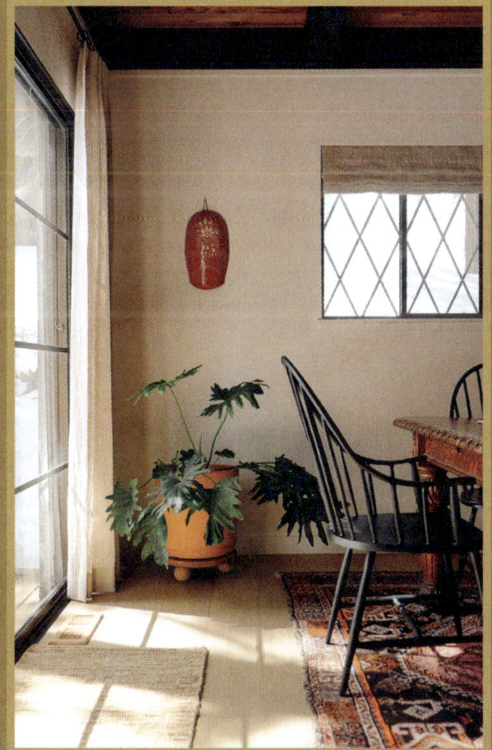

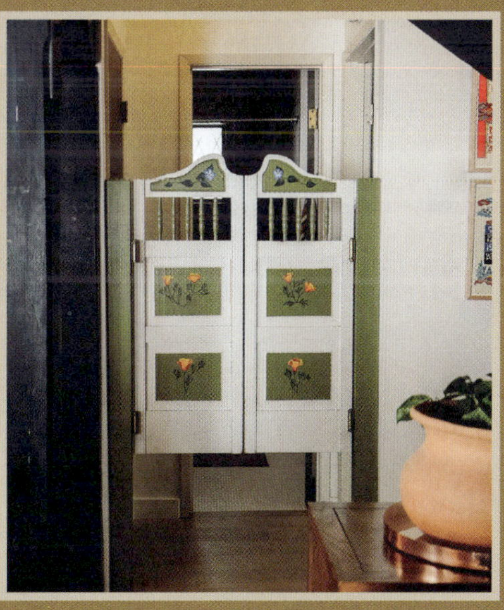

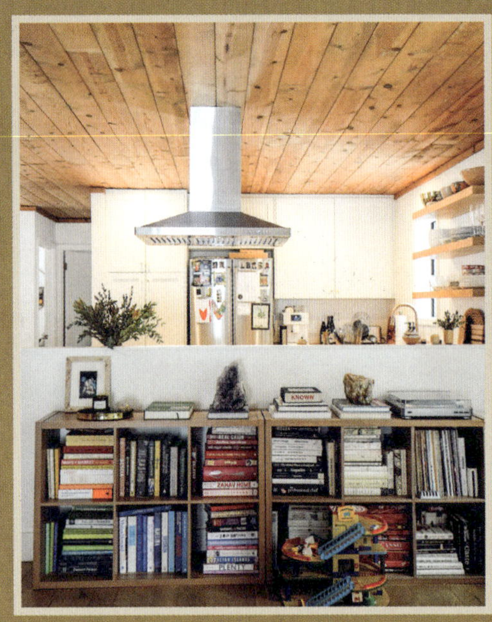

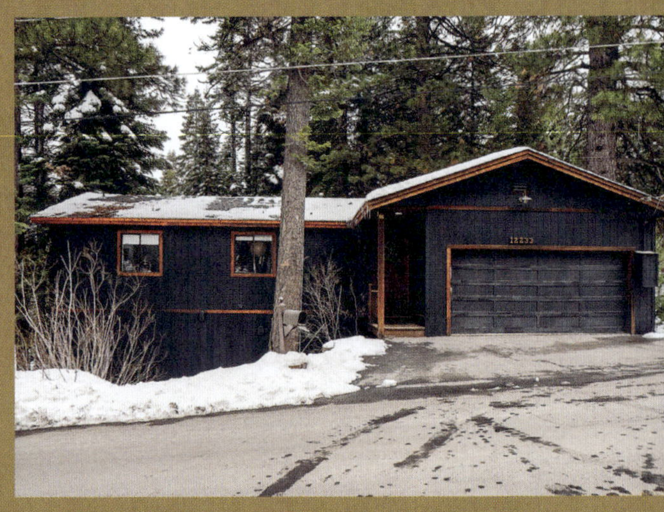

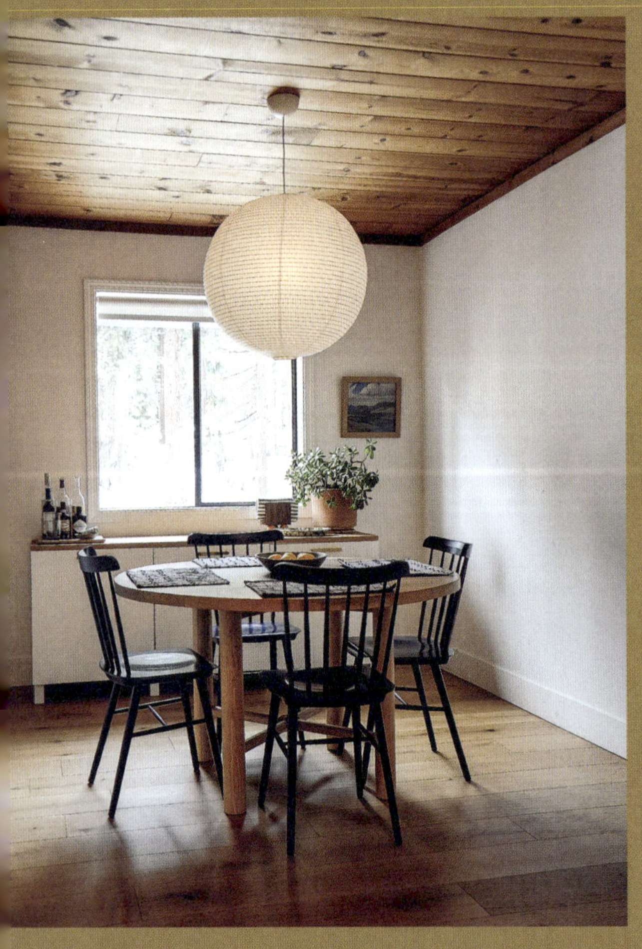

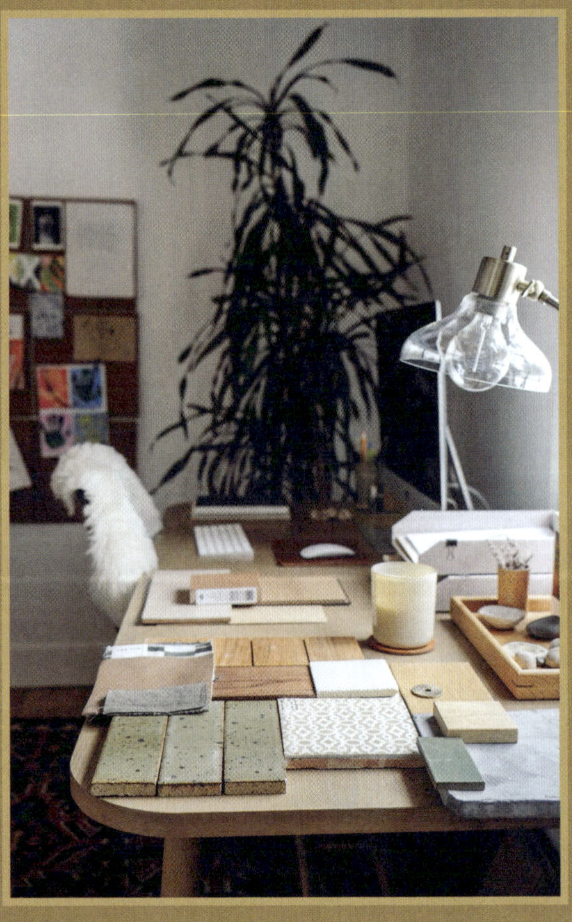

BRINGING OUTSIDE CULTURE HOME

Sometimes, living in a small town leaves you wanting to move about and travel, taking in new cultures, trying new food, and absorbing design and art from places that feel unfamiliar to you. For Allie and K.C., although they live in areas where they'd always dreamed of living and setting up their businesses, the desire to get away and travel often is still at the forefront of their minds. "Being in a small town is that kind of respite you need to relax and take a deep breath. It's where I come to be at peace and relax a little. But it's inspired me, I think, to also take on more and get out there more, and to take advantage of opportunities where I get to travel and feed that creative and cultural side that I need to be happy," shared Allie. For K.C., it's a similar sentiment. As a designer, getting out, traveling, and taking inspiration from faraway places is important both personally and professionally. Being able to come back home, take a deep breath, and use what you've found in a way which doesn't feel as frantic or fast-paced is incredibly valuable.

The sisters always knew they wanted to work on a project together but weren't sure what that would look like. With a passion for design and the food industry, the two decided to search for a hotel or bed-and-breakfast they could fix up and run and decided upon the town Saint Michaels. K.C.'s husband's family has been spending time in Saint Michaels since 1972, and it was a place Allie and K.C.

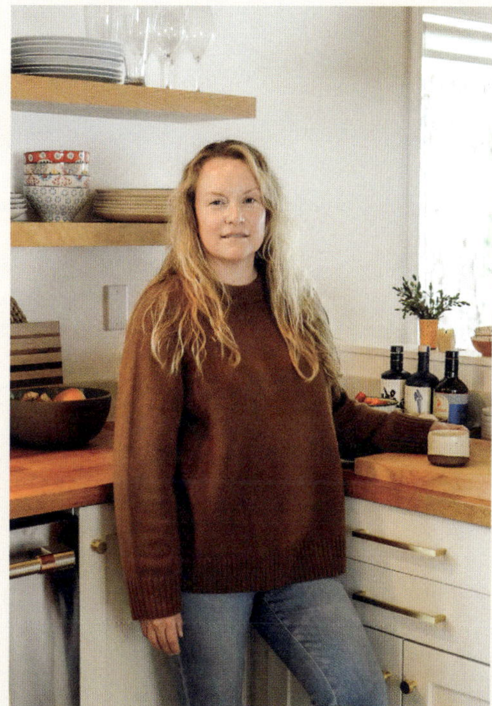

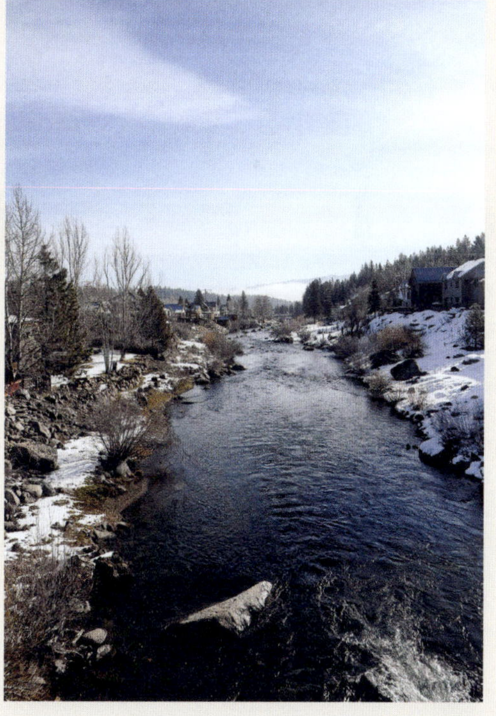

had been going to since the women were teenagers growing up in Northern Virginia. "We'd spend holidays there, and it became this place where a lot of our family got married," shared K.C., cementing the special hold Saint Michaels had on them both. They started their joint venture with K.C.'s brother-in-law, and The Wildset was born. Giving it a coastal yet refined look was K.C.'s department, turning a former B&B into a 34-room sleek, design-forward space with an on-site restaurant, Ruse, named for the town that fooled the British during the War of 1812, with a menu focused on the seafood just outside their front door, leaning heavily on oysters and shellfish. "We wanted to create something and do it in a place where we had such strong roots that made us feel excited to bring the hotel to the town. It felt great for our first project," said K.C.

Differences are few and far between, but they still exist. With such a strong culture of watermen in Maryland, fishing is a way of life in Saint Michaels, while in Truckee and Incline, it's treated with more of a recreational bend.

THE WILDSET AND BUSINESS OPERATIONS

Thanks to a reliable team at The Wildset, the sisters can run the hotel and restaurant from one coast while operating on the other. "We're fortunate. Our chef, general manager, and the assistant general manager of our hotel have been there since day one," said K.C. Both are

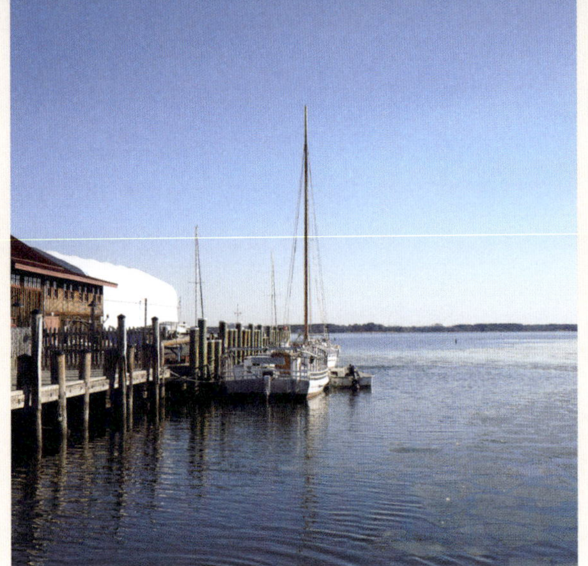

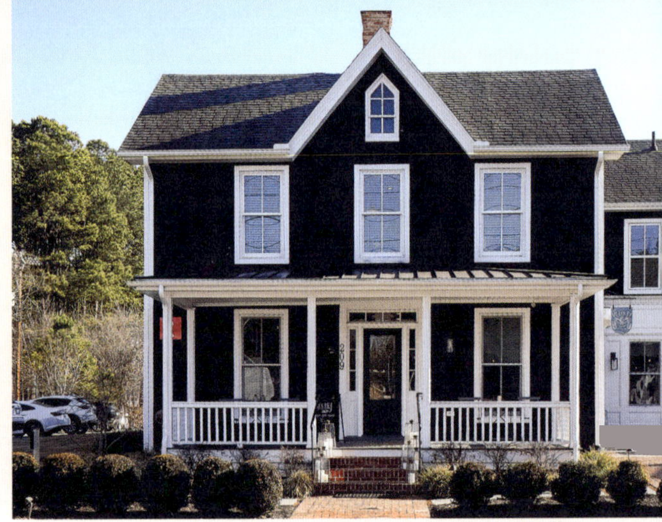

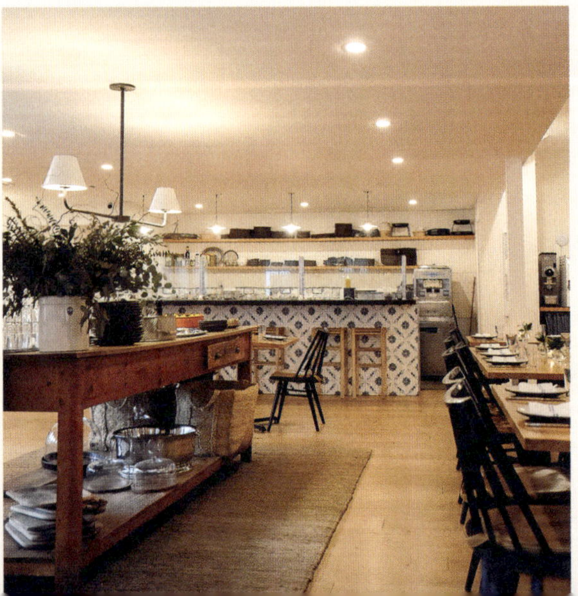

interested in looking for more hospitality projects they can work on together. Allie's got a wine distribution business, and K.C.'s work with her husband's family business to renovate residential properties gives her strong ties to the East Coast, which she visits more often than Allie.

CHALLENGES AND OPPORTUNITIES IN SMALL TOWNS

People often ask Allie and K.C. when they will open a restaurant or hotel in the Lake Tahoe area, and several factors make it a bit trickier for the sisters. Zoning is an issue, for one, with height requirements and parking stipulations in place. Construction costs are also very unpredictable. The other factor, which is often overlooked, is employee housing. Living in Truckee and Incline is costly. "Housing [costs and inventory], like so many places, are an issue, especially where people have second homes. There's just a lack of housing, especially for the people working in restaurants and hotels," expressed K.C.

COVID changed things for the Lake Tahoe area in both positive and negative ways. People from out of town found their way to Incline and Truckee alike, realizing they didn't need to be in the office anymore and could work remotely. "It brought in a ton of creatives. A lot of new businesses have opened, such as the Proper Hotel, refurbishing an existing hotel, and a couple moved from San Francisco and opened a restaurant," said Allie.

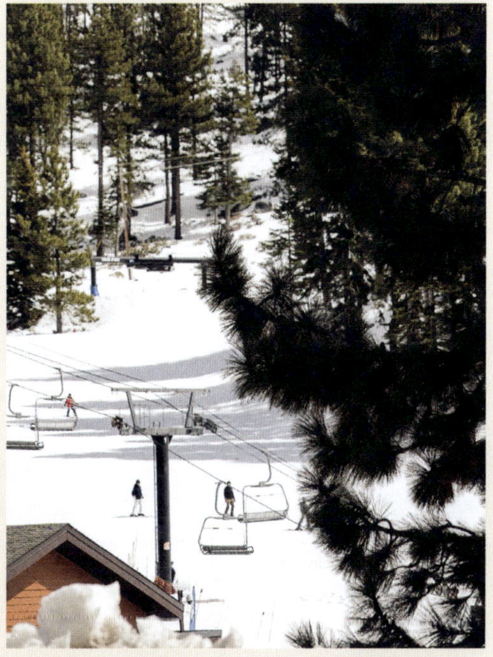

But with growth, there's been an exponential rise in property values and housing prices. In the Tahoe region, there's no place for the sprawl to overflow and a lack of labor for the new businesses. Also there are more wildfires with no new infrastructure for people to evacuate. When considering a small town, think about how you can restore a home to feel natural to the area in sustainable ways. Consider how much square footage you would use versus how big of a home you might want to build. How does the home align with the town and the other homes in the area? How can you be part of the mindset and growth of a place so that it doesn't look to change the town to the degree that people who have lived there their whole lives won't recognize it? We've lost sight of community-building when we cross that line.

TRUCKEE, CALIFORNIA

POPULATION: 17,039 full-time residents in 2024

TOWN SIZE: 34 square miles

CLOSEST INTERNATIONAL AIRPORT: Reno-Tahoe International Airport, Nevada (35.8 miles)

CLOSEST REGIONAL AIRPORT: Truckee Tahoe Regional Airport (2.5 miles)

CLOSEST LARGE CITY: Reno, Nevada (31.9 miles)

BONUS TOWNS NEARBY: Tahoe City, Kings Beach

TOWN FACTS: Truckee's downtown is listed on the National Register of Historic Places. With a yearly average of 206.6 inches, Truckee is considered one of the snowiest places in the country. With many ski lodges and Lake Tahoe nearby, Truckee gets the best of both worlds.

PLACES AND THINGS TO NOT MISS: Truckee Thursdays in the summer: Main Street becomes walking traffic only; the street is filled with food, shopping vendors, and live music.

SEASONS: Truckee has four seasons.

RIVER WATER ACTIVITIES: tubing, swimming, kayaking, whitewater rafting, canoeing, paddleboarding, fishing

WATER SPOTS TO VISIT: Donner Lake and Truckee River

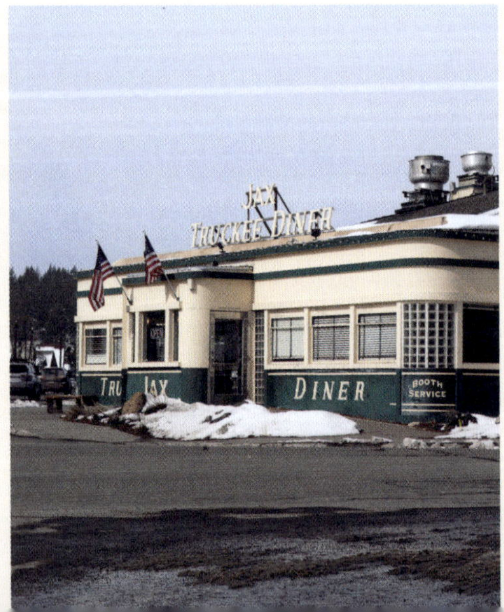

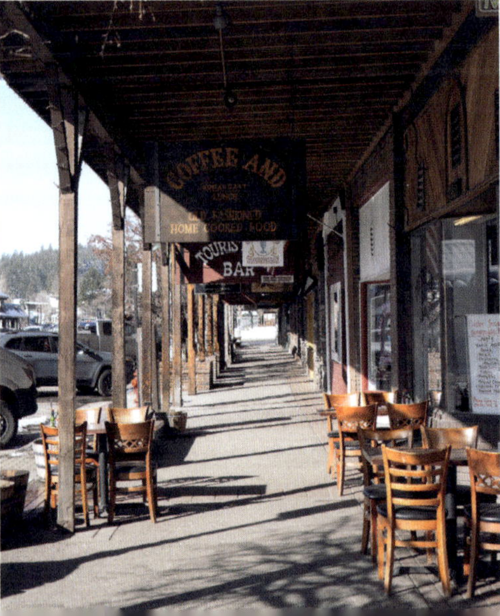

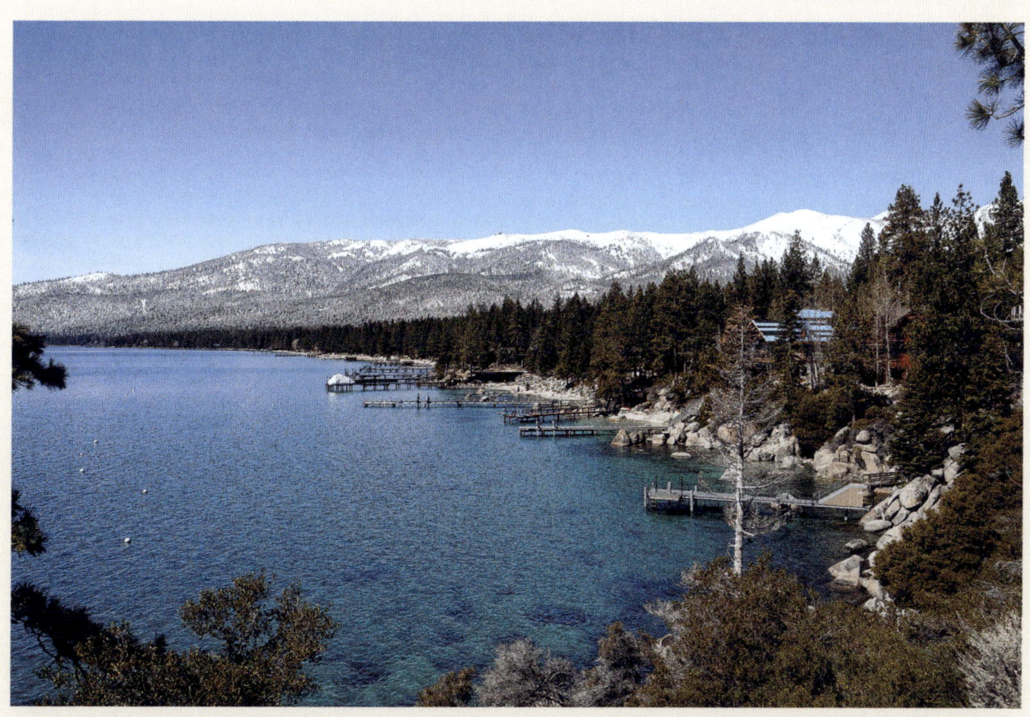

INCLINE VILLAGE, NEVADA
POPULATION: 9,163 full-time residents in 2024
TOWN SIZE: 21.7 square miles
CLOSEST INTERNATIONAL AIRPORT: Reno-Tahoe International Airport (33.1 miles)
CLOSEST REGIONAL AIRPORT: Truckee Tahoe Regional Airport, California (15.7 miles)
CLOSEST LARGE CITY: Reno (36.9 miles)
BONUS TOWNS NEARBY: South Lake Tahoe, Tahoe Vista
TOWN FACTS: Incline Village hosts the Lake Tahoe Shakespeare Festival each summer.
PLACES TO NOT MISS: Hidden Beach, The Flume Trail
SEASONS: Incline Village has four seasons.
LAKE WATER ACTIVITIES: swimming, boating, kayaking, Jet-Skiing, sailing
WATER SPOTS TO VISIT: Crystal Bay on Lake Tahoe and Kings Beach

SAINT MICHAELS, MARYLAND

POPULATION: 1,094 full-time residents in 2024

TOWN SIZE: 1.3 square miles

CLOSEST INTERNATIONAL AIRPORT: Baltimore/Washington International Airport (70.1 miles)

CLOSEST LARGE CITIES: Annapolis (50.9 miles); Baltimore (77.7 miles); Washington, D.C. (78.9 miles)

BONUS TOWNS NEARBY: Easton, Oxford, Queen Anne

TOWN FACTS: While being invaded by the British in 1812, the locals hung lanterns high in the trees to fool the approaching troops into overshooting the town, mainly saving it from cannon fire from the bay. Only one house was struck, known today as the Cannonball House.

PLACES AND THINGS TO NOT MISS: Chesapeake Bay Maritime Museum, Waterman's Appreciation Crab Festival, Phillips Wharf Environmental Center

SEASONS: Saint Michaels has four distinct seasons.

BAY WATER ACTIVITIES: kayaking, sailing, harbor cruises, Jet-Skiing, fishing, ecological kayaking tour

WATER SPOTS TO VISIT: Miles River, Broad Creek, Edge Creek, Tilghman Island Beach, and Eastern Bay

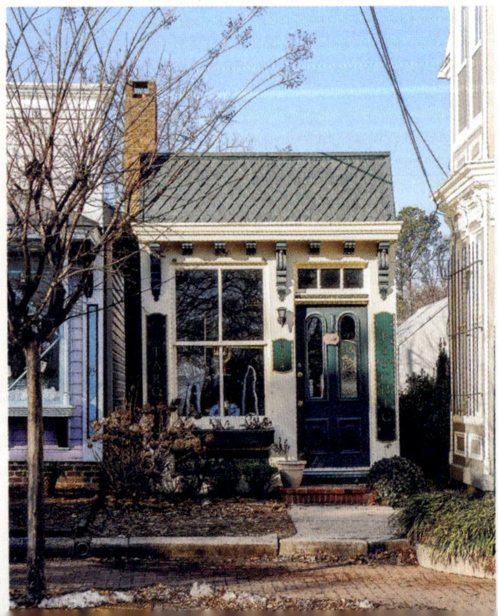

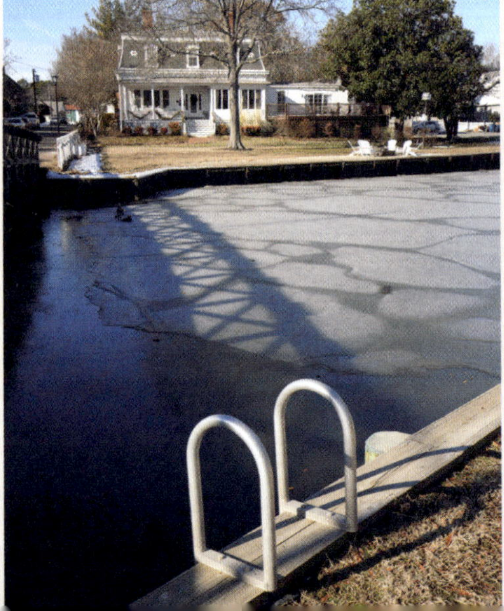

FUN EXTRAS

ACTIVITIES

WATER SPORTS

- Ice fishing
- Ice sailing, aka iceboating
- Ice-skating
- Kayaking
- Snow kiting
- Surfing
- Water biking
- Winter water sports

PLACES TO GO CRABBING

- Alaska—king crabs
- Louisiana—blue crabs
- Maryland—blue crabs
- North Carolina—Atlantic blue crabs and stone crabs
- Oregon and Washington—Dungeness and red rock crabs

LAZY RIVER TUBING FOR A RELAXING ADVENTURE

- Buffalo River Arkansas
- Clackamas River Oregon
- Comal River Texas
- Delaware River New Jersey
- Frio River Texas
- Ichetucknee River Florida
- Middle Loup River Nebraska
- Portneuf River Idaho
- Potomac River West Virginia
- Rainbow River Florida
- Root River Minnesota
- San Marcos River Texas
- Yampa River Colorado

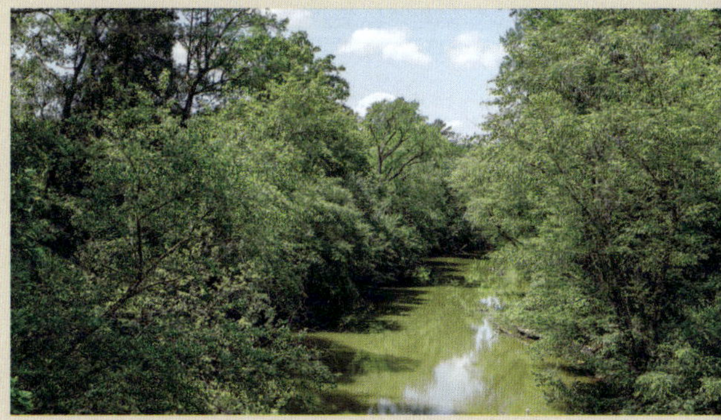

SAILING SCHOOLS

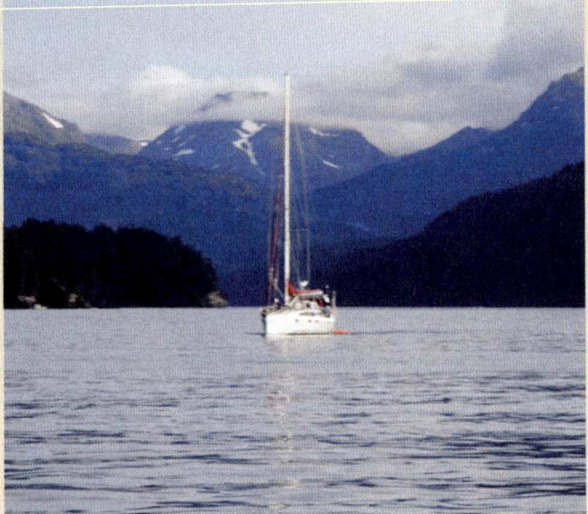

- American Sailing Academy Florida
- Blackjack Sailing Mississippi
- Griffin Bay Adventures Washington
- GT Sailing Michigan
- Kauai Sailing Association Hawaii
- Modern Sailing School & Club California
- New York Sailing Center New York
- Peaks and Tides Sailing School Colorado
- Sailing, Inc Alaska
- Sail Monterey California
- SailTime Alabama Alabama

SCUBA DIVING AND PLACES TO DIVE DEEP

- Amistad Reservoir Texas
- Blue Grotto Dive Resort Florida
- Bonne Terre Mine Missouri
- Channel Islands California
- Manta Night Dive Hawaii
- Strawberry Island Washington
- Thunder Bay National Marine Sanctuary Michigan
- U-352 Cape Lookout North Carolina
- West Bank, Flower Garden Banks National Marine Sanctuary Texas
- White Rock Park Indiana
- Wooden Fingers Alaska

TRAIL HIKES TO NOT MISS

- Alamere Falls California
- Alys Beach Nature Trail Florida
- Cape Lookout Oregon
- Catwalk Trail New Mexico
- Fern Canyon Trail California
- Kalalau Trail Hawaii
- Lost Coast Trail California
- Pictured Rocks Michigan
- Ocean Path Trail Maine
- Ozette Triangle Loop Washington

BEST SWIMMING HOLES AND COLD SPRINGS TO VISIT

- **Dolan Falls** Texas
- **Emerald Pool** New Hampshire
- **Fossil Creek Dam** Arizona
- **Goat Lake** Idaho
- **Grasshopper Point** Arizona
- **Hoyt Trail at South Yuba River** California
- **Madison Blue Springs** Florida
- **Oyster River Potholes** British Columbia, Canada
- **Seven Teacups** California
- **Sliding Rock** North Carolina

WARM AND HOT SPRINGS TO VISIT

- **Bigelow Hot Springs** Oregon
- **Crowley Hot Springs** California
- **Crystal River Warm Springs** Florida
- **Frenchglen Warm Springs** Oregon
- **Homestead Crater Mineral Dome** Utah
- **Jacob's Well** Texas
- **Keough's Hot Springs** California
- **Keyhole Hot Springs** British Columbia, Canada
- **Meadow Hot Springs** Utah
- **Remington Hot Springs** California
- **Umpqua Hot Springs** Oregon
- ***BONUS*** **Idaho Hot Springs Loop**

BIKE TRIPS TRAVERSING WATER

- **Assateague Island Bike Path** Maryland
- **Dillon Reservoir** Colorado
- **Island Line Trail** Vermont
- **Mississippi River Trail** Minnesota to Louisiana
- **Mon River Rail-Trail** West Virginia
- **Olympic Discovery Trail** Washington

STAYS

WATERSIDE HOTELS

- **Cabbage Key Inn** Cabbage Key, Florida
- **Camp Wandawega** Elkhorn, Wisconsin
- **Captain Whidbey** Coupeville, Washington
- **Dawn Ranch** Guerneville, California
- **Gulf Hills Hotel and Resort** Ocean Springs, Mississippi
- **Gurney's Montauk Resort** Montauk, New York
- **Hygge Sunrise Lake House** Lake Leelanau, Michigan
- **Just Add Water Floating Camps** Bremen, Maine
- **Lokal Hotel** Cape May, New Jersey
- **Migis Lodge on Sebago Lake** South Casco, Maine
- **Otyokwa** Bremen, Maine
- **River Cabaan** Tillamook, Oregon
- **Sage Lodge** Pray, Montana
- **Salish Lodge & Spa** Snoqualmie, Washington
- **The Sea Ranch Lodge** Sea Ranch, California
- **Sunset Beach Hotel** Shelter Island, New York
- **Tourists** North Adams, Massachusetts
- **Tutka Bay Lodge** Homer, Alaska

TOWNS

TOWNS TO FIND FRESH SEAFOOD

- Bay St. Louis, Mississippi
- Chatham, Massachusetts
- Crisfield, Maryland
- Georgetown, Maine
- Hatteras, North Carolina
- Marathon, Florida
- Marshall, California
- Mystic, Connecticut
- San Juan Island, Washington
- Yachats, Oregon

SMALL SURF TOWNS

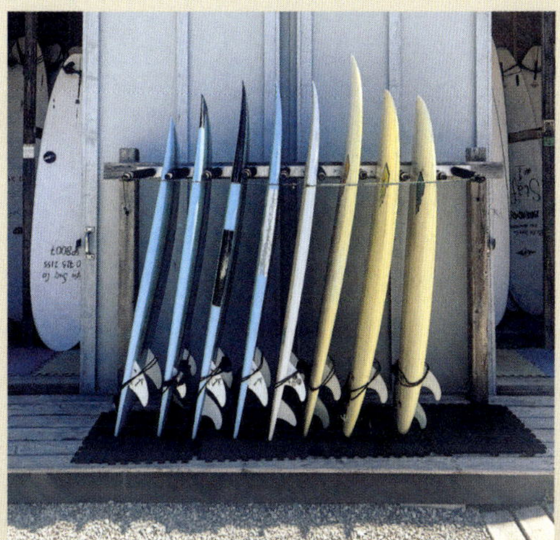

- Cape May, New Jersey
- Cocoa Beach, Florida
- Crescent City, California
- Folly Beach, South Carolina
- Haleiwa, Hawaii
- Hatteras Island, North Carolina
- Ocean City, Maryland
- Ocean City, New Jersey
- Pacific City, Oregon
- Seaside, Oregon
- Solana Beach, California
- Tofino, British Columbia, Canada
- Vero Beach, Florida
- Watch Hill, Rhode Island
- Westport, Washington

ISLAND TOWNS TO VISIT

- Beaver Island, Michigan
- Block Island, Rhode Island
- Cabbage Key, Florida
- Friday Harbor, Washington
- Jamestown, Rhode Island
- Key West, Florida
- Les Cheneaux Islands, Michigan
- Madeline Island, Wisconsin
- Monhegan, Maine
- Santa Catalina Island, California
- Smith Island, Maryland
- St. Simons, Georgia
- Sullivan's Island, South Carolina
- Tofino, British Columbia, Canada
- Vashon Island, Washington
- Vinalhaven, Maine

BEACH TOWNS WITH CLASSIC CHARM

- Anna Maria, Florida
- Bodega Bay, California
- Captiva Island, Florida
- Fernandina Beach, Florida
- Hatteras Island, North Carolina
- Jamestown, Rhode Island
- Manzanita, Oregon
- Ogunquit, Maine
- Rehoboth Beach, Delaware
- Shelter Island, New York
- Sullivan's Island, South Carolina
- Tofino, British Columbia, Canada

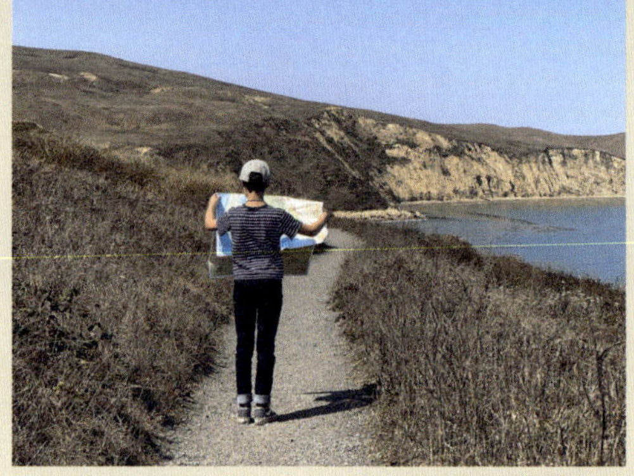

DESTINATIONS

NATIONAL LAKESHORES

- Apostle Islands, Wisconsin
- Pictured Rocks, Michigan
- Sleeping Bear Dunes, Michigan

NATIONAL SEASHORES

- Assateague Island, Maryland and Virginia
- Cape Canaveral, Florida
- Cape Cod, Massachusetts
- Cape Hatteras, North Carolina
- Cape Lookout, North Carolina
- Cumberland Island, Georgia
- Fire Island, New York
- Gulf Islands, Florida and Mississippi
- Padre Island, Texas
- Point Reyes, California

NATIONAL PARKS NEAR THE OCEAN

- Acadia National Park Maine
- Biscayne National Park Florida
- Channel Islands National Park California
- Dry Tortugas National Park Florida
- Everglades National Park Florida
- Glacier Bay National Park and Preserve Alaska
- Hawai'i Volcanoes National Park Hawaii
- Katmai National Park and Preserve Alaska
- Kenai Fjords National Park Alaska
- National Park of American Samoa
- Olympic National Park Washington
- Virgin Islands National Park U.S. Virgin Islands
- Wrangell-St. Elias National Park and Preserve Alaska

OYSTER FARM REGIONS IN THE UNITED STATES

- **Bayou La Batre** Alabama
- **Caminada Bay** Louisiana
- **Cape Cod** Massachusetts
- **Capers Island** South Carolina
- **Chesapeake Bay** Maryland
- **Damariscotta River** Maine
- **Hood Canal** Washington
- **Humboldt Bay** California
- **Long Island** New York
- **Narragansett Bay** Rhode Island
- **Puget Sound** Washington
- **Tomales Bay** California
- **Willapa** Washington
- ***BONUS*** **The Great Pacific Oyster Trail, Louisiana Oyster Trail, Maine Oyster Trail, Maryland Crab and Oyster Trail, Washington State Shellfish Trail**

STATE PARKS TO NOT MISS NEAR WATER

There are more than 9,800 state parks in the United States. This is only a small selection.

- **Assateague State Park** Maryland
- **Bahia Honda State Park** Florida
- **Baxter State Park** Maine
- **Big Lagoon State Park** Florida
- **Cape Henlopen State Park** Delaware
- **Cape Lookout State Park** Oregon
- **Custer State Park** South Dakota
- **Denali State Park** Alaska
- **Devil's Lake State Park** Wisconsin
- **Garner State Park** Texas
- **Green River Reservoir State Park** Vermont
- **Gulf State Park** Alabama
- **Ha Ha Tonka State Park** Missouri
- **Jones Gap State Park** South Carolina
- **Letchworth State Park** New York
- **Mackinac Island State Park** Michigan
- **Nāpali Coast State Wilderness Park** Hawaii
- **Palouse Falls State Park** Washington
- **Point Lobos State Natural Reserve** California
- **Popham Beach State Park** Maine

Rocky Neck State Park Niantic, Connecticut

Silver Falls State Park Oregon

Sinks Canyon State Park Wyoming

Tahquamenon Falls State Park Michigan

Tallulah Gorge State Park Tallulah Falls, Georgia

Tettegouche State Park Minnesota

Tishomingo State Park Mississippi

Thousand Springs State Park Ritter Island, Idaho

Valley Falls State Park West Virginia

Watkins Glen State Park New York

U.S. TERRITORIES TO VISIT

American Samoa

Commonwealth of the Northern Mariana Islands

Guam

Puerto Rico

U.S. Virgin Islands

RIVERS TO GET LOST NEAR

Columbia River Oregon

Elwha River Washington

Hanalei River Hawaii

Hudson River New York

Ichetucknee River Florida

Kenai River Alaska

Opal Creek Oregon

Rainbow River Florida

Snake River Wyoming

Truckee River California

Yuba River California

Tallulah River Georgia

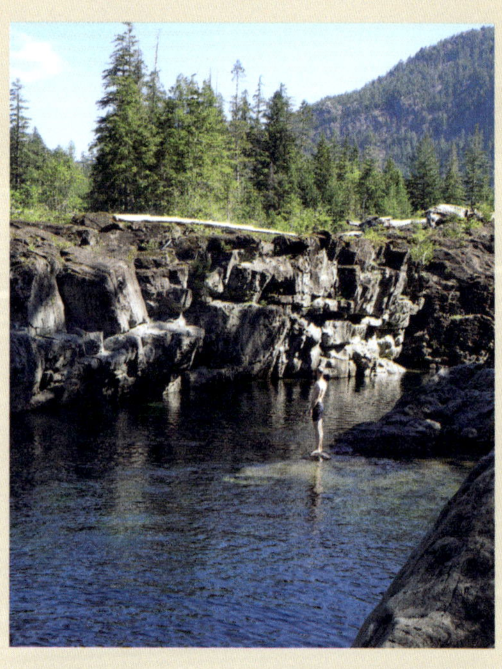

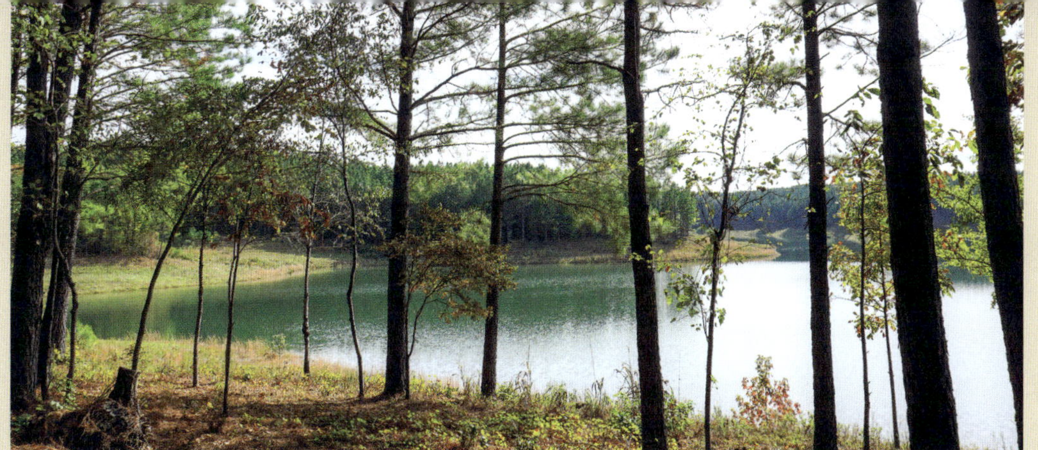

RIVER, LAKE, OCEAN, AND ISLAND ROAD TRIPS

Coastal Connection Scenic Byway	Alabama
Great River Road National Scenic Byway	Minnesota to Louisiana
Hana Highway	Hawaii
Highway 101	Oregon
M-22	Michigan
Overseas Highway	Miami to Key West, Florida
Pacific Coast Highway	California
Pacific Marine Circle	Vancouver Island, British Columbia, Canada
Rangeley Lakes National Scenic Byway	Maine
Route 6	Massachusetts to Rhode Island

MARITIME MUSEUMS AND EDUCATIONAL CENTERS

Door County Maritime Museum	Wisconsin
The Fishermen's Museum	Maine
Graveyard of the Atlantic Museum	North Carolina
Hudson River Maritime Museum	New York
Light Keeper's House Museum	Michigan
Maritime Heritage Center	Washington
Mississippi Shipbuilding and Maritime Center	Mississippi
Mystic Seaport Museum	Connecticut
Sail Power and Steam Museum	Maine
Spongeorama Sponge Factory	Florida
Tahoe Maritime Museum	California
Waterman's Museum	Maryland

TRADE THIS FOR THAT

If you are living in North America and want a travel experience to transport you to a faraway place without leaving the continent, below you will find a fun list of location dupes.

- Catalina Island, California, for the Amalfi Coast, Italy
- Florida Keys for Hawaii
- Fogo Island, Newfoundland and Labrador, Canada, for Norway
- New Brunswick, Canada, for Lower Saxony, Germany
- Newfoundland, Canada, for the British Isles, United Kingdom
- Newport, Rhode Island, for Nice, France
- Saint Pierre and Miquelon archipelago for the Brittany region of France
- Secret Beach, Oregon, for Fauskasandur, Iceland
- Tarpon Springs, Florida, for the Greek Islands

EVENTS

WOODEN BOAT FESTIVALS AND SHOWS

- Concours d'Elegance California
- Door County Classic and Wooden Boat Show Wisconsin
- Les Cheneaux Islands Antique Wooden Boat Show Michigan
- Wooden Boat Festival Louisiana
- Wooden Boat Festival Washington

SEAFOOD-CENTERED FESTIVALS

- Astoria Warrenton Crab, Seafood & Wine Festival Astoria, Oregon
- Delaware Seafood Festival Rehoboth Beach, Delaware
- Dungeness Crab Festival Port Angeles, Washington
- Florida Keys Seafood Festival Key West, Florida
- Maine Lobster Festival Rockland, Maine
- New Jersey Seafood Festival Belmar, New Jersey
- North Carolina Seafood Festival Morehead City, North Carolina
- Wellfleet OysterFest Wellfleet, Massachusetts

MISCELLANEOUS

MOVIES FILMED IN WATER TOWNS

- *Beautiful Girls*
- *The Birds*
- *CODA*
- *The Goonies*
- *Indian Summer*
- *Jaws*
- *Manchester by the Sea*
- *Moonrise Kingdom*
- *Mystic River*
- *The Notebook*
- *On Golden Pond*
- *A River Runs Through It*
- *The Shipping News*

ANIMALS TO SPOT NEAR WATER

- Black bears Vancouver Island, British Columbia, Canada
- Eagles Alaska
- Manatees Silver Springs, Florida
- Puffins New Brunswick, Canada
- Elephant seals Point Reyes, California
- Whales Washington (Travel the Whale Trail to find the best vantage point from land.)

TIDE POOL ETIQUETTE TO FOLLOW

- Watch where you walk, and avoid stepping on living rocks; look for bare ones.
- Avoid touching anything in the pools so as not to disturb the marine life.
- Leave nature where you found it: no collecting.
- Leave no trace.
- Be aware of the tide and make sure you don't get caught in a rising tide.
- Make sure children understand the rules.
- Avoid spray-on sunscreen and other products you might have on your hands, as they can disrupt the marine life.
- Wear shoes that will cause the least amount of damage to the marine life.
- Don't let dogs go in the tide pool.

ORGANIZATIONS WORKING TOWARD WATER AND LAND CONSERVATION AND EDUCATION

- American Rivers
- American Whitewater
- Center for Watershed Protection
- Clean Water Action
- Columbia Water Center
- Environmental Defense Fund (EDF)
- Friends of the Yampa
- Grand Canyon Trust
- Idaho Rivers United
- International Rivers
- Island Institute
- National Audubon Society
- National Wildlife Federation
- The Nature Conservancy
- Pacific Institute
- Riverkeeper
- Rogue Riverkeeper
- Soil and Water Conservation Society
- Trout Unlimited
- WaterAid
- Waterkeeper Alliance
- The World Water Council

COMMON BIRDS TO SPOT NEAR WATER

- Bald Eagles
- Cranes
- Gulls
- Herons
- Killdeers
- Long-billed curlews
- Ospreys
- Oystercatchers
- Pelicans
- Puffins
- Red knots
- Sandpipers
- Stilts
- Wilson's plovers

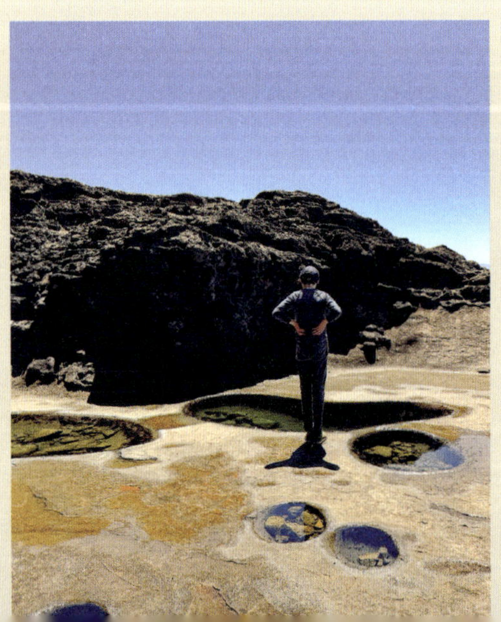

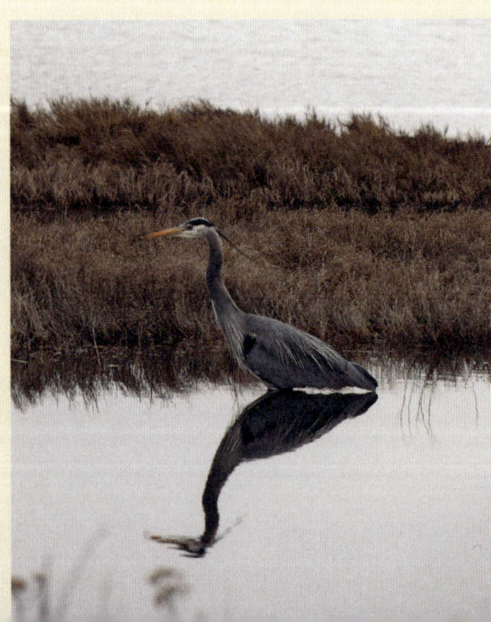

SMALL WATER TOWNS IN EVERY STATE IN THE UNITED STATES

ALABAMA

- Cullman
- Dauphin Island
- Eufaula
- Fairhope
- Magnolia Springs
- Wedowee

ALASKA

- Gustavus
- Homer
- Ketchikan
- Seward
- Skagway
- Sitka

ARIZONA

- Cottonwood
- Gila Bend
- Grand Canyon Village
- Page
- Patagonia

ARKANSAS

- Beaver
- Eureka Springs
- Heber Springs
- Jasper
- Mammoth Spring

CALIFORNIA

- Carmel-by-the-Sea
- Inverness
- Morro Bay
- Solana Beach
- Stinson Beach

COLORADO

- Buena Vista
- Georgetown
- Glenwood Springs
- Pagosa Springs
- Steamboat Springs

CONNECTICUT

- Ansonia
- Derby
- Niantic
- Old Saybrook
- Wilton

DELAWARE

- Bethany Beach
- Fenwick Island
- Lewes
- Millsboro
- New Castle

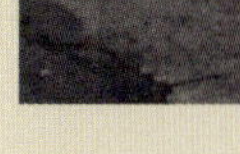

FLORIDA

- Cedar Key
- Flagler Beach
- Marathon
- New Port Richey
- Rosemary Beach

GEORGIA

- Americus
- Bainbridge
- Brunswick
- Greensboro
- Royston

HAWAII

Haleiwa
Hana
Lahaina
Poipu
Waimea

IDAHO

Priest River
Riggins
Stanley
Swan Valley
Wallace

ILLINOIS

Fox Lake
Fulton
Galena
Nauvoo
Ottawa

INDIANA

Fremont
French Lick
Knightstown
Madison
New Harmony

IOWA

Bellevue
Fort Madison
Iowa Falls
LeClaire
Marquette

KANSAS

Burlington
Cheney
El Dorado
Junction City
Mulvane

KENTUCKY

Gilbertsville
Grand Rivers
Maysville
Midway
Somerset

LOUISIANA

Abita Springs
Breaux Bridge
Covington
Mandeville
Natchitoches
New Roads

MAINE

Bailey Island
Bethel
Cape Elizabeth
Milbridge
Ogunquit
Rangeley

MARYLAND

Cambridge
Havre de Grace
North Beach
Oxford
Smith Island

MASSACHUSETTS

Concord
Manchester-by-the-Sea
Newburyport
Sandwich
Wellfleet

MICHIGAN

Frankfort
Leland
Les Cheneaux Islands
Marquette
Munising

MINNESOTA

Albert Lea
Bemidji
Lindstrom
Minnetrista
Walker

MISSISSIPPI

Bay St. Louis
Columbus
New Albany

Pass Christian

Water Valley

MISSOURI

Excelsior Springs

Hannibal

Hermann

Kimmswick

Rocheport

MONTANA

Bigfork

Big Timber

Fort Benton

Lakeside

Whitefish

NEBRASKA

Brownville

Ogallala

Plattsmouth

Scottsbluff

Weeping Water

NEVADA

Boulder City

Ely

Incline Village

Mesquite

New Washoe City

NEW HAMPSHIRE

Meredith

New Castle

Portsmouth

Rye

Seabrook

NEW JERSEY

Frenchtown

Lebanon

Ocean Grove

Seaside Heights

Spring Lake

NEW MEXICO

Abiquiu

Red River

Santa Rosa

Silver City

Truth or Consequences

NEW YORK

Cornwall-on-Hudson

Penn Yan

Sag Harbor

Shelter Island

NORTH CAROLINA

Bald Head Island

Belmont

Hatteras Island

Little Switzerland

Southport

NORTH DAKOTA

Garrison

New Town

Valley City

Wahpeton

Washburn

OHIO

Catawba Island

Geneva-on-the-Lake

Kelleys Island

Port Clinton

Yellow Springs

OKLAHOMA

Eufaula

Guthrie

Longtown

Sulphur

Webbers Falls

OREGON

Astoria

Baker City

Brownsville

Cannon Beach

Florence

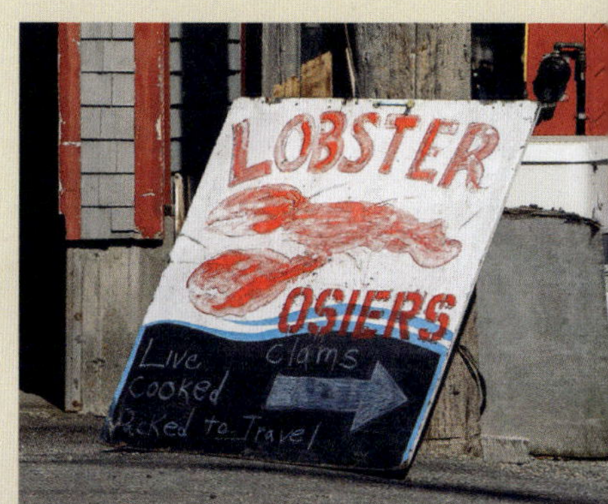

PENNSYLVANIA

- Hawley
- New Castle
- Pymatuning Central
- Sewickley
- Stroudsburg

RHODE ISLAND

- Barrington
- Narragansett
- New Shoreham
- Scituate
- Tiverton

SOUTH CAROLINA

- Edisto Beach
- Folly Beach
- Murrells Inlet
- Pawleys Island
- Sullivan's Island

SOUTH DAKOTA

- Chamberlain
- Lake Andes
- Pierre
- Vermillion
- Yankton

TENNESSEE

- Dandridge
- Erwin
- Kingston Springs
- Loudon
- Pulaski
- Tiptonville

TEXAS

- Port Aransas
- Rockport
- South Padre Island
- Uncertain
- Wimberley

UTAH

- Garden City
- Green River
- Kamas
- Kanab
- Springdale

VERMONT

- Charlotte
- Fairlee
- Newport
- South Hero
- Woodstock

VIRGINIA

- Chincoteague
- Onancock
- Tangier Island
- Urbanna
- Wachapreague

WASHINGTON

- Gig Harbor
- Ocean Shores
- Port Ludlow
- Poulsbo
- Sequim

WEST VIRGINIA

- Berkeley Springs
- Buckhannon
- Hinton
- Point Pleasant
- Shepherdstown

WISCONSIN

- Baileys Harbor
- Sister Bay
- Sturgeon Bay
- Two Rivers
- Washington Island

WYOMING

- Cody
- Green River
- Riverton
- Saratoga
- Thermopolis

CAPTIONS

66 Brandon, Vermont, a vivid corner of the Condrys' living room

67 Brandon, Vermont, a peek at Alexa's art supplies in her studio

70 Brandon, Vermont, Fern Lake in spring

71 Middlebury, Vermont, Juniper Creative mural outside of American Flatbread and Noonie's Deli

72 Frankfort, Michigan, the beach at Point Betsie Lighthouse

74 Point Comfort, Quebec, Canada, Half-Crown Island, on 31 Mile Lake, swim dock

75 Point Comfort, Quebec, Canada, Half-Crown Island on 31 Mile Lake, cabin

76 Point Comfort, Quebec, Canada, Half-Crown Island on 31 Mile Lake, my son Tom Otis kayaking in the late summer

78 Point Comfort, Quebec, Canada, Half-Crown Island on 31 Mile Lake, fresh caught fish from the lake for a traditional shore lunch; the vintage Whaler boat in a hidden cove

79 Point Comfort, Quebec, Canada, Half-Crown Island on 31 Mile Lake, sunset

82 Patagonia, Arizona, from the hills, overlooking Patagonia Lake

83 Patagonia, Arizona, the Paton Center for Hummingbirds attracts both birds and humans from around the world

84 Patagonia, Arizona, a traditional adobe-style home in downtown Patagonia; a street sign for the Queen of Cups Winery; a collection of bikes outside of Patagonia Bikes

86 Patagonia, Arizona, the Patagonia Mountains on the edge of town; a life jacket lending stand at Patagonia Lake

87 Patagonia, Arizona, the walking bridge over Patagonia Lake

88 Patagonia, Arizona, peeks around Adrienne's home in the hills above the town, outdoor patio; living room and kitchen; her dining room

89 Patagonia, Arizona, a roadside memorial shrine on Highway 82; springtime at Patagonia-Sonoita Creek

92 Sandpoint, Idaho, Lake Pend Oreille, as viewed from up in the mountains above the town

93 Sandpoint, Idaho, Katie's business, Heart Bowls, in downtown Sandpoint; Matchwood Brewing Company

94 Sandpoint, Idaho, Katie's kitchen

96 Sandpoint, Idaho, mural in downtown Sandpoint; the Panida Theater; a lifeguard chair at Lake Pend Oreille

97 Sandpoint, Idaho, clouds over Lake Pend Oreille; a Sandpoint neighborhood mural

100 Frankfort, Michigan, Point Betsie Lighthouse; Frankfort Public Beach and Playground, where you can sit and enjoy sweeping views of Lake Michigan

101 Frankfort, Michigan, Point Betsie Lighthouse

102 Frankfort, Michigan, the Garden Theater in the downtown; the sign of the classic Frankfort Dairy Maid; pick up a dozen local eggs at one of the roadside stops; a beach slide

103 Frankfort, Michigan, The Vault in downtown Frankfort

104 Frankfort, Michigan, Katie and Tim's living room and den

105 Frankfort, Michigan, curbside look at the Jones's home

106 Frankfort, Michigan, Frankfort Public Beach and Playground, where you can ride bikes along the Frankfort North Pier; a sailboat in Betsie Lake

107 Frankfort, Michigan, the reflection of Frankfort North Pier Lighthouse over Lake Michigan

110 Elkhorn, Wisconsin, Camp Wandawega, relaxing hammock at camp

111 Elkhorn, Wisconsin, Camp Wandawega, the lifeguard stand; bunk at camp

112 Elkhorn, Wisconsin, Elk Restaurant; a repurposed First National Bank turned pocket park

113 Elkhorn, Wisconsin, Camp Wandawega, a roundup of classic camp scenes: vintage car, a primitive tent, a traveling farm stand

115 Elkhorn, Wisconsin, Camp Wandawega, a roundup of classic camp scenes: a bunk house, an Airstream turned tavern, a vintage cabinet stores general goods, and the swim dock

116 Elkhorn, Wisconsin, downtown Elkhorn

117 Elkhorn, Wisconsin, Camp Wandawega, summertime at camp from the most perfect swim dock

118 Taylor, Mississippi, Splinter Creek, an electric boat on North Lake

120 Taylor, Mississippi, Splinter Creek, a fall look at South Lake

121 Taylor, Mississippi, Splinter Creek, a deck among the trees; modern architecture juxtaposed with beautiful nature; the home, aptly named the House Boat, on the North Lake at Splinter Creek; the House Boat living room

122 Ocean Springs, Mississippi, catamarans ready to set sail

126 Sausalito, California, a peek at the houseboat community with Mt. Tamalpais in the background

127 Sausalito, California, each houseboat dock works like a front yard to each boat, lined with potted plants and blooming flowers

129 Sausalito, California, the view from Blythe's front deck; inside the kitchen and living room of Blythe's well-intentioned, beautifully designed houseboat

130 Sausalito, California, a corner of the living room, Blythe's grandmother's marble table; a secret roof deck off the primary bedroom holds a collection of plants soaking up the California sun

131 Sausalito, California, neutral tones help the balance of design throughout the houseboat; Marigold's room is a tranquil spot meant for reading and relaxing

133 Sausalito, California, a regular seal sighting around Sausalito; a secret blue heron mural near the Galilee Harbor Community Association; stunning landscaping lines large flights of stairs throughout the town; houseboats

134 Sausalito, California, low tide at the houseboats
135 Sausalito, California, float plane over Richardson Bay, looking toward Tiburon, another small bayside community
138 Mystic, Connecticut, the working harbor in Mystic; Welcome to Historic Mystic sign greeting visitors
139 Mystic, Connecticut, Oyster Club, one of Renee's restaurants
140 Mystic, Connecticut, waterfront homes situated along the Mystic River
141 Mystic, Connecticut, Oyster Club and Port of Call, Renee's restaurants
142 Mystic, Connecticut, Mystic Pizza in downtown Mystic; the movie *Mystic Pizza* was inspired by this restaurant
143 Mystic, Connecticut, Sea View Snack Bar, a roadside snack shack; a waterfront home
144 Stonington, Connecticut, Stone Acres Farm, the local farm run by the 85th Day Restaurant Group, which serves for all the restaurants under their umbrella, including Port of Call and Oyster Club
145 Noank, Connecticut, Haring's Noank, dock side restaurant, part of the 85th Day Restaurant Group, can be reached by land or by sea
148 Ocean Springs, Mississippi, seagull over the docks
149 Ocean Springs, Mississippi, an exterior look at the Croom/Rankin home, designed by Tall Architects; a look down Washington Street in downtown Ocean Springs
150 Ocean Springs, Mississippi, the Croom/Rankin home, the foyer; Caroline's father's book next to a found bird's nest; the screened porch off the dining nook; the dining nook
151 Ocean Springs, Mississippi, pelicans on a local dock
152 Ocean Springs, Mississippi, Ocean Springs Harbor Boat Launch, alligators ready for dropped fish from the working fishing boats
154 Ocean Springs, Mississippi, Gulf Island National Seashore, a great egret in the marsh; the mural on the side of Lil' Market Deli & Bagelry featuring a beloved free-roaming rooster in downtown Ocean Springs named Carl; permanent fireworks stand in town
158 Arrowsic, Maine, a waterfront home in Arrowsic; Arrowsic city sign
159 Brunswick, Maine, Bicyclette Studio, one of Brian's creations
160 Brunswick, Maine, Bicyclette Studio
161 Arrowsic, Maine, Carla and Brian's home, the loft above the dining room gives a quiet spot for writing and reading; an exterior look at their home; the dining area of the open floor plan
162 Wiscasset, Maine, early spring boats in the water near the Bicyclette storefront studio; the Bicyclette storefront overlooking the Sheepscot River
163 Arrowsic, Maine, the Arrowsic town hall; the bridge that connects Woolwich to Arrowsic
164 Ocean Springs, Mississippi, houseboat
166 Rutherford Island, Maine, waterside home
170 Rutherford Island, Maine, the view from Ashleigh's family's home on Rutherford Island in late spring
171 Rutherford Island, Maine, Osier's Wharf, in the heart of Rutherford Island; a wooden boat ready to head to the water for the summer
172 Rutherford Island, Maine, a lobster fisher's truck, home for the day
174 Rutherford Island, Maine, The Blue Shaboo, Ashleigh's home, the den; thrifted lobster finds in the kitchen; the primary bathroom
175 Rutherford Island, Maine, The Blue Shaboo, Ashleigh's home, the living room; the den
177 Rutherford Island, Maine, The Blue Shaboo, sunset view over the Damariscotta River in front of Ashleigh's home
180 Shelter Island, New York, Wade's Beach on Shelter Island; vintage cars are around every turn on the island
181 Shelter Island, New York, a car ferry is the only way on and off Shelter Island, which can be accessed from the north or south side of the island
182 Shelter Island, New York, a traditional Cape Cod style home with shake siding; Black Cat Books at the heart of the island
183 Shelter Island, New York, Shelter Island Heights Pharmacy is a focal point of the Heights neighborhood
184 Shelter Island, New York, Rebecca and Watt's home, the living room; the entry; the exterior of the home
185 Shelter Island, New York, boats in Shelter Island Sound behind Marie Eiffel Market; the lifeguard stand on Sunset Beach
188 Hatteras Island, North Carolina, Frisco Beach, beach in Brooke and Jerry's neighborhood
189 Hatteras Island, North Carolina, kayak rentals on Hatteras Island; Frisco Beach, public trail to access the beach from Brooke and Jerry's neighborhood
190 Hatteras Island, North Carolina, Frisco, Brooke moving surfboard for an afternoon surfing jaunt; found shells on the home's windowsill
191 Hatteras Island, North Carolina, local surf shop in the central business district of Hatteras
192 Hatteras Island, North Carolina, a blue heron near Cape Point; you can drive on many of the beaches, with a permit, at Hatteras, but it's important to lower your tire pressure before doing so, to avoid getting stuck
193 Hatteras Island, North Carolina, surfer off the coast of Hatteras Island
196 Camano Island, Washington, the Welcome to Camano Island sign represents the local arts community
197 Camano Island, Washington, a locally made orca art installation in Freedom Park; local coffee shop shack, Shipwreck Coffee

198 Camano Island, Washington, Shogo's souped-up Subaru, parked in front of his home

199 Camano Island, Washington, a home built for an artist, the A-frame allows natural light to capture the art and color of the living room; inside Shogo's home studio

200 Camano Island, Washington, the kitchen looks out over the woods that surround the Camano Island home; firewood pile for the sauna and a found Lion's Club sign; a barrel sauna rests just outside the home

201 Camano Island, Washington, Shogo's children have a magical spot to play and explore on the property; a seagull rests at the Point Lowell Picnic Area

202 Camano Island, Washington, Skagit Wildlife Area, Leque Island Unit is an ideal bird-watching area

203 Camano Island, Washington, a hand-painted Camano Island map sits near the Camano Island Coffee Roasters

206 Greenbank, Whidbey Island, Washington, Admiralty Head Lighthouse at Fort Casey State Park; a footpath at Fort Ebey State Park

207 Greenbank, Whidbey Island, Washington, the dock at the famed hotel Captain Whidbey; Whidbey Scenic Isle Way sign

208 Greenbank, Whidbey Island, Washington, charming roadside market in the heart of Greenbank; Greenbank Pantry, the sundries and coffee shop at Captain Whidbey

210 Greenbank, Whidbey Island, Washington, Kyle's back deck, overlooking the sound; grass and moss-covered roofs in Kyle's neighborhood

212 Greenbank, Whidbey Island, Washington; popular with the tourists and locals alike, Greenbank Farm connects to wonderful hillside walking trails, great for dogs; the firepit at Captain Whidbey provides a place to sit and watch for gray whales in the migration months and spot orcas year-round

213 Greenbank, Whidbey Island, Washington, the view of Greenbank Farm from the walking trails just above the property

216 Deception Pass, Whidbey Island, Washington, you cross the green waters of Deception Pass as you enter Whidbey Island from the north, not far from Oak Harbor

217 Oak Harbor, Washington, North Whidbey Little League sign; downtown shops

218 Oak Harbor, Washington, the living room of Shannon and Jason's midcentury modern home; a LEGO Mars Rover in the bedroom of Shannon and Jason's youngest son

219 Oak Harbor, Washington, Wind and Tide Bookshop in downtown Oak Harbor; a downtown mural

220 Oak Harbor, Washington, mural in the central business district of Oak Harbor; an Oak Harbor bus stop

221 Oak Harbor, Washington, views of Mt. Baker can be seen from Windjammer Park in Oak Harbor

225 Langley, Washington, view from the Whidbey Island Ferry; a look down 1st Street in Langley; Hope the Wishing Whale and whale-spotting bell on 1st Street; a shop in Langley

228 Incline Village, Nevada, snow-covered mountains above Lake Tahoe; Allie in her Incline Village, Nevada, home

229 Incline Village, Nevada, the exterior of Allie's home; living room; swinging doors original to the home; natural light streaming into the dining area of the open floor plan

230 Truckee, California, K.C.'s home, the living room looking in the kitchen; the exterior of the home; K.C.'s in-home office; the dining room

231 Truckee, California, K.C. in her kitchen; the Truckee River, which runs through downtown

232 St. Michaels, Maryland, boats in the harbor; the exterior of the Wildset Hotel; the dining room of the hotel's James Beard–nominated restaurant, Ruse

233 Incline Village, Nevada, Diamond Peak Ski Resort overlooks the mountains and Lake Tahoe, near Allie's home

234 Truckee, California, Jax at the Tracks in early spring after a late season snow; downtown Truckee business district

235 Incline Village, Nevada, the water of Lake Tahoe stays crystal blue year-round

236 St. Michaels, Maryland, downtown St. Michaels in winter; the frozen harbor

237 Tishomingo, Mississippi, river at Tishomingo State Park

238 Homer, Alaska, sailboat in Kachemak Bay

241 Tofino, Vancouver Island, British Columbia, surf boards at Pacific Surf School

242 Point Reyes National Seashore, California, my son on his way to see the seals; Hatteras Island, North Carolina, birds over Cape Point

244 Vancouver Island, British Columbia, roadside swim along Taylor River

245 Taylor, Mississippi, late summer at Splinter Creek

248 Vancouver Island, British Columbia, tidepools at Botanical Beach Provincial Park; Oak Harbor, Washington, blue heron

249 Astoria, Oregon, Custard King in downtown Astoria

251 South Bristol Island, Maine, Osier's Wharf

252 Frankfort, Michigan, kayaks and canoes by Crystal Lake

ACKNOWLEDGMENTS

Thank you to my husband Sean and our son Tom Otis. I'm so grateful for your continued support and for living the small town journey with me. For my mom Dorothy, I don't tell you enough, but you inspire me. To both my family and married family. I'm so thankful for you all.

To my agents, Kim Perel, Margaret Danko, and everyone at High Line Literary, I'm so thankful that you have believed in me since day one. To my editor Shannon Connors Fabricant, Anna Shura, Amber Morris, Jenna McBride, and the team at Running Press, I've won the publishers' lottery. I'll be forever grateful for how you've championed this project.

I'm grateful to my local and around-the-country friends who continue to support my work. Your encouragement is something that I hold dear, and I feel validated by the projects I take on.

Thank you to my Water Valley, Oxford, and Taylor communities. You have shown me what it means to feel at home and at ease in a place. I am constantly amazed that so much creativity, generosity, and kindness can live in one area. I'm thankful for the space you allow me to share with you all.

Last but not least, I'm so thankful to everyone featured in this book for allowing me to tell your stories and share your towns with my readers. Thank you for welcoming me into your homes. I couldn't have made this book without your support.

In memory of Jason Grube, featured on pages 214–220. His life was tragically taken in August 2025 doing what he loved most, riding his bicycle. He was a great supporter of bringing art to his community and was a positive force for his family and all who knew him. He will be greatly missed.

INDEX